SO THEY WANT US
TO LEARN FRENCH

Matthew Hayday

SO THEY WANT US TO LEARN FRENCH

PROMOTING AND OPPOSING BILINGUALISM IN ENGLISH-SPEAKING CANADA

Matthew Hayday

UBCPress · Vancouver · Toronto

23 22 21 20 19 18 17 16 15   5 4 3 2 1

Printed in Canada on FSC-certified ancient-forest-free paper
(100% post-consumer recycled) that is processed chlorine- and acid-free.

Library and Archives Canada Cataloguing in Publication

Hayday, Matthew, 1977-, author
    So they want us to learn French : promoting and opposing bilingualism in English-speaking Canada / Matthew Hayday.

Includes bibliographical references and index.
Issued in print and electronic formats.
ISBN 978-0-7748-3004-1 (bound). – ISBN 978-0-7748-3005-8 (pbk.) –
ISBN 978-0-7748-3006-5 (pdf). – ISBN 978-0-7748-3007-2 (epub)

    1. Bilingualism – Canada – History. 2. Bilingualism – Social aspects – Canada.
3. Bilingualism – Political aspects – Canada. I. Title.

FC145.B55H39 2015   306.44'60971   C2015-903888-X
                                                         C2015-903889-8

Canadä

UBC Press gratefully acknowledges the financial support for our publishing program of the Government of Canada (through the Canada Book Fund), the Canada Council for the Arts, and the British Columbia Arts Council. UBC Press is also grateful to the Wilson Prize for Publishing Canadian History for its contribution toward the publication of this book.

Back cover image: Alphonse, the bilingual parrot, courtesy of the Office of the Commissioner of Official Languages.

UBC Press
The University of British Columbia
2029 West Mall
Vancouver, BC V6T 1Z2
www.ubcpress.ca

For my dad, Bryan Hayday, who told me that my books would sell more copies with (bilingual) car chase scenes in them

À haute vitesse, les policiers poursuivent le camion noir. Leur proie: Guillaume "Le Raton-laveur" Morin, un bandit célèbre accusé d'avoir volé des millions de dollars à la Banque de Montréal. Le camion se faufile entre les voitures sur la route Transcanadienne, traversant la frontière entre le Québec et l'Ontario, en tentant de leur échapper. D'en haut, les hélicoptères de Radio-Canada et CTV couvrent la scène pour les milliers de téléspectateurs qui regardent en retenant leur souffle.

Contents

Illustrations

Foreword

The history of language policy in Canada has tended to be more political than social and more likely to have been written in French Canada, where historians have examined the elimination of French-language education in English-speaking Canada, in particular in Ontario and Manitoba. The emergence of language legislation and language policy following the recommendations of the Royal Commission on Bilingualism and Biculturalism beginning in 1967 was an effort to repair the damage caused by a century of measures taken to eliminate the use of French as a language of instruction and administration outside Quebec. The five decades since then have shown not only progress but also occasional setbacks in the face of constitutional controversy and strong opposition.

One of the many refreshing things about the approach in this book is that Matthew Hayday broadens the perspective for looking at the policy-making process beyond politicians and public servants to consider other players: idealistic parents, academics, and commissioners of official languages on one side and disillusioned parents, conspiracy theorists, and anti-bilingualism crusaders on the other. As he puts it, the policy emerged from a "bureaucracy–civil society dynamic."

The result is not merely a rich account of a remarkable period in the history of Canadian public policy but also a description of key actors in a democratic society, ordinary people who mobilized on behalf of something that they thought critical: the education of their children. To achieve success, they had to defend themselves from attacks by those who were (and in some cases still are) convinced that Canada was being taken over by people who wanted to transform it into a French-speaking country.

The challenge of developing a federal policy for second-language learning is inherent in our constitutional history. As I have often remarked to foreign visitors, Canada's Fathers of Confederation gave all of the powers that they considered to be important – the military, the major tools of the economy, foreign policy – to the federal government and relegated to the provinces what they thought to be trivial – health and education. Since the Second World War, Canadians have tended to disagree with those priorities, and the result has been the source of many federal-provincial tensions.

Hayday captures the vigour and commitment of several of my predecessor commissioners, and, though Max Yalden and D'Iberville Fortier have passed away, all of the others remain charismatic and passionate about official bilingualism. It is an honour to follow in their footsteps or, as an academic might put it, to take advantage of the process of path dependency that their initiatives created.

Immersion education, as Hayday demonstrates, has gone from a small experiment in a single school to a widely acclaimed model of second-language learning adopted across the country. However, funding caps have limited its growth. In 1989, André Obadia – often cited in this book – predicted that, if the increase continued at the rate that it had achieved by then, there would be 1 million students in immersion by 1999. But the continued expansion did not happen; enrolment plateaued at about 300,000, where it has remained ever since.

The suggestion persists that immersion is simply an elite program or, as Hayday summarizes its critics' argument, "private school for yuppies on the public dime." It is a particularly frustrating argument; principals, teachers, and school board officials across the country pressure parents to remove their children from immersion whenever a learning difficulty emerges, whether or not the language of instruction is a factor. Then, when all of the children with learning problems are systematically removed, immersion is attacked as elitist. This is still happening four decades after Dr. Margaret Bruck demonstrated that there was no need to remove children from immersion, research that has been confirmed more recently by Fred Genesee at McGill University.

As Glenna Reid pointed out in 1972, immersion contributes to what she called "other-culture understanding." Anecdotally, I can confirm this through the experiences of friends of my children and children of my friends. Through them, I can name young people who went to China and learned Chinese, who taught English in Japan and learned Japanese, who worked on solar projects in India and learned Hindi or on water projects in Vietnam and learned Vietnamese, who travelled to Central America and learned Spanish or joined the expatriate musical community in Berlin and learned German. They all learned Canada's other official language first. It is easier to learn a third language than it is to learn a second language; learning French is not a barrier but a bridge to the rest of the world.

There has been progress. In 1992, Victor Goldbloom flew to Alberta to refute eloquently Premier Don Getty's claim that official bilingualism was an "irritant" that should be "removed from the force of law." No premier would say that now; in 2014, for the first time in Canadian history, a majority of Canada's premiers were bilingual. It is now taken for granted that bilingualism is a prerequisite for leadership of a political party in Canada, and it is now a legislative requirement that agents of Parliament be bilingual. There are excellent language-training programs for judges to improve the bilingual capacity of the provincial and superior courts. Some 40 percent of new employees were bilingual when they joined the federal public service.

But there continue to be challenges. Canada welcomes 250,000 newcomers every year, and it is not surprising that they are not fluent in both of our official languages when they arrive. In addition, they have not learned the history of our struggles for language equality.

And, as Hayday makes clear, second-language education and other language-learning initiatives are often the victims of budget cuts, government reorganization, and austerity measures. Constitutional or political crises can increase hostility to the French fact in Canada. And, though there were three times as many bilingual Canadians living outside Quebec in 2011 as there were in 1961 – and 142,900 more than in 2001 – the percentage slipped from 10.3 percent in 2001 to 9.7 percent in 2011.

Although it is disconcerting to see that some of the unfounded arguments made thirty years ago are still repeated, and that some of the good ideas proposed then were never implemented, the support for Canada's linguistic duality that Hayday describes is still strong. Canadian Parents for French, which has been so important in the fight for effective second-language education in Canada, is still hard at work.

This is an important story that needed to be told.

Graham Fraser,
Commissioner of Official Languages

Preface and Acknowledgments

This book examines a wide array of issues related to how bilingualism has been promoted and opposed in English-speaking Canada. In the chapters that follow, I often approach these events through local, community-based case studies from across the country. When I was conducting formal interviews, and in casual conversations about my research on bilingualism, personal experiences of and attitudes toward language learning quickly came to the forefront. Both supporters and opponents of bilingualism were passionate about this issue and eager to share their opinions. Similarly, I began the research for this book with a set of questions about a topic that matters to me personally, politically, and intellectually (the three being inextricably linked). But it is historical evidence that drives the exploration that follows, and though I cannot claim complete neutrality my goal is to provide a fair and objective evaluation of the various groups and people involved in the debates over bilingualism. Inevitably, though I set aside my personal opinions and prejudices, some personal background doubtless shaped my research. I thought that starting with a short "personal case study" might shed some light on my background, perspectives, and biases.

Both of my parents, children of postwar British immigrants to Canada, thought that their children should learn French. My father grew up in Toronto, Saskatoon, and Montreal. As a teenager in the west island Montreal suburb of Lachine, he attended an English Catholic high school in the 1960s and then university at the English and Catholic Loyola College (now part of Concordia University). Growing up in Quiet Revolution–era Quebec, he was convinced of the merits of bilingualism. My mother, born in St. Catharines, Ontario, and raised in the Toronto suburb of North York, learned French throughout high school. After university, she continued to pursue her study of French as an adult using language cassettes. However, when I started junior kindergarten in 1981, my parents did not enrol me in a French immersion program. Some of their friends had chosen to enrol their children in this exciting new program, in which, for the first few years of elementary school, instruction was entirely in French, with English gradually phased in in later grades. But my parents were of the opinion, based on anecdotal evidence, that immersion produced children who did not speak either language well. The experience of their close friends' eldest child in kindergarten and grade one reaffirmed their decision. (I will return to the temporary "immersion lag" later in my discussion of the immersion language-learning process.)

Instead, I attended a publicly funded Catholic school in North York that had core French as a Second Language (FSL) starting in grade one. My parents did take steps to increase my motivation to learn French outside the regular classroom, including speaking in French to each other in the car when they did not want my sisters and me to understand what they were saying. Eager to "break the code," I picked up some key vocabulary, including *crème glacée* ("ice cream"). In a household that strictly restricted "junk TV," we could watch unlimited hours of French television on Radio-Canada (and later on the provincially run *La chaîne française*), so I could watch as much of *Les Schtroumpfs (The Smurfs)* as I wanted.

In school, I learned French for twenty minutes a day for grades one to six, then for forty minutes a day for grades seven and eight. Unlike many people whom I know, my school benefited from having the same French teachers for several years. Madame Nazar and Madame Opdebeeck developed a curriculum that progressed from year to year. Like other core FSL programs of this period, it stressed written grammar and vocabulary and placed less emphasis on verbal communication. I enjoyed my French classes and worked part time as a French tutor for these teachers after graduation – often with students who had recently immigrated to Canada and were struggling to catch up with French.

In high school, only grade nine French was mandatory. My school offered about seven or eight French classes at the grade nine level. Perhaps 20 percent of my classmates continued on to grade ten French. Of the approximately 200 students in my grade cohort, barely a dozen took French to

This *Fisher* comic strip nicely captures my parents' approach to letting me and my sisters watch French-language television. | *Source: Fisher* comic strip, March 3, 2012. © Philip Street. Used with permission.

the Ontario Academic Credit (OAC – grade thirteen equivalent) level. Although there was some increased emphasis on spoken French at the high school level, most of the emphasis was still on the written language, and I would consider my capacities at graduation to have been good in receptive bilingualism (reading and listening), strong in written grammar, but weak in the spoken language. An undergraduate major in French language and literature (alongside my history major) helped to improve my written French and moderately improve my spoken abilities, but I envied my undergraduate classmates who had taken French immersion, for they were far more comfortable speaking French than I was. It was not until I attended the bilingual University of Ottawa as a graduate student, taking history courses in French with mother tongue francophone students and making francophone friends that my spoken French really started to improve. I still consider my spoken French to be the weakest aspect of my bilingualism. In my years at the University of Ottawa, I made a number of francophone friends and ultimately married my husband, an anglophone from Toronto pursuing degrees in translation. Issues of bilingualism and language are closely intertwined with my personal development, and I have always thought that knowing Canada's second official language has enriched both my personal life and my professional life. That said, though, I have certainly met many people who have thought differently for a variety of reasons and whose attitudes toward learning French ranged from indifference to hostility. These personal perspectives inform this book, but I have also tried to be even-handed in my analysis.

Although this book was shaped by my upbringing, and more importantly by many long years of research, it was not a solo venture. Many people contributed in various ways to bring this book to publication. I had barely started my current job at the University of Guelph when my department chair, Terry Crowley, urged me to submit an application for a Social Sciences and Humanities Research Council of Canada Standard Research Grant for a new project. I was surprised and delighted to win this grant, which helped enormously in getting the research process started. Over the years, this grant allowed me to hire research assistants – Mark Sholdice, Michelle Hebert, Mark Dorsey, Derek Murray, Anthony Hampton, and Colleen Wood – who put in long hours poring over documents and finding great material. I am also grateful for an internal grant from UBC Press and my start-up funding grant from the College of Arts at the University of Guelph, both of which contributed to the publication of this book.

A number of people were enormously helpful in facilitating my access to interviews and archival material. Graham Fraser, the commissioner of official languages, chatted with me about this project as it developed and helped to connect me with his predecessors. He also kindly agreed to write the foreword after reading the final manuscript. Many of his staff – including Luc Chabot, Carsten Quell, Catherine Scott, and Robin Cantin – provided invaluable advice and access to materials. Réjean Lachapelle, recently retired from Statistics Canada, helped me to understand how data on bilingualism have been collected and pointed me to many useful studies. I am also indebted to the people who maintained papers from the history of Canadian Parents for French (CPF) and facilitated my access to them, including Rhianna Edwards and David Mawhinney at Mount Allison University, who helped with the CPF fonds there, Robert Rothon at the BC branch of CPF, and Jim Shea, Cathy Stone, and Joan Hawkins at the CPF national offices. Judy Gibson, Janet Poyen, Berkeley Fleming, Gunild Spiess, Beth Mlacak, Carmeta Abbott, and Marion Langford all kindly gave me access to their personal papers. I would also like to thank all those people who kindly gave of their time for the interviews that enriched this study; they are listed at the end of this book.

I have been fortunate to have many kind friends, family members, and colleagues who agreed to read various chapters of this book in draft form. Particular thanks go to Adam Chapnick, Greg Beneteau, Sally Mennill, Luke Stocking, Kevin Brushett, Steven Huston, Bruce Douville, Will Stos, and members of the Toronto political history reading group. Many of my historian colleagues – including Marcel Martel, Shirley Tillotson, Martin Pâquet, Nicole Neatby, Franca Iacovetta, and Chris Dummitt – have provided helpful advice and encouragement along the way. Kirsty Bell and

Paul Forrest provided much-needed assistance with some of the images in this book. I am also incredibly lucky to work in a very supportive and collegial department in which we have a summer works-in-progress reading group. I would like to thank my friends at the University of Guelph who provided valuable insights on a number of chapters, in particular Alan Gordon, Catherine Carstairs, Susannah Ferreira, Renée Worringer, Richard Reid, Susan Armstrong-Reid, Doug McCalla, Linda Mahood, Stuart McCook, Sofie Lachapelle, and Karen Racine. My PhD students have also patiently listened to me discuss this project, and I am grateful to Serge Dupuis, Marc-André Gagnon, and Ted Cogan both for their insights and for tolerating my rants. My sisters, Catherine and Sarah Hayday, have been the source of much-needed humour and encouragement throughout this process – some of Catherine's pulp fiction–inspired alternate book jacket designs were truly awesome.

Teaching core French in Ontario schools is a difficult profession. Many teachers experience great frustration with the limitations of this program, with student apathy, and with the high rate of teacher turnover. I am lucky to have had a great set of dedicated teachers when I was growing up and want to thank Madame Malec, Madame Keeley, Gloria Nazar, Anne Opdebeeck, Ernesto Facchini, Alexandra Stefaniw, and Paul Frasca. You provided concrete proof that core French teachers can make a major contribution to second-language learning in this country.

A subtle theme in this book is that humour can go a long way toward diffusing hostility toward and skepticism about language learning. In the midst of writing this book, I saw Philip Street's *Fisher* comic strip, which appears above, which so perfectly captured my childhood experiences. It was pinned up on my bulletin board while I researched and wrote this book, and I am glad that he gave permission for it to be reproduced here.

I have been fortunate to work with such a great team at UBC Press over the past several years. Melissa Pitts took an interest in the project in its earliest days, and then, after she advanced within the ranks at the press, Darcy Cullen has been an incredibly supportive and keen editor. The anonymous peer reviewers provided helpful and thoughtful critiques of my manuscript that have made this a stronger book. I would also like to thank my production editor Ann Macklem and my copy editor Dallas Harrison for their careful work and attention to detail in shepherding this book toward its final form.

Finally, there are two people whom I want to single out for special acknowledgment. The first is my husband, Matthew Kayahara, who has put up with far too many conversations about my work, often during what was supposed to be "fun" or vacation time. He patiently let me talk through whatever issue I was grappling with and only occasionally asked "And which of your many projects is this for?" The second is my dad, Bryan Hayday, who was always an enthusiastic supporter of my academic career and loved to talk about my work with his friends. He was a role model for me in his willingness to work in two official languages and his belief in a bilingual Canada. He passed away suddenly in May 2011 while I was in the midst of researching and writing my first draft chapters. This book is dedicated to him because he always joked that my books would sell better if they had action sequences in them. I wish that he could read this one.

Abbreviations

ABC	Action for Bilingual Children
ACELF	Association canadienne d'éducation de langue française
ACFO	Association canadienne-française de l'Ontario
APEC	Alliance for the Preservation of English in Canada
AUCC	Association of Universities and Colleges of Canada
BEP	Bilingualism in Education Program
BES	Bilingual Exchange Secretariat
CABI	Canadians Against Bilingualism Injustice
CAIT	Canadian Association of Immersion Teachers
CASLT	Canadian Association of Second Language Teachers
CAUT	Canadian Association of University Teachers
CCC	Citizens' Committee on Children
CLIN	Canadian Language Information Network
CLR	Canadian League of Rights
CMEC	Council of Ministers of Education, Canada
CNA	Canadian National Association
CNLA	Canadian Network for Language Awareness
COR	Confederation of Regions Party
CPE/CF	Canadian Parents for English/Core French
CPF	Canadian Parents for French
CSTA	Canadian School Trustees' Association
FFHQ	Fédération des francophones hors-Québec

FLQ	Front de libération du Québec
FSL	French as a second language
NAER	National Association for English Rights
NCR	National Capital Region
NFER	National Foundation for Educational Research
OCOL	Office of the Commissioner of Official Languages
OISE	Ontario Institute for Studies in Education
OLEP	Official Languages in Education Program
OLMP	Official Languages Monitor Program
PQ	Parti Québécois
RIN	Rassemblement pour l'indépendance nationale
SANB	Société des Acadiens du Nouveau-Brunswick
SEVEC	Society for Educational Visits and Exchanges Canada
SLBP	Summer Language Bursary Program
SPF	Saanich Parents for French
TFS	Toronto French School
VCL	Voice of Canada League

SO THEY WANT US
TO LEARN FRENCH

Introduction
———————— Canada's Bilingualism Conundrum

In the 1960s, Canada's two solitudes encountered and clashed with each other. Quebec's Quiet Revolution signalled that French-speaking Canadians were no longer going to accept passively being treated as second-class citizens. Some, such as Jean Lesage and Paul Gérin-Lajoie, worked to expand the powers and roles of the Quebec state. Others were drawn to more radical options, such as sovereignty association or separation. While the extremist minority who belonged to the Front de Libération du Québec exploded bombs around the province, many more were drawn to René Lévesque's Parti Québécois and other separatist political parties and used political channels to accomplish their goals. Pierre Trudeau, supported by Lester Pearson, pursued another path. Trudeau went to Ottawa with the goal of making the federal government a bilingual institution so that French-speaking Canadians – including the French Canadian and Acadian minorities being left behind by Quiet Revolution Quebec – would consider Ottawa to be *their* government as well. This was part of Trudeau's vision of a "just society" in which all Canadians, regardless of language, class, or ethnicity, would have equal opportunities to thrive and succeed.

But Canada could not have a bilingual federal government and institutions without more Canadians who could speak both English and French. At least *some* more English-speaking Canadians would have to become bilingual rather than leaving this to French speakers who had been forced to learn English to work in Ottawa. It would be even better if English speakers voluntarily embraced this ideal and came to see bilingualism as part of Canada's identity. This would be a challenge. At hearings of the Royal Commission on Bilingualism and Biculturalism (B&B Commission) in the 1960s, English-speaking Canadians groused that they did not understand why all Canadians did not just speak English. Many French Canadians encountered nastier versions of this sentiment and were told to "Speak White!" when they spoke their own language. It was not a big surprise when, after passage of the Official Languages Act in 1969, many Canadians asked "Why are they trying to force French down our throats?"

English-speaking Canadians have changed their attitudes toward bilingualism since the 1960s. The majority now accepts (though not always embraces) what was once fervently resisted. This is partly because of improved opportunities for Canadians to become bilingual. Starting with a few pilot projects in the 1960s, the Canadian innovation of French immersion took off. Hundreds of thousands of English-speaking children are now enrolled in these programs. Canadian parents have fought to improve the French as a Second Language (FSL) programs offered as part of the regular school curriculum. They hoped that these classes might actually produce language learning, rather than frustration, in the children who took them. These families are part of a rather remarkable phenomenon. Despite speaking the majority language of their country and continent – arguably the dominant language of the planet – these Canadians thought that it was important for their children to learn the language of their country's official language minority community.

On the other hand, while the total number of Canadians who can speak Canada's two official languages has increased over time, as a percentage of the total population this figure has remained both fairly constant and quite low – always less than 20 percent of the total population. Bilingualism remains less common among English speakers (anglophones) than among French speakers (francophones). Although polling data have consistently shown that a majority of English-speaking Canadians accept the official languages policy and think that children should have opportunities to learn French in school, they are not actually becoming bilingual in droves. The question "Why are they trying to shove French down our throats?" has frequently been replaced by the statement "Sorry, I don't speak French." Indeed, this was the title of journalist Graham Fraser's 2006 book, which examined the limitations of Canada's language policies in reaching their goals.[1]

How do we reconcile these more favourable attitudes and increased opportunities with the rather limited increase in personal bilingualism among the Canadian population? To find the answer to this question, this book explores the various ways in which bilingualism on an individual level was promoted to English-speaking Canadians from the 1960s to the late 1990s. Over these decades, governments and social movement actors undertook major projects to recraft Canada's national identity – and others resisted these efforts. The book aims to explain how Canadians engaged with the language-related dimensions of these nation-shaping efforts. While opponents of bilingualism claimed that the government of Canada was trying to "shove," "force," or "cram" French down their throats,[2] other groups tried to make the prospect of becoming bilingual seem more pleasant, coaxing Canadians to embrace the benefits afforded by bilingualism. At present, it remains practically impossible for a day to go by without one language-related issue or another making the news. Official languages and bilingualism remain contentious and important aspects of Canada's politics and society. The debates surrounding them have deep roots, and today's dramas echo, and often repeat, those that have been ongoing for decades.

Major Research Questions and Parameters

A major objective of this book is to determine why some Canadians came to believe fervently in the merits of individual bilingualism, to the extent of being willing to fight for better educational opportunities and to promote bilingualism as a national Canadian value during a period of intense constitutional politics. Conversely, why is it that, fifty years after the B&B Commission was formed, and with over forty years of federal government funding and support for second-language education, the overall level of English-French bilingualism[3] among English-speaking Canadians has remained low? There has been only a modest increase in the total number of bilingual English-speaking Canadians over the past half century and a slighter increase when this is expressed as a percentage of the population. How do we account for the successes, and the failures, of the proponents of individual bilingualism during these decades?

My main interests in writing this book relate to questions surrounding the growth of personal bilingualism in the predominantly English-speaking Canadian communities outside Quebec. By English-speaking Canadians, I am referring to Canadians whose primary language of use was English. This includes both those who had English as their mother tongue and those who adopted English as their most commonly used language. The book emphasizes issues related to the promotion of bilingualism undertaken by civil society actors, such as lobby groups and social movement organizations, and some quasi-governmental actors, such as the commissioner of official languages. I also examine the reactions, both positive and negative, to campaigns and efforts to promote bilingualism in English-speaking Canada. What emerges are explanations of how and why progress was made in expanding opportunities for French-language learning for those who chose to pursue this goal. It also becomes apparent why these efforts encountered fierce resistance in some quarters, beyond (but not excluding) anti-French prejudice.

"Bilingualism" can mean many different things. The term is imbued with powerful negative and positive connotations, and it was not uncommon for activists, politicians, and writers to muddy the waters deliberately. In the interests of clarity, a few definitions might be useful. The main interest of this book is with *personal* or *individual bilingualism,* which means the ability of individual people to communicate in both English and French (Canada's two official languages after 1969). This is often confused with *institutional bilingualism,* which means the capacity of an institution – such as the federal government – to provide services and function in both English and French. Institutional bilingualism does not require that all individuals working for the institution be bilingual, though a certain percentage need to be to make it function. There are also several levels of language proficiency that an individual can reach, so the question of whether a person is bilingual might be answered in different ways depending on the threshold of language competency. On the issue of bilingualism as a national value, some Canadians supported both types of bilingualism, but many were resistant to the idea of individual bilingualism if it were anything other than a voluntary personal choice. Driving this book are questions related to personal bilingualism as opposed to how governments could or should be bilingual institutions (though these latter issues certainly crop up).

The Cast of Characters
When this project started, I intended to study the promotion of bilingualism aimed at all segments of the Canadian population. However, while delving into social movement campaigns and initiatives, it became apparent that little was done in Canada between 1960 and 2000 to try to increase bilingualism among Canadians older than postsecondary students, apart from language retraining programs for civil servants and the occasional reference to private language courses. The emphasis was overwhelmingly on language training for the next generation, or the "youth option," as it was often called. That emphasis is now my main focus, though I cast an eye on

initiatives targeting the non–civil servant adult population, including those aimed at convincing adults of the merits of supporting – often with their tax dollars – programs capable of raising a bilingual generation of young Canadians. This in turn required gaining broad support for bilingualism as a Canadian value.

The major focus of this book is on how individual bilingualism was promoted to English-speaking Canadians by civil society organizations. The federal government was keen to promote its new official languages policies and could provide funding for some initiatives. But it was the grassroots energies of Canadians who believed in the merits of bilingualism and the new Canadian identity with which it was connected that helped these policies to flourish. These activists undertook campaigns so that the next generation of Canadians could grow up bilingual, further cementing bilingualism as a Canadian value. In the sections of this book dealing with the period prior to 1977, the emphasis is on a number of small, often isolated groups across the country. For the period following 1977, the emphasis shifts to the nation-wide association of Canadian Parents for French (CPF). CPF is an organization of English-speaking parents – many of them unilingual – who wanted better opportunities for their children to learn French and lobbied at federal, provincial, and local levels across Canada to improve FSL programs and get French immersion programs created. Of the pro-bilingualism groups, CPF maintained the greatest array of archival and published primary sources, and many former members were willing to participate in oral history interviews. CPF was also by far the dominant organization working to improve access to bilingualism through the education system. I do consider other pro-bilingualism organizations, such as those that sponsored exchange programs, though their documentary records are more fragmentary. CPF was active in every province and territory, and I draw on examples from different parts of the country and communities of varying sizes and demographic profiles, without attempting exhaustive coverage of its activities.

Individuals and social movement organizations opposed to bilingualism and Canada's official language policies were less organized and left records that were much more fragmentary. They also – proudly – did not receive any funding from the government and thus were not subject to the same sort of reporting requirements facing groups such as Canadian Parents for French. Unfortunately, the consequence was that these groups did not maintain the same types of archival records or issue public financial statements or annual reports. The most well-known of these groups, the Alliance for the Preservation of English in Canada, did publish a newsletter from the late 1970s to the mid-1990s, but there are no formal library holdings of the full run, and my efforts to track it down in private archives have yielded only individual issues or runs of a couple of years. My analysis of these organizations is therefore rooted more heavily in the books that they published, their direct interactions with pro-bilingualism groups, and their appearances in the media. Most of the key individuals involved in anti-bilingualism groups had passed away by the time that I was conducting my research. The one key individual still alive, Jock Andrew, declined to be interviewed, claiming that my "study, no matter how good, would be little more than the record of the conquest of a nation by a determined third of its population. I watched it happen and I do not wish to relive it again."[4]

This book devotes several chapters to the Office of the Commissioner of Official Languages. The commissioner was an officer of Parliament who stood apart from the formal federal government bureaucracy. I am particularly interested in the "unofficial" nature of the commissioners' activities as champions of bilingualism in Canada rather than in their formal "watchdog" or ombudsman roles of evaluating the progress of the official languages policies within federal agencies. The commissioners and their staffs demonstrated great creativity in fostering support for bilingualism among English-speaking Canadians. Although their actions in promoting personal bilingualism were not envisioned as part of the Official Languages Act, when this office was created, the commissioners' initiatives were not opposed, and often were welcomed, by the governments of the day.

Canada's public servants encountered personal bilingualism in ways very different and important from those of the language learners central to this book. Unlike those participating in bilingualism initiatives on a voluntary basis – whether as parents, students, or otherwise civically engaged Canadians – civil servants acquired French as a second language while "on the job," where that skill was becoming compulsory. Bilingualism in their case was less promoted than mandated. How the federal government and its civil service developed official languages policies and dealt with bilingualism are questions that merit separate study. Certain aspects of this issue have been considered, whereas others await treatment.[5] In this book, governments and their bureaucracies come into view as they interact with social movements, whether as targets of lobbying efforts or as funders for some groups.

A final group of individuals keenly involved in the activities covered by this book are the education experts and front-line teachers involved in second-language education. This book does not investigate the finer points of the academic debates over second-language education, nor does it provide a comprehensive study of the teachers' associations and their activities. I am more interested in how the research conducted by experts was mobilized as part of the arguments of social movement actors for or against certain programs (and by their direct involvement, at times, within these organizations). But since both front-line teachers and education experts were engaged as allies for both pro- and anti-bilingualism groups, I tend to refer to them, their public position statements, and their activities when they came directly into contact or conflict with one of the social movement organizations. Similarly, I also look at some of the ways that groups such as the Canadian Association of Second-Language Teachers (CASLT) and the Canadian Association of Immersion Teachers (CAIT) worked together with advocates of second-language teaching to advance their mutual goals.

This period of French-language promotion in English-speaking Canada also witnessed efforts at partnership and joint action with Canada's francophone minority community associations and organizations. In some cases, francophone groups partnered with English-speaking proponents of bilingualism to pursue joint goals. In other cases, they found themselves at odds when certain FSL learning programs ran counter to the priorities of the francophone groups. Sometimes the proponents of bilingualism found themselves, uncomfortably, in tense or adversarial relationships with their would-be allies.

Theoretical Framework and Bodies of Literature
In recent years, as archival sources have been opened to researchers, there has been a flurry of historical writing pertaining to the 1960s and 1970s. A key theme in much of this literature is how Canada's national identity was undergoing transformation. This transformation could be seen in a number of ways. There were initiatives designed to promote a made-in-Canada popular culture. New social welfare programs aimed both to promote the health of the population and to build a broader sense of national community (and a larger federal government). A new politics of national identity emerged, seeking to replace an older, British Canadian model of identity with one more inclusive of the growing linguistic and ethnic diversity of the country.

Many authors point to the postwar years, particularly the 1960s, as a key transitional period between models of Canada. José Igartua argues in *The Other Quiet Revolution: National Identities in English Canada, 1945–71* that this decade saw the replacement of the British Canadian model with

English-speaking Canadians (or at least their elites) embracing a multi-cultural, bilingual approach.[6] Bryan Palmer contends that the old models were blown up in the 1960s but that nothing concrete emerged to replace them.[7] Chris Champion, on the other hand, sees strong traces of the British Canadian tradition in the new symbols and policies of the Pearson and Trudeau governments, even as they claimed to replace the old order.[8] I have argued in work related to other aspects of the Canadian government's identity policies that Igartua's thesis is at least partly correct, though I see it as more of an ongoing process.[9]

This book looks at a number of the language and cultural elements of the new Canadian identity emerging and vying for acceptance in this period. Although I have disagreed with certain aspects of Kenneth McRoberts's *Misconceiving Canada: The Struggle for National Unity*, I do agree with his premise that the Trudeau government attempted to "implant a new Canadian identity" that transformed the way that many English Canadians think about Canada.[10] Certainly, the new order seemed to have its adherents, but it was not universally accepted, which suggests that Champion's arguments have at least some merit. There was a rearguard of English-speaking Canadians – many of whom were what Eva Mackey terms "unmarked," white, "Canadian-Canadians," or "ordinary Canadians" – who resented or resisted the new identity politics and did not see themselves, the "silent mass" of the majority, as being reflected in this new Canada.[11]

The study of official languages, language learning, bilingualism, and English-French relations has received growing attention in recent decades from a wide array of scholars in different fields. Marcel Martel and Martin Pâquet have written an excellent overview of Canada's language politics – available in both official languages – that provides a concise introduction to the major themes and questions that have animated these debates over the past four and a half centuries in North America.[12] Their survey makes evident, however, that most of the scholarly work in political science, sociology, socio-linguistics, and history in Canada – and this is not a unique situation – deals largely with the political and social questions that relate to language rights and services for linguistic minorities. Indeed, these have long been the animating questions that seem to guide language laws and policies in many countries. How does one accommodate linguistic diversity? How far should services in the minority language be extended? To what extent should minorities be permitted to control their own educational systems or be educated in their mother tongues? How much autonomy could or should be provided to minority-language communities? What are the sociological impacts of living in a minority situation and of bilingualism on the minority-language community individual?[13] How can language laws be crafted to protect minorities? There is a wealth of literature on this topic in both Canada and other countries, not surprising since it deals with fundamental issues of cultural survival and preservation, issues often dear to the hearts of scholars from these communities studying these topics.[14]

Education specialists, with Canadian experts among the leaders in the field, have made great strides in analyzing the "how" questions related to best practices in second-language instruction. They have also identified key issues related to student motivation and parental support and how these issues relate to success in language learning. But those studies, by and large, are not primarily interested in the broader national or regional political and cultural contexts in which this education takes place. The issues of how to craft policies and how to create broad support among the *majority* population for enhancing bilingualism have not really been addressed, and these issues animate this study.

In both the Canadian and the international literature, some attention has been paid to resistance to bilingualism among majority populations, particularly with regard to the Official English or English-only movements in the United States. This research emphasizes resistance among the majority population to extending any official recognition to other languages, particularly in education. Raymond Tatalovich considers these campaigns of resistance to be intimately tied to nativism and anti-immigration discourses.[15] James Crawford and Carol Schmid add that these English-only or anti-bilingualism campaigns serve as proxies for concerns over any recognition of diversity that might create "special status" for a group or render acceptable a civil society that operates in a language other than English.[16] Although these works do not directly address the issue of English-speaking Americans who choose to learn another language (such as Spanish), they do provide useful concepts for understanding Canadians who opposed all forms of bilingualism, ranging from government services in French, to French minority-language education, to FSL education for English-speaking Canadians.

Bilingual countries in Europe are of limited value as points of contrast with Canada in terms of second-language learning because, in many cases, the "minority" language learned as the second official language by students has greater prestige as an international or regional language. This is the case in Belgium, for example, where until recently the numerically larger Flemish community was more likely to learn the other official language because French had greater international status than Dutch. Although almost a third of Finland's population speaks Swedish as a second language, the language of their small linguistic minority and numerically more populous neighbour, this pales next to the more than 60 percent who speak English. Recent experiments with immersion education in the province of Andalusia, Spain, use languages such as English and French, not Spain's minority languages of Basque and Catalan. In any case, there appears to be something distinctive about countries in the so-called Anglosphere in terms of their resistance to learning second languages that sets them apart from continental Europe and other parts of the world. This resistance seems to be linked to the growing international predominance of English and its popularity as a second language among people with other mother tongues.[17]

I examine much of bilingualism promoters' activism through the lens of social movements, even though the actors in this book do not really resemble the stereotypical militant 1960s social activist. This stereotype, admittedly, is overblown and unrepresentative of the diversity of social movement activism. Even in the 1960s, for instance, Canadian peace activists in Voice of Women were keen to maintain their image as "respectable" women and indeed used it to their advantage.[18] In their 1998 book, David Meyer and Sidney Tarrow posited that, in the decades following the 1960s, social movement activity became more widespread and socially acceptable or at least less subject to social opprobrium. A much wider array of actors could engage in a more established array of social movement activism tactics and strategies, and governments were becoming much more used to dealing with social movements. They argued that a "social movement society" had emerged by the 1990s.[19] More recent scholarship has reconsidered the timing of the emergence of this society and qualified some of its premises.[20] Many of its conclusions have been borne out in the Canadian context, often with an earlier start date for the "normalization" of social movement–government relations than posited by Meyer and Tarrow. Indeed, even before the appearance of their work, Leslie Pal had convincingly argued that the Trudeau and Mulroney governments, through the Department of the Secretary of State, had been directly funding a host of different social movement organizations, with the partial objective of bolstering public support for their social and cultural policy objectives. Pal had argued that this did not mean direct government control over these groups, though it did channel their social movement activism in certain directions.[21] Historians – including Dominique Clément, Kevin Brushett, and Andrew Nurse – have further developed our understanding of this important government–social movement dynamic in post-1960s Canada.[22]

Historical institutionalist approaches to public policy are key to my understanding of how social movements related to bilingualism operated in the Canadian context. This approach, which owes much to the scholarship of Theda Skocpol and Paul Pierson, and much earlier theoretical work by sociologist Max Weber, attaches great importance to the state as an active and autonomous participant in public policy debates, often acting through bureaucracies and civil services.[23] As Paul Pierson observes, policy legacies also matter a great deal, since policies put in place during one historical period will shape politics and policy development in future periods. This is referred to as "path dependency," since it creates a preference for a given set of policy choices that is often difficult to change.[24] This is particularly important for understanding the role of the commissioner of official languages. The first commissioner, Keith Spicer, took the office in an unanticipated direction, with major ramifications for how the office later maintained its involvement in bilingualism promotion. Neo-pluralist scholars, building on historical institutionalist theories, have added governments and bureaucracies to the repertoire of key actors that can seek to shape public policy. They acknowledge that the bureaucracy might deliberately seek to cultivate and support certain social movement actors and citizen groups to support its policies.[25] The relationship between Canadian Parents for French and the Department of the Secretary of State (as well as the Office of the Commissioner of Official Languages), examined in the middle chapters of this book, is much more easily comprehended in light of this theoretical framework.

In examining the social movements involved in these debates, my focus is somewhat different from that of theorists who seek broad explanations for how and why social movements arise. My analysis does draw on a number of the concepts from social movement scholarship to explain the successes or failures of the social movements discussed in this book. However, rather than being wedded to a single theoretical framework of social movement theory and applying it systematically to all aspects of pro- and anti-bilingualism social movements, my research suggests that elements from various (sometimes competing) theoretical schools are applicable to different points in the history of these movements. No single theoretical framework fully captures the history of social movement activism around the issue of bilingualism, but many of the concepts and tools from this literature are useful in helping to explain certain elements of both how these social movements operated internally and how they interacted with both the state and Canadian society.

In particular, I draw on aspects of both resource mobilization theory and the political process models developed by Sidney Tarrow, Doug McAdam, John McCarthy, and others.[26] Resource mobilization theorists have emphasized how social movements mobilize supporters around a common cause and then attempt to maximize the diverse resources that they can bring to bear – people, expertise, money, and so on – in support of that cause. The political process model acknowledges the importance of mobilizing these resources and adds the concept of the political opportunity structure, which refers to key windows of opportunity when social movements can have impacts on policy. These windows are affected by various factors, including openness of the political system, sympathetic allies, divisions among elites, and stability or instability of political alignments. This model posits that there are key points in history when a political system might be more open or more closed to the possibility of change and that movements can capitalize on these points. In other words, a social movement's success is determined not solely by its own resources but also by external factors in the system that it seeks to change.[27]

Within the theoretical literature on political opportunities are heated debates about whether these opportunities spawn social movements or whether pre-existing social movement actors create and foster the conditions that lead to more open political systems. In some respects, this is a "chicken-and-egg" problem, since the conditions that foster political opportunities for one social movement can result from the actions of *other* social movements. Tarrow's "cycles of contention" model is useful here.[28] Tarrow notes that historically there have been waves of social protest and social movement activity. A given social movement's activities, if successful, can spur additional social movements into action, because they either demonstrate the existence of political opportunities or in fact bring them into being. The actions of this next wave of social movements can in turn lead to greater openness by the state to change or to a period of repression. They can also trigger actions by counter-movements opposed to the new directions taken by the state and society. These interactions are extremely complex. They are also historically contingent, which makes developing a predictive theoretical model highly problematic. As a tool for explaining events in the past, however, the concept of political opportunities is useful to my analysis.

Early theoretical models of both political opportunities and resource mobilization tended to be dismissive of earlier psychological and sociological scholarship on collective behaviour that focused on the role played by grievances in instigating social movement activity; their emphasis was on external political structures and concrete resources that could be brought to bear on social movement organization activity.[29] More recent scholarship has brought these two schools together, adopting a broader conceptualization of collective behaviour theory that encompasses other motivational factors, such as emotions, values, and discontent with existing structures and governance. Together they feed into larger debates about the concept of "framing," which applies both to how social movements define the types of injustices and problems that they seek to address and to how the movements define themselves and their values and how they conceptualize the states and societies in which they operate.

These new approaches are also the products of interactions between North American scholars and European scholars of the "new social movement theory" school who were studying concepts such as the creation of collective identities.[30] The new social movement school has been challenged, however, on its initial argument that many post-1960 social movements (unlike their predecessors from the labour movement, for example) were primarily driven by identities and values rather than a material basis. Many scholars have argued that this distinction is perhaps not so clear-cut. Nevertheless, the conceptual tools of framing and collective identities have been incorporated into revised versions of the political process model. Indeed, as will become evident when I consider the motivations of those who advocated for bilingualism and French-language education for their children, issues around values and considerations of potential economic advantages were both in play.

My analysis of social movements is also influenced by Miriam Smith, who does not see a stark division between social movements (or social movement organizations) and interest groups in terms of their actions or organizational structures.[31] The same concepts can be productively employed to analyze the behaviour of both groups, if clearly definable differences between them even exist. Throughout this analysis of social movement and interest group activity, evidence drawn from the actions of these groups is the driving force, with concepts and tools from these theoretical models applied as appropriate. My main objective is to explain how and why these pro- and anti-bilingualism social movements succeeded and failed, not to prove or disprove a particular theoretical model.

Engaging with how bilingualism was received among the English Canadian population from the 1960s on also requires considering the many factors that social, political, economic, and cultural historians apply more

broadly to their analyses of all events. Debates over the merits of bilingualism related intimately to the shifting terrain of and debates over Canadian
national identity and took place against the backdrop of major constitutional
debates, including the 1967 Confederation of Tomorrow Conference, the
1980 Quebec Referendum, the 1980–82 patriation of the Constitution, the
Meech Lake and Charlottetown Accords, and the 1995 Quebec Referendum. They must all be borne in mind as the context in which Canadians
considered the place of English and French in their country's politics and
society. Nor is this an issue that can be discussed in solely national terms.
Significant regional differences from province to province, and within individual provinces, not only played a role in shaping intellectual attitudes
toward bilingualism but also determined the practical considerations about
whether resources to improve bilingualism among the population were
available.

Issues of race and ethnicity also played a complicated role in the debates
over bilingualism. Much of the anti-bilingualism rhetoric was couched in explicitly racist language, casting aspersions on both the French language and
the "French Canadian race" that spoke it. Although it might seem peculiar
now to think of French Canadians as a "race," it is important to bear in mind
that many aspects of race are a social construction. French Canadians were
certainly treated as a different racial group in the 1960s and 1970s. This treatment, indeed, led Pierre Vallières, an intellectual sympathetic to the Front
de Libération du Québec (FLQ), to title his manifesto *White Niggers of
America*, likening French Canadians to African Americans.[32] On a less con-
frontational level, there was active debate about the merits of biculturalism
versus multiculturalism in forging a new Canadian identity. Many of Canada's racial and ethnic communities felt alienated from the bilingualism
discourse. This fed into concerns, particularly linked to French immersion,
about the inclusion or exclusion of new immigrants and racial minorities.

Class-based analysis was routinely a part of critiques of the French programs advanced by opponents of bilingualism. French immersion, in particular, was often subject to allegations of upper-middle-class privilege and
elitism. Gender was also a crucial factor in how resources were mobilized,
particularly in the pro-bilingualism camp. Gender-based factors also played
into discussions on whom bilingualism was perceived to benefit, particularly with respect to jobs for teachers and which students took French
classes. Age and generational identity also shaped people's opinions about
bilingualism. There was often a fairly stark divide along age lines (and, to a

certain extent, by ethnic identity) between the most fervent pro- and anti-bilingualism advocates.

Broad trends in the economy also came into play in the debates about how best to advance bilingualism. Not always the merits of language learning but sometimes the perceived costs of these programs in a contracting economy were at issue. The personal stakes of individuals and their livelihoods and jobs cannot be ignored. And, of course, the changing demographic tides, particularly those affecting Canada's student-aged population, which waned and waxed over the decades covered in this book, added broader structural considerations of which programs would be sustainable.

There were broader intellectual debates over educational philosophies and over opportunity and equity in society that fed into the specific debates about French-language education and bilingualism. Arguments related to special French programs, whether French immersion or extended French, were often not about the merits of the programs themselves, and how effective they were in teaching the language, but about broader concerns over equality of opportunity and streaming. Opponents of expanded French programs, even optional ones, frequently cast this in terms of a zero-sum game in which some students would benefit and others would not. Similarly, proposals to expand the amount of core French within the regular curriculum were opposed because of how other programs or subjects might suffer. Debates over which students could benefit from second-language learning were often framed as concerns about students with learning disabilities or special needs.

All of these aforementioned factors combined and interacted in diverse ways, in different local contexts, and at different points during the years covered in this book. No single factor provides an adequate explanation of how and why certain groups achieved their objectives regarding personal bilingualism, but together these factors shape the arguments that this book advances.

The Progression of Bilingualism in English-Speaking Canada

This book advances a number of arguments related to developments in individual bilingualism in English-speaking Canada. Supporters of bilingualism largely agreed with the vision of Canadian identity that valued two official languages as framed from the 1960s on. They actively articulated and advanced this conception of Canada. Beyond this conception, they were sold on the educational, intellectual, and economic merits of individual bilingualism. As the decade progressed, they became increasingly convinced of the merits of bilingualism in the context of globalization. The key activists in the social movements favourable to bilingualism were often, but not always, concerned about the national unity dimensions of the language question. Much of their success, at least in terms of creating new optional language programs, can be attributed to a favourable political opportunity structure, particularly in the 1970s and 1980s, when there were key governmental supports in terms of both program and organizational funding.

There were also a number of key positive factors related to resource mobilization. This was particularly the case from the late 1960s to the early 1980s, when the pro-bilingualism groups could draw heavily on the energies and skills of relatively young, and often university-educated, mothers not in the paid workforce. They could also count on supportive allies in the media, business community, bureaucracy, and all three major political parties. Many of the pro-bilingualism activists had previous experience in other social movement activities and organizing. Educational research was a crucial tool in the arsenal of bilingualism's promoters. The new French programs, especially immersion, were extensively studied by academics, and the results were positive. Canadian Parents for French actively disseminated the results of this research, which played a major role in overcoming myths and fears about French immersion. Parents flocked to enrol their children in these programs because of the job opportunities and the intellectual and cultural benefits that they believed would result.

Opponents of bilingualism arrived at their position for an array of reasons, and this affected the intensity of their opposition. There was some opposition from teachers' unions and administrators in the English-speaking stream of the provincial education systems. This often stemmed from fears of potential job losses, pointing to the merits of the economic grievance–based theories of social movement mobilization. At the other end of the spectrum were xenophobic individuals who saw no merit in the French language and were hostile to Quebec's culture (the terms "priest-ridden" and "backward" were bandied about freely). Between these two poles were various individuals and groups fearful or uneasy about the rise of a new conception of Canada in which bilingualism challenged their privileged position, whether on the personal level or on the broader level of institutional bilingualism. They were often unlikely to separate the two completely in their rhetoric. Emotions, particularly anger and fear, were also potent motivators for action among these actors. Many of them expressed variants of the argument that the language question "should have been settled with the conquest." This speaks to their conceptions of political and social power and how it was challenged by the new value attached to bilingualism.

Broader national questions played a role in determining the general sympathies of English-speaking Canadians for French second-language education specifically as opposed to second-language instruction more broadly. Turmoil over Quebec separatism from 1976 to 1980, and again in the constitutional crises from 1987 to 1995, dampened support for French second-language learning. The spectre of Quebec separating diminished the appeal, for many English-speaking Canadians, of pushing for French-language instruction for their children. Some linked this to a quid pro quo for what they saw as diminished English-language rights in Quebec, while others thought that the value of French-language skills would be lessened in a Canada without Quebec. Although a substantial number of Canadians were willing to contemplate bilingualism as a gesture of national unity in the 1960s and 1970s, they were less likely, in the later period covered in this book, to think that it would have any impact.

New programs to enhance French education did have costs, and the extent to which concerns over costs, particularly in recessionary periods, could be allayed by the promise of federal funding played a major role in the success or failure of many local campaigns for FSL and French immersion. Federal government cutbacks to funding of bilingual programs and organizations that supported bilingualism made in two major rounds – the late 1970s and early 1990s – came at the worst possible moments in terms of waning sympathies for French-language learning because of constitutional turmoil and heightened economic concerns about the costs of these programs. Although we should shy away from counterfactual arguments and historical "what-ifs" regarding what might have happened if the federal government had sustained, or even increased, its budget for official languages programming during these periods, we can observe what did happen. Those indicators – stalled provincial investment in French second-language programming, plateauing enrolment in French immersion in the mid-1990s, and plummeting public support for mandatory FSL learning in the 1990s – indicate that these cutbacks certainly did not help. The emphasis of this book is not on the bilingualism policies in the federal public service, but one might make the case that there was a failure of nerve in the federal government to defend strongly the principle that, in some cases, mandatory bilingualism would be part of how it operated. It might also have been more forceful in asserting that Canadian individuals and provincial governments should not have assumed or expected that Ottawa would bear sole responsibility for training a bilingual workforce.

The development of policies for and debates about bilingualism in English-speaking Canada did not take place in a completely linear fashion, and the chronology of events in one community did not always line up with what was happening elsewhere in the country. I was overwhelmed, in conducting the primary source research for this book, by the richness of the material available, the revealing interviews that I was able to conduct, and the detailed stories that I would be able to tell for so many Canadian communities. Naturally, not all of their stories could fit into this book. I have selected individual case studies that illustrate particular points about social movement activities or factors influencing a given debate. As a result, though the chapters that follow are organized both chronologically and thematically as much as possible, the individual case studies are not always confined to the chronological boundaries of the chapters.

In an effort to try to situate these events for readers, Chapter 1 provides a broad historical overview of the period covered by this book, identifying the key political events, constitutional debates, and social, demographic, and economic trends that formed the backdrop for the specific debates over bilingualism. Readers familiar with post-1960 Canadian history might wish to proceed straight to Chapter 2, which examines the early activism of groups interested in bilingualism prior to the 1969 Official Languages Act and federal funding for educational programs. Chapter 3 begins the discussion of the curious role played by the Office of the Commissioner of Official Languages. The first commissioner, Keith Spicer, went beyond the formal mandate of his office to try to foster greater appreciation of bilingualism among English-speaking Canadians, and he attempted to create more focus on the youth-oriented dimensions of these efforts. Chapter 4 examines developments in the social movements during the Spicer years, from 1970 to 1976, in the years leading up to the election of the Parti Québécois. This chapter pays particular attention both to the often isolated parent groups attempting to use federal funding to convince their school boards to offer better French programs and to the early anti-bilingualism activists who felt deeply threatened by the Official Languages Act and hoped to stop official bilingualism in its tracks.

Chapters 5 to 7 cover the first decade of Canadian Parents for French, from 1977 to 1986. In Chapter 5, I examine the national-level activities of this new social movement of English-speaking parents as it established its infrastructure, published materials on French-language learning, and lobbied the federal and provincial governments to provide funding for French-language learning. It also faced off against increasingly high-profile anti-bilingualism individuals and groups, including Jock Andrew and the Alliance for the Preservation of English in Canada. Chapter 6 discusses the role played by Maxwell Yalden, who became the commissioner of official languages as CPF was getting started. He held this office in a period spanning both the first Quebec Referendum and the creation of the Charter of Rights and Freedoms, and the chapter analyzes his efforts to continue and deepen the initial work done by Spicer. Chapter 7 takes a community-based approach to CPF, looking at a number of local efforts to expand FSL programs and French immersion and considering the challenges that these parents faced.

By the mid-1980s, the Office of the Commissioner of Official Languages was retreating from activist promotion of individual bilingualism, and Chapter 8 looks at what remained of those efforts during the terms of D'Iberville Fortier and Victor Goldbloom in the late 1980s and 1990s. In Chapters 9 and 10, I look at the incredibly tumultuous decade of constitutional crisis from 1986 to 1996 and study the clashing pro- and anti-bilingualism activism that took place against the backdrop of the Meech Lake and Charlottetown Accords, Quebec's revived language debates, the economic recession of the early 1990s, and the 1995 Quebec Referendum. In Chapter 9, I note that Canadian Parents for French still had some momentum and provide evidence of improved Canadian attitudes toward bilingualism (particularly through polling) in the late 1980s. In Chapter 10, though, which covers the first half of the 1990s, I note that financial cutbacks and a strained constitutional climate caused enrolments in French immersion to stall and public support for French-language learning to decline. Anti-Quebec sentiments fuelled the growth of the Alliance for the Preservation of English in Canada and other groups that took direct aim at French immersion and FSL programing in Canadian schools. This decade sapped much of the momentum and optimism of bilingualism's supporters. Chapter 11 covers the turn of the millennium, a period when activists and politicians tried to figure out how to move forward and revitalize the bilingualism dossier. Finally, the conclusion pulls together the major findings on how and why activists on both sides of the individual bilingualism debate succeeded or failed in achieving their objectives, and it offers some explanations of the relatively limited progress in making English-speaking Canadians, as a group, more bilingual than they had been in the 1960s.

For advocates of bilingualism, these were exciting decades. They thought that they were helping to build a better Canada and a brighter future for the

next generation. Learning French would open doors and provide enrichment for their children. For opponents of bilingualism, its spread was connected to the decline of the vision of Canada that they cherished. The
expansion of French-language learning was deeply threatening to them, and
they reacted with hostility and vitriol. It all made for a spirited atmosphere
as these social movement activists engaged with society and the state, trying
to make the case for their vision of Canada and the place of languages within
it. There was creativity along with conflict, perseverance along with passion.
Bilingualism was anything but boring; it got to the root of how Canadians
thought about themselves. It is to the story of how their campaigns played
out that I now turn.

1

Bilingualism and Official Languages in Canada

The progression of issues related to bilingualism in Canada often happened at different paces in different regions of Canada, and the timelines of what occurred in various sectors of activity do not always align perfectly. Similarly, much of the analysis in subsequent chapters will not follow a strict chronological progression. In the hope of avoiding too much repetition, this chapter presents the timeline of major events that formed the political, economic, and social contexts of debates over bilingualism in Canada. Readers familiar with the major political and constitutional issues related to bilingualism, official languages, and English-French relations from the 1960s to 2000 might wish to skip to Chapter 2.

This chapter provides a brief overview of the political events, major laws, policy shifts, constitutional changes, and economic, demographic, and social trends that helped to shape the reactions of the Canadian public to the new initiatives related to bilingualism. Readers interested in a more thorough treatment of the history of language policy issues and English-French relations in Canada will be well served by Marcel Martel and Martin Pâquet's excellent overview, *Speaking Up: A History of Language and Politics in Quebec and Canada* (originally published in French as *Langue et politique au Canada et au Québec: Une synthèse historique*).[1] The finer details of the development of federal funding programs for official languages in education (both minority-language education and second-language instruction) and how this played out in various provinces from the 1960s on are covered in my book *Bilingual Today, United Tomorrow: Official Languages in Education and Canadian Federalism.*[2]

In the text of the 1867 British North America Act, perhaps surprisingly in light of the cultural and linguistic tensions of the pre-Confederation period, there was very little about how language issues would be handled in Canada. The sole section reads thus:

> 133. Either the English or the French Language may be used by any Person in the Debates of the Houses of the Parliament of Canada and of the Houses of the Legislature of Quebec; and both those Languages shall be used in the respective Records and Journals of those Houses; and either of those Languages may be used by any Person or in any Pleading or Process in or issuing from any Court of Canada established under this Act, and in or from all or any of the Courts of Quebec.
>
> The Acts of the Parliament of Canada and of the Legislature of Quebec shall be printed and published in both those Languages[3].

When Manitoba joined Confederation in 1870, section 23 of the Manitoba Act mimicked this wording:

> 23. Either the English or the French language may be used by any person in the debates of the Houses of the Legislature and both those languages shall be used in the respective Records and Journals of those Houses; and either of those languages may be used by any person, or in any Pleading or Process, in or issuing from any Court of Canada established under the *British North America Act, 1867,* or in or from all or any of the Courts of the Province. The Acts of the Legislature shall be Printed and published in both those languages.[4]

Although education was considered to be the sector in which issues of language and culture were most important and likely to be protected, no wording in these constitutional documents explicitly dealt with language rights in education. Confessional education rights were explicitly protected, and this was a sector assigned to the provinces. Moreover, nowhere in these documents was there any explicit wording to indicate that the legislatures, courts, and acts of Parliament were the *only* places where French could be used in an official capacity. However, in the 1960s, a number of historians and anti-bilingualism proponents would claim that the wording of these documents suggested that in all other realms of government activity only English had official status.

In the decades that followed, Canada's federal government and the governments of the provinces other than Quebec did act as if English were the only official language. Most provinces took steps between the 1890s and 1920s to curtail the use of French as a language of education and to eliminate any use of that language in provincial legislatures and courts. English was by far the dominant language of the civil service as it grew and professionalized in the twentieth century. French speakers were underrepresented in the senior ranks of the civil service and overwhelmingly bilingual. French was used in a limited capacity in providing federal government services in Quebec and some other bilingual regions, though it was common for French speakers, even in areas where they were heavily concentrated, to be unable to obtain services in their mother tongue.

The public face of Canada's government was English. It would not be until 1927 that Canada started issuing bilingual stamps. The Bennett government approved bank notes issued separately in English and French in 1934, and the King government replaced them with bilingual currency in 1936.[5] The federal government created its translation bureau in 1934, but it would be another twenty-two years before John Diefenbaker, during his 1958 election campaign, promised simultaneous French-English interpretation in the House of Commons, and this occurred the following year.[6] Three years later, as the culmination of a long-standing campaign by French Canadian groups, the federal government started issuing bilingual cheques.[7]

The major shift in Ottawa's approach to issues of language was largely prompted by pressures from French-speaking Canadians and challenges to its legitimacy and power from the government of Quebec. Although there had been a long-standing approach of defensive federalism under Quebec's provincial governments, which culminated with the Union Nationale administration of Maurice Duplessis (1935–39, 1944–59), it was the election of the Liberal Party of Jean Lesage in 1960 that kicked off an activist phase. His government launched the Quiet Revolution, a major expansion of the provincial government's spheres of activity, with the aim of improving the lot and life of the francophone majority.[8] Indeed, the situation even in Quebec for the status of French was dire. Canadian National Railways president Donald Gordon thought nothing of naming his new landmark hotel in Montreal the Queen Elizabeth in 1954, rebuffing a multi-year campaign by Quebecers, including Mayor Jean Drapeau and a petition with 200,000

signatures organized by the Ligue d'Action Nationale, to rename it the
Château Maisonneuve.[9] In 1962, Gordon engendered massive hostility and
protests from the Quebec Federation of Labour, student groups, and the
separatist Rassemblement pour l'indépendance nationale (RIN) when he
claimed that no French-speaking persons were qualified to hold vice-
presidential positions with the railway.[10]

In January 1962, in the midst of the Quiet Revolution, *Le Devoir* editor
André Laurendeau called on the federal government to respond to the aspirations of French Canadians within Confederation. Inspired by this, Lester
Pearson, who assumed power with a minority government in 1963, called
on Laurendeau to become co-chair of the Royal Commission on Bilingualism and Biculturalism.[11] The commission was established on July 19, 1963,
with a mandate to

> inquire into and report upon the existing state of bilingualism and bicultur-
> alism in Canada and to recommend what steps should be taken to develop
> the Canadian Confederation on the basis of an equal partnership between
> the two founding races, taking into account the contribution made by the
> other ethnic groups to the cultural enrichment of Canada and the measures
> that should be taken to safeguard that contribution.[12]

Over the next eight years, the commission undertook a massive array of
research studies, held public hearings, received over 400 briefs, and consulted with Canada's federal and provincial governments to fulfill these
objectives, ultimately producing a preliminary report and a six-volume final
report between 1965 and 1971. The year that the B&B Commission (as it was
usually called) was founded was also the first year of violent actions, including bombings, of the radical Quebec separatist group the Front de libération
du Québec (FLQ).

The B&B commissioners were struck by the depth of feelings over the
language issue in Canada and by the extent of mutual incomprehension
between the two main language groups. The depth of anti-French bigotry
at the hearings often caused Laurendeau to despair in his diary. A French
Canadian factory worker from Maillardville, British Columbia, recounted
often hearing the comment "Why don't you go back to Quebec?" when he
spoke French with his colleagues. It was a variant of the "Speak white!" insult
encountered coast to coast by French Canadians and Acadians.[13] At another
public hearing in Vancouver, English-speaking participants launched into

a series of negative comments on Quebec on the theme of a "retarded people."[14] An Irish Protestant pastor from Saskatoon opined that

> what is going on here reminds me of what I've gone through in my native country. The Irish were never willing to accept that they were beaten. They withdrew into their corner, licked their wounds, and it just got worse. Here, I see the same unfortunate thing happening: the French Canadians never accepted their defeat, they retreated within Quebec, they too licked their wounds, and today they are rebelling. As long as they don't accept the Canadian and North American reality as fact, problems will never cease.[15]

Meanwhile, in Quebec, francophone participants at a hearing in Sherbrooke, a city that was 85 percent French speaking, recounted that it was impossible to communicate with the English except in English. Young French Canadians in Quebec knew that they had to learn English, while young English Canadians did not feel obliged to learn French.[16]

The situation prompted the commission to produce, in February 1965, a preliminary report in which it observed that "Canada, without being fully conscious of the fact, is passing through the greatest crisis in its history."[17] The commissioners believed that major action was needed to prevent the country from splitting apart. In the same year that this report was issued, Pearson's Liberal government called an election, hoping for a majority. The election returned a Parliament with almost the same number of seats for each party, but it did bring the "three wise men" from Quebec into the House of Commons: journalist Gérard Pelletier, labour union leader Jean Marchand, and law professor Pierre Elliott Trudeau, appointed as Pearson's parliamentary secretary and then promoted to minister of justice in 1967. Quebec's Liberal government fell in the provincial election of 1966, bringing to power an even more nationalist administration under Daniel Johnson. The new Union Nationale premier adopted a slogan of *Égalité ou indépendance* (Equality or Independence)" for his dealings with the federal government.

By the latter half of the 1960s, tensions between the Quebec government and the federal government had escalated dramatically, with power struggles for control over social welfare policy and over foreign policy in areas related to provincial jurisdiction. Separatist political parties were attracting increasing interest, and even the mainstream provincial party leaders were far from deferential to Ottawa. The wrangling over French president Charles de Gaulle's visit to Expo '67, held in Montreal during·Canada's centennial, and his infamous "Vive le Québec libre" speech added to these tensions.

The federal government, for its part, was aware that it needed to reinvent itself as a government relevant to French-speaking Canadians and to be the government of all of Canada, not just the British Canadian elements. This was at least partly why the Pearson government pushed for a new official flag, adopted in 1965, to replace the Red Ensign. On April 6, 1966, Pearson announced a new policy for the public service that introduced bilingualism as an element of merit in hiring and promotion so that the federal government could serve the public in both official languages. In making this announcement, Pearson also noted that "the achievement of bilingualism is in itself a desirable objective for any Canadian citizen."[18] Although the Progressive Conservative and Social Credit Party leaders expressed concerns about launching this policy before the B&B Commission had submitted its final report, they generally approved of its thrust while cautioning of the need to consult with the civil service organizations. The New Democratic and Créditiste Parties were more overtly supportive, arguing that these changes were long overdue.[19]

In 1967, the Royal Commission on Bilingualism and Biculturalism issued its first report, *The Official Languages.* It called on Ottawa to take a major step forward by making English and French the two official languages of the country and by making services available in both official languages in all head offices as well as in regional offices where there were substantial populations of the official language minority. The commission proposed a system of "bilingual districts" to determine how services would be provided. In 1968, it produced a second major volume dealing with education, which called for major federal government action, and financial investment, to promote minority official language education from coast to coast and to encourage second-language learning by more Canadians.

By 1968, Quebec's place within Canada was front-page news. Early in the year, Premier Johnson sparred with Justice Minister Trudeau at the federal-provincial conferences on the Constitution. Whereas Johnson called for new powers for Quebec to reflect its special status in Confederation and to carry out its role as the main government of French Canada, Trudeau argued that the federal government had a key role to play as the government of all Canadians, both English and French speaking, and advanced proposals to entrench language rights in the Constitution and to take steps to make the federal government a bilingual institution. Before the year was out, Pearson had stepped down as Liberal leader, making way for Trudeau to take over as head of the party and then win a majority in the 1968 election. Meanwhile, in Quebec, René Lévesque, who had left the provincial Liberals over issues related to Quebec's place within Confederation, transformed his Mouvement Souveraineté-Association into a new political party, the Parti Québécois (PQ).

Over the following year, Trudeau's government introduced and passed the Official Languages Act, 1969, which made English and French the two official languages of the country, and guaranteed services in both official languages from the federal government and its institutions. The government of New Brunswick passed its own Official Languages Act the same year. Over the next year, the apparatus to put these laws into effect was developed, including the Office of the Commissioner of Official Languages and the Bilingual Districts Advisory Board.[20] Meanwhile, through a subcommittee of the ongoing constitutional conference, a committee of federal and provincial officials was negotiating an agreement to give effect to another set of key recommendations of the B&B Commission. In 1970, the committee announced the agreement that gave birth to the Bilingualism in Education Program, under which the federal government agreed to contribute a percentage of the costs of provincial programs in minority-language education and second-language instruction. The first agreement, to run for five years, had an estimated budget of $300 million.[21]

In Quebec, tensions over language education rights had led to street demonstrations in the Montreal suburb of Saint-Léonard in the fall of 1969. This activism prompted the provincial government of Jean-Jacques Bertrand to pass Bill 63, A Law to Promote the French Language in Quebec, which gave parents the right to choose the language of education for their children. It also required that high school graduates have a working knowledge of French.[22] Although well received by English-speaking Quebecers, it outraged many nationalist Quebec organizations. Partly in an effort to appease these groups, the provincial government also appointed a Commission of Inquiry on the Position of the French Language and of French Rights in Quebec, headed by linguist Jean-Denis Gendron (the Gendron Commission).

On April 29, 1970, Liberal Robert Bourassa won a majority government in Quebec's provincial election, but perhaps more notable was the fact that the sovereignist Parti Québécois captured 23 percent of the popular vote. The new Bourassa administration immediately faced a major challenge with the eruption of the October Crisis. Cells of the FLQ kidnapped British Trade Commissioner James Cross and Labour Minister Pierre Laporte. Bourassa asked for Ottawa's help to combat the FLQ, and the Trudeau government invoked the War Measures Act. By the time the provisions of the act were lifted in December, Laporte had been murdered, and Bourassa appeared weak in the public eye for having turned to Ottawa.

Some have speculated that it was in part to firm up his credentials as a strong Quebec nationalist that Bourassa ultimately decided not to follow through on his commitment to sign the Victoria Charter in 1971. The charter, to be the culmination of the constitutional talks that had been ongoing between Ottawa and the provinces since 1968, would have included constitutional entrenchment of the two official languages at the federal level and additional language rights that applied to the provinces willing to accept them.[23] Later that year the federal government announced its policy on multiculturalism, partly a response to the many ethnocultural communities that had felt excluded or marginalized by the very premise of the B&B Commission. It was also rooted in Trudeau's belief that there should be no "official" cultures endorsed by the government and thus a rejection of the "biculturalism" dimension of the 1960s commission.[24]

Moving through the 1970s, the Trudeau government and the Public Service Commission gave meaning to the provisions of the Official Languages Act. Although language training was provided for civil servants, various promises were made to those already working for the federal government that, at least in the short term, their careers would not be harmed because of an inability to speak French. Those in existing positions were protected from being fired even if their positions were designated "bilingual" for future occupants. Willingness to learn French was accepted in lieu of actual proficiency for those wishing to apply for bilingual positions.[25] The process of designating "bilingual districts" remained mired in political and jurisdictional battles and was ultimately abandoned in 1976,[26] replaced by a more informal system of bilingual regions for bilingual service provision.

In 1974, the federal government renewed its commitment to teaching in the official languages at the provincial level with another five-year commitment to the Bilingualism in Education Program (BEP). It had also added, in the early 1970s, annex programs to the BEP to enhance teacher education and research on language learning. In 1971, the Secretary of State started funding the Summer Language Bursary Program (renamed the Explore Program in 2004), administered by the Council of Ministers of Education, Canada (CMEC), permitting university-aged students to spend several weeks immersed in the other language community. In 1973, it added the Official Languages Monitor Program (renamed the Odyssey Program in

2004), also with the CMEC, that funded university-aged students to work as teachers' language assistants in communities across the country. The federal government was also taking action on a symbolic level to enhance official languages in the public sphere with the passage, in 1974, of the Consumer Packaging and Labelling Act, which extended requirements for bilingual packaging to an array of goods, including many foodstuffs. Although critics of the law would often indicate this as the point at which they were forced to have "Flocons de Maïs" on their Corn Flakes box, the Kellogg's company had in fact made these boxes bilingual in 1907.[27]

Meanwhile, the Quebec government, which since Confederation had been by far the most generous of the provinces in its treatment of its linguistic minority, was moving away from bilingualism and toward an emphasis on the French language. This move was inspired at least partly by the 1972 report of the Gendron Commission, which noted that measures were needed to improve the status of French in Quebec's economy and to encourage new residents to integrate into the francophone majority.[28] In 1974, the Bourassa government adopted Bill 22, the Official Language Act, which made French the only official language of the province, created incentives to encourage businesses to make French their working language, and instituted a regime of language tests for students who wanted to be admitted to the province's English-language schools. The law provoked outrage from both nationalist Québécois organizations, which thought that it was too easily circumvented, and English Canadian and anglophone and allophone Quebecer groups, which thought that it was an assault on English-language rights.

These tensions over language rights were central to the 1976 *gens de l'air* bilingual air traffic controller crisis over the right of pilots to communicate in French with air traffic control towers at Quebec airports, a crisis that provoked a national debate over the use of French.[29] Later that year, on November 15, René Lévesque's Parti Québécois won a surprising majority government, having campaigned on an incrementalist approach to sovereignty-association. Although it did not immediately hold a referendum on this issue, the PQ government moved swiftly to bolster the province's language policy, passing Bill 101, The Charter of the French Language, in 1977. The charter made French-language use mandatory for Quebec-based businesses, prohibited the use of English on commercial signage, and tightly restricted access to English-language schools in the province to children of parents who had received this type of education in Quebec or had older siblings who met this criterion. It provoked a backlash across the country for its perceived assault on the English language and caused many to question (often in a hostile manner) the point of making the federal government bilingual and offering French-language education in other provinces if Quebec was going to restrict access to English schooling and free expression.

In addition to this political turmoil over language issues and national identity, Canada was coping with two other major shifts. After decades of sustained economic growth in the immediate post-Second World War period, the economy stalled in the 1970s. A period of "stagflation" – high inflation mixed with stagnant growth – created major budget strains for governments throughout North America and Western Europe. Canada's federal government routinely began running budget deficits. In an effort to control this, the Trudeau government announced large cutbacks to all major spending initiatives in 1977, a move that hit directly at the budgets for its official languages initiatives, greatly scaled back after the 1977–78 fiscal year. The combination of a reduction in federal funding and conflict over jurisdiction and accountability resulted in a lengthy delay of a new agreement for the renamed Official Languages in Education Program (OLEP). OLEP subsisted on year-to-year agreements from 1979 to 1983 before a new multi-year protocol agreement was finally reached.[30] It certainly did not help that Canada faced a major recession in the early 1980s, with interest rates leaping into double digits.

Canada was also facing a major demographic shift in this period. The years of sustained high birth rates of the "baby boom" ended in the mid-1960s (many scholars pin 1966 as the end year), and the birth rate began to drop steadily. The new availability of legal contraception, a substantial increase in women's participation in the workforce, and a concomitant set of delays in getting married and starting families meant that the birth rate continued to decline throughout the late 1960s and early 1970s, with the lowest number of births in 1973.[31] The birth rate remained low throughout the rest of the decade. In the education sector, this meant that school systems, which had rapidly expanded, built new schools, and hired new teachers to meet the demands of the baby boom generation, were now faced with the opposite problem of an oversupply of teachers and insufficient student numbers to keep all of the schools open. This created great insecurity among a number of teachers' unions, whose members feared for their jobs.

In the spring of 1979, the Trudeau government, deeply unpopular in a period of hard economic times, had to call an election, which it lost to Joe Clark's Progressive Conservatives, who won a minority government. Shortly thereafter, René Lévesque's government announced its platform of sovereignty association and its plans for a referendum. Although Lévesque might have hoped not to have Trudeau, who had announced his retirement from politics, as an adversary, the Clark government was toppled on a budget vote in December and forced to call an election. Trudeau returned to lead the Liberals to a new majority government in February 1980. He was a key player in the May 1980 referendum on sovereignty-association, which saw Lévesque's proposal defeated by a 59 percent–41 percent margin, including a majority of francophone voters. Trudeau, who had promised that a "no" vote would not be interpreted as acceptance of the constitutional status quo, launched a new round of constitutional negotiations. His central aim was to get a Charter of Rights and Freedoms, including language rights – particularly minority language education rights – entrenched in the Constitution. After a year and a half of constitutional wrangling, involving televised hearings on the charter and high-profile constitutional challenges that went all the way to the Supreme Court of Canada, Trudeau came to an agreement on a constitutional package with all of the premiers except Lévesque. The new Charter of Rights and Freedoms included the right of official language minorities to be educated in their mother tongue where numbers warranted doing so and entrenched the two official languages of Canada. These sections of the charter, notably, were not subject to section 33, the override clause. The Quebec government refused to sign the new, patriated Constitution, which nevertheless received the approval of the British Parliament and was signed by Queen Elizabeth II on April 17, 1982.

Trudeau retired from politics in the spring of 1984. His successor, John Turner, was unable to prevent the new Progressive Conservative leader, Brian Mulroney, from winning a landslide majority government in the fall election. The fluently bilingual Mulroney owed much of his victory to widespread support in Quebec for his promises to take steps to allow Quebec to sign the 1982 Constitution "with honour and enthusiasm." A resurgent Liberal Party under Robert Bourassa defeated the Parti Québécois in the 1985 election in Quebec. Shortly thereafter, Mulroney began talks with the Quebec government on the conditions under which Quebec might agree to sign the Constitution. The result of these talks, broadened to include the other premiers, was the 1987 Meech Lake Accord, a deal that, among other things, would recognize Quebec as a distinct society. The accord had to be ratified by all the provincial legislatures and the federal Parliament within three years to come into effect. One short-term impact of the accord was that it added fuel to growing western Canadian discontent, particularly to the argument that the federal government, regardless of the political party in office, was overly focused on central Canadians', particularly Quebecers', interests. The Reform Party of Canada held its first major conferences that year, with strong interest in and support from the prairie provinces. It became an official party on November 1, 1987, with opposition to official bilingualism among the planks of its platform.

In the early months of ratification of the Meech Lake Accord, the federal government committed itself to the identity-based legislation of the Trudeau years. In 1987, the Mulroney government introduced a bill to revise and give more clout to the Official Languages Act. The revised act, passed in 1988, gave additional official power to the Secretary of State to support linguistic duality and official language minority communities. It also introduced new provisions for the public service, including the right of civil servants to work in the official language of their choice. That year the Mulroney government also passed the Multiculturalism Act, giving concrete legislation to the policy that had existed for the past seventeen years largely on the basis of the 1971 policy statement in the House of Commons. It also renewed the Official Languages in Education Program protocol for another five-year period, to run until 1993, with modest funding increases built into the agreement.[32] On issues related to official languages policy and multiculturalism, there was thus great continuity between the Trudeau Liberals and the Mulroney Progressive Conservatives despite their differences over the status of Quebec within Confederation.

By late 1988, concerns had been raised about the Meech Lake Accord in a number of quarters, including a major condemnation by Trudeau, and opposition marshalled in the west by the Reform Party. But the ratification process had been moving smoothly through the provincial legislatures, and public opinion on the issue had been fairly muted. Arguably, this process was derailed in late 1988 when the Supreme Court of Canada issued its decision on the *Ford* case regarding commercial signage in Quebec. It ruled that the prohibition on English signage of the Charter of the French Language contravened the freedom of expression provisions of the Canadian Charter of Rights and Freedoms. Premier Bourassa responded by passing Bill 178 in December, which reintroduced many of the provisions struck down by the courts, using the notwithstanding clause of the charter.[33] This action sparked outrage among English-speaking Quebecers. Further anti–Meech Lake Accord sentiment spread through English-speaking Canada as a reaction to Bourassa's statement that invocation of the notwithstanding clause might not have been necessary if the accord was already in force, because the distinct society clause would have permitted Quebec to have those laws. The Meech Lake Accord was viewed (rightly or wrongly) as a measure that would strip away the rights of Quebec's English-speaking minority. Over the next year and a half, ratification unravelled as provincial governments moved to hold public hearings on the accord. These hearings provided opportunities for oppositional sentiments to be voiced. A couple of provinces rescinded their approval of the agreement, and ultimately two provinces failed to ratify the deal by the June 23, 1990, deadline, killing the accord.

In the wake of the demise of the Meech Lake Accord, Lucien Bouchard, Mulroney's Quebec lieutenant, led a cohort of disaffected Conservative and Liberal MPs to form a new separatist political party, the Bloc Québécois. Bourassa's government launched a series of commissions both in his party and in the legislature to investigate options for Quebec's future. The federal government tried to develop a substitute for its failed constitutional package, launching its own series of commissions of inquiry to gain the input of Canadians and their provincial governments. All of this was set against the backdrop of another major economic recession in the early 1990s and the plummeting popularity of the federal Conservative government. The result of all this consultation was a new constitutional package, the Charlottetown Accord, submitted to the Canadian electorate in a referendum held on October 26, 1992. The accord, a hodge-podge of constitutional amendments designed to appeal to both Quebec and other groups that had felt excluded or marginalized by the Meech Lake process, pleased few people. Only three Atlantic provinces had clear majority votes in favour of it, Ontario and Nova Scotia split almost evenly, and Quebec and the western provinces, along with the majority of the Canadian vote, rejected it by wide margins. Overall, 54.2 percent voted against the Charlottetown Accord, whereas 44.8 percent supported the deal.

The 1993 federal election was deeply polarizing. Jean Chrétien's Liberal Party won a majority government, but the major story of the election was the rise of the Bloc Québécois, which won fifty-four seats in Quebec and formed the official opposition, and the Reform Party, which won fifty-two seats, all but one of them in western Canada. Both the Progressive Conservatives and the New Democrats lost official party status in the House of Commons. The renewal date of the Official Languages in Education Program in 1993 passed without a new deal, and the program shifted to incremental, one-year funding arrangements, with a shrinking budget. Like all federal programs, it was subject to the major deficit-slashing budgets of the early years of the Chrétien administration, under the guidance of Finance Minister Paul Martin. When a five-year protocol agreement for the program was finally reached in 1996 to cover the 1993–98 period, its budget had been slashed by 36.6 percent and was down, in total annual dollars, to a level not seen since 1975.[34]

The intervening years had been bleak on the national unity front. Jacques Parizeau led the Parti Québécois to a majority in the 1994 provincial election. He rapidly launched a process for holding another referendum, this time on sovereignty partnership in collaboration with Lucien Bouchard's Bloc Québécois and the soft-nationalist Action Démocratique du Québec under Mario Dumont. Their proposal was only barely defeated by the Quebec electorate on October 30, 1995, with 50.6 percent voting "no" and 49.4 percent voting "yes."[35] In the aftermath of the narrow victory, the Chrétien government placed a reference on secession before the Supreme Court. The government then passed the Clarity Act, which spelled out, in accordance with the Supreme Court decision, which conditions would compel the federal government to negotiate secession with a province in the advent of a clear majority vote on a clear question. In 1998, with its budget stabilized, the federal government renewed its commitment to official languages, with a substantial injection into the OLEP of new funds, increased with the 2003 protocol.[36]

It is probably fair to say that by the late 1990s constitutional "fatigue" had set in across Canada and that many Canadians were fed up with discussing issues of language, identity, and the Constitution. The last four decades of the twentieth century had been particularly active in terms of changing approaches to language, identity politics, English-French relations, and constitutional affairs, and they had seen a fair bit of economic volatility and a number of major demographic changes. All of this provided a tumultuous and important backdrop to the efforts of those trying to promote bilingualism and the learning of French by English-speaking Canadians and of those opposed to bilingualism, who often thought that it posed a threat to "their" Canada. It is to these campaigns that I now turn.

2

From *Chez Hélène* to the First French Immersion Experiments

Canadian interest in French-language learning began to expand even before the B&B Commission and the Official Languages Act, though they certainly accentuated the trend. Of particular interest in the decade from 1959 to 1969 is the way that parent groups across the country mobilized to try to provide better French-language learning opportunities than they themselves had experienced. Although some of these initiatives were limited, they demonstrate the grassroots interest in improving opportunities for bilingualism in English-speaking Canada even before it became an overt part of federal government policy.

From *Chez Hélène* to *Sesame Street:* Early Exposure on the CBC

Before the Quiet Revolution, before the B&B Commission, before Pierre Trudeau made the national scene, there was *Chez Hélène*. A fifteen-minute program that aired weekdays coast to coast on the English-language CBC network from 1959 to 1973, *Chez Hélène* was many Canadian children's first introduction to French. The show was hosted by Hélène Baillargeon, a French Canadian folk singer born in Saint-Martin, Quebec, who sang songs and spoke French to her child companions (who included, over the years, "Marianne," "Peter," and "Louise"[1]) and a puppet mouse named Suzie. Hélène always spoke in French, her companions spoke in English, and the dialogue often featured Hélène responding to English questions with variations of what the children or Suzie had said in French.

The show was based on the Tan-Gau method of language learning, developed in part by Robert Gauthier, the Ontario Department of Education's director of French instruction (in collaboration with Burmese educator Tan-Wan Yan).[2] The method emphasized that second languages should be learned in the same way as first languages, so the teacher always spoke in the target (second) language. It emphasized the repetition (and variation) of complete phrases rather than isolating individual words and explicitly teaching formal grammar. Baillargeon was approached by Dr. Lambert,[3] head of the CBC's children's services in Toronto, to host a show aimed at preschoolers, working from the theory that, the younger the children were, the easier it would be for them to acquire a second language. They believed that their preschooler audience would not have prejudices against learning the language when they got to school because they would have been exposed to it as part of their upbringing.[4]

Chez Hélène received a lot of favourable press, which described the show's approach of having Hélène speak only in French but convey meaning by means of pictures and pantomime, mimicking the way in which children learn their first language from their parents. All of this aimed to make learning a second language as pleasant and entertaining as possible.[5] The show's two main aims were "1) educational, in that a second language opens a window on to a wider world; 2) social, because the study of French by English-speaking Canadians will contribute, more effectively than any other means, to a deeper and friendlier understanding between the two major ethnic groups of our country."[6] The show was certainly popular: 25,000 children responded to a 1962 offer to receive a picture of the cast. *Chez Hélène* ran for fourteen years and over 3,500 episodes before the CBC cancelled it in 1973. Baillargeon claimed that she was shocked and bewildered when the show was cancelled "for no apparent reason."[7] But CBC's head of children's and youth programming, Dan McCarthy, believed that the time was right to end the show before it "lost any of its vibrancy." McCarthy wanted to move on to other programming that would appeal more to children.[8] *Chez Hélène's* time slot was filled by a new show, *Mon Ami*, starring Gilbert Chénier. However, the CBC did not mask the fact that the real replacement was the new, Canadian edition of *Sesame Street*. Commissioned by the Secretary of State in 1970, it started airing in 1972.[9] The producers of the Canadian edition sought to expose children to a Canadian cultural context, specifically one that featured French. The Canadian edition featured fifteen minutes of Canadian content mixed into the American version. Starting in 1973, 50 percent of the Canadian *Sesame Street* segments were in French.[10] As of 1975, many children had the option of watching the French Canadian edition of the show, *Bonjour Sesame*, dubbed in Quebec.[11]

North York: The Struggle for More Core French

Chez Hélène opened the door to greater interest in French second-language teaching among Canadian parents. A clear example of its impact is Gunild Spiess. Spiess and her husband, Fritz, a cinematographer, had immigrated to Canada from Germany in 1951 and settled in the Toronto suburb of North York. They started a family, and their eldest daughter, Lorraine, was enthralled by *Chez Hélène,* to the point that Gunild wrote to the CBC in 1960 to thank the corporation for the program. An exchange of correspondence about the Tan-Gau method and the *Chez Hélène* program ensued.[12] Although German speaking, the Spiesses were believers in the bilingual nature of Canada – it was one of the few things that they knew about Canada before they immigrated. They wanted their children to have the benefits of learning a second language through the school system (in addition to the German that they were teaching them at home) and thought it only natural that French would be taught. However, at their local school, McKee Avenue Public School, and throughout the North York Board of Education, FSL instruction started in grade seven. Between *Chez Hélène* and her growing awareness of the theories of Dr. Wilder Penfield of McGill University, who argued that language learning should begin in childhood, Gunild Spiess wanted to create greater opportunities for her children to start learning French at a younger age. With this in mind, she joined the local Home and School Association and approached the principal of McKee in 1962 with the idea of a noon-hour French program for interested children or a program that would run directly after school hours.[13] However, regulations of the North York Board of Education made it difficult to get a permit to use the school during these time slots.

Undeterred, Spiess worked on her Home and School Association to get a French committee created and found a way to work around the regulations. In 1963, a group of parents arranged for after-school supervision for students from 3:30 to 4:00 prior to an after-school French program that would run once a week from 4:00 to 4:30. The parents, led by Spiess, found a teacher to run the class, and this popular program persisted for over a decade, eventually adding classes of ten to twelve students for different age and skill levels.[14] By the 1970s, McKee parents would pay between eight and twelve dollars for sixteen to twenty lessons over two school terms. As they were told, "Don't expect your children to be bilingual by the time the 20 lessons are over. What we are trying to do is to instil a good feeling towards the language and if we succeed with that – the children will be learning their second language with great pleasure, when they get to grade 6."[15]

The McKee after-school classes were a limited introductory French program, but the process of creating them familiarized Spiess with the dynamics of organizing parents and working in a school to get a program established. She also became familiar with the challenges of dealing with a school board and the resistance of authorities to broadening French-language instruction. This proved to be useful background training for Spiess in the post–Official Languages Act period when she began working to get North York's French curriculum changed, as I will discuss in Chapter 5.

The Toronto French School and Kitchener-Waterloo Bilingual School

When scholars and activists talk about the success of the French immersion movement in Canada, they invariably identify the pilot project in St. Lambert, Quebec, in 1965 as the groundbreaking experiment that paved the way for the bilingual education revolution. However, the St. Lambert project was not entirely the first of its kind in Canada.[16] Three years earlier the first long-running immersion experiment was launched in Toronto by Harry and Anna Giles. The Toronto French School (TFS) was intended from the beginning to be a private school offering an alternative to the publicly funded education system. It did not attract much research attention or act as a model for parents interested in changing the programs offered by publicly funded school boards. It thus tends to be overlooked in the broader histories of language education in Canada. Indeed, the parents who launched the St. Lambert experiment were not aware of it when they started their campaign. However, once their project got under way, they learned of TFS and drew some encouragement from its success and some inspiration from its methodology.

The Toronto French School, in many ways, was a product of the North Toronto milieu in which it was created. Like many other parents, Toronto lawyer Harry Giles and his wife, Anna, were not impressed by the quality of the French spoken or written by graduates of Ontario schools. Together with two other couples, the Gileses hired a private French tutor to instruct their three-year-old children in French for several hours three times a week. The couples considered bilingualism to be important and a link in Canadian culture.[17] Not wanting the progress that their children had made to be lost when they entered kindergarten, Giles approached the Ontario Department of Education for a charter to operate a private school and a day nursery that would operate with an English-French kindergarten and an all-French environment in grade one. The school opened in September 1962 with Nicole Corbi, an Egyptian-born, Université de Sherbrooke–trained teacher for both the kindergarten and grade one classes. Initially, the classes were housed in the Sunday School facilities of Saint-Léonard's Anglican Church. The program differed significantly from the English-language schools of Toronto. Giles wanted the school eventually to produce graduates who could qualify for France's Baccalauréat Français, the highest secondary school rating. This international orientation led him to select textbooks from France, Belgium, and Switzerland. He rejected most Quebec textbooks on the basis that they had too many grammatical errors. Class sizes were capped at fifteen students per grade, and tuition was initially set at thirty dollars per month. The initial plan was to add a grade per year and eventually offer courses all the way through high school.

The Toronto French School proved to be extremely popular. It drew its first cohort of students largely from children of teachers and university professors but also started attracting a number of families from the city's economic and cultural elite.[18] The school not only promoted French-language learning but also started adding third-language courses (including Russian taught at the grade three level). It had a very advanced curriculum, including French poetry from Hugo and Rimbaud taught to grade two students. Although Giles did not follow the Ontario curriculum, he rooted the school's aims in Canada. As he noted in a 1965 interview,

> as a Canadian nationalist I firmly believe in bilingualism and biculturalism ... Should we fail to become seriously bilingual, this country will not continue to exist. The misunderstandings between French- and English-speaking Canadians will continue if we make the mistake of setting up French-language schools only for French-Canadians. In that way we will destroy Canada – we will make sure that it breaks up.[19]

By 1965, Giles, thirty-five, had taken over as principal of the school, which now had classes up to grade three and had opened "campuses" in Port Credit, Peterborough, and Kitchener.[20] Lacking permanent facilities in Toronto, Giles and other parents appeared before the Toronto hearings of the B&B Commission and asked for federal assistance in the form of a building that the school could lease for a nominal fee.[21] At the time, B&B Commission co-chair Davidson Dunton questioned the idea of a federal role for the school given provincial responsibility for education. University of Toronto political science professor Paul Fox, who had children at the TFS, suggested that the federal government could encourage provincial interest by offering grants on a fifty-fifty basis. Ultimately, the B&B Commission would not endorse the TFS request for federal funds, though the fifty-fifty model would later come into effect for publicly funded pilot projects.

One spinoff of the Toronto French School was the Kitchener-Waterloo Bilingual School, which Giles initially intended to be a campus of his Toronto-based project. This school emerged out of the desire of a number of professional parents in the Kitchener-Waterloo area to create an enriched education program for their young children in a political context in the mid-1960s in which they believed that a proposal for a French-language school would be a non-starter with local school boards. The parents invited Giles to come from Toronto to speak. Inspired by the story of his school, they had drummed up enough parental interest by August 1965 to create an immersion program for kindergarten and grade one classes. One of the key parents was Carmeta Abbott. She was bilingual and had benefited greatly from a one-year exchange to France set up by her high school French teacher in Columbus, Ohio. When she and her husband, a university professor hired at the University of Waterloo, moved to Canada, they hoped to find French-language learning opportunities for their four-year-old son. The Abbotts were surprised that they could not even buy a bilingual book of poetry.

The first year was rocky, involving problems with one of the teachers, who had been recruited at the last minute. At Easter, Giles told the Waterloo parents to switch the classes over to English so that their children could be reabsorbed by the public school system. However, the parents were happy with the progress of their children. A group of them secured a bank loan to buy an abandoned two-room school in the region. Ongoing fundraising and tuition fees paid the mortgage and teacher salaries.[22] The parents opted for a fifty-fifty bilingual format for their children, partly to assuage fears that they would not develop their English skills. After a few years of running with minimal funding, the school became more stable. By 1976, it was celebrating its ten-year anniversary. The board invited the commissioner of official languages (discussed in Chapter 3) to attend the anniversary celebrations. Although he did not attend, he recalled the school when he was thinking of ways to bring parents together with expertise in establishing French-language learning opportunities.[23] This bilingual school has now been in operation for over four decades, and it has survived despite the eventual creation of French immersion programs in Waterloo County school districts.

As for the Toronto French School, its student population continued to grow, with 650 pupils by the fall of 1966, thirty-eight teachers, and a growing student wait list. Tuition was between $350 and $400 per year. The TFS board organized a "French week" at Yorkdale shopping centre to fund a permanent building, including a gala opening featuring VIPs Paul Martin, the secretary of state for external affairs; François Leduc, the French ambassador to Canada; and Pierre Laporte, Quebec's public works minister.[24] After several years of these fundraisers, Ontario's premier, Bill Davis, attended the opening of the new permanent school building in 1971 for the now 750 students. In later years, adjacent mansions were purchased and added to the main campus.[25] The Toronto French School capped its enrolment at 1,000 students in the mid-1970s (when tuition was about $2,225 a year) and began benefiting from federal funding under the Bilingualism in Education Program in 1977, when the provincial government agreed to let private schools, including Catholic secondary schools (for grades eleven to thirteen), receive grants at the same rates as public schools.[26]

Harry Giles remained a long-standing critic of Quebec-trained teachers, their grammar, accent, and vocabulary, as well as textbooks from Quebec.[27] Although defending immersion to the hilt, and thinking that Quebec was an integral part of the country, he believed that the French language was taught poorly even within that province and that students were being taught "the simplified language of the semi-literate."[28] With such views of Canadian[29] and Québécois French and teaching approaches, it is not surprising that his Toronto French School, though still a thriving private enterprise, failed to become the model for bilingual education in Canada. For that model, I turn to St. Lambert, Quebec.

The St. Lambert French Immersion Experiment

It is not particularly surprising that the major breakthrough in FSL learning for English speakers would take place in Quebec in the 1960s. Canada's first large-scale pilot project in a public school board with French immersion was undertaken in 1965 in the community of St. Lambert, on the South Shore of Montreal Island. By this point, Quebec was making major strides toward making French the working language of the province (though not yet through language laws). What *is* surprising, however, is how much work it took for the English-speaking parents who wanted to experiment with French-language education for their children to get their proposals approved and then to keep the program moving along. This is also one of the most documented educational programs in Canada. Pedagogical experts played a vital role in this program as part of a strategic manoeuvre not initially part of the parents' plan. It was a crucial dimension, however, that explains much about how this experiment got off to a strong start and established foundations that would last for decades.

To explain the drive for French immersion in Quebec, one must consider that French-language instruction in the English-language schools of Quebec was poor and did not usually produce fluency in the students. Also key was a cluster of researchers at Montreal's prestigious McGill University who had a keen interest in language acquisition. Most notable were Wilder Penfield, a neurosurgeon with the Montreal Neurological Institute, who had developed a number of theories about neuroplasticity and the ability of younger children's brains to master languages (many Canadians of my generation are familiar with Penfield as the neurologist famous for his work on mapping the brain and the "I smell burnt toast!" Canadian Heritage Minute), and Wallace Lambert, who studied psychological and cognitive aspects of bilingualism. In the past, Lambert had counselled parents who sought better French fluency for their children to send them to one of the French-language schools. However, many principals were reluctant to admit many anglophone children out of fear of undermining the French-language atmosphere of the classrooms.[30]

What was being considered in St. Lambert went far beyond this. On October 30, 1963, a group of twelve English-speaking parents from St. Lambert, at the time 50 percent anglophone and 50 percent francophone, met to discuss their options for improved French education for their children. Some wanted their children to learn French for the "instrumental" reasons of increased job opportunities, whereas others were driven by "integrative" motivations such as cultural, intellectual, and social connections with French Canadians. All thought that the Protestant English schools did not provide adequate language training. Although some had put their older children in French Catholic or French Protestant schools, these avenues were closing down because of overcrowding. At this meeting, the parents established their goal of a fully French-language teaching environment for the first three grades but in an English-language school under the jurisdiction of the St. Lambert Protestant School Board. They also elected officers to shepherd their organization's work.[31] Three women in particular took on leadership roles in this campaign: Murielle Parkes, Valerie Neale, and Olga Melikoff.[32]

The parents' first step was to approach the local supervisor of the school board, who indicated that consideration would be given to their request if enough children could be found for one French kindergarten class of twenty students. Networking through their connections, they drew up a list of parents and asked them to sign up their children if they were in sympathy with the four-year French program that they were proposing (kindergarten to grade three). Within two months, over 100 families returned the forms, creating a list of a few hundred children aged one to nine. Upon presenting the signatures to the St. Lambert School Board, the parents were informed that educational policy was handled at a higher level, and they were re-directed to the regional Chambly County Protestant Central School Board. The initial response was not favourable. The St. Lambert commissioners were conservative and hostile to the proposal, whereas those from other communities seemed to be more open. Moreover, there was an under-current questioning the merits of the proposal, which threatened the board members' long-held view of the superior quality of education offered by the English school system.

The issue was referred to a two-member committee – the supervisor for the district and one of the conservative St. Lambert members – who would create a questionnaire and consult with twenty "experts," largely from McGill University, Macdonald College, and private schools. The parents were not allowed to see this questionnaire (which they claimed misrepresented their goals).[33] They realized that these experts would determine the fate of their proposal, so they got in touch with both Penfield and Lambert, who seemed to be supportive. The parents were able to get these two experts onto the list of those consulted by the board. It turned out that they were the only two supportive of the proposal; others questioned whether it would work for children of less than superior intelligence or whether it would harm children's development in their mother tongue. The board dismissed the parents' request.

However, the parents were already aware that the deck was stacked against them. Accordingly, they engaged in their own research and mobilized evidence from a 1962 UNESCO report on the teaching of second languages, which cautiously endorsed doing so from an early age. The parents noted that most current programs around the world had not managed to increase contact hours in the second language without cutting into time spent on subject matter. They reasoned that the skills required in learning to read and write in one language were transferrable, so learning them in

French first should work and then be applicable to the mother tongue of English. Another key consideration was the concept, endorsed by Penfield, that some aspects of language learning, including pronunciation, were best learned at a young age. These considerations formed the basis of a new brief compiled by the parents and circulated to fifty experts of their choosing as well as to the Chambly board members. The parents also courted media attention, with the *Montreal Star,* among other outlets, endorsing the "revolutionary" proposal in January 1964. Although the parents received encouraging letters from this campaign, and supportive responses from the experts, the Chambly board ignored the brief and counterarguments.

Faced with this roadblock, the parents tried other approaches. They decided to sponsor their own French-language immersion sessions. Renting spaces in church halls and from the Catholic school commission, they hired a French teacher to work with groups of ten to fifteen children for a "language bath," organizing three summer and two winter sessions. The parents also took political action, announcing their intention to put up candidates for the two vacancies on the St. Lambert board that would open in June 1964, breaking a long-held pattern of uncontested elections. The board was reluctant to see a public debate over the radical proposal emerge and indicated that it would accept one of the parents' candidates if the parents would agree not to oppose the board's choice. The parents agreed and thus got a guaranteed seat on the board for the next three years. They also organized well-attended meetings through the local Home and School Association, wrote a series of articles in the local press on the advantages of early bilingualism, and managed to convert their local French supervisor. The supervisor visited the Toronto French School and the parent-sponsored classes and declared that he now had no objection to an experiment at the kindergarten level, since the early immersion method was "undoubtedly extremely effective." The parents' persistence and the favourable publicity received by their proposal eventually converted the St. Lambert board and won over the Chambly board. The central board agreed to set up one experimental kindergarten for the fall of 1965. On registration day, the cap of twenty-six students was reached in five minutes, leaving about half of the interested parents disappointed.[34]

The parents continued to play an active role as the program began. They found the teacher for the first class and played an ongoing role in encouraging her and the principal of Margaret Pendlebury Elementary School. With the program under way, the parents reconstituted their organization, creating the St. Lambert Bilingual School Study Group, with two members from the original St. Lambert Protestant Parents' Group, two members from the St. Lambert Home and School Association (who had also been part of the original group), and a member from the St. Francis (English Catholic) Parent Teachers' Association. This group would play a watchdog role for the next five years (eventually adding an English consultant from the South Shore board). It was important for the group to put the experiment on more solid footing, so it began work on a second brief to try to broaden support. It was submitted to Minister of Education Paul Gérin-Lajoie in December 1965 and circulated to board members and about fifty others, including the members of the B&B Commission, the heads of teaching colleges, and the local MP (Pierre Laporte). The Bilingual School Study Group proposed changing the original plan to start introducing English in grade two to appease fears on the school board and among English teachers. It also proposed expanding the experiment to include Catholics. Almost all parties responded favourably to the brief, though the minister never acknowledged it directly.

Despite this positive response, the future of the experiment was in jeopardy. Some board members saw this project as "selling out" to French Canadians and as putting the English system at risk. Other emotional factors were evident to the parents. They responded in detail to practical concerns about finding teachers, locating textbooks, and minimizing expenses. Board members also feared being held responsible if the children in the program were unable to function normally in English at a later date or if some other aspect of their education was found to have suffered. As a result, the board dithered on whether the program would be expanded to offer other kindergarten classes in 1966 and whether the lead class would be allowed to continue in a French-language grade one.[35]

To solve this problem, the St. Lambert Bilingual Study Group took a step that would make its program the model for other Canadian jurisdictions. The group approached Wallace Lambert of McGill University to see if he would be willing to participate in an evaluation program. He agreed, and so did the Chambly board, which then agreed to carry the immersion experiment into grade one and to start two additional kindergarten classes. It was also at this point that members of the group, the grade one teacher, and the school principal visited the Toronto French School. Connections made with this program were invaluable in terms of inspiration and advice. But the St. Lambert group also realized that the TFS program, with its emphasis on enrichment, went beyond what it wanted from its own program. The TFS approach weeded out students on the basis of academic ability and ability to pay, whereas the St. Lambert group wanted to make its program accessible to children of any intellectual capacity and at public expense, with the goal of bilingualism at the end of elementary school. The group hoped that Lambert's involvement and testing would demonstrate that the program reached this goal – without other subject learning suffering as a result.[36]

Provincial changes rolled the Chambly board into the new South Shore Protestant School Board, which continued the program. Lambert's research established control groups in other Montreal-area schools against which the St. Lambert classes were measured for their mother tongue, French-language, and other subject achievements.[37] Wallace Lambert found himself drawn into the project in non-academic ways as well, including speaking to parent groups in other districts. He also provided in-person annual reports to the parents. As the program grew, members of the St. Lambert Study Group maintained their involvement with the program. They served on the board's education committee as well as its committee on teaching French. The reports of this latter committee, informed by Lambert's evaluations, helped to spread the immersion experiment to other areas of the South Shore. The march of the Quiet Revolution meant that there were more adults in the district, including board members, who found themselves needing to learn French and struggling with adult-oriented courses. This led to more sympathy for the "Bilingualism without Tears" approach aimed at children (which became the title of a pamphlet produced by the St. Lambert Study Group).[38]

Pockets of resistance continued to exist. At no point did the school board authorize more than a one-year extension at a time. Parents reported that there were concerns among the English-language community that such bilingual education programs might imperil their right to an English-language education and jeopardize the positions of English-language teachers. For example, the brief of the Association of (English-speaking) Catholic Principals of Montreal to the Gendron Commission in 1969 stated that

> while we favour bilingualism and the effective teaching of the French language from kindergarten to grade XI, we reject the so-called bilingual school which attempts to give equal or nearly-equal importance to two languages as media of instruction. We are of the opinion that the average child cannot cope with two languages of instruction and to try to do so leads to insecurity, language interference and academic retardation ... We have all met people who in adult life suffer from chronic linguistic confusion.[39]

By 1971, programs modelled on the St. Lambert experiment had been picked up in the Protestant School Board of Greater Montreal and a number of local Catholic boards. The St. Lambert experiment, which now counted 700 children in six communities on the South Shore, was also providing the model for experiments elsewhere in Canada. It was emulated largely on account of the favourable evaluation by Wallace Lambert, published after the lead class finished grade five. Perhaps most importantly, Lambert stated that the students were showing no negative impacts on their home language of English on the key measures of reading ability, listening comprehension, knowledge of concepts, and verbal expression. Their progress in French was also far above those in the English control group, with comprehension skills comparable to those of the French controls. Their fluency and overall expression were not equivalent to those of the French control group, but their verbal sentences were long and complex. Lambert believed that their productive skills could be brought closer to native-like competence with more correction by the teacher and more interaction with French children outside a classroom setting. Performance tests in other subjects, specifically math, showed that they were performing at the same high level as the control groups. There was no impact on the measured intelligence (IQ) of the students. If anything, they were slightly advanced.

In terms of attitudinal tests, the children tested after grades two and three were more fair and charitable in their attitudes toward French-speaking people than either control group, and less ethnocentric and biased toward their own group, though they were still showing healthy views of themselves. Surprisingly, after grade four, they were in line with the English control group. Lambert's team hypothesized that the FLQ crisis of the prior year might have had an impact. A test a year later, after the atmosphere of crisis had faded, showed a return to more favourable attitudes toward French Canadians.[40] Lambert noted the importance of a supportive parental approach, and he believed that this positive attitude helped the children to thrive. These were positive results indeed and would be referred to constantly over the decades to come as keen parents in other jurisdictions tried to convince their school boards to pilot similar programs.

The Citizens' Committee on Children in the National Capital Region

The Ottawa-Carleton region is a good example of how pre-existent social movement networks allowed new bilingualism-specific groups to emerge.

An initial organization in the region interested in promoting bilingualism in education was the Citizens' Committee on Children (CCC). Formed in the late 1940s out of a variety of groups in the National Capital Region interested in the welfare of children, the CCC's efforts contributed to the creation of daycares, preschool parent centres, early childhood education courses, and the Children's Hospital of Eastern Ontario. The committee also had publication experience, with a bulletin that dated to 1948, and topic-specific guides on issues such as television viewing and winter activities for children.

By the early 1960s, the CCC had a particular emphasis on education and had begun to consider the issue of learning French.[41] In 1965, the group published a pamphlet entitled "Three Dozen Steps to Bilingualism," which included lists of simple French-language songs, books, and records suitable for preschoolers.[42] The group built on this with a six-page "French for Children" chapter in the fourth edition of their booklet "What's What for Children" in 1967, which tried to answer parents' questions about which school-based programs were available, the arguments for and against different options, how to help children learn French, which opportunities existed beyond the school programs, and at what age it was best to start learning a second language. The chapter provided a bibliography of books and records suitable for children at different ages, prominently featuring the records of Hélène Baillargeon as well as popular children's books such as the *Madeleine* and *Babar the Elephant* series.

Mrs. C.A. Brigden, a board member of the Toronto French School, authored the section on introducing French to English-speaking children. She identified the years between infancy and age eight as the best time to start exposing a child to a second language, noting that after that age accent and vocabulary become more difficult to master. Brigden argued, however, that children with physical or emotional health issues should not be introduced to a second language because it would cause additional stress.[43] The methodology for teaching French to children outlined by Brigden resembled the immersion method, emphasizing that the instructor should speak only in French during the lessons and use a game- and music-based approach to learning for younger children. For learners aged six to nine, she suggested a more formal structure, including simple reading and word games, but still without any formal grammar.

At this point, the first immersion programs in Canada had barely been created, and no such program existed within the school boards of the National Capital Region, so the instructional suggestions were oriented to parent-organized classes that ideally would run daily for thirty minutes or more. Brigden told parents not to worry about vocabulary confusion, claiming that it would sort itself out over time. She also stressed that parents should not try to "show off" their children's French learning or force it on their children. Brigden stressed that it made the most sense to learn French as a second language for Canadian children because, next to English, it was spoken by more Canadians than any other language, and, "in Canada, French and English should go hand in hand." She also noted the importance of French as a language of diplomacy, the richness of French culture in literature, drama, and art, its value as "an expressive and beautiful language," and that both English and French were derived from Latin and interlaced with the vocabulary of each other.[44] When this 1967 edition was released, Ottawa was still a couple of years away from the first public school board–based immersion programs (discussed in Chapter 4), but the interest and organization to create and improve French programs were present.

The Calgary French School

Alberta in the mid-1960s was a wasteland for public education in languages other than English. Although it was possible to take second-language courses, the provincial Schools Act forbade the teaching in languages other than English after the midpoint of the grade one year. For Franco-Albertans with the financial means to afford it, there were some private school options subsidized by the Catholic Church. But for English speakers who wanted opportunities for their children to become bilingual, there was nothing on offer. This was the situation that faced Calgarians Mary Stapleton, an American who had moved to Canada in the 1960s; Louise Moore, a francophone Nova Scotian who had been educated in English; and Jane Carrothers, who had moved west when her husband, Alfred, was appointed as president of the University of Calgary. The three would be responsible for founding the Calgary French School (CFS), a privately run nursery and kindergarten that operated in French. The CFS ran for ten years before it began expanding in 1979 to form a private school that ran to the end of high school.

The genesis of the CFS was the friendship between Moore and Stapleton, who had known each other since 1965, when their children were born. They later met Carrothers, who moved into Moore's neighbourhood. Moore had grown up bilingual, and Stapleton, raised in California, had started learning Spanish at age six. Both believed in the advantages of learning languages from an early age and wanted their children to have the opportunity to learn a second language fluently. In 1967, they began researching existing programs in Canada and the literature on teaching children a second language from an early age. Moore, a trained teacher and translator, was familiar with the St. Lambert experiments and the pedagogical theories of Wilder Penfield.[45] Stapleton was also friends with Gertrude Laing, the only anglophone westerner (and only woman) on the B&B Commission. They were aware of the federal government's efforts to promote French and thought that it, the other major language in Canada, was what their children should be taught.

Initially, these parents found no interest among the public and separate school boards in Calgary to run such a program, nor was there any action from the minister of education, Lou Hyndman, though many people expressed moral support.[46] The head of the separate school board did point out, however, that there were no regulations governing the language of a preschool or kindergarten. Offering a French program at these levels would not engender any bureaucratic red tape, and this was a rare point of flexibility in the Alberta education system. Stapleton and Moore got in touch with their friends and generated enough interest to form a class of eleven five year olds for an initial preschool group that would start in the fall of 1969. It was through Carrothers, whose husband had connections with the Toronto French School group, that they were able to track down the first teacher for the group, a woman from France with a degree in teaching école maternelle. At the time, teaching materials in Canada for the preschool level were limited, so the group used materials from France, echoing the TFS model. The first classes took place in the basement of Christ Church on 8th Street SW.[47] Within a couple of years, they had more parents interested in enrolling their children than there was space to accommodate. The parents came from a wide array of backgrounds and were unified by an interest in second-language learning. A survey showed that most of the parents understood another language, but that language was not always (or even mostly) French, and there were at least fourteen ethnic groups represented among them.

The Calgary French School persisted and thrived as a private venture at the preschool and kindergarten levels. Full-day French immersion could not expand to higher grades until the late 1970s (it was limited to 50 percent from 1968 to 1976), when the Alberta government finally lifted the full restriction on teaching in other languages and started permitting their use for up to 80 percent of the school day. By this point, the initial parents who had started the CFS had moved on, and the public and separate school boards had started their own pilot projects in French immersion in the province. In 1979, the Calgary French School opened its first grade one class and would expand over the years. It currently operates as the Calgary French and International School. Most notable about this school is how a small group of parents worked within their pre-existing networks, and the limitations of the education system, to create better language-learning opportunities for their children. Although some of the other parents who sent their children to the school were generally interested in the value of second-language learning, the organizers were parents committed to French in particular as the other national language of Canada and were inspired by the climate of the B&B Commission.[48]

Conclusion

By the late 1960s, the political culture surrounding Canada's official languages had changed dramatically, and new institutional and financial supports for French-language learning were about to emerge. Whereas most of the efforts in the 1960s in bilingual education had been, of necessity, private initiatives, there was also the St. Lambert public education model, new research, and reservoirs of parent energies that could be tapped to develop new programs. These community groups and early initiatives of the 1960s demonstrate that there was a keen appetite for new approaches to teaching and learning French and a fertile terrain to be exploited as Canada's language-learning revolution was launched.

3

Playing Games with the Language Czar

The First Commissioner of Official Languages

"Bonjour, mon ami! How are you, my friend? Ça va très bien, thank you!" The chipper bilingual folk song by Angèle Arsenault plays as flimsy singles spin on record players. A parrot named Alphonse wisecracks while four Canadian cousins travel the country in a magical flying bathtub. Canadian children translate phrases from English into French, and from French into English, to advance in a board game that will take them from Grand Banks, Newfoundland, to Victoria, British Columbia, to Inuvik, Northwest Territories, and back again.

It hardly sounds like the stuff of a fearsome inquisitor with the power to dismiss thousands of civil servants for their linguistic failings, nor does it sound like the activities that one might expect in the star chamber of the language czar. Yet, in the 1970s, over 2 million "Oh! Canada" kits, consisting of a record of bilingual songs, a board game, a comic book, and an activities book, were distributed by the Office of the Commissioner of Official Languages to schools, service groups, and parents across the country. The kits were part of the "youth option," an initiative launched by the first commissioner of official languages, Keith Spicer, to foster more positive attitudes toward language learning among Canadian children. This was just the tip of the iceberg of unconventional activities undertaken by this office as part of a broader effort to foster public acceptance of official languages in Canada.

Created as part of the Official Languages Act, 1969 (OLA), to oversee the implementation and administration of Canada's new official languages policy, the men and women who occupied the post of Commissioner of Official Languages, an independent officer of Parliament, were granted significant latitude to fulfill their mandate. And so, rather than simply investigating complaints launched against various federal government offices for failures to deliver services in both official languages, the commissioners undertook efforts to shape the climate and discourse of language issues in Canada. They hoped to fulfill the spirit as well as the letter of the country's language laws. Theirs was not an uncontroversial role, and there were certainly blunders along the way. However, the creative efforts of the commissioners and their teams had decisive impacts on shaping attitudes and approaches to bilingualism in Canada.

Keith Spicer (like his successors Maxwell Yalden, D'Iberville Fortier, and Victor Goldbloom, discussed in Chapters 6 and 8) attempted to foster positive attitudes toward linguistic duality, official languages, and bilingualism in a decade of significant challenges to national unity, during which questions of language were usually front and centre. It was a complex task in which Spicer played "the long game." The commissioners' roles were somewhat constrained by the nature of their position and the discourse of federal language law and language policy. These factors curtailed what the commissioners might have wanted to pursue in terms of approaches to individual bilingualism among Canada's population. However, they also showed great ingenuity and were able to expand the scope of action that the framers of this office might have originally intended. Moreover, they did so without prompting a backlash in official Ottawa. Spicer in particular established a path of action that others could follow.

Roles of the Commissioner and Officers of Parliament

Canada's commissioners of official languages have not escaped scholarly attention, and a few words are needed on how others have considered this office and on how it fits into our broader understanding of Canadian political life. Bureaucratic and state structures created over time play a significant role in shaping policy, and the individuals who work within these structures can have impacts on which policies are proposed and pursued. As Donald Savoie argues, the extent of the impact can vary over time, depending on the extent to which the executive branch of the government permits bureaucratic autonomy and innovation.[1] In the early 1970s, when Spicer was setting up the initial structures of the Office of the Commissioner of Official Languages, there was still a fair deal of latitude for bureaucratic mandarins and their officials. As Paul Pierson notes, even this initial period of openness could have long-term consequences for policies and institutional structures, which persist in the future, even with shifts in terms of the bureaucratic freedom that elected officials permitted.[2] As theorists of historical institutionalism have noted, early decisions made in an institution tend to set the course of action, and subsequent decisions that reinforce these early decisions make it more likely that this path will continue to be followed.

This also has consequences for social movement activism, since a supportive bureaucracy can provide a window of opportunity for movement actors to influence the direction of government policy.[3] As Leslie Pal and others have noted, the 1970s were a fertile time in Canada for collaboration between bureaucratic actors and social movement groups. Direct funding was provided by the Department of the Secretary of State to a variety of organizations interested in social changes that broadly aligned with federal government objectives.[4] Pal argues that this was not simply a matter of funding puppet organizations. The organizations that received federal funding were often critical of federal programs and lobbied with varying degrees of success to change these policies. As I have noted in other work, in the dossier of official languages there was certainly a bureaucracy–civil society dynamic at play.[5] Although the commissioner of official languages, as an officer of Parliament, and his or her office are not, strictly speaking, part of the federal civil service, the broader concepts of how state-funded institutions and non-elected officials play roles in shaping public policy and state-society interactions and dialogues are nevertheless relevant.

Most analyses to date have focused on the official roles of the commissioner, identifying three major dimensions. The first role is that of ombudsman, in which the commissioner investigates complaints levied against various government departments about their failure to deliver language services. The second role is that of auditor. This office, of its own accord, can initiate studies of various departments to try to identify problem areas of service, make recommendations for best practices, and monitor ongoing compliance with the OLA. The third role is that of policy adviser, in which the commissioner acts as an advocate for new language policies or for changes to how these policies are crafted. Scholars such as C. Michael MacMillan, for example, have identified the increasing importance attached to this third role, particularly in the 1980s as the commissioner played a key role in revamping the OLA and in the constitutional debates of the post-charter era.[6]

These studies reflect broader questions: to understand the functions of Canada's officers of Parliament and to determine how much scope for action and true independence these officers can exercise.[7] On the whole, these authors have argued that the commissioner, and indeed most of Canada's officers of Parliament, have been granted wide latitude in the exercise of their functions. Carl Cosman argues that the commissioners often strayed from their mandate, becoming involved in political debates tangential to their officially defined roles under the OLA.[8] Delving into the archival record of the Office of the Commissioner and speaking with commissioners themselves and their main interlocutors reveal a far more extensive history of broad interpretation of the commissioner's mandate. However, before one accuses them of "exceeding" or "violating" their mandate, it is important to note that they were broadly supported in their actions by all major political parties. They also had broad support at both national and provincial levels when their activities skirted the formal delineations of responsibility in Canada's federal system.[9] There was remarkable continuity among the Trudeau, Mulroney, and Chrétien governments in terms of how they engaged with the commissioners and the latitude that they permitted for operations of the office. Although some MPs were critical of the commissioners and their statements, such criticism tended to be the exception, not the rule.

Star Chambers, High Priests, and Non-Political Humanism

The idea to create a commissioner of official languages originated with the Royal Commission on Bilingualism and Biculturalism, appointed in 1963 by Prime Minister Lester Pearson. In their first report, published in 1967, discussing a proposed federal Official Languages Act, the commissioners envisaged that this legislation would require a "high state official, independent of the government" (s. 429), to oversee its implementation. Several sections spelled out more fully the roles and authority envisaged for the commissioner. As ombudsman, he would be "the active conscience – actually the protector – of the Canadian public where the official languages are concerned" (s. 435). As auditor, he would "offer criticism of the manner in which the federal Official Languages Act is implemented" (s. 436). The commissioners also suggested that he might play a provisional advisory role to the governor in council until the bilingual districts were established.[10]

The B&B commissioners envisioned much autonomy and authority for the commissioner of official languages, who should have "wide powers" to question public servants under oath, who should make public any complaint raised about implementation of the act, and who should "enjoy wide discretionary powers" within federal jurisdiction for this purpose. They recommended that the commissioner be appointed for a seven-year term, renewable until retirement, to "allow him the fullest freedom from federal government interference, and ... the necessary authority to carry out his duties." The commissioner would be accountable directly to Parliament rather than the governor in council. The commissioners hoped that he "would have high moral authority through his influence on the Canadian public and the government and Parliament of Canada, and could well become one of Canada's most effective instruments making for equality of the two official languages." Accordingly, they recommended "a) that the federal Parliament adopt a federal Official Languages Act; and b) that the Governor in Council appoint a Commissioner of Official Languages charged with ensuring respect for the status of French and English in Canada" (s. 439).[11]

As the recommendations of the B&B Commission were translated into legal wording in the form of the Official Languages Bill, a certain degree of paranoia accompanied it. In debates over second reading of the bill, Progressive Conservative MP Jack McIntosh (Swift Current) argued against it and the "high priests" of bilingualism, Secretary of State Gérard Pelletier and Prime Minister Pierre Trudeau.[12] He contended that the new law would be "the end of the dream of one nation, with one citizenship and one nationality," and that the ministers were not to be trusted when they said the bill would not be prejudicial to unilingual civil servants. McIntosh raised the spectre of airports in which everyone from "taxi drivers and waitresses to char staff and porters" would be forced to be bilingual.[13] Although expressing support for the bill in principle, Robert Stanfield, leader of the Conservative Party, voiced the more moderate concern that new language requirements in the civil service might be difficult, particularly for older civil servants. Many members of his caucus voiced concerns about the ability of individuals to learn a second language, especially at an older age, and what it might mean for their prospects for promotion.[14]

Speaking directly to the issue of the commissioner of official languages, Stanfield's predecessor as Conservative leader, John Diefenbaker, was far less temperate, referring to the proposal to create this office as "an abrogation of parliament beyond anything that has taken place in any generation in our country excepting during the days of war."[15] He railed broadly against the Official Languages Bill, and the commissioner in particular, who would be, he argued, a puppet of the government.[16] Diefenbaker joined sixteen other Conservative MPs, all but one from the prairie provinces, in voting against the bill on second reading.[17]

Although several dimensions of the proposed Official Languages Act were subject to scrutiny, the provisions dealing with the potential role of the commissioner attracted particular fears. Moving an amendment designed to limit the powers of inquiry of the commissioner, Melvin McQuaid (Conservative MP for Cardigan) expressed concern over a provision of the bill that referred to investigations conducted in private, raising the spectre of a "star chamber" and maintaining that hearings should be held in public to allow individuals to clear their names.[18] The image of the star chamber reoccurred in the speech by Eldon Woolliams, the Conservative justice critic, who spoke at length about the procedural concerns of his party about the proposed commissioner, who would be acting alongside the "czar of culture and language," the secretary of state.[19] Minister of Justice John Turner dismissed these concerns and others raised in subsequent Conservative amendments as unfounded, given that the purpose of the commissioner's inquiries would not be to target individuals for their personal actions but to address the overall practices of government departments.[20] The extent of the debate over the prerogatives of the commissioner indicates the level of fear and concern about this office and the desire to circumscribe its scope of action – at least insofar as it pertained to the commissioner's influence on the careers of federal public servants.

The Official Languages Act was passed in the House of Commons on July 7, 1969, without a formally recorded division.[21] Of its forty sections, sixteen pertained to the formal roles and responsibilities of the commissioner of official languages. The first commissioner, Keith Spicer, was fluently bilingual and charismatic, and he had a high media profile thanks to his appearances on a variety of CBC and Radio-Canada television shows throughout the 1960s. He held a PhD in political science and had worked as a researcher for the B&B Commission, a speech writer for Pearson-era Liberal minister Guy Favreau, a writer for the *Globe and Mail,* a professor of political science at the University of Toronto, and a policy analyst under Trudeau's secretary of state, Gérard Pelletier. It was in this last capacity that Spicer had been asked to sketch a strategy for promoting the Official Languages Act after consulting with newspaper editors across the country. In his autobiography, he relates this report as an exercise in "thinking aloud how I would do the job myself."[22] The report clearly impressed Pelletier and Trudeau, who then offered him the job of commissioner.

The decision to appoint an anglophone to this position was key. It was in English-speaking Canada that the task of selling Canada's official languages policy would prove to be more difficult. A media-savvy individual who would not be viewed as "imposing" the policy was needed. Despite the many sections of the Official Languages Act, 1969, outlining the formal processes for inquiries and complaints, Spicer identified section 25 as encapsulating the key aspects of his mandate. The section read thus:

> It is the duty of the Commissioner to take all actions and measures within his authority with a view to ensuring recognition of the status of each of the official languages and compliance with the spirit and intent of this Act in the administration of the affairs of the institutions of the Parliament and Government of Canada and, for that purpose, to conduct and carry out investigations either on his own initiative or pursuant to any complaint made to him and to report and make recommendations with respect thereto as provided in this Act.[23]

In his first annual report, Spicer indicated that his reading of this section was that his role was to do more than simply defend the institutional bilingualism of the federal government as prescribed by law; rather, it was "actively, if indirectly, to help promote it." He viewed phrases in this section – such as "take all actions," "spirit and intent of this act," and "on his own initiative" – as indicating that his mandate was to go beyond the denunciatory role of an ombudsman to take a more proactive role in fostering the spirit of the OLA.[24]

Spicer identified his underlying philosophy as one of "non-political humanism" that would promote a trusting and relaxed dialogue on issues of bilingualism. Speaking specifically about state bilingualism, he viewed justice in this respect as "an ideal of human dignity and as one of the much-needed long-term bridges to understanding among Canadians." He signalled that his plan was to avoid using the coercive powers granted to his office under the OLA whenever he could, stressing instead informal diplomacy and low-key persuasion. Spicer believed that official bilingualism would succeed only if it had the willing support of federal employees.[25] In his first year, his main tasks were to set up his office, hire staff, and establish relationships with the various government departments with which he would be dealing. Although these tasks demanded the lion's share of his time, one can also detect hints of how this low-key approach to building bridges among Canadians was not, in his mind, to be limited to government institutions.

As early as the first year of his mandate, his office received requests for funding for second-language schooling and other inquiries aimed at a much broader swath of issues related to bilingualism. Although many of these requests were redirected to provincial authorities, Spicer did make a number of speeches in favour of funding for interprovincial youth exchanges designed to foster language learning.[26] He also signalled in his first report that it was through youth that the "recognition, by Canadians as a whole, of the equal dignity and value of their two main language communities" could best be achieved and that more needed to be done to make the teaching of second languages more realistic.[27] He believed that Canada needed to address, during childhood and youth, "the root of the problem: intercultural misunderstanding (with the mutual denial of dignity which that implies) and involuntary unilingualism."[28] Although Spicer was taking up the formal mantles of linguistic ombudsman and auditor provided for under the OLA, clearly he also believed that the issues of individual bilingualism and access to second-language learning opportunities were intimately connected to his mandate, and he found wording in the act to support this view.

The Creative Provocateur

One could easily write an entire book on the seven years of Keith Spicer's term as the first commissioner of official languages. My focus here is on how Spicer "broadened" his mandate to tackle the underlying issues related to Canadian attitudes toward official languages and bilingualism. He was clear about what form of bilingualism was required under the Official Languages Act. Many Canadians feared that the OLA was a tool to shove French down their throats – a misconception so widespread that the federal government released a pamphlet designed specifically to address this critique.[29] Spicer was clear that it was institutional bilingualism – the ability of the federal government to provide services in both official languages – that was at stake. That said, he also observed in his second annual report that "the Official Languages Act imposes no obligation on private citizens to learn a second language. [Yet] well-perceived self-interest ought to." Moreover, he argued that the encouragement of young people to learn a second language "should get backing from all enlightened Canadians."[30] Over the course of his mandate, Spicer would attempt both to make institutional bilingualism more palatable to those on the front lines and to develop a broader Canadian culture supportive of this approach to language policy. This would make institutional bilingualism easier in the future.

Civil Servants and the General Public

Sex and humour. These were the two hallmarks of the public face of Spicer's approach to his roles as ombudsman and auditor. In tackling the challenging

issue of encouraging an anglophone-dominated federal civil service to live
up to the obligations of the Official Languages Act, Spicer largely succeeded
in disarming his critics. He was provocative in his statements but almost
always coupled necessary provocations with humour and wit. As federal
language training courses came into effect, Spicer challenged those charged
with organizing these courses – the Treasury Board and Public Service
Commission – to make them relevant and ensure that they would be useful,
going beyond what he termed "cocktail party bilingualism." It was widely
believed, and indeed later studies backed this up,[31] that much of what was
learned in government language training courses was either not used or
quickly forgotten by the senior civil servants who had taken them. This left
the government wide open to allegations of waste and the program vulner-
able to criticisms as an obstacle to the promotion of unilingual civil servants
who failed to accomplish its objectives. Confusion also reigned over what
exactly was required under the new language policy.

Spicer developed a decidedly cheeky strategy to address these potentially damaging concerns. For civil servants struggling to determine their
obligations under the OLA, trying to make their way through what Spicer
himself termed the "bureaucratic jungle" of inadequate information,[32] his
office developed the "Safari Kit" for civil service managers, with distribution
beginning in October 1973. Packaged in a small box that resembled a travel
satchel, the kit contained a pamphlet on the OLA, a Q&A brochure entitled
"Twenty Questions ... and a Few More, on Canada's Official Languages," and
a booklet entitled "The Jungle Book on Official Languages." All components of the kit attempted to spell out, in plain language, the official language requirements of the federal civil service. "The Jungle Book" is notable
for its format. Although primarily textual, it has illustrations centred on an
intrepid male explorer making his way through the jungle of Canadian language policy. Eventually, in the series of illustrations, he encounters a pro-
vocatively dressed, buxom woman seductively standing in a glen holding a
copy of the Official Languages Act.

Selling language policy with sexy images was key to the strategy of
Spicer's office. It would be difficult, for instance, to miss the innuendo im-
plicit in the subheading "The Adam and Eve Syndrome: Who Is Covered
(by the Official Languages Act?)."[33] In his fourth annual report, Spicer noted
that the national capital region was "blessed with a rich selection of television, radio, theatre and splendidly racy French movies – not to mention
soothingly bilingual body-rub parlors – which should enable English-
speaking graduates of French courses to reinvest a few minutes each day in

The intrepid explorer of the language policy jungle. |
Source: "The Jungle Book of Official Languages," Safari Kit, Office
of the Commissioner of Official Languages, 1973.

protecting the public's investment in them."[34] A reader of this particular
report would have been tipped off that this advice was coming given that
it fell under the subheading "Duty Calls: Shall We Slip over to Hull for a
Skin-Flick?"

Playfulness was also evident in Spicer's reports. His third annual report
drew inspiration from literature with subheadings related to *The Jungle Book*,
I'm OK, You're OK, and various works of Shakespeare. It is safe to assume
that few government departments ever began sections of their reports with
"Nightly she sings on yon pomegranate tree: Believe me love, it was the
nightingale" or "I do begin to have bloody thoughts."[35] The departmental
wrap-up of 1975, entitled "The Book Fair: Slim Volumes of Verse and Other
Titillating Tomes (Departments and Agencies 'Evaluated')," gave each agency
its own subheading, ranging from *Animal Farm* (Agriculture) to *Murder on*

The seductive keeper of the Official Languages Act. |
Source: "The Jungle Book of Official Languages," Safari Kit, Office
of the Commissioner of Official Languages, 1973.

the Orient Express (Canadian National Railways).[36] For 1976, Spicer turned
to the classics, with the annual "Read-Out" of departments captioned "*La
commedia non è finita:* The Divine Comedy of Bilingualism – Being a
Dantesque Account of Places Saintly and Sulphurous Where Each Is Found
Classified According to His Linguistic Deeds and Misdeeds."[37] Humour
served to engage readers and perhaps attracted a greater readership than
might otherwise be expected for the report of a government ombudsman.
It also served to disarm those reading what could sometimes be scathing

commentaries on the failure of certain departments to make progress in meeting the standards of the Official Languages Act. But his playfulness, while periodically landing him in hot water in the media (a reference to Montreal's anglophone elites as Westmount Rhodesians went over particularly poorly), aided Spicer in advancing various issues related to official languages and bilingualism.

The Youth Option

"The notion of two neighbourly societies which respect each other must germinate in the minds of today's children and teenagers."[38] Targeting the attitudes of Canadian children and directing additional government resources toward their language learning were high priorities for Spicer. His first annual report referred to exchange programs, and in subsequent years his office would dedicate attention and funds to these programs. By the third year of his mandate, the Information Services Division had developed a twelve-minute film entitled *Bons Amis* aimed at explaining Canada's official languages policy to Canadian youth. The film featured teenagers Pierre Fournier and Mary Sawyer interviewing Spicer as part of a school project to learn about Canada's two official languages. The interviewers asked him about a number of common misconceptions about who had to learn both languages, what the government's obligations were, and what the role of the commissioner was. Toward the end of the film, there was a brief dramatization of how the new Official Languages Act allowed people to get government services in their own language. Following Spicer's approach of selling language policy with sex, this entailed replacing a dialogue between two increasingly frustrated unilingual middle-aged men with a scene in which the English-speaking male government staffer called for a lovely blonde "mademoiselle" to assist the (suddenly flustered) francophone male client at the "Department of Improvements" who declared this to be a great "amélioration."[39] By January 1974, about 500,000 citizens in movie theatres across the country had seen the short film.

By his fourth annual report, Spicer was explicitly calling for a shift in strategy of the federal government's approach to language learning. He called for a reorientation of emphasis from civil service training programs toward youth, in what would be called, by the following year, the "youth option." This entailed a major redirection of funds toward schoolchildren. Spicer believed that the major agents of the official languages program, the Treasury Board and Public Service Commission, should prepare an information program aimed at high school students five to eight years away from entering the job market, motivating them to prepare for a bilingual civil service.[40] By this point, the federally funded Bilingualism in Education Program was already channelling funds for second-language instruction to provincial education departments, but Spicer argued that much more needed to be done to deal with the stagnation of second-language learning in Canada's elementary and secondary schools and the "persisting tragedy of woodenly taught second languages in secondary schools."[41]

Direct funding to assist language learning went well beyond the budget and mandate of the commissioner's office. But motivation and attitude were issues that Spicer and his team thought could be considered. Since education was under provincial jurisdiction, his office needed to tread carefully. So it was in full consultation with the Council of Ministers of Education, Canada (CMEC), that members of his team, coordinated by Gabrielle Kirschbaum and author/illustrator Madeleine Kronby (formerly of *Chez Hélène*), worked with four Ottawa-area school boards to develop a new information kit called Oh! Canada aimed at children aged eight to twelve. The kit was intended to be a motivational tool for language learning among children, with the objectives of "aim[ing] to underpin the motivation of children to learn second languages, and to strengthen their interest in Canadian studies"; "help[ing] not only teachers and students who seem eager for materials on Canada but parents interested in seeing their children develop healthy, positive attitudes to their country, in particular to its language challenges and opportunities"; and "instilling in [children] a wish to communicate with members of the second-language community [and] convincing them that learning can be fun."[42] An initial 50,000 kits were sent out in the spring of 1975, with an additional 500,000 printed and distributed by March 1976.

The Oh! Canada kit consisted of five main components. The most striking was a board game built into the design of the fold-out cardboard kit that held the other components. The game board was a stylized map of Canada. Players could start at one of four cities, and the objective was to make their way all around the country. To advance from city to city, they had to spin a dial. The results of the spin corresponded to numbers on one of four game cards, which contained lists of English and French phrases (which increased in difficulty depending on which card was used). To advance to the next city, players had to translate the phrase into the other language or simply read it in both languages – thus providing various options and levels of difficulty for game play.

Oh! Canada, whether consciously or not, drew on traditions of fostering nationalism and identity formation using maps and games. As Benedict

The Oh! Canada board game. Players advanced to the next city either by translating words from English into French (or vice versa) or by reading the words aloud, depending on the level of difficulty chosen. | *Source:* Oh! Canada Activity Kit, Office of the Commissioner of Official Languages, 1975.

Anderson points out, maps have long been used to reinforce sentiments of nationhood and in effect put boundaries on what geographical territory "belongs" to the nation – or empire – as the well-known use of red to denote British imperial territories reinforced the adage that the sun never sets on the British Empire.[43] Or, if one wants to draw on Canada's French heritage, the *jeu de l'oie* ("game of the goose") was used in post-revolutionary France to teach children about the French Revolution.[44] One can see echoes of each in a board game in which children moved game pieces across a map of Canada (marked with both the English name and the French name of each province) learning about the country's geography and official languages.

The second component was a comic book, thematically linked to the board game. It told the story of four Canadian cousins from the two major language communities – Hildie, Michel, Jamie, and Lise – who travelled across the country with their wisecracking bilingual parrot Alphonse and their love-struck pet turtle Geneviève in a soda pop–powered flying bathtub invented by Lise's uncle Albert. Along the way, the children visited every province and territory, learning facts about each (provided by the provincial ministries of education and tourism) and meeting people from the two major language communities, Aboriginal communities, and other multicultural groups. The comic book was bilingual in the sense that it alternated between the two languages – necessitating use of a glossary or dictionary for full comprehension.

The third component of the kit was an activity book with puzzles, crosswords, and other exercises related to the comic book. The fourth was a 33 ⅓ rpm record with bilingual songs, including "Dans mon pays" performed by Edith Butler and "Bonjour, My Friend" performed by Angèle Arsenault. And the fifth component was a backpack patch featuring Alphonse.

The Oh! Canada Activity Kit was the first major element of what became a two-decade program of information kits, games, and posters aimed at Canadian youth. Over 2 million kits would be printed in its five-year run, and the games would continue to circulate for some time.[45] The kit was highly popular with the public, with a 1978 evaluation reporting that 100 percent of children found the kit to be "fun." Officials in the commissioner's office were extremely pleased with the overwhelming public demand for the game. However, the response from ministerial officials and pedagogical experts was somewhat more mixed and is interesting for what it reveals about the delicate balance that the commissioner's office had to maintain in promoting bilingualism among Canadian children.

Alphonse, the bilingual parrot, Oh! Canada backpack patch. |
Source: Oh! Canada Activity Kit, Office of the Commissioner of Official
Languages, 1975.

Before Oh! Canada was given widespread national distribution, the initial print run of 50,000 copies was tested in Canadian classrooms and distributed to a number of Ministry of Education and school board officials, second-language teachers, and other parties connected with the process of development. For the most part, response to the kit was very positive. Robert Gillin, curriculum services officer for the Ontario Ministry of Education, referred to it as "superb" and observed that "youngsters will get the message that learning a second language can be both exciting and fun."[46] An evaluation conducted for the Carleton Board of Education by André Obadia yielded extremely positive comments from teachers, such as "très bon pour l'avancement du bilinguisme et pour l'attitude" and "elle prouve aux élèves que l'étude d'une langue seconde peut être agréable et simple. Lorsqu'on a atteint cet objectif je crois qu'on a déjà gagné la bataille."[47] Reports from Newfoundland claimed that the activity book was excellent and that the songs on the record were catchy.[48]

As distribution increased in 1975 and 1976, provincial ministers and deputy ministers, including Minister of Education Julian Koziak (Alberta) and

Deputy Minister of Education Harvey Malmberg (New Brunswick), testified to the high appeal of the materials. Deputy Minister of Education George Waldrum (Ontario) noted that "the general enthusiasm for the Oh! Canada kits has certainly been overwhelming in Ontario, as reflected in the number of requests you quote for this province."[49] Federal MPs of various political stripes were enthusiastic in their support as well. John Fraser, Progressive Conservative MP for Vancouver South, who encountered the game through his daughter, observed that "I think it has been a valuable contribution to the language policy in this country."[50] Liberal MP John Stanbury, representing York-Scarborough, believed that the kit "will be a valuable aid in promoting bilingualism among young Canadians."[51] Positive responses came in from Quebecers as well, including Pierre Blanchard, principal of École Secondaire Gamelin in Hull, who considered the activity book to be "une perle pour nos professeurs d'Anglais."[52]

Yet pedagogical criticisms were levied by a variety of experts, who viewed the kit not through the lens of a language-learning motivational tool (the main objective of the commissioner's office) but as a language-teaching tool for second-language classrooms. Robert Cousin, of Saskatchewan's Ministry of Education, was extremely critical of the systematic translation that was key to the game and comic book, which he noted "only serves to confuse French as a second language students and is contrary to the philosophy and methodology of our three French programs."[53] The reports from Newfoundland French specialists Marie-Christine Demessine and René Enguehard raised concerns about the mixture of English and French in the comic book, which they thought created difficulties in comprehension for children.[54] Manitoba's Raymond Hébert noted that the material, though well presented, did not correspond to the province's pedagogical principles of second-language acquisition and ran counter to those used in its French immersion programming.[55]

These concerns were echoed by Henri Tanguay, director general of the Commission Scolaire Ottawa-Hull, whose pedagogical officer, Jean-Pierre Prud'homme, claimed that language learning by translation had been rejected by most language teaching centres over twenty-five years earlier as ineffective and had thus been eliminated from schools in the 1950s and 1960s.[56] He went further to claim that "la méthodologie et la démarche ... peu[ven]t avoir des effets désastreux sur la langue de nos enfants."[57] Armed with this pedagogical critique, the newly appointed Parti Québécois education minister, Jacques-Yvan Morin, stopped distribution of the kits in Quebec schools in March 1977. He claimed that the methodology of the kit would result in "l'apprentissage du franglais," and he claimed that the content of the comic book was "faible, pour ne pas dire trivial," giving what he considered to be misinformation that French could be used throughout Canada, when in fact French Canada "lutte avec peine pour la reconnaissance de sa langue et sa survie."[58]

The Oh! Canada kits were explicitly sent out not as second-language teaching tools but as motivational tools designed as supplementary materials for classroom and home use. Spicer and his team were clear that the kits were intended not to teach the second language but to develop an appetite for second-language learning and for learning more about Canada. Indeed, had the commissioner produced a pedagogical tool, it would have been unlikely to get past the CMEC, with which the kit had been designed. Moreover, response to the kits from second-language teachers did not produce the uniformity of pedagogical approaches implied in the reports by Hébert, Prud'homme, and Cousin. Many teachers noted how the kits helped in their classrooms. In a survey of 110 teachers commissioned for a formal evaluation of the kit in 1978, 90 percent reported that it had motivated their students to learn a second language and had provided them with a better knowledge of Canada.[59] A similar percentage believed that the kit should continue to be distributed and that a kit for older students should be developed.

The evaluation of Oh! Canada was somewhat problematic. Requested by the Treasury Board in order to authorize future printing and the development of new kits, it was not possible, given time and logistical constraints, to conduct before-and-after evaluations of student attitudes toward and interest in second-language learning, so the evaluator's report was based on educators' opinions and observations. An additional component of the evaluation was based on letters received by the commissioner's office regarding the kit, with only 0.2 percent reporting negative comments. In response to letters that complained about the principle of the kit and its cost, the commissioner's office responded that "to bring up children who cannot communicate with other people in this world is simply not defensible. A unilingual education is out of date." It also believed that "providing our children with second language instruction should be considered as basic as making sure they learn history and mathematics." The cost of $1.71 per kit was defended as a "cheap price to pay for bringing about understanding between members of the two language groups of this country."[60]

The Oh! Canada kits were wildly popular through repeated print runs. In 1975, a recorded version of the comic book was released on cassette for classroom use. There were even discussions about an animated television series on CBC/Radio-Canada based on the comic book. Beyond the classroom, the kits were ordered by a number of private organizations, including CN Rail, which requested 82,000 kits for its trans-Canada trains. Many organizations also saw national unity–enhancing potential. In the aftermath of the PQ election of November 1976, a number of organizations, including the Mouvement Québec-Canada, and Quebec Liberal MPs ordered tens of thousands of kits for distribution in the province after Minister of Education Jacques-Yvan Morin barred their distribution in schools. Every month letters from Canadians poured in in response to the kit. Many came from children who wrote thank-you notes to the commissioner as part of the kit's activity booklet. By August 1977, over 100,000 letters had been received.[61] Given this enthusiastic response, it is not surprising that, when deciding on the formal evaluation format for the kit, the commissioner's officials chose to balance the more tepid pedagogical evaluations with this popular form of support. The Oh! Canada kit thus provided the gold standard for future information kits produced by his office, and the commissioner's staff hoped to continue working in this vein under Spicer's successors.

Travel the Country, Meet Fellow Canadians

Not all of Spicer's initiatives met with enthusiastic responses. Spicer had long championed linguistic exchanges for students. In 1976, he pushed this concept further, trying to incorporate adults who were not civil servants into his language advocacy. He proposed a variety of measures that he hoped would increase openness, and possibly personal bilingualism, among Canadian adults. The measures included relatively low-cost proposals such as encouraging the government to publicize the section of the Income Tax Act that allowed for tax deductions when over twenty-five dollars were spent on job-related training and urging the relevant ministries to interpret this section generously when it came to language training.[62] This represented existing policy, and the relevant ministers responded positively.[63] Much bolder, and much more expensive, was Spicer's proposal, first raised in 1974, then actively pursued in 1976, to have the government subsidize one vacation per year for Canadian families who travelled over 1,500 miles within Canada. He argued that this initiative would induce intercultural mingling by Canadian families.[64]

Most of the ministers whom Spicer contacted played a pass-the-buck game of arguing that his proposal did not fall under their purview. The transportation minister, Otto Lang, was more definitive, arguing that, though the idea had some merit, there was no instrument through Transport Canada to permit this scheme. As Lang pointedly noted, "transportation has been used as a tool to attempt to achieve a variety of national goals, but I believe there is a limit to the number of ends an efficient transportation system can be expected to serve."[65] Spicer engaged in a parallel effort with the presidents of Air Canada and CN Rail, encouraging them to offer a once-per-year low-cost trip.[66] The response to this initiative was tepid; the executives were interested only if the federal government would foot the bill and particularly if the scheme could bolster off-season travel.[67] As will become evident in later chapters, though Canada's private sector leaders often spoke about the merits of personal bilingualism, and complained about shortages of qualified bilingual personnel, rarely were they willing to put company money behind initiatives to promote bilingualism.

After this discouraging initial response, Spicer and Maxwell Yalden, his successor, engaged in a more detailed study of how the proposal might be developed, incorporating Gallup poll studies of how Canadians thought this travel might help national unity and figuring out the economic spin-offs.[68] The proposal still received a cool reception from the federal government. Prime Minister Trudeau thanked Yalden for his renewed efforts and indicated that the project would be studied, but he observed that any new initiative would have to line up with broader conclusions of a review of Canada's tourism policy. Trudeau expressed doubt about the potential success of the project given "il faut admettre que la réussite d'un projet comme le sien dépend, avant tout, de la population canadienne."[69] This latest venture to promote bilingualism and tolerance through adult travel largely fizzled out, though efforts to promote student exchanges remained a priority for the commissioner's office.

Instigating Activism: Canadian Parents for French

One of the final para-mandate activities undertaken by Keith Spicer had perhaps the most enduring impact on personal bilingualism in Canada. Since the early 1970s, with the leverage provided by the federal Bilingualism in Education Program, parents' groups across the country had been working to encourage their schools and school boards to improve language teaching and the options available to their children. Lacking was any substantial degree of interprovincial or national cooperation in this respect. Toward the end of his term, on a trip to Calgary, Spicer encountered this problem directly, meeting with a group of parents frustrated at the limited number of opportunities for their children to learn French as a second language and regularly blocked by trustees in their efforts to expand programs.[70] In the winter of 1977, Spicer used his office's budget to bring together parents from across the country to meet in Ottawa to "discuss ways and means of ensuring that their children receive good-quality instruction in the French language."[71] The parents were put in touch with resource people such as teachers, pedagogical experts, and exchange program directors. To select this group of individuals, Spicer drew on his extensive personal networks, many of which predated his term as commissioner. Norman Webster, editor of the *Globe and Mail,* and his wife, Pat, who had been active in campaigns for French immersion in Toronto and Oakville, were contacts from Spicer's journalist days who helped to draw up the initial list of invitees. Spicer played only a limited role in the event (discussed in detail in the next chapter), allowing the parents to run the show, with his adviser on youth issues, Gabrielle Kirschbaum, checking in from time to time.

This first conference generated an incredible amount of enthusiasm and concluded with the decision to form a new national organization to improve opportunities for second-language learning. Canadian Parents for French (CPF) held its founding convention, again in Ottawa, and with the financial support of the commissioner's office, in October 1977. The organization attracted a membership of over 2,000 people in its first months. Spicer observed that initially the main francophone cabinet ministers, such as Marc Lalonde and Trudeau himself, were reluctant to meet with CPF's leaders, considering the promotion of French-language learning to English speakers a low priority. Spicer persisted in urging Trudeau to receive the group and boost their profile, driven by his belief that this was a key way of "seducing" anglophones to support the Official Languages Act, by showing them that, beyond the law itself, there could be benefits for their children.[72] This persistence would ultimately pay off.

CPF would be highly influential in the campaign for Canadian individual bilingualism, as will be evident in later chapters. In terms of the commissioner's role, however, what occurred in 1977 was that an officer of Parliament, of his own initiative, effectively convened a new national and provincial lobby group and provided it with start-up funding from his budget. This was not atypical for Canadian political life of the 1970s; Leslie Pal and others have noted comparable activities of the Department of the Secretary of State. What differs somewhat in the case of CPF is that the commissioner's office was beyond the direct control of the elected government of the day, and as such there was, at least initially, less direct government endorsement or control of this group and its mandate (though that would change over time as the secretary of state started funding the group).

Conclusion

Keith Spicer wrapped up his seven-year term in 1977, leaving behind very large shoes to fill. He had been outspoken, wry, disarming, and provocative. He had also clearly established the independence of his office and his willingness to take on all opponents. Although Spicer had clearly gone beyond the strictest literal interpretation of the Official Languages Act with his activities, he had generally received the approval of not only the Liberal government but also the opposition parties. He had also been careful, when venturing into provincial waters, to do so with caution and deference to Canadian federalism and thus avoid provoking major outbursts or condemnations. It remained to be seen whether his successors would take advantage of the precedents that he had set for public engagement or retreat into a milder form of linguistic review and the ombudsman role.

4
Social Movement Activism, 1969–76

Passage of the Official Languages Act (OLA) and creation of the Bilingualism in Education Program served as spurs to action for social movement activism on both sides of the bilingualism debate. Groups organized both in opposition to and in support of the federal government's new language policies. However, the two groups tended not to interact directly with each other in the period leading up to the election of the Parti Québécois in November 1976. Anti-bilingualism groups were more national in focus, concerned with the constitutionality of the OLA and opposed to the conception of Canada that it supported. Pro-bilingualism groups were more local in focus and interested in the educational implications of these policies. They took a particular interest in creating better French-language learning opportunities. Although most active at the local level, pro-bilingualism groups were increasingly aware of the need to build their networks and tap into expertise from across the country. Although the main case studies in this chapter of expanding French programs are drawn from Ontario, there was similar activity in communities across the country (which unfortunately left behind fewer records). Pioneering immersion programs were created from Coquitlam, British Columbia, in 1968 to Halifax, Nova Scotia, in 1976.

Joseph Thorarinn Thorson and the Single Canada League
Opposition to the idea of bilingualism and two official languages circulated during the hearings of the Royal Commission on Bilingualism and

Biculturalism (the B&B Commission). A small cohort of MPs, primarily from western Canada and the Progressive Conservative caucus, voted against the Official Languages Act on its first two readings. But the extent of organized opposition to the new language policies was relatively limited in civil society. Once the act was passed, Prime Minister Trudeau indicated that he had received letters from only seventy-nine individual Canadians objecting to the bill, and eight organizations had submitted petitions. Petitions from the Maritime Loyalist Association and the Grand Orange Lodge of Manitoba were no surprise. Half of the groups that submitted petitions were from Edmonton, including the Edmonton Chamber of Commerce and the Voice of Western Canada.[1] The most significant anti-bilingualism group, and the one with the most staying power, was the Single Canada League, founded on June 3, 1969, in Edmonton.

The Single Canada League was born from the opposition of Joseph Thorarinn Thorson to the OLA and more broadly to what he called the imposition of a "dual French-English Canada" by the Pearson and Trudeau administrations. This campaign against bilingualism and biculturalism is fascinating not least because it pit Thorson indirectly against his son Donald, a lawyer with the federal Department of Justice who had drafted the OLA. Thorson was born to Icelandic parents in Manitoba. His illustrious career included a Rhodes Scholarship in Oxford and a term as dean of the University of Manitoba's law school. He was a Liberal and Liberal-Progressive MP from 1926 to 1942 for the ridings of Winnipeg South Centre and Selkirk, rising to the post of minister of national war services in 1941–42. He then became president of the Exchequer Court of Canada. As an MP, he learned French (making him trilingual, with the Icelandic and English that he had learned as a child), and as a judge he heard cases and wrote decisions in French.[2]

It was a curious background for a man who would contest the Official Languages Act right up to the Supreme Court of Canada and serve as counsel to the anti-bilingualism mayor of Moncton, Leonard Jones, in his court case against the act. From 1968 to 1974, Thorson was the champion of the most vocal group opposing implementation of the Official Languages Act and "compulsory bilingualism." His advocacy included a speaking tour of forty-two Canadian Clubs from Arvida, Quebec, to Victoria, British Columbia, prior to the 1968 election, and a Single Canada League speaking tour of Ontario and western Canada in 1971.[3] Thorson hoped that the book version of his arguments, *Wanted! A Single Canada,* would be in print in time for the 1972 federal election, but McClelland and Stewart did not publish it until 1973.[4]

Thorson claimed to support the increased teaching of French but objected fervently to the promotion of bilingualism as a matter of national policy and to making French an official language on the ground that this status was needed for national unity. He strongly opposed language requirements in the civil service, which he saw as a departure from the merit system and "discriminatory against the many persons who find it difficult to learn French." On the other hand, he supported special status for Quebec to give it as much jurisdiction as possible to handle its own affairs – provided that this did not hamper national considerations and development of the rest of the country.[5] Thorson strongly believed that section 133 of the British North America Act was a legal limitation on the use of French as a language of government. He considered any extension of its use beyond the areas spelled out in that section a "breach of an essential condition of Confederation."[6] (He was notably silent on the fact that this is also the only section of the BNA Act that mentions where English can be used.) Thorson saw the Official Languages Bill as an attempt to change Canada's character, and in a 1969 speech in Edmonton he called for an organization to fight this attempt. At that meeting, the 400 people present chose him to be president and leader of the organization with the name that he suggested: the Single Canada League.[7] He proposed to challenge the constitutionality of the new bill through the court system.

On June 26, 1970, Thorson filed a lawsuit against several people, including the attorney general of Canada, the B&B commissioners, and the secretary of state, charging them with foisting an unconstitutional law on the Canadian people and spending their money to implement it. On March 5, 1971, Chief Justice Dalton Wells of the Ontario High Court of Justice ruled that Thorson, as an individual, lacked the standing to challenge the law. Following this decision, Thorson went on a speaking tour of western Canada to rally opposition to the Trudeau government's language policies. Letters that he received in response to his speeches showed that at least some of his listeners disagreed with him. Agnes Enns, an immigrant from the Netherlands who heard him speak in Victoria, thought that the French had earned equality in the country and had the right to teach their language in any part of Canada.[8] She believed that his proposals would "lead to hatred, malice and violence" and even "terrorism."[9]

Enns seems to have been in the minority of Thorson's audiences (both live and on call-in radio), which attracted many people virulently opposed to official bilingualism and French-language instruction. W.H. Dunne of Toronto wrote "I wish you luck with your league but think that Quebec is going to separate from the rest of Canada and I say let them and the sooner the better. This is the only and best way to get rid of the damn French on every thing that we pick up here."[10] Harry Luck of Vancouver observed that almost all of those in attendance at the talk were over fifty years old (including himself). He thought that Thorson needed to reach out to younger Canadians to win this fight. Luck then argued that the Single Canada League should urge all of its members to purchase a Red Ensign for flying on Canada's national days, noting that Canada "fought 2 wars under this flag with very little assistance from Quebec, I may add," and that "it is time determined people took down Pearson's flag of appeasement."[11] Thorson agreed with Luck on the need to reach youth but not on the flag issue. Another supporter of the League, R.W.F. James of Toronto, sent $200 to help launch a court case to charge Minister Jean Marchand with mischief for his actions in the October Crisis after he "[misled] Canadians with his story of rifles and machine guns and dynamite that would blow up the core of Montreal."[12] Thorson declined this suggestion as well, preferring electoral means to remove Marchand and noting that this was the method that he suggested in his speeches in western Canada, Hamilton, and St. Catharines. The Single Canada League was proving to be a lightning rod for a more general anti-French (and pro-British) element of the Canadian public, which often tapped into resentment over Quebec's anti-war stance in the Second World War.

In 1972, Thorson took his legal challenge to the Ontario Court of Appeal, but again his appeal was refused on the ground that he lacked standing. His book, *Wanted! A Single Canada*, was finally published in 1973. His version of a Single Canada (his capitalization) was "based on the sacredness of individual personality," "in which all Canadians, regardless of differences in ethnic origin, whether British or French, or neither British nor French, stand on the footing of equality with one another, both in the enjoyment of their rights and in the fulfillment of their duties, without any preferential treatment to the members of any component of the Canadian nation." This contrasted with what Thorson called "the French-English duality that is in the course of being foisted on us."[13] He claimed that the current policies would not lead to national unity and that Canadians "strongly resent the compulsion involved in the bilingualism policy that is being forced on them and the attempt that is underway to make Canada not only a bilingual country but also a dual French-English one. This resentment is deep-seated and widely spread."[14] Thorson drew heavily on the statements of Union Nationale premiers Daniel Johnson and Jean-Jacques Bertrand, and various

Parti Québécois supporters and leaders, to make the case that they did not want bilingualism but autonomy for Quebec. He cited conservative histor- ian Donald Creighton to argue that any status for the French language be- yond that found in section 133 of the British North America Act would be unconstitutional and "a breach of an essential condition of Confederation."[15]

Thorson boldly claimed that "the truth is that Canada never was a bilin- gual country, it is not a bilingual country now, and it may fairly be predicted that it never will be a bilingual country. The contention that it is a bilingual country is a deliberate 'false pretence.'"[16] He argued that it was a distortion of history to claim that Canada was founded on two distinct linguistic groups, and he rejected the idea that language rights are a type of human rights.[17] He railed against the "imposition" by Lester Pearson of bilingualism on the civil service, "making it a condition of employment and of promotion in it,"[18] which he blamed on "militant" French Canadian cabinet ministers such as Jean-Luc Pépin.

Although Thorson spoke both official languages, he was strongly opposed to what he called "compulsory bilingualism." He believed that "it is contrary to the basic policy of our country that a person should be compelled to learn a language other than his own as a condition of employment in the public service of his country or of promotion in it."[19] He clearly assumed that the "person" in question had English as his or her "own" language. He expressed no qualms about francophones having to learn another language.

Thorson thought that public money should not be spent to expand bi- lingualism, including the "Bilingualism Development Program" and the Bilingualism in Education Program. He opposed Secretary of State Gérard Pelletier's desire to use public funds to create French-language schools in every city and expand French-language CBC television.[20] Thorson was critical of a 1971 civil service plan to recruit French-speaking university graduates in advance of positions opening up, and then place them as positions were posted, an attempt to create units of the federal civil service in which the working language was French, expansion of bilingualism in the Armed Forces, plans to expand labelling laws to encompass more consumer products, and the OLA plan to create bilingual districts.[21] He claimed that there would be "enormous cost[s] to the public" attached to these programs, costs that would be a waste since "Canada will never become a bilingual country."[22]

Thorson was particularly concerned that bilingualism policies for the federal civil service would affect all groups that did business with the gov- ernment. He observed that, "whether there is justification or not, the belief is growing in Public Service circles that the real purpose of the proponents of the bilingualism policy in the public service is to secure jobs in the service for French Canadians."[23] There was occasional slippage by politicians or senior administrators between their use of ethnic-based terms such as "francophone" or "French Canadian" and linguistic-based terms such as "bilingual" when referring to hiring targets. This conflation of terms fed the argument of opponents that "bilingual" was government code for "francophone."

Thorson did not oppose Quebec's right to decide to secede, but he thought that this should be a take-it-or-leave-it proposition. He thought that no changes should be made to make Quebec happier to remain in Canada, observing that "the Canadian people must not allow themselves to be diverted from their decision to reject the concept of a dual French-English Canada by the implied threat that Quebec will separate from the rest of Canada if its demands are not met."[24] French Canadians, in his rhetoric, were holding Canada back: "How can there be national unity in Canada as long as the Quebec leaders insist that the integrity of the French-Canadian nation must be maintained and that French Canadians remain French? How can there be any Canadian identity as long as that attitude persists?"[25] Canada, he argued, would never become a great country if its people allowed it to become a dual French-English country. Thorson proposed blunt majority rule by non-French Canadians to reverse the policies of the Trudeau and Pearson governments. He observed that "it is within their power to defeat any attempt to make French an official language across Canada with a status equal to that of English in every aspect of our national life ... by voting against the candidates of any government that makes such an attempt whenever they have the chance to do so."[26]

Interviewed about his activism a few years later, Thorson claimed that his main opposition was not to the French language "but [to] what he perceived as its compulsory imposition on the Canadian people, and the political bribery with which he felt Quebecers were being bought." But the interview also makes it clear that his Icelandic parents brought their children up within the English milieu. Although some Icelandic culture was passed on to them, as he put it, "Canada would come *first*." It was a libertarian upbringing based on "the sacredness [that] we afford individualism," to which compulsion was anathema.[27] Yet, as Royce Firth points out in a book review, there were huge blind spots in Thorson's worldview about the extent to which an English-only policy would be viewed as compulsion by French Canadians, who were not part of the "us" and "our dreams" that Thorson wrote about with an "unrelenting bias."[28] In his profile of Thorson, Val Ross chalked some of this up to his belonging to "Canada's third solitude: the immigrants from Europe and Asia who feel forgotten in the struggles of English and French Canadians."[29] Thorson does appeal in his book to the more than 5 million Canadians of origins other than English or French who, according to him, resented the "preferential treatment that has been accorded to French Canadians."[30]

Ultimately, the Supreme Court of Canada granted Thorson standing for his legal challenge in 1974.[31] He never took advantage of this standing directly, because the case of Leonard Jones was heard first, and the Supreme Court ruled decisively, in *Jones v. A.G. of New Brunswick*,[32] that the Official Languages Act was in fact constitutional, rendering most of Thorson's case moot. The Single Canada League continued to run advertisements for members describing their mission to assist in building a Canada based on "absolute equality" of ethnic groups in which, outside section 133 of the BNA Act, "English should be the only official language." The ads spoke of "unit[ing] Canadians in opposition to any attempt to change the basic character of Canada or to establish a dual Canadian nation or create a dual Canadian nationality" and "in opposition to the use of public funds for the preferential promotion of any particular culture." Anyone "opposed to the imposition of bilingualism on the Canadian people" was invited to send the five-dollar membership fee to Thorson, as president of the league.[33] However, its activities were starting to wane with the failure of the court case. By 1976, the league was dormant, and Thorson was returning donations that continued to trickle in.[34] As will be seen in Chapter 5, a successor was waiting in the wings to pick up the torch of anti-bilingualism and anti-dualism.

Thorson's story came to a bittersweet end in 1978. Backing his car out of the driveway of his Ottawa residence in April, Thorson accelerated and collided with the Austrian Embassy across the street. He spent most of the next three months in a body cast. On July 5, he was taken unconscious to the hospital. He regained consciousness long enough during a visit to find out that his son Donald (drafter of the Official Languages Act) had been appointed to serve as a justice on the Ontario Court of Appeal. Donald had been the deputy minister of justice from 1973 to 1977, and most recently he had been Trudeau's constitutional adviser. Joseph grinned with pleasure at the news and passed away a few hours later.[35]

The Canadian National Association, Dominion of Canada Party, and Voice of Canada League

A number of other anti-French and anti-bilingualism organizations cropped up in the 1960s and early 1970s. Like the Single Canada League, most of them were centred on a single activist with a group of passive (or financial) supporters. They opposed the expansion of French as an official language and the "imposition" of French on the civil service. Voluntary French-language learning by Canadians did not figure substantially in their rhetoric or publications, though it did crop up. They generally opposed greater visibility for the French language and thus worked against some of the secondary goals of pro-bilingualism groups. Although with short lifespans and limited impacts, these groups did help to shape elements of the anti-bilingualism discourse that persisted in future decades.

The Canadian National Association (CNA), through its secretary, William Busby, a lawyer from Toronto, wrote to J.T. Thorson prior to founding of the Single Canada League asking him to consider supporting the CNA. This group wanted English to be the single official language for all of Canada, including Quebec, and to do away with the clauses of section 133 of the BNA Act referring to the French language. Their literature argued that "two languages will divide us into a weak nation, which creates situations now existing in Belgium and Cyprus." As they rhetorically asked their readers, "do you want education costs and taxes to increase in order that all school children shall be taught French?" A few paragraphs later they claimed that "we want to keep Canada a free nation where people may use any language they please (as we now have freedom of speech) but without concessions to any group. As a true Canadian, wouldn't you learn and use one official language willingly for the sake of your country and to build a stronger democratic nation?" It was a peculiar balancing act of trying to appeal to various ethnic groups, who "have the right to maintain their individual language and culture," yet showing hostility toward French. Although the group argued that "Canadians have the right to any second language of their choice but will not force it on others,"[36] which made them appear to be striving for some degree of openness to second languages, they opposed other languages being taught in schools or having any public status.

Busby made it clear to Thorson that his association wanted only English in Canada's public schools and wanted the CBC abolished. Apparently, the group had trouble attracting members because "we do not have enough prominent Canadians who are willing to state their views publicly."[37] Thorson declined the invitation, thinking that the CNA's proposals to restrict section 133 and do away with the CBC went too far. He suggested that Busby's group was unlikely to make progress unless it conceded some status to French in Quebec (and possibly New Brunswick).[38] The CNA maintained a presence for a few more years, running ads in newspapers with the text of section

133 of the BNA Act and a caption: "This is the Law of Canada – If you believe in upholding the law, your contribution to repeat the publication of this information will be appreciated."[39] But the group did not appear to gain much traction and faded from view.

Members of the Canadian National Association might have thrown their support behind the Dominion of Canada Party. The party was founded in 1969 by Flo E. Frawley of Calgary, a fifty-six-year-old grandmother opposed to the "rapid sellout of English-speaking Canada to Quebec."[40] In 1970, the group Voice of Western Canada merged with Frawley's party.[41] The Dominion of Canada Party's rallying cry was "one language, one Canada." It was a good match with the "one language for Canada" motto of the CNA, which Frawley addressed in Toronto (along with the Canadian Loyalist Association) in July 1970. In the early 1970s, she refused to release official membership numbers but claimed that she had members in up to 100 communities and that her party was "going to mushroom overnight." By 1977, she claimed "thousands" of supporters in 235 communities.[42] Frawley did not draw huge crowds – only twenty-six turned out to her Toronto meeting – and she did not have an official platform other than "one official language for Canada" and rejection of "compulsory bilingualism."[43] Appearing before a joint parliamentary hearing on the Constitution in Calgary in 1971, Frawley was alternately booed and laughed at by the committee members and 400 people in attendance. Undaunted, she delivered a brief claiming that her party would form the government and rescind all legislation on bilingualism.[44] Her party was willing to accept French only within the limitations of section 133 of the BNA Act. She thought that second-language education should be solely on a voluntary basis and that those who wanted to learn another language should pay for it themselves.[45]

Frawley claimed that communists had caused the conflict between French and English Canadians, alleging that this was also the case in Northern Ireland.[46] She detested the replacement of British Canadian symbols, referring to elimination of the Red Ensign as one of "a multitude of diabolical schemes" by the Liberal government.[47] In later years, she deemed the renaming of Dominion Day to Canada Day "an illegal vote by a few, without a quorum."[48] Frawley was a fervent believer in the monarchy, expressing concern that the release of a special series of stamps featuring Canada's Plains Indians was "but another attempt to phase out Queen Elizabeth on our 8-cent stamps."[49] The Dominion of Canada Party would never win a seat in a Canadian election. It is nevertheless significant for how its rhetoric echoed that of other groups who saw section 133 of the BNA Act as the absolute limit for official use of French in Canada, who expressed fear and concern about the replacement of British and British Canadian symbols, and who linked the spectre of communism to changing Canadian identity politics.[50]

The Voice of Canada League (VCL), led in the late 1960s by Stanley Petrie of Ottawa, was even more inflammatory than the other anti-bilingualism and anti-French organizations of its period. The VCL cast its fight as one for freedom itself and against the advance of fascism under French rule.[51] Its rather hysterical manifestos are nicely summed up in the following extract from a 1969 letter to members:

> If our English speaking culture is to be submerged in favour of a French culture, if our Monarchical and Democratic form of Government is to be Exchanged for a Republic with a French accent, if the secular State is to give way to a Roman Catholic State, and a Vatican incumbent in Ottawa, if the choice is to be between the French and English language, and whether we have State Governments with super power over a Dominion Government, then we English Speaking people have a choice, either we submit or we stand firm. We have everything to lose, and everything to gain.

Petrie's writings were classic conspiracy theories, claiming evidence of a French takeover of Canada on the basis of things such as French-first naming conventions on signage at Canada's embassies, meetings of the Quebec caucus of Liberal MPs ("to plot the take-over of English speaking Canada's rights"), and Quebec ministers' control of Canada Post. Petrie believed that the CBC was "a principal media of propaganda against English-speaking Canadians" and that the press in the country was biased and "deliberately keeping silent" on how the English were being discriminated against. He claimed that "all French organizations, some visible and some not, are applying pressures on their own Provincial government, on the Federal Government, and on all other Provincial Governments to insist on French first and even exclusively wherever possible." VCL bulletins were peppered with other allegations of a takeover of the military (with due reference to Quebec's support of the collaborationist Vichy-era French government). Closest to a "positive" take on French was the line "French language by choice, yes! By co-ercion, No!" The Voice of Canada League was appalled by Bill C-120, which would "impose upon the country the French language" and lead to a state in which "people will be subject to censors, and censorship and scrutiny as to their willingness to accommodate to the French fact, the minority will be aided and abetted by the French managed

Liberal Government who will support the aims and claims of any minority French group to impose their will upon the majority, anywhere in Canada."[52]

The VCL did not gain much public notice even during the OLA debates. It popped up again in a splashy way at the height of the bilingual air traffic controllers dispute in June 1976 with a full-page ad headed "Our Government: Racist and Arrogant" in the *Globe and Mail*, with the particularly provocative claim that, "in its hysterical pursuit of Bilingualism at ANY price, the present government has pursued a racist policy worthy of South Africa."[53] The ad was paid for by a private citizen who asked to remain anonymous and was greeted mainly with mockery and condescension; columnist Geoffrey Stevens said that "League of Anglophone Bigots would be a better description."[54] Vitriol did exist in Canada, albeit at this point largely confined to extremists unwilling to go public and put their names behind their actions.

BMG Publishing: Anti-socialism Meets Anti-bilingualism

In the mid-1970s, another group of Canadians opposed to official bilingualism came together to form a publishing consortium under the brand of BMG Publishing. The group clustered around Kenneth McDonald, a British-born pilot in the RAF posted to Canada during the Second World War. He worked for Canadair after the war, then became a full-time author in 1969. He ran into difficulty finding a publisher when McClelland and Stewart, which had published J.T. Thorson's work, refused to publish books penned by him and his colleague, Winnett Boyd. Boyd was an engineer, the chief designer of the Chinook and Orenda engines and the Chalk River nuclear reactor. Initially a Liberal, Boyd left the party after Pierre Trudeau became its leader and ran as a Progressive Conservative in York-Scarborough in 1972.[55] Together with their friend Orville Gaines (the G in BMG), they would self-publish and publish eight books between 1975 and 1979 by like-minded authors who had been turned down by mainstream publishers, and they claimed that each book sold at least 10,000 copies.[56]

Although individual bilingualism per se was not the target of their first two books, *The National Dilemma and the Way Out*, authored by McDonald and Boyd with illustrations by Gaines, and *Red Maple: How Canada Became the People's Republic of Canada in 1981*, by McDonald, the books are indicative of the worldview and conception of Canadian identity that these author-publishers hoped to promote and particularly how they considered French Canadians, Quebec, and the French language to be hostile to that vision.

These 1975 books claimed that Canada had become a socialist state and that all three major federal parties subscribed to this ideology to varying degrees. Boyd's *The National Dilemma* was primarily committed to proving how socialism had advanced in Canada and proposing an alternative economic model. McDonald's *Red Maple* projected the complete end of Canada's liberal pluralistic society and complete state control of the economy. McDonald claimed that Canada's heritage had been deliberately erased – citing the 1965 flag debate as an example[57] – and that the rise of powerful unions and social welfare programs was fuelling the growth of the bureaucracy and civil service. The core of this rise, he argued, was Quebec: "The Quebec machine delivered the seats to Ottawa in return for money."[58] He claimed that Quebec had consistently failed to realize the economic potential of its advantages and blamed *les Anglais* for its shortcomings. "Pierre Trudeau's answer was to make the country, but especially the federal government, bilingual ... Most of those senior positions would be filled sooner or later by French-speaking Quebecers ... To be bilingual in Canada was to be a French-speaking Canadian who had learned to speak English."[59] McDonald thought that Quebecers would continue to vote for socialist policies indefinitely, allowing the Trudeau government to pursue its objective of "establishment of the People's Republic of Canada."[60] Bilingualism, in the minds of the BMG group, was a sop to Quebec voters to give them jobs and a decoy to allow the promotion of socialist policies and further the expansion of authoritarian government. And all to appease a population, McDonald argued, unable or unwilling to work for success on their own.

Neither book attracted much public attention. But the effort of getting the books published meant that the infrastructure was in place for other authors who wished to publish such tracts. The most dramatic example would come a couple of years later when a retired lieutenant commander in the Canadian navy sought a venue for his theories of Canada's takeover. BMG's highest-profile author, Jock Andrew, will be discussed in Chapter 5.

Immersion and Language Program Development in the NCR

Meanwhile, the pace of change on the issue of bilingualism in education had accelerated greatly, in terms of both the new federal-provincial funding arrangements and research on and experimentation with early French immersion. In Ottawa, responding to the explosion of programs and research, the Citizens' Committee on Children (CCC) published a new, nineteen-chapter booklet in 1972 entitled *What's What for Children Learning French*, edited by Glenna Reid. Funded by a grant from the National Capital

Commission, it contained a wealth of information compiled primarily by Ottawa-Carleton–area mothers (all of the articles were by women) to help parents make decisions about French-language learning and to support their children while they learned. Reid noted that the parents who put together the booklet were convinced that, by learning French, "our children may attain a higher level of other-culture understanding than we ourselves have known. It is not easy, but no doubt it is worth our efforts." They hoped that language skills would help their children to overcome negative attitudes toward both the French language and its speakers.[61]

In her chapter, "Why Bilingualism? An Anglophone Point of View," Diana M. Trent noted that parents were no longer satisfied with the programs of the past. Earlier programs had emphasized grammar, vocabulary, and translation, and French was taught "with the tacit assumption that students were never going to 'use' it anyway." Parents wanted their children to learn to express themselves in both languages and have French serve as a means of personal enrichment and interpersonal communication. Trent posed a couple of questions: "Why do we bother? Why should we go to the trouble of learning the language of a minority?" She offered the obvious and pragmatic reasons for the national capital. With the Official Languages Act, the policy of institutional bilingualism would not work without a relatively high level of individual bilingualism in the local population, and there would be job-related advantages. But she noted that "it is also an expression of the growing spirit of Canadian nationalism. We have discovered that the co-existence of French and English cultures is one of the most important distinctive features of our country." Learning French was part of acknowledging the right of French Canadians to their culture and language and allowing them to flourish. Bilingualism among anglophones, she believed, was a positive way of promoting the health and vigour of French Canadian culture.[62]

Trent had little time for those who opposed learning French, noting that "any level of bilingualism is useful and some level of proficiency is attainable by any well-motivated adult with application." Furthermore, "English is not in danger on the North American continent and we have nothing to lose and much to gain by supporting bilingualism. It is said that sensitivity to the needs of a minority is one of the indicators of a healthy democracy. The onus is on English Canadians." Trent did not believe that bilingualism meant that everyone had to meet the (apparent) Trudeau standard of "equilingualism" or seemingly equal comfort and facility in both languages. Rather, she thought, "the goal for each individual should be to be bilingual *enough* –

enough to permit equality of self-expression to all Canadians at whatever level they may meet."[63]

The collection approached French-language learning from a variety of perspectives, including a Franco-Ontarian view from Jacqueline Neatby urging parents to bear in mind that the French first-language schools for Franco-Ontarian children served purposes different from those of the newly piloted French immersion classes for anglophones. Janice Yalden, a professor at Carleton University, laid out the state of research on language teaching, including the early favourable results from the St. Lambert experiment.

The booklet also contained sections on the French-language learning options for the four school boards in Ottawa-Carleton (public and separate for each region) and in western Quebec. It is striking how varied the programs were from board to board. The Roman Catholic boards in both districts led the way, with Ottawa's board having offered a half-day optional kindergarten program starting in 1969 in twenty-eight schools. By 1971, the Carleton board was offering the same option to all students (who could be bused to one of the 13 of the 24 schools where this option was offered). By then, 98 percent of kindergarten children in the Carleton Catholic board were taking the half-day immersion program, and it was offered as a pilot up to grade two, with extended French options starting to be introduced at the grade two level for other students. An immersion kindergarten had started in Rockcliffe in 1969, and then six schools in the Ottawa public board added immersion kindergarten in 1970.[64] An additional grade of immersion was added to each school in 1971, and the kindergarten program expanded to ten more schools. Two public schools in the Carleton board offered immersion at the kindergarten and grade one levels. In all of these boards, core French was limited, with most students in a twenty-minute program per day, with plans to expand it to forty minutes for elementary grades by 1975. French was optional after grade nine in all of the school boards.[65]

Other chapters in the booklet listed child-friendly books, periodicals (including the popular *Tintin* and *Astérix* comic books), television shows, and records. In what would become a familiar trope over the years, Donalda Hilton's discussion of television observed that, when it came to non-educational television, some parents took the attitude that, "if they must watch junk, it might as well be in French." She suggested that perhaps the bar for "junkiness" might be set a little lower if the show would reinforce language learning.[66] *What's What* also contained listings for French-language nursery schools, summer camps, weekend programs, and interprovincial exchanges.

Although the Ottawa-Carleton region was leaps and bounds ahead of most jurisdictions in Canada in terms of new programs for French-language learning, it was still a struggle to get them established and a challenge to defend them against attackers. It took hard work to make Ottawa into what French immersion advocates of the 1990s would refer to as a "paradise."[67] One challenge was dealing with the high parental demand for French immersion for children who could not benefit from the pilot early French immersion programs being created. These programs usually started with only a kindergarten or grade one class, with an additional grade added each year. In Ottawa-Carleton, where the realities of civil service bilingualism requirements hit home, parents did not want their older children to miss out on a better language learning program. Fortunately, the federal government was keen to try one of the new "special projects" funded on a fifty-fifty basis under the Bilingualism in Education Program in the National Capital Region. The Ontario minister of education, Thomas Wells, expressed concern about preferential treatment for one board but ultimately agreed in 1972 to a large-scale special project to develop French immersion and core French programs in the region. Wells simultaneously pressed Secretary of State Gérard Pelletier to agree to fund all French immersion programs in the province (and by extension the country) at the higher rate allocated for minority-language education (of 9 percent) under the Bilingualism in Education Program agreements.[68] The official announcement of this funding arrangement was made on March 16, 1973.

Both provincial funding and federal funding were crucial in helping parents to persuade their boards of education to add new programs as soon as possible. For Beth and John Mlacak of Kanata, there was a certain urgency. Their eldest son, Bill, was set to enter grade seven in the fall of 1973, and they wanted to have him enter a late French immersion program if possible. They already planned to have their youngest daughter, Siobhan, repeat the first grade so that she could enrol in the local French immersion program. The Mlacaks started discussions with the local French and classroom teachers at their children's school – Stephen Leacock – to explore options, and then they worked their way up to press William Ross McGillivray, the superintendent of the Carleton Board of Education, to get a late immersion program started.[69] McGillivray was supportive of the idea and had begun planning for a late immersion program at W. Erskine Johnston school, but the provincial government had not yet granted approval.[70] Beth Mlacak escalated the issue to the local MPP, Sidney Handleman, urging rapid confirmation of funding, which Handleman conveyed to Minister Wells.[71] The campaign succeeded, and their son Bill was among the students accepted into the program.[72]

Extension of this program to a grade eight class the following year was not guaranteed. The Mlacaks had to lobby the school board for continuation and expansion of the program.[73] There were a number of key allies in this work, including dedicated French program consultants and coordinators with the Carleton board, such as André Obadia (who would go on to become a leading professor in French immersion research at Simon Fraser University) and Superintendent McGillivray. The Carleton board parents drew support and information from other parents in the region, including the Citizens' Committee on Children and a new group called Action for Bilingual Children (ABC).[74] Most of the key parents in the group were mothers, who conducted the research and wrote the correspondence. However, Beth Mlacak noted that occasionally they would strategically send one of their husbands, including her husband, John, a reeve for the Township of March, to deliver the presentations because they were sometimes received with greater authority.[75] Op-eds in the community papers were sometimes necessary, as in 1976, when members of the board imposed a cap on immersion enrolments and Trustee Lloyd Wright of Nepean seemed to be trying to eliminate immersion and replace it with a combination of core and extended French.[76]

In 1976, the Citizens' Committee on Children produced an updated version of its booklet *What's What for Children Learning French*, edited by Elaine Isabelle, a member of ABC. She noted that the first booklet's initial print run of 3,000 copies had been exhausted within weeks. A reprint had been distributed across the country, even up to the Northwest Territories. This revised edition was once again produced with financial support from the National Capital Commission and funds for broader distribution from the federal secretary of state. Keith Spicer, the commissioner of official languages, wrote the foreword, observing that he "view[ed] with unguarded optimism the activities of groups such as the Citizens' Committee on Children" and considered their handbook one of the most serviceable ones since Dr. Benjamin Spock's![77]

The CCC wanted to present balanced and unbiased information on available French options, so experts joined parents in providing their viewpoints. For the most part, these were positive but cautious endorsements of the new methodologies. Experts also tried to deal with overinflated expectations. H.P. Edwards, of the Department of Psychology at the University of Ottawa, touted early immersion as the best option for developing functional bilingualism, with "close to native like competence." He noted that though "students do become fluently bilingual ... it is unlikely ... that they would be indistinguishable from native French language speakers unless they associate sufficiently with native French-speaking peers."[78] Peggy Wightman, a parent of three sons in immersion and a graduate student in education at the University of Ottawa, noted that immersion students, though far superior to those in basic FSL, did not match native francophones in terms of vocabulary, grammar, or accent. There were also some problems with students using incorrect or uncolloquial terminology and reinforcing it among their peer groups unless it was caught and corrected by the teacher – or through contact with members of a francophone peer group.[79]

Wightman cited research showing that, after a lag of a year or two, immersion students' competencies in English caught up and that their performance in other subject areas did not suffer. She cited early research by Maggie Bruck and H.P. Edwards on students with learning disabilities, noting that for some French immersion was not a particular obstacle, though many immersion programs lacked the special service supports of their English counterparts. Studies showed that children from working-class backgrounds and with lower IQs performed at levels comparable to those in the regular English stream. On the issue of late versus early immersion, Wightman noted that some students did thrive in late immersion, developing skills comparable to those of early immersion learners. However, she noted that there tended to be lotteries or other types of limited selection for late immersion programs, which required more motivated language learners. It was a foreshadowing of the problem of elitism that would swirl for decades around French immersion.

The 1976 edition of *What's What* also featured a contribution from a researcher who would later be routinely cited by anti-immersion groups. Ronald L. Trites, the director of research at the Royal Ottawa Hospital, was in the midst of conducting research on learning disabilities in association with French immersion. Trites was somewhat more skeptical of the merits of bilingual education, noting an absence of research on children who would not benefit from the program or tests to screen out these children. Most of his qualms were based on research from other countries on bilingual education showing that the children in these programs performed poorly compared with control groups. (Conversely, other researchers in the collection noted that these were usually situations of socio-economically disadvantaged minority groups learning the majority language.) Trites suggested that students with lower than average intelligence, or those with delayed language development in their first language, perhaps should be considered at risk in immersion environments. His article did not condemn French immersion, but it did call for research on which types of children might have problems in this environment.[80]

By 1976, the language-learning landscape had changed radically in Ottawa-Carleton. All boards in the region had French immersion offered at least until the grade four level, with some schools extending it as far as grade six. There were also many experiments under way with extended core and late immersion. The public school boards had started hiring resource teachers for students with remedial needs in immersion, though there were only six for both boards.[81] A few other troubling issues appeared on the horizon in this edition. A new Ontario bachelor of education program requirement that applicants hold a BA degree hit the supply of francophone teachers particularly hard, compounding a shortage of French teachers.[82] Despite the advances made in French program options, they seemed to be constantly subject to the threat of budget cuts. Isabelle wrote that it was time to start thinking of these programs as an integral, self-sustaining part of the education system and second-language programs as the right of every child "whether or not supplementary funding is available." The boards needed to think of these programs not as being "opposed to" or "instead of" essential services, such as remedial reading or psychological services, but as being an integral part of the education system. She argued that it was necessary to support these programs "whether or not the federal government continues to do so."[83] Isabelle was clearly aware that provincial and local buy-in to their responsibilities in the area of bilingualism was still limited and tentative at best.

Meanwhile, Ottawa-Carleton parents were pushing for more French-language courses at the high school level to continue progress made in the immersion programs. This was a particular challenge when dealing with the lead class of a pilot immersion program in one school that had numbers too small to justify offering more high school credits in French. Parents in the Ottawa-Carleton region benefited in this case from not only geographic proximity but also personal connections to the commissioner of official languages. Spicer's son Nicholas was in the same early French immersion class as the Mlacaks' daughter Siobhan.[84] It is thus not surprising that Beth Mlacak was one of the people invited to the conference hosted by Spicer that gave birth to Canadian Parents for French. Mlacak, however, was in an accident the day before the conference, so she asked her activist friend Mary Ann Rainer to attend in her place; Rainer would become the first executive secretary of the new organization.

The Gillin Report

Robert Gillin, a curriculum services officer with the Ontario Ministry of Education, would come to have his name attached to one of the landmark reports on French-language learning in Canada with wide-ranging implications for the promotion of bilingualism. Gillin was appointed by Minister of Education Thomas Wells in June 1973 to chair a ministerial committee to develop improved curriculum and techniques for teaching French to the English-speaking students of the province.[85] Gillin was to prepare recommendations on all aspects of the province's French-language program, in particular with respect to a program for kindergarten to grade six. The elementary school French programs in Ontario were diverse. A 1972 survey of the province's boards found that the starting point for French ranged from kindergarten to grade nine and had a wide array of hours on task.[86] Secondary school programs had become more divergent since the elimination of the standardized grade thirteen departmental exams in 1967, the end of university French-language admission requirements, and the creation of the credit system in Ontario high schools in the late 1960s.[87]

The most important aspects of the 1974 Gillin Report, with its sixty-eight recommendations, had to do with clarifying the objectives of French-language instruction programs and assigning meaningful hours to those targets. It aimed for a target of 180 "daily" minutes accumulated between grades one and six, arguing that it was the total number of hours spent learning French that mattered.[88] This target, significantly higher than what was offered in most school boards around the province, was necessary as a starting point so that, combined with the French offered in grades seven to thirteen, a student could meet the "basic level" of French proficiency.

This idea of "levels" or "thresholds" of French proficiency was another important part of the report. Gillin argued that it was necessary to set real goals for the French curriculum and to be clear on what level of "bilingualism" might be accomplished at each level. His report spelled out three levels – basic, middle, and top – and the two upper ones, he noted, would also require regular opportunities to interact with French-speaking peers through exchanges, summer camps, and travel.[89] This was groundbreaking, for past French-language curricula in Canada did not try to spell out these goals clearly. Three years later the provincial government attached total hours of

French study required to reach each threshold (1,200, 2,100, and 5,000+), adopted the "basic" level as the goal for the province's regular core program, and provided incentive funding to boards to expand their program offerings at each of the three levels.[90] For advocates of French immersion, extended French, and improved core French programs, the Gillin Report set the standards for which local school districts should aim for their French programs and the time on task required to reach those objectives.

Parent Activism and Collaboration in Toronto
Although Gunild Spiess, as discussed in Chapter 2, had managed to get an after-school French program started in her local school in North York, by the 1970s there was still no elementary school French instruction prior to grade six in the local school board. The Toronto area was a hodge-podge of FSL programs. The Metropolitan Separate School Board (covering the Catholic schools) had moved in 1969 to start French instruction in grade one, but the public school boards of Metropolitan Toronto (Metro) varied widely. In 1971, the York and Etobicoke boards started French instruction in grade three, the East York and Toronto boards generally started it in grade four, and the North York and Scarborough boards started it in grade six. The creation of French immersion programs had also been very tentative. The first early French immersion program in the Toronto board was started in September 1971 at Allenby Public School with a pilot project involving forty-eight students. An organized group of parents helped to create a second French immersion pilot project at Brown Public School in 1972.[91] Many parents across Metro wanted to create more immersion programs and expand the core French programs at the elementary school level. However, their approaches to school boards in the early 1970s were often met with the response that expansion was not possible under current funding formulas.[92]

In North York, Spiess and other parents, with the support of their trustee, Marion Gordon, and the chair of the school board, Dr. Lynn Trainor, approached the board to try to expand the French-language programs. They were directed to EDUCOM, the North York Education and Community Council, and Spiess was brought into this organization to represent "French concerns." Through EDUCOM, the McKee group was granted leave to present a brief on French instruction and French programs to the North York Board of Education's Management and Academic Program Committee. The brief cited the latest research on French-language learning in the early grades, including the work of Wilder Penfield, urging the creation of both total immersion as an option and an enriched French program through the primary grades. It noted federal funding for bilingual programs and called for much greater experimentation with French programs. The brief observed that French was not only an official language but also "recognized as the most widely used international language as well – used as a means of communications in business, science and politics all over the world." It claimed that the "very survival of Canada as a nation will depend on better communication among the provinces in general, and between the two most populated ones in particular."[93] In the fall of 1973, the North York board created its first immersion pilot project at Brian Public School.[94] Otherwise, movement on the McKee group's brief was slow and frustrating. It was eight months before the North York board even passed a resolution to approve the principle of extending French below the grade six level, on an experimental basis, where interest, conditions, and funding warranted it.[95]

The North York board delayed implementation of its 1974 resolution several times. Funding from the Metro-wide board was seemingly the major obstacle.[96] Opponents of expanded French on the North York board, the Metro board, and within the Ministry of Education were also starting to point to the research of Dr. Clare Burstall from the United Kingdom as a reason not to expand elementary school French. Burstall was brought over in 1975 to present the results of her longitudinal study for the National Foundation for Educational Research (NFER), which showed dubious progress, she claimed, in French-language learning in a pilot project in the United Kingdom.[97] Spiess and other parents feared that Burstall was brought over to counter the encouraging recommendations and directions of the recently released Gillin Report and thus give the various governments excuses for further heel-dragging.

In the process of preparing briefs, responding to the Burstall Report, and addressing concerns over funding at the Metro level, Spiess and her McKee group had come in contact with many other allies. They included Kathryn Manzer and a group of parents in the Don Mills region of North York calling themselves the Parent Group for Extended French. Spiess also met Marion Langford, a friend of Keith Spicer, who had taken French courses at the University of Toronto and taught elementary school before she had children,[98] and a group of parents in Toronto who had been fighting for expanded French in the Toronto board. In 1973, the Toronto parents had managed to organize a survey of elementary school parents in the board showing that 85 percent supported the creation of an optional twenty-minute-per-day French program in the primary grades.[99] Crucial for media exposure, they came in contact with *Globe and Mail* columnist Norman Webster and his wife, Pat, who had been fighting, unsuccessfully so far, to convince the Halton Board of Education to create a French immersion program in their home community of Oakville. Norman Webster penned several columns and articles between 1973 and 1975 about the issue of French instruction in Toronto (and Canada more generally) to put pressure on Minister Thomas Wells and the school boards.[100] Spiess, Langford, Manzer, Pat Webster, and others in the Greater Toronto Area began meeting with each other, and by 1974 they had constituted the Toronto Metropolitan Parent Group for Extended French.[101] This group of women began exchanging notes about their experiences and pooling research efforts to find out how to overcome their obstacles and determine the flow of funding. They lined up supportive allies on the school boards, among elected officials (including Barney Danson, the MP in the riding where Spiess lived), and journalists with both the major papers and the community weeklies (Dave Toole of the *North York Mirror,* for instance, was a sympathetic ally). Their volunteer time was crucial to this effort, and there were struggles to balance childcare responsibilities with their activism.[102]

By June 1975, after a series of correspondence and meetings with representatives of local school boards, the Metro board, the province, and the federal government, the parent group had become convinced that the funding blockage was at the Metro level and not with provincial funding structures.[103] A meeting was called for September 1975 in an effort to get all interested parties into the room at the same time.[104] The mothers were careful to line up all of their financial data and statistics in advance of the meeting to be able to handle any evasions by the board. Marion Langford believed that the Metro board officials had underestimated the mothers' preparation and were caught unprepared for the deluge of hard numbers, which made it impossible to continue passing the buck.[105] Over the next two years, the Metro board became less of an obstacle, and new funding formulas announced by the province in 1977 for French instruction certainly helped the expansion of French programming in the Toronto-area boards. By the fall of 1975, even the North York board had started expanding core French to the grade four and five levels.[106] Sustained pressure from other affiliated groups, including the University Women's Club of North York and the Canadian Federation of University Women, maintained pressure on the Ministry of Education and local boards to improve funding for these programs and keep expanding them.[107] However, by 1977, none of the North York programs was yet in a position to reach the Gillin Report's recommended

1,200-hour threshold for basic French competency, so ongoing efforts were required.[108]

The joint efforts of these parents across Metropolitan Toronto had created a core group of mothers (and supportive fathers, though they were less directly active) interested in improved French-language learning opportunities for their children. Many of these women, particularly Pat Webster, who actually lived outside Toronto, would be instrumental in setting up a new provincial organization called Ontario Parents for French in April 1977,[109] and shortly thereafter the new national organization of Canadian Parents for French, discussed in Chapter 5.

Conclusion

By late 1976, when the surprise election of the Parti Québécois dramatically changed the political climate for language issues, activists supportive of bilingualism had begun successfully organizing new French programs, despite the inertia of their school boards and struggles over funding. Although they were still trying to find additional allies for their cause and were unaware of all of the resources available, they were beginning to make connections with other interested parents who could advance their goals. They were also making the most of their resources, including time, education, and contacts, to lay the foundation for a broader movement.

Conversely, a few key individuals vociferously opposed to bilingualism were publishing books and articulating attacks on bilingualism that framed it as being connected with anti-meritocratic hiring practices, socialism, and an assault on the British North America Act and British Canadian heritage more broadly. Although few supporters openly endorsed these vocal critics of bilingualism, they were establishing a discourse and a publishing infrastructure to allow for expansion and diffusion of their messages. Pro- and anti-bilingualism movements were usually not in direct confrontation with each other yet, for each was still oriented toward specific dimensions of language policy and targeted at a different jurisdiction. As these movements expanded in the following decade, they started clashing more openly.

5

Canadian Parents for French and Its Adversaries, 1977–86

Keith Spicer played a key role in launching Canadian Parents for French (CPF) in the final weeks of his term as commissioner of official languages. This organization, still in existence, quickly became one of the most influential players in promoting bilingualism among English-speaking Canadians. In its first decade, CPF undertook major initiatives at the national level to bolster its credibility and to mobilize evidence in support of bilingualism and better French-language learning opportunities. It also found itself faced with more organized and increasingly vocal opponents of the programs and policies that it supported. In particular, author Jock Andrew and the Alliance for the Preservation of English in Canada, inspired by his writings, were starting to challenge the educational goals of this social movement. In this chapter, I consider the origins of CPF and the first decade of its development and activities at national and provincial levels.

The Beginnings of CPF

Twenty-eight parent delegates, representing every province, attended the Parents Conference on French Language and Exchange Opportunities organized by Spicer with the help of Pat and Norman Webster. It was held at the Four Seasons Hotel in Ottawa, March 25–27, 1977, and over two-thirds of the parent delegates were mothers. They included veterans from the early creation and expansion of immersion programs, including Louise Moore of the Calgary French School, Beth Mlacak from Carleton, and Carmeta Abbott of the Kitchener-Waterloo Bilingual School. Also in attendance were resource people on second-language education and exchange programs, including representatives of the Council of Ministers of Education, Canada; Department of the Secretary of State; Bilingual Exchange Secretariat; Canadian Council of Christians and Jews; Ontario Ministry of Education consultant Robert Gillin; Merrill Swain of the Ontario Institute for Studies in Education (OISE); Carleton Board of Education's André Obadia; and, of course, McGill University's Dr. Wallace Lambert. Clearly, this was no casual undertaking.

In his opening remarks to delegates, Spicer referred to the conference as being a "little bit of creative subversion" to help isolated groups of parents in just about every city in Canada who had been "fighting epic battles to get what they consider is normal for their kids – a decent chance to plug into another world, a different culture." Spicer shared parents' frustration in trying to "find a way of getting through the Byzantine university of federal/ provincial jurisdictions."[1] He hoped that the conference would help parents to deal with this issue and, more broadly, help them to advance their goal of better French-language education for their children. As he observed, "the whole conference [was] probably illegal and unconstitutional in the first place, but necessary."[2] Beyond the initial step of bringing together keen parents, Spicer was quick to state that "any other approach you want to take in the whole orientation should be exclusively yours." He stressed that the purpose of the conference was to provide a venue for sharing information not only on the pedagogical side of language education but also on the "difficult, political challenges only parents can meet by talking to school boards and governments."[3] Formally, the conference program laid out four key goals:

(1) to give young English-speaking Canadians at the elementary, secondary, and university levels access to a more useful knowledge of the French language and French Canadian culture.

(2) to pool ideas regarding objectives and methods on French-language instruction in schools.

(3) to favour greatly expanded youth exchanges between English and French Canada.

(4) to establish and maintain communication between interested parents, experts, and government authorities in this field.[4]

With these opening words and thoughts, delegates adjourned to evening cocktails, energized for the weekend ahead.

Over the next two days, the conference alternated among sessions to provide information, opportunities for questions, and time for discussion and strategizing. It included panels on second-language learning, immersion, and youth exchange programs. A panel on jurisdictional issues included representatives from all levels of government. Each panellist noted areas in which parents could productively take action to work around the jurisdictional barricades. In the final afternoon, parent groups presented problem areas and then had a group session to identify priorities and discuss future methods of information exchange.[5]

At this initial conference, the parents decided that a national association of parents was needed and that it would have three main goals:

1) To promote the best possible types of French language learning opportunities;
2) To assist in ensuring that each Canadian child have the opportunity to acquire as great a knowledge of French language and culture as he or she is willing and able to attain;
3) More specifically, to establish and maintain effective communication between interested parents and educational and government authorities concerned with the provision of French language learning opportunities.[6]

The conference elected a provisional executive committee of five delegates, each representing a different region, to advance six tasks. These tasks included producing publications to popularize and disseminate research and case studies related to their goals; creating a directory of resource people and organizations and a bibliography of research; representing the association with authorities and the general public; and refining and consolidating the recommendations of the conference. Committee members were to organize a larger national conference before the end of the year at which a constitution, administrative arrangements, a budget, funding, and resolutions could be worked out.

Three months later the first of these tasks was accomplished with publication of the first newsletter of Canadian Parents for French. The newsletter had financial support from the commissioner of official languages, Keith Spicer, and an introductory editorial by him.[7] Beyond forming an organization, the parents had external objectives. They called on the Council of Ministers of Education, Canada (CMEC), to establish a clearinghouse for research and information on second-language learning, to devote more of the federal funds that it received to developing curricula for intensive FSL programs, and to develop a network of regional resource centres for distributing French cultural resources for educational purposes. They asked the CBC to provide more French-language and bilingual programs and perhaps to experiment with increased subtitling in French. The parents also wanted the Department of the Secretary of State to subsidize French courses at the local level for interested parents and to provide tax deductions for any accountable costs for parents or their children in learning the second official language. Exchanges were another priority area. The parents sought a lowering of the age for exchange participants below fourteen, the creation of family exchange programs, and expanded remunerative exchanges for young Canadians. Teacher training and staffing were proving to be major roadblocks in expanding FSL. The parents wanted to develop a way to deal with the fears of job losses that many unilingual English teachers associated with the growth of French immersion while also being firm that, when student needs conflicted with those of the teaching community, the former needs must prevail. Finally, and this was to become a greater priority than the parents perhaps realized, they called on the CMEC to provide much better accountability for the costs of French programs and to ensure that local boards used funds allocated for French for this purpose.[8]

The first newsletter of Canadian Parents for French was used in the summer months of 1977 to alert parents and government officials to the existence of the new organization and its mandate. It outlined the conference resolutions and included an overview of FSL programs available in each province. The executive committee was able to secure a grant from the Department of the Secretary of State to hold its first official conference in October 1977, with sixty parent delegates from across the country. The new commissioner of official languages, Max Yalden, delivered the keynote address. In addition to education researchers, including Henry Edwards of the University of Ottawa and Fred Genesee of McGill University, Jean-Luc Pépin, co-chair of the Task Force on Canadian Unity, addressed the participants.

Pépin spoke directly to the role that could be played by FSL programs in the promotion of national unity. He observed that

> our best hope is to start our children off with positive attitudes in the first place ... Our belief is that proper teaching of our country's other official language, along with the culture that accompanies it, can make a real difference. It will not, in itself, save the country, but it is a useful step that English-speaking parents and their provincial education systems can take.[9]

Pépin also urged the provincial branches of CPF (inaugurated at the conference) to submit briefs or give presentations to the task force, then touring the country in search of solutions to constitutional reform. In the following months, briefs from CPF's New Brunswick and Manitoba chapters stressed links among language learning, positive attitudes to other cultures, and Canadian unity.[10] CPF's national executive committee's brief noted that "bilingualism is not only good in itself but cultural understanding also develops in children and this cannot help but bring about positive feelings between English and French speaking Canadians. We believe our very existence is a support for Canadian unity."[11] This discourse of national unity and cultural cooperation was extremely prominent in the founding years of Canadian Parents for French.

CPF held its first business meeting at the October 1977 conference, establishing its constitution and bylaws and electing an executive. Pat Webster was selected as the first president. CPF established a structure that entailed a presence at all levels of government, with a national office and board composed of the directors of each provincial branch. Below the provincial branches (charged with issues at the provincial level), some provinces would ultimately opt to create local chapters. This approach was taken up most enthusiastically in British Columbia.

Members passed a number of major resolutions for action by the national board. The board was to urge the government of Canada to provide a deduction from personal income tax for any accountable costs expended by parents for themselves or their children in learning the second official language. CPF recommended that English-language universities and colleges across Canada be urged to re-evaluate their policies regarding French requirements for both entrance and graduation. A CPF committee would investigate core FSL programs and suggest improvements to the CMEC. Another committee would investigate and report on the implications of urging the federal government to reduce domestic air fares to facilitate travel within Canada for exchange visits and other purposes related to CPF's objectives. Finally, a committee was struck to investigate the effectiveness and availability of summer camps and exchange visits. These last two resolutions, which passed by only bare majorities, would be the most difficult to address and ultimately ended in failure.[12]

At its first board meeting, the newly elected executive voted to use some of their grant money to hire a part-time executive secretary based in Ottawa, Mary Ann Rainer, to handle a series of tasks. They laid out plans and topics for the next year's newsletters. They also began considering issues such as long-range fundraising, publicity guidelines, plans for the next conference, and liaising with other groups, such as the Fédération des francophones hors-Québec and Canadian School Trustees' Association.[13]

The first couple of years of activity at the national level for Canadian Parents for French were spent trying to implement resolutions adopted by the membership and providing support to local campaigns for improved FSL programs. In addition to the national newsletter, CPF wanted to pull together a handbook for parents interested in French-language learning. CPF began by collaborating with Elaine Isabelle and the Citizens' Committee on Children on a publication modelled on *What's What for Children Learning French*.[14] It was to be a comprehensive booklet on issues of strategy, choices available for parents, and the latest research on second-language instruction. Ultimately, the CCC withdrew from the final stages of production but was still given authorial credit. In late 1979, *So You Want Your Child to Learn French! A Handbook for Parents* was published and greeted with significant demand from members. Funds to assist its publication came from the Language Programs Branch of the Department of the Secretary of State to encourage teaching and learning English and French as second languages.[15]

Volunteer members of CPF were responsible for *A Bibliography of Articles and Books on Bilingualism in Education*, commissioned by CPF and compiled in 1979 by D. Anthony Massey of the Faculty of Education at Queen's University. CPF continued printing an annual *Immersion Registry*. CPF also printed booklets and pamphlets on various aspects of French learning. The first booklet was "How to Get What You Want," which dealt with issues such as generating interest among parents, dealing with school boards, finding out facts about funding and second-language programs, and answering typical questions about French-language learning. In short, it was a primer on what local parent groups would encounter as they started to pressure their school boards and schools for new programs.[16]

Although French immersion supporters were the core constituency for CPF activists, the group was careful, even in its earliest years, not to neglect an interest in core French. At least part of this attention stemmed from the second CPF president, Janet Poyen. She had learned French while growing up in Alberta and held a BA in French from McGill University. She returned to Alberta in the early 1970s and obtained a teaching certificate and then taught core French in both Edmonton and Calgary. She moved to Victoria, British Columbia, in the mid-1970s; her older daughter was too old for the immersion program there, but she enrolled her younger daughter in the immersion kindergarten and became involved in a local parents' group pushing for expansion of the program.[17]

Poyen attended the first official conference of CPF in October 1977. Initially, she was the alternate director for British Columbia but was promoted to director in February 1978 when Judi Madley moved to England. When Pat Webster also moved to England and resigned her position, Poyen found herself thrust into the presidency of CPF at its second conference, held in Calgary in the fall of 1978.[18] Judy Gibson wrote the chapter of *So You Want Your Child to Learn French!* entitled "What about Core?" and the CPF pamphlet on core French.[19] For Poyen, it was crucial to reach out to core French parents and to fight for improvements to the program. Doing so would help to defuse the argument that CPF was an elite group interested only in their own children and immersion programs. Moreover, core French, by necessity and practicality, would be the main way that most Canadian children were introduced to the French language. A 1979 issue of the CPF newsletter was devoted to the question of core French: "Are we in CPF content to see the vast majority of students denied exposure to French?"[20]

Much of CPF's initial activity was tied to initiatives for which the group could secure grant money, including publications such as *So You Want Your Child to Learn French!* In 1978, the group had a total budget of $43,694.[21] Funding to support the annual conference had to be applied for each year from the Department of the Secretary of State. As a result, some initiatives fell by the wayside when funding failed to materialize. Such was the fate of a proposal for a Canadian Festival for Bilingual Children. The basic premise was that 300 children – 150 anglophone immersion students and 150 Quebec francophone students from grades four to six – would be brought together for a weekend in Quebec City to foster cultural understanding and bilingualism.[22] But it was an expensive proposition to fly that many children and their guardians to Quebec City, and the proposal was abandoned when it became apparent that Secretary of State funding would not be forthcoming.[23] Carmeta Abbott, the Ontario CPF director, asked board members to think about possible alternative activities, such as a correspondence exchange program. CPF continued to work on promoting exchange programs, dedicating its third and sixth newsletters to the topic.[24] The national office of Canadian Parents for French, run by Executive Director Jos Scott from 1979 on, also worked closely with Sandy McKay and Jane Dobell (formerly of the Secretary of State) of the Society for Educational Visits and Exchanges Canada (SEVEC) as it began expanding beyond Ontario-Quebec exchanges to cover other provinces.[25]

Although members of CPF approached a succession of finance ministers regarding tax deductibility for courses taken by parents or children to learn a second language, there was little progress on this issue under the Trudeau government.[26] John Crosbie, Joe Clark's finance minister, ultimately rejected the proposal, stating that "tax deduction is not an appropriate method of promoting bilingualism."[27] CPF efforts to secure low-cost or discount air fares for language exchanges also ran into blockades or simple passivity.

Establishing Operational Funding and Gauging Community Attitudes toward French

In its early years, CPF applied for a series of project grants from the Department of the Secretary of State to provide it with enough additional revenue to staff its central office. It took this approach because federal regulations at this point did not permit direct funding for administrative costs of groups. CPF tried to set these projects up in such a way that they would further its mission and organizational development. In 1979, it won a grant for a pilot study to determine parents' reactions to opportunities for their children to study French language and culture. Viewed a certain way, the Secretary of State was providing money to CPF to find out who its potential supporters were. It was also, from the perspective of the Language Programs Branch, which provided an initial grant of $46,500 to cover about 75 percent of the costs of the project, a way of determining how Canadians were responding to the ideals of second-language learning and hopefully which values were informing supporters of these programs.[28]

The pilot study proved to be a major networking opportunity for the fledgling organization, but it was also a huge drain on volunteer energies. Each of the five initial provinces – Alberta, Saskatchewan, Ontario, New Brunswick, and Prince Edward Island – adopted its own methodology to meet the project's objectives. Methods ranged from the rather slick, province-wide survey in Alberta coordinated by members who were professors at the University of Lethbridge to the more informal, community-oriented approaches of Prince Edward Island and New Brunswick, where information gathering occurred through interpersonal contacts, door-to-door interviews, and community meetings where members were concentrated. In Ontario, questionnaires were distributed along with CPF newsletters, and radio spots advertised meetings in major cities for members of the public to voice their views.[29] Most participating provincial branches were able to develop new chapters, gain media coverage, and establish better communications among parent groups, school boards, and francophone organizations. In some provinces, especially Alberta, there was close cooperation between the francophile CPF and the local francophone minority associations.

CPF then sought and received funding to go into greater depth in the initial five provinces and expand the study to cover the remaining provinces. The national study aimed to answer a series of broad questions for all provinces: "Why do parents want their children to learn French? What are their expectations of French language programs? Are these expectations being met? What regional differences can be found? What is the number and location of interested parents? What is the impact of this interest upon the francophone community?" The study attempted to find out more in the pilot provinces about expectations at the postsecondary level, bilingual exchanges, and interactions with francophone communities. This also allowed CPF groups to make presentations to provincial governments regarding programs, bilingual opportunities, curriculum development, teacher training, and resource materials.[30] CPF was positioning itself as a third-party, arm's-length promoter of the federal government's agenda for bilingualism, a promoter that was rich in volunteers but lacked the financial ability to carry out a study of this scale unassisted. The federal grant also provided, indirectly, the money to pay core staff of the organization.

A sampling of the key results of these surveys and studies helps us to understand the perceived benefits of expanded FSL learning opportunities as well as some key obstacles. A PEI study of 103 parents, 69 of whom were CPF members, and an Ontario survey of CPF members revealed the following responses regarding why they wanted their children to learn French (see Table 5.1). In both provinces, though disparate in size and socio-economic

TABLE 5.1
Reasons why Canadian parents want their children to learn French, 1980

Reason	PEI (%)	Ontario (%)
Intellectual enrichment	86	92
Cultural enrichment	71	82
Job prospects	84	72
Travel	58	68
Support for Canadian bilingualism	42	64
Family tradition	22	16

Sources: Canadian Parents for French Questionnaire – PEI raw data, 1980, MAUA, CPF fonds, 2000.23/2/13/2; evaluation of Canadian Parents for French Pilot Study into parents' reactions on French second-language learning, 1979–80, May 9, 1980, MAUA, CPF fonds, 2000.23/2/13/4.

profile, support for Canadian bilingualism trailed behind the more pragmatic issues of intellectual and cultural enrichment and job prospects.

In many provinces, support for compulsory French was limited, particularly for secondary and postsecondary education. In New Brunswick, only
41.6 percent of the parents surveyed thought that French should be required
for university entrance.[31] In Prince Edward Island, 42 percent of the parents
surveyed thought that French should not be a compulsory subject in high
school.[32] In British Columbia, between 60 and 70 percent thought that core
French should be taught to all students at the elementary level (most districts did not offer French before grade six), and 46 percent thought that
it should be taught to all students at the secondary level.[33] Levels of satisfaction tended to be much higher among parents of children in immersion
programs compared with those in core French. Parents tended to identify
lack of money, lack of community interest, and uncooperative trustees as
the key reasons for a lack of satisfactory program choices.[34]

Some of the provincial surveys also revealed a rather disturbing amount
of misinformation on and misconceptions about FSL learning. Saskatchewan's survey of 1,000 parents in three communities found that 70 percent
believed that it was not possible for a school to teach in French and still
maintain a satisfactory level of training in other subjects. Most Saskatchewan parents did not know which French programs their school boards offered.[35] The survey also revealed gross misperceptions of French immersion
families; only 29 percent knew that the students came from predominantly
English-speaking homes.[36]

British Columbia Parents for French aimed for a more professional approach to its opinion polling, contracting with Gallup. BC parents were
asked a specific question: "Do you think children residing in BC should
learn French in school so that they may become bilingual?" Fifty-one percent of respondents answered yes. In terms of the main advantage that they
thought knowledge of French would provide, 26 percent said employment
opportunities, 22 percent intellectual development, 17.7 percent cultural enrichment, 13 percent travel, and 7 percent enhanced national unity. Interest
in French education was driven primarily by practical considerations, not by
political reasons.[37] This professional approach to determining public opinion seemed to hold much potential for future CPF activism.

Project grants were of short duration and drained CPF staff and volunteer energies. More stable funding was needed for long-term viability. CPF
instituted membership fees in March 1979 (initially set at five dollars per
family), split between the national organization and its provincial branches.[38]

The branches had the option of giving part of their share of these fees to community-level chapters, where they existed. By March 1981, 3,210 families had taken out paid memberships. The fees were introduced partly to demonstrate that CPF was an "independent, viable organization." It was also careful to document volunteer hours as in-kind contributions made to the organization. Both types of data were considered very important in making the case to the Department of the Secretary of State that the organization should receive operational funding.[39] The board also hoped that this information would convince corporate and private sector sponsors that the organization was worthy of funding.[40] Efforts to attract corporate funding, however, were disappointing. Although donations were made in 1980 by both the RHW Foundation and Dascon Investments, both had direct ties to the Webster family.[41] The membership of the organization, on the other hand, grew steadily over the years, despite doubling of the fee in 1983 to ten dollars for individuals and families. By 1986, there were more than 17,000 individual/family members plus an estimated 4,000 people covered by associate organization memberships.

The Department of the Secretary of State was filled with officials who supported CPF and its goals, but the trick was how to provide long-term funding to the organization. Funding for conferences and newsletters had tracked through the Languages Acquisition stream, whereas funding for projects such as the national study had come through the Promotion of Official Languages budget. In contrast, the major francophone organizations received funding through the Official Language Minority Groups program. Secretary of State officials struggled to fund CPF without providing sustaining funds for administrative costs (against regulations) or diverting funds that might otherwise go to the francophone minorities.[42] Some longer-term sustainability was worked out in 1982. The national office began receiving funding from the Promotion of Official Languages directorate, and the provincial branches received funding through the citizenship branches of Secretary of State regional offices. All told, this amounted to about $250,000 annually – a substantial increase from CPF's first couple of years (see Appendix 5 for details).

Jock Andrew, BMG Publishing, and APEC
While CPF was revving up its efforts to expand French-language teaching, opponents of bilingualism were also entering a new phase. In 1975, Jock Andrew, a retired lieutenant commander in the Canadian navy, began work on a book that would become one of the best-selling conspiracy theories

ever penned in Canada. Between starting his manuscript and its publication, Quebec's newly elected Parti Québécois government introduced Bill 101, which ultimately became the Charter of the French Language. Published in March 1977 by BMG Publishing, Andrew's *Bilingual Today, French Tomorrow: Trudeau's Master Plan and How It Can Be Stopped* posited the remarkable thesis that Canada's official languages policies were part of a grand conspiracy to make the entire country French speaking. The conspiracy, Andrew argued, was orchestrated by Prime Minister Trudeau with the collaboration of Quebec-based French speakers fanning out across the country to demand services in French. Their goal was to convert the federal civil service to an all-French one, then all the provincial and municipal governments, and then businesses that worked with the government, and then the private sector, until eventually the entire country was forced to speak French. Andrew argued that this was already happening in the Department of National Defence and that the process was spreading rapidly. His book apparently sold 120,000 copies in its first year – a veritable Canadian bestseller – and was frequently cited by opponents of bilingualism over the next couple of decades.

Mixed into Andrew's anti-Quebec, anti–French Canadian screed are some choice words about bilingualism. At one point, Andrew appears to be conciliatory, noting that "Canadians are confusing the business of two languages in one country with the very desirable personal attributes of being able to speak two or more languages ... Such an ability is to be admired."[43] However, in the same paragraph, he states that "there is no positive attribute whatsoever to having two languages in one country" and that "there are a dozen different ways we could better use our time without any thought to languages at all." Andrew considered French immersion courses problematic because there was no equivalent for French-speaking children in Quebec.[44] Although he noted that being seriously schooled in both languages was one of three ways to become fluently bilingual (in addition to having one parent from each language group and one language at home and one at school and work), he doubted that immersion would work: "Consider the organization involved. Furthermore, most Canadian kids can't get serious enough to make it through school now in one language. Imagine them trying to do it in two."[45]

Andrew argued that "bilingualism is in fact a mechanism for converting Canada from a predominantly English-speaking country to a totally French-speaking country ... [It] is just a tool which will be scrapped once the job is done."[46] When it came to English Canadians, he argued, we have nothing against French-Canadians, but we would be a lot happier if they were in their own country, preferably a million miles away, busy trying to be French without trying to do the same for us ... We don't like having French thrust upon us, either on the labels of everything we buy, or as a qualification for every job in English-speaking Canada which has heretofore been done reasonably well without benefit of having been French.

Ultimately, he proposed that the only solution to Canada's language problem was partition into two countries, each speaking its own language.[47]

There is a curious preface to Andrew's book written by Winnett Boyd (author of *The National Dilemma*). Boyd opposed Andrew's option of Quebec separatism. He also wrote that "no intelligent Canadian could seriously disagree with the idea of promoting bilingualism by education and persuasion ... What everyone does object to is bilingualism by coercion." Boyd thus proposed rescinding official bilingualism back to the level of section 133 of the BNA Act but accompanying it with a federal government pledge to promote conscientiously the advantages of social – but not official – bilingualism throughout Canada; this could include federal encouragement of provincial educational authorities to teach both languages enthusiastically. In this way, those with aptitude would benefit, but "those who lacked it would not suffer."[48] Boyd's proposal would become completely lost over the following decades among adherents of Andrew's book, even though they would occasionally mouth platitudes about having nothing against individuals who chose to become bilingual. Andrew himself disagreed with the notion of provincial education systems spending time on more intensive teaching of or in French.

Bilingual Today, French Tomorrow helped to feed the growth of a new anti-bilingualism organization. Irene Hilchie, a fifty-five-year-old civil servant in Bedford, Nova Scotia, believed that her career was being hampered by language requirements in the federal civil service. To combat this problem, she joined six other people in 1977 to form the Alliance for the Preservation of English in Canada (APEC). Within two years, the group reported about 6,000 members, including 3,500 in Ontario and 900 in Nova Scotia, who paid two dollars per year in membership fees and received a monthly newsletter.[49] Although Hilchie would not remain as head of the organization for long, she was its secretary well into the late 1990s. In addition to opposing the spread of bilingualism and language requirements in the federal and provincial civil services, APEC's Nova Scotia branch suggested that French-language instruction be de-emphasized and English-language instruction encouraged. Mary Gillis, APEC's head in 1979, claimed that the growth of French-language instruction was a threat because there was no firm way of knowing whether the material being taught was what young Canadians should be learning: "How can we know if those classes are being taught Canadianism in the right way?"[50] APEC's growth in Ontario owed much to Jock Andrew and Ronald Leitch of Richmond Hill. Leitch later traced the genesis of APEC's Toronto branch to having purchased 100 copies of Andrew's book and mailing them to like-minded friends.[51] It would not be until the mid-1980s that APEC made a big splash on the national scene (and particularly in Ontario), but Andrew's book helped to fuel this new wave of conspiracy-oriented activism against official languages, and campaigns to promote individual bilingualism would suffer collateral damage.

BMG Publishing followed up Andrew's book with two other titles in a similar vein. David Somerville's *Trudeau Revealed by His Words and Actions* drew on a number of Trudeau's past travels, public statements, and published writings to build the case that Trudeau was a socialist who frequently consorted with communists and spent time in communist nations, coupling this assessment with statements about his desire to provide greater status for French Canadians.[52] Sam Allison's *French Power: The Francisation of Canada* was less oblique in its approach. Allison, a Montreal high school history teacher born in Scotland and educated in the United Kingdom, supported Andrew's claim that there was an ongoing colonization of places in Canada that had never been French. He claimed to expose the "myth" that Quebec's anglophones were better treated than French Canadian minorities elsewhere in the country. Allison crafted a tale of an English Quebec minority under siege, educated in a system that received less funding than the French one.[53] He tried to build the argument that authoritarianism was systemic in Quebec and married to chauvinistic conservatism and a belief in the cultural superiority of French Canadians.[54] He claimed that the French language itself was in international decline and that it was structurally inadequate, with an overly small vocabulary insufficient in the modern era. He asked rhetorically if French, like Latin, was "a luxury we can no longer afford."[55]

Columnist William Johnson of the *Globe and Mail* considered Allison's book part of a new literary genre of "French-bashing," and he called it "a torrent of chauvinism, of bitterness, of half-truth and error ... used to develop an ugly thesis." For Johnson, Allison's work contrasted "the genius, the tolerance, the virtues of the English-speaking" with the "arrogant, authoritarian, incompetent" French, and he believed that it was a tract "apt to incite anger against French Canadians." Although Johnson dismissed the book's arguments, he noted that "the virtue of such books is that they articulate publicly the contemptible thoughts that so many people reserve for the privacy of their homes or bull sessions in the pub with their pals. Perhaps once they are out there, they can be better dealt with."[56] From a social movement perspective, it is also arguable that these books legitimized the views of those who privately held anti-French and anti-bilingualism attitudes. Such views published in book form (even if by a fringe press) had greater status.

In 1979, Jock Andrew published a sequel to his first book. *Backdoor Bilingualism: Davis's Sell-Out of Ontario and Its National Consequences* was ostensibly focused on the spread of "Frenchification" in Ontario, squeezing out anglophones from government and other jobs, to make space for bilingual people, allegedly francophones from Quebec (it did not seem to occur to Andrew that there were actual Franco-Ontarians).[57] Several chapters were devoted to a follow-up to his first book and his allegations of a conspiracy to block its distribution and silence him.[58] He reprinted several letters from fans. Andrew had clearly found a constituency, and letter writers supplied anecdotes of how they, or someone they knew, had lost a job or feared losing opportunities because of bilingualism. Some were filled with nasty rhetoric referring to Hitler, Goebbels, and gulags in connection with these policies.[59]

Backdoor Bilingualism contained virulent attacks on bilingual education. Andrew claimed that "millions of dollars have been spent to brainwash Canadian parents into having their children schooled in French. The carrot for such schooling is called culture. The stick is a self-fulfilling threat: 'No French, no jobs.'"[60] "So English-speaking Canadian children grow up speaking French and are indoctrinated in the French Canadian persuasion ... Each immersion-French teacher hired" puts one more English-speaking teacher and potential teacher out of a job."[61] Andrew tried to cast doubt on the legitimacy of Canadian Parents for French as an association of English-speaking parents: "Note that although many of the surnames of many of the people involved in pushing French immersion may be English names, quite often the Christian names of the married women are French ... Once again we think we are being led when we are being conned." Oddly, this was in reference to an article about French immersion in West Vancouver that referred to Denise Izzard, Judi Madley, and Pat (short for Patterson) Webster.[62] For Andrew, the voluntary embrace of another culture was inconceivable, and French immersion had to be the result of a French Canadian, government-backed conspiracy.

Learning Disabilities, Elitism, Program Growth, and Caps

One of the longest-running challenges for CPF was how to deal with charges of elitism levelled against French immersion. It was a particular conundrum because some of the proposed "solutions" themselves could reinforce charges of elitism or engender other problems. One of the first big challenges linked to the charge of elitism was the issue of who could benefit from immersion. Was it merely another form of enrichment aimed at only the brightest and strongest students? Was it a program only for children from upper socio-economic backgrounds? Could only children with bilingual or francophone parents succeed?

There was a veritable thicket of pedagogical issues attached to the charge of elitism, and pro-immersion groups did their best to advance and disseminate the research being conducted. One of the biggest concerns was that immersion would siphon off the strongest students, leaving behind a mix of children with parents who opposed French and children with learning disabilities. The strongest research on this concern in the 1970s came from Dr. Margaret Bruck of the McGill-Montreal Children's Hospital Learning Centre. She argued that, for most children with learning disabilities, there was no need to remove them from an immersion program. Needed was a firm commitment of parents to the program along with remedial help in the classroom. Bruck noted that most learning difficulties did not relate to the language of instruction, with the exception of students with auditory difficulties. For the majority of students with learning disabilities, issues could be dealt with in the immersion environment. Bruck responded to those who claimed that moving students out of the program dealt with the problem that doing so was in fact externalizing the problem to an outside source, putting the blame on French, and not dealing with the root problem. Testing of children who switched programs showed that most had the same learning difficulties as before. Parents (and teachers) simply had a better sense of well-being. Students with learning disabilities who stayed in the programs with support did improve, albeit not to the same level of accomplishment as students without problems, but this was really the best that could be hoped for and what one would expect in the regular stream.[63]

This was not a unanimous opinion. Dr. Ronald Trites of the Royal Ottawa Hospital, who later went into private practice, claimed that children in immersion programs developed a host of psychological problems from the "schizophrenic" learning environment. His was the minority voice, however, in the debate. Fred Genesee noted that his sample pool was skewed, drawing on children referred for clinical assessment, and that the conclusions of his follow-up studies were also called into question by researchers, including Jim Cummins.[64] Regardless, the bigger problem was that the solution proposed by Bruck and others – hiring assistants for those with learning difficulties – was difficult for cash-strapped boards, and those who spoke French were in particularly small supply in many regions.

The harder-hitting criticism faced by French immersion advocates was that the program was elitist on socio-economic grounds. Critics contended that French immersion was private school education by another name. They pointed to the fact that French immersion class sizes, particularly in the upper grades of middle and secondary school, were smaller on average than those in the English program. They argued that weaker students were being filtered or screened out of the program. They further claimed that the students in these programs were overwhelmingly drawn from families that were at least second-generation Canadian with university-educated professional parents who earned salaries that placed them in the upper class or at least upper middle class. French immersion, in essence, was private school for yuppies, paid for on the public dime. This last claim resonated when the most active parents in lobby groups fighting for French immersion did tend to come from these strata.

Similar criticisms were voiced in the academic community, providing critics with scholarly sources that could be cited as evidence to "prove" their case. Canadian Parents for French faced a minor crisis when two sociologists from the Ontario Institute for Studies in Education (OISE), Paul Olson and George Burns, published an article entitled "Immersed for Change: Politics and Planning in French Immersion."[65] Critics of French immersion claimed that the study provided evidence that French immersion was elitist, selective, and targeted at upper-middle-class Canadians, and they tried to build an argument that the program should therefore be abandoned. Newspapers and magazines seized on a quotation from Olson that the program was creating a new cultural elite.[66]

A closer read indicates that the critics were only partially right about the study's findings. Olson and Burns had engaged in a study of how French immersion was being implemented on the ground in Sudbury and other northeastern Ontario communities. They noted that only a minority of immersion parents were motivated by more altruistic objectives such as national unity and that their main motivation was access to better jobs – suggesting more venal aspirations. They contended that they had found evidence of many immersion teachers weeding out their weaker students (most often with lower IQs or from the working class). And they noted that the lead classes of the program had been elitist because interest in the program had been highest among the professional class. Unilingual anglophone teachers, they noted, feared for their jobs. In short, the schools *as they currently functioned* tended to be divisive and elitist.[67]

However, Olson and Burns were not opposed to French immersion. They wanted attention paid to the issues that they raised, such as developing guidelines to prevent teachers from streaming children out of the program. They sought more coherent and structured training of teachers and principals and increased long-term planning. They also opposed restrictions on growth of the program. These were all points that CPF was quick to highlight in its newsletter article addressing the controversy. CPF noted that Olson and Burns were calling for more federal funding to support bilingualism in education, for major improvements to teacher training, and for school board action to recruit and retain students from all parts of society. Overall, they were recommending many of the policy changes for which CPF had long been calling.[68]

At CPF's 1982 national conference, Burns reiterated that French immersion should be improved so that all Canadians could have equal access to bilingualism. He observed that elitism had thus far been the de facto status of immersion because parents of high socio-economic status tended to be more willing to gamble on innovation. This was compounded by school boards that tended to hinder a policy of universal admission and teachers and principals who tracked out students. Burns called on school boards to make all ratepayers aware of immersion programs and facilitate accessibility, providing supports to the full range of student needs.[69] In *Contact*, a review for French-language teachers, Burns said that the elitist nature of immersion programs could be addressed with additional funding and support programs and if barriers to admission such as tracking out, enrolment caps, and lack of funding for transportation were addressed.[70] CPF was able to contain the demoralizing impact of the media kerfuffle that erupted when the Olson-Burns study was released and use it as a lesson in bad publicity.[71] However, critics of immersion would continue to take the "elitist" charge and terminology out of context and use it to bludgeon proponents of immersion for years after the study was released.

Although many parents considered French immersion a form of enrichment, this was only partly true. The Olson-Burns study had raised red flags about how immersion programs could be elitist, particularly if they were tracking out students with learning disabilities. There was also the issue of what was being done for particularly bright students who, were they in the regular English programs, would be sent to enrichment or "gifted" programs. Margaret Bruck argued that most students with learning disabilities would have them regardless of the language of instruction, so it was better to leave them in French immersion programs and provide supports there. Despite this recommendation, by the mid-1980s there did not seem to be a coherent set of policies in most provinces on this issue. With that in mind, CPF sponsored a national study, conducted by CPF Saskatchewan in 1985, on the need for and availability of remedial and enrichment education in French immersion.[72]

A questionnaire was sent to all school boards in the country that offered French immersion and every twelfth parent on the CPF membership list: 143 boards filled out the questionnaire, as did 318 parents. The resulting study had good national coverage, though there was fairly high representation from boards with small French immersion programs. Overall, it appeared that there was not a significant problem with parents transferring out their children because of remedial issues. Boards indicated that from 1 percent to 5 percent of students were transferred out for this reason. However, 27.5 percent of parents said that no remedial supports were available. Most school boards offering remedial supports did so via a withdrawal program, though in 34 percent of cases this meant an English-language support teacher. About 34 percent of parents were unsatisfied with the degree of support provided for remedial education, and almost 40 percent thought that needs were not being met. An even greater percentage of school board representatives (57.3 percent) indicated that some remedial education needs were going unmet. Funding was identified as the major reason, followed by a lack of perception of the need, limited space, and/or a lack of qualified personnel.

Although parents of children not in French immersion programs considered them a sufficient form of enrichment, this was not the perception of parents of children in the programs: 31.8 percent responded that their children had needs for enrichment that were not being met. Over half of those parents indicated that there were no enrichment programs for French immersion children, and another quarter indicated that their children went to enrichment programs taught in English. Board officials felt even more strongly than parents that this need was not being met (62.9 percent of board members versus 47.2 percent of parents) but acknowledged that it was rare that this would lead to students withdrawing from the program. The remedial issue was much more pressing. The most important finding was that in many boards French immersion numbers were too small to justify hiring special remediation or enrichment teachers. This meant that there was an acute need for training in these techniques for French immersion teachers and that CPF's provincial chapters would need to work with teacher training institutions on this priority.[73]

The issue of how best to deal with students with learning difficulties remained a theme in CPF's work. The organization continued to stress that removing children from French immersion programs should not be the default response. This was the message of Kate Saunders, a French immersion consultant with the Regina School Board;[74] Mary Jane Cioni, a tutor and former FSL teacher in Calgary;[75] and even the incoming commissioner of official languages, D'Iberville Fortier, when he addressed CPF's 1985 conference, which had the theme of "Special Needs in Learning French."[76] At that conference, Bruck noted the importance of attitudes toward French and school in general. She reported on a study of seventy-five students with problems with learning, attitude, and behaviour. Compared with that of a control group, the academic performance of students who transferred out of immersion between grades two and four did not immediately improve. After the first year, students' negative attitudes remained, though their parents believed that they were happier. After two years, their academic ratings started to improve, as did their behaviour. CPF concluded that attitudinal factors were key in deciding whether or not to transfer a child out of the program for behavioural reasons, as doing so could indeed hamper his or her progress, but it argued that this decision was shaped by both parent and teacher opinions. Bruck stressed that special support services could be offered in-stream to French immersion students and that, if they were in place, students should not be transferred out for academic reasons.[77] Fred Genesee noted that, when it came to lower-IQ students, there was no reason not to admit them to French immersion, since they performed at the same level as their peers in the regular programs. He observed that studies showed that socio-economic background was not a hindrance to success in French immersion.[78] To combat the charge of elitism, but also to provide the best-quality second-language education programs, CPF had to do what it could to prevent French immersion from becoming a boutique program in which students with learning disabilities were perceived to be unwelcome.

The Constitution and the OLEP

CPF was born in a period of extreme turmoil and dynamism in which language issues, finances, and the Constitution were factors. It was thrust into the constitutional melée from an early date and soon faced with a country slipping into a serious recession. CPF was created the same year that the federal government announced deep cutbacks to the Bilingualism in Education Program (BEP), which had been a valuable tool for advocates of new programs. As the five-year BEP agreement reached its expiration date without a commitment to a new agreement, members worried about what might happen to their programs.

As I have discussed more extensively in other work,[79] facilitating a new agreement between the federal government and the provinces became a key and time-consuming goal of Canadian Parents for French during Janet Poyen's and Carolle Anderson's presidencies. The group was well placed to act as an intermediary between the two levels of government, though it had to act delicately since it received the bulk of its funding from Ottawa. CPF engaged in extensive correspondence with both the federal secretaries of state and the provincial ministers heading up the Council of Ministers of Education, Canada, as well as bureaucrats and officials working for both levels.[80] Poyen presented a detailed brief to the CMEC urging the two parties to reach a long-term agreement.[81] CPF kept its own priorities in the forefront, noting the need for more guidance for school boards on how Official Languages in Education Program (OLEP, renamed in 1979) funds were to be used, issues of teacher training shortages, and program evaluation. CPF staff and directors met with representatives of the Department of the Secretary of State to determine the sticking issues for Ottawa and to find out how they might help.[82] In essence, CPF acted as a citizen intermediary group during federal-provincial negotiations.

CPF clearly had its own agenda when it came to securing ongoing funding of language programs. It thought it imperative that bilingualism funding not be lumped in with other (shrinking) transfer payments: "We can think of no better way to create a backlash against French programs than to tie their funding to decreases in post-secondary education funding, health and welfare, or any other federal-provincial agreement."[83] Without a firm commitment from Ottawa, CPF feared that cutbacks might cause Canadians to question how committed the government actually was to bilingualism.[84] CPF appears to have won great respect from the provinces, with even

Quebec's minister of education, Camille Laurin, writing to Poyen to acknowledge the sensitivity of CPF to provincial positions.[85] OLEP negotiations were a long process, but ultimately they did end in a new agreement in 1983.

CPF had also been active on the constitutional front. After the defeat of the Quebec Referendum on sovereignty-association in 1980 and the Trudeau government's revival of its constitutional reform efforts, members of CPF approved a resolution endorsing "the right of all Canadian children to education in either or both of this country's official languages, and ... we hereby affirm our strong support in principle of all legislation which will advance and guarantee such rights for our children now and in the future."[86] This resolution, which originated with the Alberta branch, was part of CPF's efforts to have the proposed Charter of Rights and Freedoms contain an expansive approach to language rights. CPF sought a guarantee that all Canadians, regardless of mother tongue, have the right to an education in either English or French.[87] In essence, it was seeking constitutionally protected access to French immersion. After the charter was adopted in 1982, CPF chapters tried to have section 23, on minority language education, interpreted this way.

Partnerships and Collaborations

By the mid-1980s, CPF was able to realize one of its founding goals of a national clearinghouse on second-language teaching. Its creation was the product of years of work with the Office of the Commissioner of Official Languages, the Association canadienne d'éducation de langue française (ACELF), the Canadian School Trustees' Association (CSTA), the Association of Universities and Colleges of Canada (AUCC), and the Canadian Teachers' Federation. The collaborative efforts ultimately led to joint action by the Department of the Secretary of State and CMEC to launch, in 1985, the Canadian Language Information Network (CLIN), a computerized network for French-language learning materials.[88]

CPF saw itself as an ally of francophone minority associations, even if it was not always seen this way by its funders and the associations themselves. In western Canada, advocates of French immersion and provincial francophone associations worked hand in hand to create French-language schools. In areas with small francophone populations, the creation of a French immersion school was seen as the only viable option to get some form of French education. Parents of children in French immersion bolstered the numbers to create a critical mass in places such as Coquitlam, British Columbia, and many parts of Alberta. It was this partnership model with which many CPFers were familiar and comfortable.

However, while there was often cooperation between CPF and francophone organizations, there was also tension that required negotiation or delicate balancing. Occasionally, the two sides found themselves opposed. There was significant tension when the Société des Acadiens du Nouveau-Brunswick (SANB) took the provincial government to court to prevent francophone students from attending French immersion. The SANB was concerned about the financial stability of the new French-language schools and school districts established in the 1970s. To maintain these schools, they needed as many students as possible. However, many mixed-marriage couples with one Acadian and one anglophone parent were sending their children to these schools, thinking that this was the best way for them to grow up functionally bilingual. The court ruled in favour of the SANB in a case involving the Grand Falls School District. Justice Richard wrote that, though parents had the right to choose to educate their children in English or French, children with a working knowledge of French could not be admitted to the French immersion schools.[89] At the 1983 CPF national conference, two provincial branches sponsored resolutions condemning the New Brunswick Department of Education testing regulations that blocked students with too much knowledge of French from attending immersion schools.[90] The policy remained in place, leaving strains between CPF and the Acadian group. Such incidents created frustration and the perception among some staff working for the Office of the Commissioner of Official Languages that CPF was not sufficiently sensitive to francophone minority concerns.[91] They were critical of what some perceived as CPF's "me-first Anglo approach to bilingualism."[92]

There was also some friction over parents who attempted to send their children to francophone schools in jurisdictions where there was no French immersion. The Fédération des francophones hors-Québec (FFHQ), the major national umbrella organization for francophone minority groups, issued statements that anglophones were not particularly welcome in francophone schools.[93] There was rarely direct opposition from francophone organizations to the growth of immersion and French programs for English-speaking Canadians, but this was not the top priority for groups that had been fighting for survival and recognition of their language rights for decades. There was a much stronger element of cultural preservation in the work of francophone community groups and francophone minority education. It was a factor recognized by the federal government in how it funded both types of organizations. Following adoption of the new OLEP protocols in 1983, the Department of the Secretary of State set up clear granting formulas for both types of organizations but kept funding streams completely separate. CPF funding fell under programs that dealt with promoting awareness of the minority language among the majority population, and FFHQ and provincial francophone groups were funded under the Official Language Minority Communities Program.[94]

There was ample opportunity, however, for collaboration and cooperation. For instance, amid the hubbub of Manitoba's official languages crisis of the early 1980s, when the Supreme Court of Canada ruled that Manitoba's abrogation of section 23 of the Manitoba Act in 1890 had been illegal and mandated the reinstitution of language rights in the province, CPF passed a resolution supporting the rights of Manitoba's French-speaking minority.[95] CPF directors actively sought new venues for cooperation with francophones, as will be evident in Chapters 9 to 11. This was due not only to pressures from the Office of the Commissioner of Official Languages and the Department of the Secretary of State but also to the sensitivity of some CPF presidents to this issue, particularly Stewart Goodings, president from 1983 to 1985, who used to work for the latter department.[96]

Partnership and collaboration among organizations dedicated to French-language learning remained important throughout the early 1980s. CPF assigned one member to sit on the board of SEVEC, which ensured close liaison with this organization dedicated to exchange programs for language-based learning. When SEVEC's funding was threatened with major cutbacks by the Ontario government in 1982, CPF's Ontario director and national president wrote to provide support for continued funding, stressing the importance of these exchanges as intense language-reinforcement experiences.[97] Pedagogical experts from OISE, McGill, Simon Fraser, and other universities were fixtures at CPF's conferences, and its newsletters routinely featured the latest research on French-language learning. It was therefore a natural step forward in this collaboration when, in 1981, OISE professor Sharon Lapkin approached CPF to see if it would be willing to provide funds for a new publication on French immersion targeted at eleven to fifteen year olds who might be considering options for secondary school French immersion.[98] The national board agreed to provide partial funding for *French Immersion: The Trial Balloon that Flew,* co-written by Lapkin, Merill Swain, and Valerie Argue, in exchange for a share of the book's royalties, deepening the collaboration between CPF and education experts.[99]

In the late 1970s, there had been some discussion of whether CPF could sponsor a national French public speaking competition for English-speaking students, but it lacked a budget for flying children and their chaperones across the country. At the provincial level, however, British Columbia Parents for French had participated in a public speaking festival, the Concours d'art oratoire, organized by André Obadia, formerly of the Carleton School Board, who had moved to Simon Fraser University. Obadia approached the CPF national board again with the idea of funding a national contest for 1984.[100] The national board investigated other provincial events, noting that there were similar ones in Saskatchewan and Ontario.[101] It decided that, if co-sponsors could be found, this could be an excellent publicity event for French second-language learning.[102] By the winter of 1985, plans were well under way for a national oratorical festival. Alan Roberts was hired to coordinate the first national event, held at Carleton University. CPF planned a series of public relations spots featuring the students while they were in town.[103] The Festival national d'art oratoire was set up as more of a celebration than a contest. The participants were usually the winners of the provincial public speaking competitions, but they were not placed in direct competition with each other. Instead, the festival was an opportunity for interprovincial sharing of the joy of French-language learning. The French Embassy provided the prize of a trip to France, with the winner selected by a draw.[104] The 1985 event was seen as a major success, and plans were launched for the following year. Over time, grant and private sector funding became more essential to the continuation of this high-profile but costly festival.

BilinguAction: Do It! *Faites-le!* Do It!

Collaboration with the private sector proved to be a greater challenge. At the start of his term as CPF president, Stewart Goodings approached Max Yalden, nearing the end of his term as commissioner of official languages. Goodings had an idea for a new campaign to promote bilingualism in Canada. Inspired by the popular ParticipACTION campaigns to promote physical fitness in Canada,[105] Goodings thought that a media-based campaign might be a way of moving away from selling bilingualism on the basis of linguistic rights and toward "selling bilingualism to the Canadian public as something positive and enjoyable" and stressing the personal and cultural benefits of speaking both languages.[106] His proposal stressed the use of humour, the need for private sector involvement, and the avoidance of guilt as a motivating principle. Goodings suggested that it would be important for the campaign to include testimonials from key high-profile personalities such as Maureen Forrester, Patsy Gallant, Karen Kain, Larry Robinson, and Steve Podborsky.

Goodings also suggested, capitalizing on the fervour for board games (including both Spicer's Oh Canada! Activity Kit and Yalden's Explorations game, described in Chapter 6), that a language game for adults similar to Trivial Pursuit might also be a feature.[107] Yalden's aide Pamela Wiggins thought that the proposal had merit and that a key first step would be to hold an exploratory meeting with a small group of private sector leaders. At their fall 1983 annual meeting, CPF members passed a resolution to have Goodings pursue this idea with the commissioner in greater detail.[108]

Yalden supported the idea in principle and was willing to provide both financial and moral support for a feasibility study.[109] He did caution, however, that there were pitfalls in "trying to sell a less than desirable product," and he wanted it to be clear that, though his office could try to serve as convenor, the project could not afford to be seen as a federal or commissioner-driven venture.[110] Stuart Beaty, one of Yalden's key advisers on citizen engagement, noted that bilingualism did not lend itself as easily to an ad-man strategy as physical activity did and that there was a danger that attempts to do so might be perceived as simplistic, provoking "howls that the Feds – or their agents – are once again trying to slop French into our Corn Flakes."[111] Yalden suggested that Spicer was the ideal person to undertake the initial feasibility study, given his extensive contacts in the business and media worlds. Spicer agreed to undertake the study, charging only costs, for "the idea of developing a more popular public information campaign in support of the two official languages."[112] He worked directly for CPF on this study but with funding provided by the commissioner's office.

Spicer conducted interviews with twenty-five leading business, media, and language experts, and he exchanged views with another thirty individuals. He reported back in the fall of 1984, and the final report from CPF was submitted to the Office of the Commissioner of Official Languages in November 1985.[113] CPF's basic premise had been that, since language tensions had eased somewhat by the mid-1980s, a continuing program of public education might foster long-term understanding among Canadians and galvanize public support for bilingual education opportunities in universities, at the key moment when the first cohort of immersion graduates reached this stage in their education. Spicer himself was cautious and feared that any such campaign might be viewed as either a Liberal Party plot, rekindling the fires sparked by the Official Languages Act and Bill 101, or a put-down of the dignity of multicultural groups. Accordingly, the project pitched by Spicer to his interlocutors was based on four key concepts: (1) stressing all languages, not just the two official languages, as freely chosen opportunities; (2) using utilitarian principles, stressing jobs, profits, travels, and pleasures to be derived from bi- or multilingualism; (3) ensuring a good-humoured mood for the campaign; and (4) securing private sector sponsorship that appeared to be broadly based and voluntary. Spicer found support in his focus group, with about a dozen people agreeing potentially to serve on a steering committee and to give money – though with none immediately volunteering to chair this effort and be the leader to drive it forward. Spicer argued that a launching grant from the Department of the Secretary of State of about $500,000, and perhaps ongoing costs for administration, coupled with another $2–3 million annually in corporate donations for funding creative work, would make the project viable. Support for the idea seems to have been premised on the principle of "letting personal needs guide each person to decide which extra language, if any, he and his children ought to learn," and the primacy of Canada's official languages was not part of the appeal.[114]

Efforts to find someone to chair a follow-up meeting to explore future steps did not go anywhere; none of the individuals suggested by Spicer thought that he or she was in a position to take a lead role. Although CPF's board thought that his more subtle approach to the campaign – promoting all second-language learning to avoid the "stigma" of French being foisted upon English-speaking Canadians – had some merit, since most Canadians would likely opt for French, given local course availability, it was unlikely that CPF could take a lead role, given its mandate. Directors from the western provinces in particular thought that a multilingual approach would detract from a necessary emphasis on preserving the rights of French minorities and making the case for better French programs in their schools. Given this prospective orientation of the campaign, CPF decided that it could play at best an advisory role, but it was not willing to drive the project forward as the lead player.[115] With CPF's idea for a mass-media campaign in favour of bilingualism thus sidelined by a multilingual approach, and with no champion among private sector leaders willing to take the lead, the media campaign idea fizzled out.

Despite the failure of BilinguAction, CPF tried to marshal private sector support to promote second-language learning and bilingualism. When corporate executives, such as Walter Light, the chairman of Northern Telecom, made comments such as "in the markets of the world, multilingualism separates the winner from the losers," CPF made sure to report this to its membership.[116] It also reprinted reports that ran in corporate publications, such as a report on French immersion that ran in the *Imperial Oil Review* in 1985.[117] Corporate Canada did believe in the importance of language learning and Canadian bilingualism, but unfortunately none of its leaders could be convinced to take independent action to run a campaign to promote bilingualism.

Core French and Postsecondary Bilingualism

Although struggles to create French immersion programs were usually the most visible aspects of the activities of Canadian Parents for French, it maintained activities in the field of core FSL. In 1983, provincial chapters were tasked with carrying out studies of core French availability as the organization attempted to develop strategies for reaching parents with children in these programs. CPF developed a pamphlet entitled "What Makes Core French Work?" It noted the best practices of that approach to language learning, since the organization pushed to have core French programs reflect the minimum threshold of 1,200 contact hours recommended by the Gillin Report.[118] Articles in the CPF newsletter continued to feature core French, including how immersion French was affecting and enhancing core French.[119] In 1985, CPF completed its document on the availability of core French programs across the country.[120] As a follow-up, past president Janet Poyen agreed to be part of a national team under the direction of H.H. Stern of OISE. His National Core French Study was a wide-ranging approach to rethinking and redesigning core French to improve this long-neglected dimension of language learning to make it more effective. He was backed by an initial grant of $220,000 from the Department of the Secretary of State.[121] The final report on new approaches to and enrichment of core FSL was published in 1990.

CPF members were also concerned about opportunities for their children to maintain their French-language skills once they graduated from high school. As the lead classes of the first immersion programs started to reach the end of secondary school, the issue of how these graduates could pursue postsecondary education at least partly in French became a higher priority. CPF's main concern was convincing English-language universities to offer some French courses in disciplines other than literature. Representatives of various universities who attended the annual CPF conference in 1982 indicated that there might be faculty-driven willingness to offer some introductory courses in French in various subjects or to have French-language tutorials to accompany regular English-language courses. This was already being attempted at the University of Toronto.[122] In western Canada, though there was interest in growing some of the bilingual degree programs – which existed at the Faculté St-Jean in Edmonton and the University of Regina – there were more pressing priorities at the postsecondary level. While the popularity of French immersion had boomed, and provinces had expanded their core French offerings, teacher supply had not kept up. So the priority had to be on developing greater teacher training capacity at western Canadian universities. The University of British Columbia and Simon Fraser University had immersion methodology courses, but there was a sense that much more was needed in terms of locally training teachers who would be inclined to work in the region.

To support parent efforts, CPF held a series of conferences at Glendon College in Toronto in September 1983, the University of British Columbia in May 1984, and Carleton University in September 1984.[123] Meetings were also held on this topic in other regions, including in Calgary and Charlottetown, and then in a national conference in Ottawa in March 1986.[124] The major outcome was a commitment to increased collaboration with the francophone community. CPF members decided that the priority was advancing the needs of provincial francophone minorities for postsecondary education in their own language. CPF president Carolyn Hodych met with her counterpart at FFHQ. That organization considered the push for French courses at English-language universities compatible with its own objectives, and it was supportive of a certain number of anglophones attending francophone postsecondary institutions if they already spoke French.[125] With this in mind, CPF produced a publication urging secondary students to maintain their studies in French at the postsecondary level and held workshops to this end.

Public Relations Strategies

With a more stable base of federal funding, CPF moved to increased professionalization of staff. The national office met with public relations consultant Cynthia Steers in 1984 about increasing its profile and promoting its objectives. Steers outlined a series of specific projects, including intensive publicity campaigns on the national conference and an upcoming Gallup poll release, a series of speaking engagements with decision makers by the

CPF president and vice-president, and the development of media spots such as public service announcements.[126] These were steps in the direction of a slicker media presence. Steers was put on retainer for the organization and hired to replace Harvey Linnen, a CPF Saskatchewan member stepping down in 1985 from editing the national newsletter, which he had done since the late 1970s.

The National Gallup Poll

Although they can be problematic because they rely on voluntary responses and assume that respondents are willing to reveal their true beliefs, polls are among the few tools that we have to gauge broader public opinion on issues such as language learning. Polls are also useful to social movement activists who want to demonstrate broader public support for their objectives and counter claims made by their critics. Bilingualism had attracted much pollster interest since the era of the B&B Commission. In 1983, the Canadian Institute of Public Opinion (CIPO) released a Gallup report dealing with bilingualism. The pollsters found that support for compulsory second-language teaching of the official languages had rebounded somewhat after a 1978 post–Bill 101 dip in support.[127] CIPO reported that the question "Do you ... or do you not think that French should be a compulsory subject like Reading, Writing and Arithmetic in all grades of public schools in English speaking Canada?" received the following responses over the last three polls (see Table 5.2).

Although there was support for some degree of mandatory French-language teaching by 1983, there was not yet majority support outside Quebec. However, support had risen since the low point of the Bill 101 era. For Canadian Parents for French, these national figures, coupled with its

TABLE 5.2
Canadian opinion on whether French should be a compulsory subject

Region	Yes	No	No opinion
National 1983	58	39	3
National 1978	52	46	3
National 1974	61	34	5
Canada outside Quebec 1983	48	50	2
Canada outside Quebec 1978	42	55	3
Canada outside Quebec 1974	51	43	6

Source: Gallup, "Quebecers Show Most Interest in Bilingual Classes," press release, September 1983, Canadian Parents for French National Office files (hereafter CPFN), file Surveys/Opinion Polls.

1981 poll of British Columbians, provided useful material when lobbying school boards. But in some respects, the generic national poll data were almost a tease since they did not provide the detailed breakdown of opinions that would be useful to CPF, and the question asked was not the one that CPF might have chosen to ask.

Thus, CPF applied for and received a $24,000 grant from the Department of the Secretary of State for a Gallup poll in 1984.[128] Between June 14 and July 7 that year, 3,152 English-speaking Canadians were asked eight main questions.[129] The poll was rich in detail, with seventy-five pages of cross-tabulated results provided to CPF, allowing for analysis of answers by region,[130] level of education, age, gender, mother tongue, occupation, community size, and whether respondents had children of school age.[131] As one drills down to these smaller subcategories of the analysis, the reliability of the data decreases, but a number of interesting trends emerge.

The first major question pertained to whether the respondent thought that children living in his or her province should learn French in the schools to become bilingual. Nation wide, 68 percent of respondents were in favour, while 27 percent were opposed. There was a sharp decline of support for French-language learning as one moved west, dropping from highs of 83 percent in Atlantic Canada and 95 percent in Quebec to 73 percent in Ontario and about 56 percent in the western provinces. There was also a significant gender spread on this issue, with 61.5 percent of men versus 74.5 percent of women saying yes. Support for second-language learning also rose steadily with education levels, rising from 62 percent among those with public school education to almost 77 percent among university graduates. Support declined as one moved up the age categories.[132]

Opponents of having French taught in the school system gave a number of reasons for their opposition. The most common reason was personal choice, with 33 percent giving this response, particularly common among younger respondents, students, and university graduates. About 18 percent thought that there would not be much use for French, a response frequently given by students but uncommon in Atlantic Canada. There was then a series of reasons related to negative issues regarding the position of French in the country or community: 15.2 percent said that they resented the growing French influence in the country,[133] a little over 9 percent thought that Canada should be a unilingual country, 8 percent said that the majority of their province spoke English, and 12 percent said that French was no more special than other languages.[134] Men, labourers, lower-income, and less-educated Canadians were less likely to see the utility of a second language and more likely to reject bilingualism and special status for French outright. Women, professionals, and younger Canadians were among the most likely to frame their opposition in terms of personal choices or options.[135]

There were also significant variations among supporters of learning French regarding the main advantage for children. The pragmatic response of better employment opportunities was the most popular, given by 44.9 percent of respondents. This reason declined sharply as one headed from east to west, ranging from a high of 82.4 percent in New Brunswick to a low of 28.4 percent in British Columbia.[136] Cultural enrichment was named by 13 percent overall.[137] This factor rose in importance with both level of income and level of education. Similar trends occurred for the response "intellectual development," named by 15.1 percent overall.[138] Travel possibilities were named by 12.9 percent, with higher levels among those with lower incomes, labourers, and housewives. Finally, contribution to national unity was named by 6.5 percent overall, with decidedly higher levels among those with the most education (10.2 percent) and among students (13 percent).

It appears that Canadians wanted their children to have opportunities to become bilingual mostly because of jobs or intellectual/cultural development. The more pragmatic reasons of job opportunities and travel possibilities appeared to be more evident to those with less education and lower incomes, whereas the slightly more abstract benefits of intellectual and cultural enrichment appealed to those with more education, working in professional or executive positions, and those who lived farther away from bilingual regions of the country.[139] On the issue of which type of French instruction respondents would prefer for their children, there was remarkable consistency across all the subcategories. Overall, early French immersion was picked by 40.8 percent of respondents, followed by French as a subject by 29.9 percent, an undefined "bilingual instruction" by 18.7 percent, and late French immersion by 7 percent.[140]

Of respondents favourable to the idea that children should learn French in school, 59.3 percent said that they would enrol their children in early French immersion if it were available in their region.[141] Willingness to send children to immersion schools tapered off both as one moved west and, perhaps surprisingly, as income levels increased. People working in sales were the most likely to endorse this option (64.5 percent), suggesting that, for Canadians in working-class and lower-income groups, French immersion education was perceived as a means of social or economic advancement for their children.[142]

Those polled were asked to indicate whether they had studied French in school and their level of satisfaction with the French instruction. Only 9.3 percent were very satisfied, and 24.6 percent were quite satisfied. An additional 35.4 percent were either not too satisfied or not at all satisfied, and 28.3 percent had not studied French in school.[143] Disturbingly, the most common reason for dissatisfaction was that the teachers were unqualified or not fluent in French (24.5 percent), a particularly common response in western and Atlantic Canada.[144] About 17 percent noted that they had started taking French at too late an age, and another 21.6 percent noted that there was not enough French taught or not enough classroom time devoted to it. A fairly low percentage indicated that they were unsatisfied with their French instruction because they disliked French or were not interested in learning it (7.9 percent) or because it was forced on them (2.6 percent). Dislike of French was much more likely to be noted by those with only an elementary school education (17.2 percent), who indicated this dislike five times as frequently as those with a university education (3.3 percent).[145]

Respondents were asked their opinions about mandatory French as a subject at various levels of the education system. Only for elementary school did this question garner a slight majority of support, at 50.1 percent yes to 46 percent no. But there were fairly clear majorities of support in Atlantic Canada (62.7 percent) and Ontario (57.4 percent) and clear opposition in British Columbia (59.2 percent) and the prairie provinces (63.8 percent).[146] Support was highest among those with university education, in the top income bracket, and among women, students, and professionals.[147]

At the secondary school level, there was overall a majority opposed to mandatory French, at 44.9 percent yes and 50.3 percent no. Only in Atlantic Canada and Quebec was there majority support. Women slightly favoured this approach (50 percent to 45.5 percent), whereas men were much more clearly opposed to it (55.3 percent to 39.5 percent).[148] As for university entrance and graduation requirements of French courses, the overall response was a vehement no to both: 66.9 percent opposed French instruction as an entrance requirement, and 76.1 percent opposed it as a graduation requirement.[149]

Cynthia Steers coordinated the release of the poll. After the raw data were analyzed to develop CPF's strategy, news releases and media alerts were drafted and translated into French. A communications strategy for provincial chapters was developed, and then the alerts were released to national and local news media and education and consumer publications. CPF

president Stewart Goodings announced the results at a formal press conference at the Ottawa press building on September 27, 1984. Follow-up news
releases were also developed to maintain momentum.[150] Local chapter
presidents were provided with material to communicate to local radio and
TV talk-show producers and local and weekly newspaper editors.[151]

The national news release led with the results that two out of three
English-speaking Canadians had responded that they wanted French instruction in school to enable children to become bilingual and that 50 percent had indicated that French instruction should be compulsory at the
elementary level. Moreover, 40 percent thought that early French immersion was the most effective form of French instruction, and 60 percent of
respondents with children indicated that they would send their children to
immersion schools if available. Also positive, from CPF's perspective, was
that support for French instruction in schools was highest among younger
age groups and that support for it was over 60 percent at all levels of
income, education, and occupation. The press release mentioned the main
advantages of French instruction: better employment opportunities, intellectual development, cultural enhancement, and national unity. It noted
that over a third of Canadians had expressed dissatisfaction with their own
French-language instruction.[152] CPF trumpeted that this poll was believed
to be the most comprehensive one on language education ever taken in
Canada. As Goodings observed, "these impressive and encouraging results
show that English-speaking Canada has accepted the value of having two
languages." He also noted that this growing acceptance of French immersion
should have a beneficial impact on teaching core French, carefully maintaining the message about CPF's dual interests and keeping this larger constituency in mind.[153]

The national Gallup poll was a benchmark event for Canadian Parents for
French. As the press release established, it provided CPF with a "good news"
angle on the level of support – at least in principle – for French-language
learning in schools. It did reveal a significant gap between support for the
ideal of French-language learning and belief that courses should be mandatory parts of the curriculum. It also demonstrated that there would not
be a groundswell of demand for postsecondary institutions to provide
leadership by reinstating language requirements. With these detailed demographic breakdowns, CPF could carefully consider how it should frame its
publicity campaigns in the future and which groups would need to be
more carefully managed and actively courted. There was clearly a divide in
Canada along class, gender, regional, income, and education lines in terms

of how Canadians had experienced French-language learning and the degree to which they were now willing to support the policy changes advocated by CPF.

The Making Choices Campaign

Cynthia Steers proposed a major nation-wide information campaign as a follow-up to the Gallup poll. She designed a campaign themed Making Choices that included professionally produced television and radio spots and placard ads on public transportation.[154] The theme played to the positive messaging that CPF wanted to endorse. It emphasized that French immersion was one of a number of options that parents had for their children and would not be forced on them (a concern evident in the poll results). It stressed making *informed* decisions about a child's education as opposed to simply accepting the status quo. The campaign would also raise, board members hoped, the relatively low public awareness of CPF that had been revealed by the poll. Prompted with the name Canadian Parents for French, about 10 percent of respondents had claimed to have heard of the group.[155]

Making Choices kicked off with an event at the National Arts Centre in January 1986, including the launch of the new CPF edited collection *More French, S.V.P.!* The event was attended by major political figures, including Progressive Conservative Secretary of State Benoît Bouchard, Liberal MP Sheila Copps, *Ottawa Citizen* editor Keith Spicer, FFHQ president Gilles Leblanc, and Andrew Kniewasser, president of the Investment Dealers Association of Canada (which had recently declined to run the BilinguAction campaign).[156] Over the next couple of months, a thirty-second TV spot was run in several markets, including on CBC and Global television, four public service announcement scripts ran on radio, and print ads ran for free in the *Globe and Mail, Saturday Night,* and *Chatelaine,* among other print media. Members reported seeing bus cards in at least ten communities, covering at least 60 percent of Canada's transit ridership. CPF also prepared an informational pamphlet distributed at meetings. Overall, the national board was very pleased with the scope of the campaign and how well it reached Canadians.[157]

As a follow-up to the Making Choices campaign, Steers prepared a briefing document for the 1986 national CPF summer board meeting outlining major challenges and recommending tactics to use and strategies to employ. She contended that the economic climate had grown more stagnant and that there was a shift in focus to economic rather than social issues. She thought that a general satisfaction with public education had given way to a proliferation of private schools. Moreover, the federal government's strong support and promotion of bilingualism, though not abandoned, was veering more in the direction of multiculturalism. Steers also identified key criticisms to be faced head-on, including that immersion programs were perceived as elitist, that children did not retain what they learned in FSL, that the quality of French learned in either FSL or immersion was insufficient for jobs, and the old canard that French immersion impeded student progress in English, math, and science. Steers recommended that publicity materials stress the practical, real-world economic advantages offered by a bilingual capability. She urged the group to seek out solid statistical research proving that job and career opportunities were greater for bilingual applicants, and she recommended the collection of more information on why immersion and core French students dropped out of those programs, so that CPF could checkmate anticipated criticisms with factual knowledge.[158] Many of these suggestions would inform strategies as CPF moved forward into a much more difficult second decade.

Conclusion

As Canadian Parents for French reached the end of its first decade, it could point to a substantial amount of success at the national level. It had burgeoned from a small group of parents to a nation-wide social movement organization with 17,000 paid members. Several of its initial objectives had been accomplished, including a national clearinghouse of second-language education information, several key publications, and an ongoing commitment from both the federal government and provincial governments to fund the expansion of second-language instruction. French immersion enrolments continued to grow rapidly, and there were now signs, with the launch of the new National Core French Study, that core FSL would now get some needed attention. Relationships with groups such as the Canadian Association of Immersion Teachers (CAIT), CASLT, and FFHQ established key partnerships in both English- and French-speaking communities of people interested in fostering stronger official languages policies.

Many challenges remained. Federal funding for second-language education was still subject to a process of renewal every three to five years, and private sector partners, though making positive statements about the need for bilingualism, were not keen to take on leadership or funding. Many school boards from coast to coast continued to cap enrolments, refused to improve their programs, and did not provide necessary support services for students with learning disabilities. This local dimension will be discussed further in Chapter 7. Myths about the perils of French immersion continued to have great currency among parents.

Overall, though, it had been a positive period for advocates of bilingualism in Canada that showed growing popular support for this concept. Admittedly, support was often tied to material benefits such as job opportunities that bilingualism might provide for children, or the intellectual and cultural development that it might support, as opposed to broader, and perhaps more altruistic, conceptions of intercultural bridge building and national unity. Although Jock Andrew's book made a big splash and featured prominently on bestseller lists, it did not create a huge groundswell of support for a mass anti-bilingualism movement. Formal anti-bilingualism social movement organizations such as APEC, though having some structures in place, had only modest impact or media presence during much of this period. But maintaining this initial momentum, particularly as the energies of some of the initial activists began to wane, would be a challenge for promoters of bilingualism as they moved forward.

6

Internationalization and Higher Education

The Second Commissioner
of Official Languages

Maxwell Yalden, the second commissioner of official languages, took over the office in 1977, shortly after the election of the Parti Québécois and in the midst of the turmoil over the Quebec government's introduction of Bill 101, the Charter of the French Language. His background differed substantially from that of Keith Spicer. Although Yalden also held a doctorate (in philosophy from the University of Michigan), his career trajectory had not been that of the public intellectual. Yalden was a career civil servant, starting out in External Affairs with postings to Moscow and Paris. He returned to Canada in the late 1960s to become assistant deputy minister in the Department of the Secretary of State, where he was a key figure implementing the government's official languages agenda. Indeed, it was Yalden who, in 1969, had arranged for Spicer to write the report on how to implement the Official Languages Act that had landed Spicer the first commissioner's job.[1] Yalden became deputy minister of communications in 1973, the position that he held when Spicer's term came to an end.

How would this career path affect his approach to the commissioner's role? In his memoirs, Yalden notes that he was "determined not to come across as a grey bureaucrat in comparison" to Spicer, "as colourful a personality as had been seen in Ottawa for quite some time."[2] Or, as he put it in a recent interview, "I was damned if I was going to be characterized in the press as a wimpy bureaucrat."[3] Accordingly, Yalden set out to follow in

Spicer's ambitious footsteps, though with additional priorities and emphases that reflected his background in academia and international affairs.

Save Geneviève! Travel the World!

One of the clearest examples of continuity between Spicer's and Yalden's approaches to the office of the commissioner was in regard to the Youth Program and the information kits. Oh! Canada's success had been clear, but the kit was somewhat dated and in need of an update, preferably one that could be produced for a lower cost. There was also a desire to build on this initial foundation with a follow-up kit for teenagers who had been exposed to Oh! Canada.[4] Madeleine Kronby, the lead developer for the first kit, proposed a follow-up kit aimed at the same cohort of eight to twelve year olds, building on the characters from the first comic book. She suggested a mystery story involving the disappearance of Geneviève the turtle. For teenagers, she envisioned a somewhat more sophisticated approach that would show how using both official languages could help or change their lives. The idea of using high-profile bilingual Canadians was key to this approach. Names ranging from Conrad Black and Eugene Forsey to Maureen Forrester, Dave Broadfoot, Guy Lafleur, and Ginette Reno were bandied about as role models who could be used for this purpose. An international dimension was also part of these initial proposals, with the suggestion that it would be worth emphasizing the global reach of English and French.

Over the course of 1979, the Oh! Canada 2 kit took shape under the direction of Kronby, who worked closely with Diana Trafford at the commissioner's office. The kit was streamlined in format and size. It contained full-colour comic and activity books and a new board game with much simpler graphics and printed on much thinner cardboard, with a detached spinner wheel. In most respects, the format and style of the original kit were retained, with a bilingual language-switching comic book and a translation approach to advancing through the board game. One notable difference from the original kit is that there was no audio component. Alphonse, the iconic parrot of the first kit, was gone, in favour of the missing Geneviève. Children were invited to write to the commissioner's office to join the Geneviève fan club and receive a free iron-on transfer.

The objectives of this kit were much the same as those of its predecessor, emphasizing making seven to twelve year olds aware that English and French were Canada's two official languages. The kit also aimed to reinforce their motivation to learn the second official language by convincing them that learning languages can be fun and that learning the second language

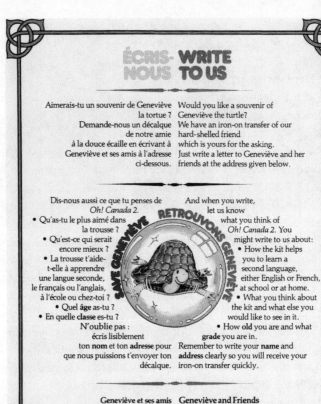

ÉCRIS-NOUS / WRITE TO US

Aimerais-tu un souvenir de Geneviève la tortue ? Demande-nous un décalque de notre amie à la douce écaille en écrivant à Geneviève et ses amis à l'adresse ci-dessous.	Would you like a souvenir of Geneviève the turtle? We have an iron-on transfer of our hard-shelled friend which is yours for the asking. Just write a letter to Geneviève and her friends at the address given below.
Dis-nous aussi ce que tu penses de *Oh! Canada 2.* • Qu'as-tu le plus aimé dans la trousse ? • Qu'est-ce qui serait encore mieux ? • La trousse t'aide-t-elle à apprendre une langue seconde, le français ou l'anglais, à l'école ou chez-toi ? • Quel **âge** as-tu ? • En quelle **classe** es-tu ? N'oublie pas : écris lisiblement ton **nom** et ton **adresse** pour que nous puissions t'envoyer ton décalque.	And when you write, let us know what you think of *Oh! Canada 2.* You might write to us about: • How the kit helps you to learn a second language, either English or French, at school or at home. • What you think about the kit and what else you would like to see in it. • How **old** you are and what **grade** you are in. Remember to write your **name** and **address** clearly so you will receive your iron-on transfer quickly.
Geneviève et ses amis Bureau du Commissaire aux langues officielles Ottawa, Canada K1A 0T8	**Geneviève and Friends** Office of the Commissioner of Official Languages Ottawa, Canada K1A 0T8

Feedback page from the Oh! Canada 2 Activity Kit. | *Source:* Oh! Canada 2 Activity Kit, Office of the Commissioner of Official Languages, 1980.

The theme of the Oh! Canada 2 comic book and activity book was finding the lost turtle Geneviève. | *Source:* Oh! Canada 2 Activity Kit, Office of the Commissioner of Official Languages, 1980.

would be useful.[5] Communication and mutual understanding among Canadians were key to the kit's message, which attempted to instill in children a desire to communicate with members of the country's other official language community.

Another team was working on a game and information package for teenagers, tentatively entitled Citoyen du monde – Citizen of the World. Yalden outlined the project in a meeting with the Council of Ministers of Education, Canada (CMEC), on January 23, 1979, and production proceeded throughout the year. This kit aimed to make thirteen to seventeen year olds aware of the international importance of Canada's two official languages and the linguistic diversity of humanity. It stressed that there are few truly unilingual countries and that English and French are spoken on all continents of the world.[6]

The kit had three main components. The first was a board game with the objective of becoming an honorary citizen of as many cities of the world as possible, determined by "knowledge" of world languages. Through game play, players earned cards with the names of various languages printed on them, which could be cashed in to "win" cities. English and French were key to many of those cities and by far the most required language cards. Once a city was "won," the player placed his or her coloured peg (similar in shape and style to those used in the children's toy Lite Brite) into the city's hole in the world map mounted in the centre of the game board.

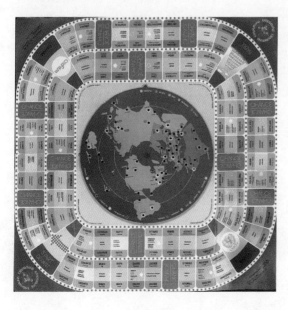

Explorations board game. Players "won" cities by turning in cards with the names of the languages used in that city. | *Source: Explorations Activity Kit, Office of the Commissioner of Official Languages, 1980.*

The second component of the kit was a world map, produced in conjunction with the Department of Geography at the University of Ottawa, showing the global distribution of official (or administratively used) languages. And the third component was a "magazine" with articles and activities designed to show the diversity of the world and how knowledge of languages was beneficial. Yalden entered into an arrangement with the CMEC to have an advisory committee of provincial education officials guide the magazine's development and provide feedback on the kit's other components.[7] Production of the game involved some long and agonizing meetings in which the development team selected which languages would be needed to "win" each city, trying to show global use of the two official languages in a believable way. The final name of the kit, Explorations, was chosen in the spring of 1980 as a simple, one-word name that worked in both languages and captured its global approach.[8]

Distribution of both Explorations and Oh! Canada 2 began in 1980. One MP, upon receiving his copies of the kits (routinely sent to all MPs and senators), was particularly cantankerous. Don Blenkarn, the Progressive Conservative MP for Mississauga South, started his letter to Yalden by congratulating him on the Oh! Canada 2 kit as a potentially invaluable tool for teachers of French or English. He then asked what authority the commissioner had to produce teaching material and where such authority could be found in the Official Languages Act. Since education is an exclusively provincial purview under the BNA Act, Blenkarn argued, "your educational activities not only abuse your mandate, but are unconstitutional." He went on to note that the position of commissioner of official languages did not allow Yalden to explore the full scope of his considerable talents as an educator, and he suggested that perhaps Yalden should consider a new career in teaching.[9] Otherwise, the response of the public and government to both kits was overwhelmingly positive as tens of thousands of the kits were rolled out to schools across the country. The limited number of negative public responses to the kits had less to do with the elements dealing with English and French than with how the map addressed the status of the Ukrainian language![10]

Initial stocks of both kits were quickly exhausted. A new climate of accountability in place in Ottawa required that both kits be subjected to formal evaluations in 1981. A team from the Ontario Institute for Studies in Education (OISE) conducted formal pedagogical and user evaluations of Explorations as well as a pedagogical evaluation of Oh! Canada 2. User response to Oh! Canada 2 was assessed by a private contractor.[11] The

Explorations kit passed the evaluation with flying colours. The OISE evaluation team of Anthony Smith, Gila Hanna, and Sharon Lapkin found that curriculum experts lauded the form and content of the kit as both clearly focused on its objectives and successful in achieving them. Teachers noted a very positive student response to the kit, particularly the board game. Their only suggestion was to tweak the rules of the game so that it could be played more quickly. The Information Branch team at the commissioner's office touted the positive evaluation in their request to the Treasury Board for funds to have the kit reprinted.[12] Explorations would be reprinted several times throughout the 1980s, with over 500,000 copies ultimately distributed before the kit was finally discontinued at the end of the decade.[13] With its emphasis on global themes, and activities that did not require knowledge of the other official language for users to be exposed to its messages, Explorations was seen as an excellent motivational tool for young people to learn official languages. Subsequent discussions on reprinting the kit highlighted the fact that the commissioner's office was "the only organization providing teachers with the tools to 'convert'" young people on the issue of language learning.[14] As well, this type of kit was useful for message reinforcement.[15]

Oh! Canada 2 did not face as easy a ride through the evaluations. OISE's evaluation of the kit, undertaken in consultation with a curriculum expert in each province, raised several major concerns. Eight of the ten experts were critical of the usefulness of the kit as a second-language learning tool. Many thought that the reading level was too advanced for the target age group in their second language (unless they were in French immersion), and several experts were highly critical of the translation dimensions of the kit, which they thought were inappropriate for teaching language at the primary level.[16] Most thought that the issue of translation would render the kit inaccessible to children and thus be problematic for at-home use. In a related vein, they were critical of the language switching in the comic book and pleaded for an audio component so that children could learn how the words sounded – stressing an audio-lingual approach to language learning. The evaluators believed that, "left to their own devices, 8–12 year old[s] would make little attempt at the second language in the kit."[17] These pedagogical experts were highly critical of the dimensions of the kit that required knowledge of a second language or would force children to translate in order to engage with Oh! Canada 2 and its intended messages, echoing the "expert" response to the original kit.

However, as was the case with the first Oh! Canada, children reacted extremely well to the kit.[18] The telephone-based survey with actual kit users demonstrated that the experts were wrong in practice. Although the survey was intended for parents, most parents contacted for this part of the study, conducted in New Brunswick, Quebec, Ontario, and British Columbia, turned the phone over to their children. The children were regular game players and readers of the comic book. Although some had trouble with vocabulary or pronunciation, they turned to their parents, siblings, or fellow players for help in looking up words, and they were not deterred from game play because of this feature.[19] The evaluators opined that difficulty with the second language did not translate into a decision not to use the kit. Rather, this was seen as a challenging and fun aspect. Consequently, after the first batch of 300,000 kits had been distributed, Information Branch staff submitted a report to the Treasury Board acknowledging the mixed evaluation but emphasizing the kit's popularity with children, teachers, and the public. Treasury Board officials authorized a second printing of 400,000 more copies in the winter of 1982. This fine line between the kit as a motivational tool and the kit as a second-language learning device proved to be a stumbling block for evaluators, but end users of the kit, Canadian children, did not seem to be dissuaded by their second-language limitations. This challenge was viewed by the commissioner's team as a positive factor in motivating children to learn a second language and become bilingual. Responding to the other critique raised by the evaluators, the commissioner's office developed an audio component to accompany the kit, Telephone, a playful record based on an extraterrestrial communicating with children across Canada via the telephone.[20]

Keeping an Eye on the Children

Although Canadian Parents for French (CPF) was born under Keith Spicer's watch, it was during Maxwell Yalden's first term that the organization really began to flourish. As discussed in the previous chapter, CPF grew rapidly and engaged in direct action at local, provincial, and federal levels. Much of this activity would have been significantly more difficult without the direct patronage of the commissioner's office. The commissioner paid for the first few CPF newsletters and helped with start-up office funds. Yalden was a regular speaker at the annual conferences of the organization, and his officials provided advice on how to get access to federal funding through other departments and how to strategize. There was always a member of the commissioner's staff assigned to the role of liaison with CPF. Moreover, his office was supportive of initiatives, such as the ultimately ill-fated BilinguAction campaign, that CPF proposed to foster public support for bilingualism.

Student exchange programs had been another major preoccupation of Spicer. A number of interprovincial language exchange programs, such as the Ontario-Quebec exchanges operated by the Bilingual Exchange Secretariat (BES), had qualified for federal matching grants as special projects under the Bilingualism in Education Program. However, organizations such as the BES were operating within a time-limited framework, for special project funding could last only for five years. This created major headaches when federal-provincial talks over renewal of the Official Languages in Education Program (as the BEP was renamed in 1979) ran into a log jam from 1979 to 1983. Early plans for renewal included creating a new envelope of funding explicitly targeted at exchange programs. During the interim period, not only did this not exist, but also federal funding was reduced by 20 percent. To mitigate this, Yalden played an important role as go-between, intervening on behalf of the BES to argue for exceptional circumstances to continue funding beyond the five-year cap.[21]

Yalden was a believer in the approach and mandate of these exchange programs. As the BES described its approach,

> students are immersed in a second language environment and involved together in activities to let them learn the way of life of their counterparts, to develop their self-reliance and character, to make them realize the similarities and differences which exist between the two cultures and to develop tolerance for others, to acquaint them with a different region of Canada and its economy.[22]

From 1980 to 1982, this required annual interventions by Yalden or his staff to support Jane Dobell and the board of the BES and its successor organization, born from a merger with Visites interprovinciales, the Society for Educational Visits and Exchanges Canada (SEVEC). Yalden argued forcefully for continuing federal and provincial support for exchanges. He saw them as contributing to national unity and respect, which, as he put it, "depends very much on how individual Canadians feel towards each other. Which in turn depends very much on the extent to which they actually have an opportunity to get to know each other – not merely through the information that filters through the press, or books, or TV, but through what can be learned on a one-to-one basis."[23] Thanks to his interventions and fierce lobbying by SEVEC's board, planned cutbacks from the Ontario Ministry of Education and the federal Department of the Secretary of State were scaled back.[24] However, funding for exchange programs remained tenuous. The commissioner frequently noted how important these exchanges were yet how little funding was devoted to them on an annual basis.

The flipside of arguing for more funding for youth programs was the commissioner's attack on the federal government's bilingualism bonus. Yalden claimed that the bonus, paid out to 40,000 civil servants, many of whom learned the second language at public expense on the job, was extremely costly at $30 million per year. It was harmful to morale and out of line with the government's language policy.[25] Yalden pointedly noted that money spent on the bilingualism bonus would pay for a significant number of language exchanges.[26] Despite this, the bonus continued, and he characterized it as "an overextended houseguest who cannot take a hint – unloved but unbudgeable."[27] Public sector unions refused to consider its termination. Every year the bilingualism bonus appeared in Yalden's annual report as his frustration with its persistence grew. By 1983, Yalden noted that the budget for the bonus was $40 million, compared with $13 million spent between the Summer Language Bursary Program, which had to turn away two out of three applicants, and the Official Languages Monitor Program, in which only one in four applicants got a position. When it came to advocating for youth exchange programs to receive part of the civil service's share of federal bilingualism funding, Yalden was up against an immovable object.

Tilting at Ivory Towers

Armed with a doctorate in the philosophy of language, and married to a French professor, it is not surprising that Yalden took an interest in second-language teaching in Canada's high schools and universities. Most Canadian high school systems had moved away from compulsory courses in the 1960s, and mandatory French courses were among those dropped. Most universities also dropped the second-language admission requirement. Consequently, though the new federal funding being pumped into provincial education systems led to significant increases in second-language course enrolment at the elementary level, secondary school enrolments tumbled in the 1970s. Yalden thought that this shift in requirements was damaging to second-language acquisition because it sent a powerful signal to Canadian students that these skills were neither valued nor necessary.

Over the seven years of his term, Yalden gave many public speeches and corresponded directly with ministry officials, university presidents, and interuniversity task forces on the issue of reinstating the language requirement. For the most part, his efforts were to little avail. In Ontario, Premier

Bill Davis was supportive of expanding second-language teaching, but he opposed making it a requirement for university admission or graduation, citing the ever-increasing diversity of his province and how the language requirement would be unfair to new immigrants. Davis went further in a response to a question from Liberal MPP Sean Conway, firing off the zinger that "I had not heard, prior to this morning, that the Liberal Party of Ontario wants us to legislate the degree qualifications of our great universities in this Province."[28] This issue of university autonomy vis-à-vis governments cropped up frequently when the issue of legislating entrance or graduation requirements was broached with education officials.

Targeting the universities directly often resulted in an equally disappointing response. In a 1978 exploratory report on the potential of pushing the issue, Yalden's officials noted that morale was low in Canada's universities, faced with declining enrolments at the end of the baby boom. Introducing "hard" required courses or new admission requirements was not likely to occur. Put bluntly in an internal memo, "lack of 'warm bodies' equals reduction in grants."[29] By 1979, few universities had language requirements for either admission or graduation, as a study conducted by a team at Laval University for the Association of Universities and Colleges of Canada (AUCC) discovered.[30] Among fifty-four universities (out of seventy-one) that responded to the questionnaire, only four had across-the-board second-language requirements, while some others had program-specific requirements (usually for language programs). Those that did were bilingual institutions – the University of Ottawa, Royal Military College, Université Ste-Anne, and Faculté St-Jean of the University of Alberta. While organizations such as the AUCC, the Council of Ontario Universities,[31] and the Association of Atlantic Universities discussed these concerns and even appointed task forces, the result was always the same. They agreed to take measures to encourage and facilitate second-language study, but imposing new requirements was a non-starter.

Even within university French departments, where one might have expected support for Yalden's proposal, there was reluctance. The narrative of modern languages units in the early 1980s was one of severe financial cutbacks, failure to replace retirees, and swelling class sizes.[32] French professors cast severe doubt on the sincerity of their presidents' commitment to second-language learning when the on-the-ground story was one of diversion of university resources to other priorities.[33] There was concern that French departments would be turned into second-language learning mills for reluctant students fulfilling course obligations rather than students with interests in literature or linguistics, which tended to be faculty specializations. There was also a chicken-and-egg problem. Without high school French graduation requirements, the calibre of students entering university courses would be extremely variable, making it challenging to offer appropriately pitched courses. Consequently, even in officially bilingual New Brunswick, the University of New Brunswick decided, after studying the issue, not to change its stance on entry and graduation requirements.[34] Without even UNB on side, it was unlikely that a national approach had any chance. Indeed, though the Canadian Association of University Teachers (CAUT) invited Yalden to speak at its 1982 annual meeting on the issue of bilingualism in universities, the organization's executive secretary, Donald Savage, was clearly doubtful. He suggested that there was little merit in proposing that the University of Saskatchewan's agriculture school or the University of British Columbia's forestry program should require French for graduation and that instituting language requirements in humanities and social sciences programs might accelerate the rush away from them. As Savage snarkily put it in his letter, "it seems to me that whatever proposals you may have should have some possibility of working."[35]

Yalden's efforts to have universities reinstate some language requirements were not entirely without success. As of 1982, the University of Toronto's huge Faculty of Arts and Sciences began requiring that students complete either a senior mathematics course or a language course for admission. French was not explicitly required, though it could be expected that, given Ontario high school offerings, it was the most likely language credit.[36] Surprisingly, it was in British Columbia that his proposals had their greatest success. The University of British Columbia announced in 1977 that it would require all students to have both a grade eleven science credit and a grade eleven language credit for admission, effective in the fall of 1981, giving notice to students entering high school of what would be required of them.[37] Over the following four years, the number of BC students graduating with both of these requirements leapt from 55 percent to 80 percent. Simon Fraser University made the same decision in 1981, to be effective in the fall of 1985,[38] and the University of Victoria followed suit in 1982, despite a debate in 1983–84 to rescind the decision.[39] While the University of Victoria issue was under debate, Yalden worked closely with supporters of the policy to provide information on studies linking second-language training to cognitive skill development and job opportunities. The challenge to the new requirements ultimately dissipated, since the pathway to the new requirements had been smoothed by British Columbia's vastly improved second-language instruction programs. It also helped that at the time there were only three universities in British Columbia, and the change was initiated at the most prestigious of the three. This made the fear of students choosing another university with fewer requirements less pressing in the province. In terms of Canadian bilingualism, French per se was not the required course, but for the vast majority of BC students it would have been the course available. In 1983, of 187 secondary schools in British Columbia, 172 offered French 11, compared with only 18 offering German, 17 offering Spanish, and 4 offering Latin.[40] Perhaps it was not the ringing endorsement of English-French individual bilingualism that might have been Yalden's dream, but it was nevertheless a breakthrough for language learning in a province not known to be the most supportive of bilingualism.

Conclusion

It is fair to say that Max Yalden managed to avoid being "another wimpy bureaucrat." He successfully carried on and enhanced Keith Spicer's legacy on the youth option with his support for Canadian Parents for French and the educational kits. He ran into significantly more frustration, though, in his efforts to recruit allies for the cause of bilingualism among Canada's adult population. His attempts to phase out the bilingualism bonus ran into fierce resistance from the public service unions. The campaign to promote French-language learning at the postsecondary level achieved only modest success in a few universities and programs and was otherwise blocked by provincial governments, university administrations, and even French professors. And, as discussed in the previous chapter, Yalden's collaboration with CPF to get private sector businesses to take a leadership role in promoting bilingualism, via BilinguAction, met with nice words but a lack of real engagement. It was among youth, it seemed, that passions could be raised and greater action was possible in the 1980s.

7

Canadian Parents for French and Local Activism, 1977–87

Although the broad national initiatives of Canadian Parents for French and the Office of the Commissioner of Official Languages were important for maintaining federal and popular support for the overarching goal of bilingualism, it was at the local level that programming decisions occurred. School boards, and often individual schools, were where decisions were made on whether a French immersion program would be started or continued or whether core FSL would be expanded and enhanced. Provincial governments also played a role in creating frameworks, funding, and requirements for French programs. CPF's national and provincial newsletters are filled with stories of how the local chapters provided support to French programs, including the organization of summer camps, fundraising drives for library materials and tours of francophone performers, and the organization of winter Carnaval celebrations. It was also at this level that parents had to organize to lobby their school boards for new French programs, to promote their expansion, and to defend them from threats of closure. It is difficult to get precise numbers on how many local chapters of CPF existed at any given time, for these chapters were not tracked centrally. Some provinces, particularly British Columbia, actively developed local chapters, whereas others relied more heavily on the provincial branch. Moreover, local chapters would often pop up with the short-term objective of getting a program started and then fade away or become inactive once it was established.

By the time that the national CPF organization was established in 1977, interest in improved French programs had spread across the country, reaching many smaller communities far from the bilingual belt and francophone centres. This chapter focuses on four communities that experienced challenges with their French programs. I selected these communities partly because their local CPF chapters kept good records on their activities. In other communities, the documentary record of a given campaign for a French program is often fragmentary, depending on the extent to which chapter presidents archived their correspondence and materials. The challenges faced in these four communities were, in many respects, typical of those faced across the country. However, they also highlight the intensely local character of campaigns to promote and defend bilingualism, the central roles of key individuals to these efforts, and how local and provincial concerns nuanced or intersected with nation-wide critiques. Although the emphasis here is at the community level, it will also be evident that simultaneous activism targeting provincial government policies could play a significant role in how local efforts succeeded or failed. Political opportunities and challenges existed in many different forms and at different levels of government, and the ability to exploit them was crucial when key junctures were reached in a French program's development.

Sackville, New Brunswick

As noted in Chapter 5, the issue of elitism became particularly pressing as French immersion expanded and demand for the program grew. Most boards started with a pilot program, with one class per grade level. However, demand often swelled to the point where this could not physically accommodate all of the students seeking admission. Many boards refused to add classes for a variety of reasons, including cost and potential teacher layoffs, raising the question of which lucky students would be accepted. Some prioritized younger siblings of students already enrolled, reinforcing the "elitist" nature of the program. In other communities, school boards tried to avoid the appearance of preferential treatment for professional parents and used a first-come, first-served approach. This led to parents queuing up overnight to enrol their children. Others used a lottery system, drawing names from a hat to determine who would be enrolled. This last system was used in the community of Sackville, New Brunswick, home to Mount Allison University, to determine who would be admitted to the grade one class in the fall of 1980.[1]

Sackville's French immersion program was created in 1973. The town (population of 5,635) had recently played host to a regional mini-conference of Canadian Parents for French that had generated great enthusiasm for immersion. Twenty-eight spots were available for the 1980 incoming grade one class, but forty-seven parents wished to enrol their children. The local school board refused to budge on creating an additional grade one class. This created a minor crisis. Defeated at the school board level, the parents waged a letter-writing campaign in the *Sackville Tribune-Post*, trying to combat the letter writers who continued to insist, despite the lottery system, that the program was elitist. Parents used a variety of arguments. Child-centred rhetoric was deployed by James Purdy, who asked how he was to explain to his child that he could not attend French immersion when his friends and siblings could. Gerrit Moleman asked how he was to explain to his six-year-old daughter, who had attended an immersion kindergarten, that she would not be allowed to continue in the program where her mother taught. Others threatened the local Conservative MLA with the wrath of parent voters in a swing constituency. At the local level, however, there was little movement.

Parents escalated the campaign over immersion caps to the provincial level. There they used arguments about job opportunities and the bilingual nature of New Brunswick. They also called into question Premier Richard Hatfield's commitment to bilingualism during the 1980–82 constitutional patriation talks. Parents demonstrated in front of the provincial legislature, which resulted in a meeting with the premier. Following this meeting, Minister of Education Charles Gallagher overrode the school board and authorized school superintendent Dale Aitken to run the district's schools. Aitken authorized conversion of the second grade one class to French immersion in September 1980. In July 1981, a revised policy on French immersion was implemented by the New Brunswick Department of Education. Policy 501 required that "a school district shall implement an immersion program where there is sufficient interest to ensure that immersion classes are of comparable size to other classes in the district at that level of instruction."[2] Although this policy would not endure indefinitely in the province, in the short term the provincial government proved to be responsive to well-timed political pressure during a window of opportunity. Sackville parents hoped that this would help to defuse the charges of elitism aimed at French immersion and accommodate the burgeoning demand for it.

Prince Rupert, British Columbia

Farther from Canada's "bilingual belt," the process of creating a French immersion program and expanding FSL in the community of Prince Rupert,
British Columbia, illustrates how proponents of bilingualism had learned
from experiences in other communities yet faced many of the same challenges. A port city in the northwest, Prince Rupert had a population of
about 16,000 people during the early to mid-1980s. Two elementary schools
offered an FSL program in all grades, whereas the others offered a twenty-
minute program in grades six and seven, and all schools offered the provincially mandated grade eight course.[3] The high schools offered French as
an elective.

In September 1981, Gail Holmgren, a parent in the district and the wife
of a mill worker, wrote to the trustees of School District 52 announcing
the formation of Prince Rupert Parents for French (PRPF) and the group's
intention to request the introduction of French immersion. She provided
information about French immersion and urged the trustees to contact her
if she could provide any assistance.[4] In the months that followed, Prince
Rupert Parents for French placed ads in local papers announcing an information booth set up on January 16, 1982, at the Pride of the North mall.[5]
Parents staffing the booth asked visitors to sign a petition supporting the
creation of a French immersion program. Visitors could also peruse materials on French immersion or listen to a cassette of children singing in French.[6]
PRPF presented a brief to the school district's board later that month. The
board followed up by placing a questionnaire in the local newspaper inquir-
ing about parents' interest in the program.[7]

Meanwhile, members of PRPF obtained letters of support from Mayor
P.J. Lester, local MLA Graham Lea, and MP Jim Fulton.[8] Lester's letter noted
that the additional costs of the program were to be covered by federal grants,
at no additional cost to local taxpayers. Lea's letter indirectly addressed the
issue of access to the program, noting that "it is my sincere hope that the
funding of such a program will be adequate, so that as many families wishing to participate may do so." Fulton's approach was clearly affected by pedagogical research: "The ability to speak a second language is exciting and can
best be learned at an early age."

PRPF's briefs touched on many of the concerns that had derailed the creation or continuation of immersion programs elsewhere in the country. The
group tackled the issue of tracking out weaker or learning-disabled students

head on. It cited European experiences, and McGill University researcher Fred Genesee, to point out that students with lower intelligence, less favourable economic status, and non-English backgrounds could perform just as well in French immersion as in the regular English program if given comparable supports. The group also strongly suggested that guidelines be developed to restrict teachers from streaming children out of immersion classes.[9] In their formal pitch to the board, the parents stressed that French immersion would not affect the availability of the regular English program and highlighted the pedagogical benefits of starting language learning at an early age. They noted the increasing number of jobs demanding French fluency and how immersion graduates were able to accept French-language job positions. They pointed to student scores showing that immersion students fared as well or better than students in the regular program, and they noted how these programs would allow children to pick up third and fourth languages with greater ease. PRPF also defused the standard concerns about French immersion and English-language learning using the national CPF informational pamphlets.[10]

Although there was favourable response to the mail-in cards, and the board was impressed by the research, there was no follow-up in 1982.[11] Round two began in the spring of 1983, with another information meeting for parents and another request to the board. However, the board voted against establishing a French immersion lead class for the fall of 1983, citing the need for a complete study of community demand, availability of facilities and francophone teachers, and budget. Superintendent Lowe noted that the board was not opposed in principle to the program but thought that a full study was needed.[12]

Disappointed but undaunted, Holmgren and the other parents offered their support for the study and urged the board to hear from Geoff Mills of the Ministry of Education's Modern Languages Services Branch.[13] They then reached out to other parents and other BC chapters urging them to write to the board. They also garnered support from the president of the Prince Rupert District Teachers' Association.[14] Mills spoke to the board and parents in October, and a survey of parents' interest in French immersion was finally launched in January 1984.[15] Prince Rupert Parents for French urged the board to create multiple lead classes so that, even with attrition, senior grades would remain viable.[16] The district's education committee met on March 8, 1984, with almost all board members in attendance. The committee endorsed the proposal to start with a new kindergarten and grade one class in the fall, with plans to expand immersion up to grade four, with the proviso that regular program students would not be forced to attend schools outside their areas and that, if numbers dropped, the board would move to split grades or eliminate the class.[17] All that remained was a formal vote of the Board of Trustees, most of whom had appeared to be favourable at the education committee meeting. It was thus a major blow when the board voted 3:2 on March 14, 1984, to reject the committee's recommendation. Chair Helen Stamnes was "shocked."[18] Trustee David Bull argued that, though the program had its merits, he thought that it would mean the reduction of other programs, that parents' interest would decline over time, and that the board could not afford to introduce it during a period of declining budgets.

The parents attempted to rally. The *Prince Rupert Daily News* ran an editorial stating that "it would indeed be unfortunate if Prince Rupert lost a progressive and, nationally, highly-successful program."[19] Holmgren penned an open letter to service clubs, political parties, politicians, and the city council asking them to write to the school board, stressing that twenty-one other jurisdictions in the province had introduced this successful program and that "Prince Rupert must not be left behind."[20] Elaine Jaltema pointed out that other small communities in the province, such as Dawson Creek, 100 Mile House, and Mission, had successfully launched programs the previous fall. She identified ways to minimize the start-up costs of the program and echoed the "opportunity for Prince Rupert children" rhetoric.[21] But even with support from the local NDP chapter, aldermen, and editorialists, the board voted 3:3 on April 10, 1984, to maintain their original position.[22]

For Jaltema, who had been involved in Prince Rupert Parents for French since its inception in 1981, and who had met Holmgren when the two worked on a campaign for a child-care centre, it was now too late for her eldest son to enter the program. Her middle son could still have a shot at a grade one entry point if the board could be convinced to adopt a program for the fall of 1985. Together with Pat Wilson, a local teacher and parent, and other members of the local chapter, they decided to target their efforts at getting a supportive Board of Trustees. Wilson and Jaltema worked on the campaign of trustee candidate Fred Beil, a French immersion supporter, and helped to get out the vote on election day. The election of Beil tipped the balance on the board, which voted to start French immersion with kindergarten and grade one classes for the fall of 1985.[23] When persuasion failed, direct political intervention in the electoral process was sometimes necessary.

Saanich, British Columbia

Neighbouring communities could have thoroughly different experiences with campaigns for FSL programs, and the experiences of one could shape those of the other in both good and bad ways. So it was with the Vancouver Island school boards of the capital city, Victoria, and its neighbour, Saanich. The Saanich board encompassed the north end of Saanich, a suburb of Victoria, and extended north on the peninsula through suburban and rural areas. Although urban Victoria was among the first communities in British Columbia to have French immersion (since 1973), it would prove to be a much more difficult challenge in Saanich.

Many of the early challenges of Saanich were faced head on by Yvonne Rolston. She was born in Scotland, then moved to British Columbia, where she took a few of the regular core French courses offered in high school and a year of French in university – enough for her to have familiarity with the language but not enough to speak it. As a young married woman in Saanich in the mid-1970s, Rolston came across an article discussing French immersion in *Chatelaine* magazine and discussed it with her neighbour. At the time, she did not have any children – her first of two sons was born in 1977 – but the program struck her as an excellent opportunity. Initial conversations with the local French coordinator were positive, and seventeen parents expressed interest in creating a lead class. However, the local school board, when approached, responded that attrition would likely make a French immersion program difficult to sustain.

The Saanich group got in touch with the newly formed CPF for help in preparing additional briefs for the board. However, briefs, presentations to board meetings, and personal meetings with trustees were met with "a resounding *no*."[24] It became clear to this new chapter of CPF – Saanich Parents for French (SPF) – that a direct political approach was needed. The group found three well-educated and well-respected candidates to run in the 1978 fall school board elections and campaigned for these supporters of French immersion. Two of those candidates, John Betts and Roy Hyndman, were elected, creating the critical majority on the board to adopt French immersion.[25] The first kindergarten and grade one classes started at Keating Elementary School in September 1980. However, the board decided that no more than 50 percent of the school population could be taken up by immersion students, and parents who lived outside the catchment area were required to provide their own transportation for children.

Plans were made for a second entry-level class for the fall of 1981, but a group called Better Education for Everyone tried to block its creation. Their rhetoric tapped into fears that the regular program would be eroded by the success of French immersion. Proponents of immersion noted that the anti-immersion stance was rooted in reasons ranging from outright hostility to French – Rolston was phoned at home on more than one occasion and accused of being a Québécoise infiltrator trying to force French on British Columbians (on the basis of her first name being Yvonne) – to anti-urban and anti-"city slicker" sentiments expressed by farmers in the district who saw no point in French-language instruction.[26] Efforts behind the scenes helped to settle fears, and a second class started at Deep Cove Elementary School. The two schools kept adding a class per year, with the result that, by the fall 1985 term, both schools had reached the 50 percent limit imposed on the program.[27]

As president of Saanich Parents for French, Rolston approached the board in the late winter of 1985 to propose a late French immersion option and extension of the regular FSL program into the earlier grades. She also urged the board to determine the demand for early French immersion (EFI). There was enough demand to create two additional kindergarten classes for the fall of 1985. However, other parents were pushing the board to stop extending French immersion until there was FSL for all grades. Their representatives claimed that a majority in the district would prefer thirteen years of FSL over French immersion.[28] The board rejected SPF's proposals for new programs in light of current economic circumstances and fears of having to lay off teachers.[29] A crisis was brewing because of the high demand for immersion.

The issue of the program's success came to a head in the spring of 1986. A series of meetings of the education directions committee to try to find a home for an expanded French immersion program failed to reach a resolution. Following these meetings, Trustee Marilyn Loveless put forward a surprise motion at the board meeting of April 14 calling for the phasing out of EFI. The motion narrowly passed, by a vote of 4:3. Joe Lott, one of the trustees who voted to phase out immersion, claimed that it had been impossible to come to an agreement. He raised the issue of maintaining neighbourhood schools in a division with many small elementary schools. More troubling was his comment that French teachers were taking the place of English teachers, and he feared that more jobs would be lost. "I've also found," he noted, "that it has been extremely difficult to communicate with some of our francophone teachers. They are literally French-speaking people and they speak French in the staffroom and other teachers feel excluded when that kind of thing happens."[30] The solution to this divisiveness, Lott suggested, was to phase out early immersion and perhaps introduce a late immersion program down the road.

Faced with this surprise decision to cancel a very successful and popular program, Saanich Parents for French swung into action on a variety of fronts. A petition was signed by over 70 percent of the family physicians and specialists at the Saanich Peninsula Hospital, who expressed "strong disagreement with [the] school board's decision to end the option of Early French immersion schooling."[31] Parents were asked to make frequent phone calls to trustees – though not after 10 p.m. Members of SPF were asked to call in to radio and TV programs in support of EFI and to attend the upcoming board meetings.[32] A committee of lawyers met to consider possible legal recourses on both procedural and charter grounds, hoping to use section 23 of the Charter of Rights and Freedoms to secure continuation of the program.[33] The group also prepared briefs for the board citing the results of a parent survey showing huge demand for EFI in the years to come. They also noted that late French immersion tended to be more elitist than early French immersion because there was more self-selection by students.[34] Cancelling the program, they observed, would likely lead to the best French teachers fleeing in search of more secure jobs backed by supportive school districts. Furthermore, they noted that the principals did not support claims that teachers from the two programs did not get along. All of the teachers at Deep Cove Elementary School signed a statement attesting to the positive and amicable relations between staff and students.[35]

At the board meeting held on May 12, 1986, Saanich Parents for French presented a petition from 245 parents in the district supporting French immersion. SPF followed this up with a second petition on May 26 that had particular emphasis on parents from Trustees Esther Galbraith's and Marilyn Loveless's (both opponents of the program) constituencies. Of the 666 households that answered the door and did not have children in French immersion, 72 percent opposed the board's decision, 20 percent had no opinion, and only 8 percent supported the cancellation of immersion.[36]

Not all parents supported French immersion, and opponents expressed their hostility. Their letters speak to a variety of fears and insecurities. Bonnie Heyldig, a parent of two children in the English program at Deep Cove, thought that a presentation given to parents of kindergarten children in 1982 had left them with the impression that those who did not opt for EFI were depriving their children of the best possible education, and "their attitude certainly implied I was narrow-minded and lacked insight." She further complained that French-speaking teachers spoke French in the staffroom deliberately to exclude English teachers.[37] Janet and Chris Wakefield complained that class sizes in the English program were swelling to more than thirty students apiece and alleged that French immersion classes were smaller and diverted learning assistants who would otherwise be in the English classes. The Wakefields also said that traffic in the school area was a risk for children who rode their bikes to school.[38] The discourse of a program pitting a privileged minority against the majority resonated with opponents in Saanich and was apparent in a document that called French immersion parents "a highly-organized, special interest group [that] chooses to lobby the board for special treatment for a small group of children." They raised the spectre of school-wide split classes, forced busing of children out of their home districts, and amalgamation or closure of schools. For these parents, Saanich was too small to support what they called a "parallel system in the French language."[39]

The board agreed in early May 1986 to review their decision, which gained support from the local French teachers and French department heads.[40] By the end of the month, a compromise was reached. EFI would be maintained, and new classes would be admitted in the fall, but there would not be an incoming cohort of immersion students at the kindergarten level in the fall of 1987; that would not be reinstated until the fifty-fifty balance was re-established in these schools. The immersion program would not be permitted to expand beyond the existing two schools. A single switch vote permitted this reprieve for the program for another year. In its report to the national organization, SPF credited the success to framing the issue as one of providing choices, and avoiding threats or demonstrations, thus allowing the board a means to save face. SPF also noted how important it was both to mobilize broad community support and contact all three levels of government and local francophone groups. The group tried to sustain pressure on the board with what they called "uncomfortable numbers."[41] Moving forward, they hoped to let the dust settle at the local level and then work to obtain a common provincial policy on French immersion.

Over the summer, letters to the school board continued to flow in. There was a high degree of collaboration among the francophone communities of British Columbia, including the Société Historique Franco-Colombienne of Vancouver, the Association des francophones de Nanaimo, the Association des parents du programme cadre de Français, and the Fédération des Franco-Colombiens.[42] School board officials hastened to reassure them that the limits on the French immersion program at the kindergarten level were intended to be temporary and did not mean that the board was rolling back its commitment to improved French education. But despite pressure from SPF, the decision not to offer a kindergarten French immersion class in 1987 was maintained.[43] In the fall 1986 school board elections, a slate of trustees less favourable to immersion was elected.

Saanich parents tried to get a court ruling that section 23 of the Charter of Rights and Freedoms meant that anglophone parents had a legal right to French immersion. However, in a decision rendered on September 2, 1987, Madam Justice Proudfoot ruled against the parents.[44] Her decision noted that Jean Chrétien himself, the federal justice minister, had indicated that, when the charter was drafted, section 23 rights did not apply to the linguistic majority. The provincial attorney general had also weighed in against the parents, arguing that, if this right was deemed to exist, it might deter school boards from experimenting with the programs because they would become legally bound to retain them indefinitely.

There had been parallel developments at the provincial level. In the summer of 1987, the BC Ministry of Education adopted a new set of guidelines stating that French immersion programs must parallel the English program and that districts with EFI were required to offer it at the kindergarten level. Although this opened the door to a new avenue for pressure, Yvonne Rolston noted her concern that "there is a sense of being left to the mercy of a local board whose private vision of language education is coloured by a personal need to save face and a fear of the popularity of bilingual education."[45] The Saanich parents feared that, if they pushed too hard with this new policy, the board might just decide to cancel the program altogether, so they decided to work behind the scenes with ministry and board officials. Over time, much of the heated rhetoric diminished, while large wait lists for French immersion, coupled with the ministerial guidelines, put pressure on the board to reinstate the kindergarten classes.[46]

The Saanich case is instructive for a number of reasons. This was not a district that had particularly active anti-French organizations, yet there was a current of suspicion that it was francophones who were working for bilingualism. It was also a clear example of urban-rural tensions playing out in a semi-rural district. The pedagogy of French immersion was never really in question. Rather, issues of elitism versus "the majority" played out in a district that had opted to limit enrolments because of the program's popularity. Added into the mix were concerns over job losses and alleged tensions between "regular" and immersion students and teachers. Issues of class and opportunity were at the forefront of these disputes. On a tactical level, it was a district where a mix of strategies was needed at different phases of the program's development. The most heated battles played out at the trustee level. Parents had to elect supportive trustees to get the program started, but once it was partially established they had to be careful about how much pressure they placed on the sitting trustees if they were to avoid being perceived as snobby elitists and risk cancellation of the program. Careful management of allied groups, and a major grassroots outreach to parents without children in the program, using the language of opportunities, while also being active proponents of a better core French program for all students, were all crucial in terms of positioning Saanich Parents for French as a viable intervener with widespread support.

Ferryland and St. John's, Newfoundland

Elitism and program caps were also at the centre of a furore in Newfoundland in 1986–87. A press firestorm was spurred by Frank Galgay, school superintendent for the Roman Catholic School Board in Ferryland, on the Avalon peninsula. Galgay called immersion elitist and alleged that the program was robbing funding from the core program.[47] He claimed that the costs of French immersion were borne by the school boards after the lead classes, that class sizes were much smaller in French immersion, and that the program was leading to overcrowding in the regular program – all critiques that arose elsewhere in the country. It was all couched in the rhetoric that this was "at the expense of the majority of students for whom the school system has a responsibility to provide a well rounded education." Galgay saw French immersion as "further penaliz[ing] the majority of students," and this was "of great concern to the silent majority of this province." His solution was to relegate French immersion to a "private school system," possibly with limited government support.[48]

The St. John's chapter of Canadian Parents for French responded to Galgay with an op-ed piece in the *St. John's Telegram*. Susan Knight and Nina Beresford pointed out the ongoing nature of federal funding for both core and immersion programs, including a detailed discussion of the Official Languages in Education Program (OLEP). They cited pedagogical studies proving the "scientific fact" that more time on task produced greater fluency, and they pointed to the 1984 Gallup poll on Canadian support for French-language programs. On the issue of class sizes, they noted that French immersion classes were often just as crowded as English ones, citing numbers from St. John's elementary schools.[49]

This debate spilled over into the letters to the editor section, continuing for four months. Parents from St. John's wrote that "we believe it is unfair to fund an elitist program like French immersion" until core French had been expanded from kindergarten to grade twelve, when most students did not get core French until grade seven or eight.[50] E.R. Patrick, a regular anti-French correspondent, questioned the benefits of French immersion if there were no jobs in which students would get to speak French and raised the class issue by asking "How many longshoremen's sons are in the program? How many cleaning ladies' daughters?" Patrick and others voiced variants of "How many English immersion schools are there in Quebec?"[51] Anti-French sentiments abounded, including a letter whose writer "thought [that] we had our problems solved with the French back in 1904 when they were finally booted off the French shore."[52] "Fed Up" claimed that bilingualism was to blame for the deficit and that "French is now being pushed down our throats and that is what I and hundreds and thousands of English-speaking Canadians resent."[53] "Frustrated Proud Taxpayer" complained of money being spent to import teachers to "educate our pupils for non-existent jobs" when there were hundreds of unemployed and highly qualified teachers in the province. This taxpayer resented French immersion parents because "they think they are part of a privileged group who feel money is no object when it comes to educating their children; if children beyond the overpass cannot ride their school bus over bad roads that is just too bad."[54]

Other Newfoundlanders countered these anti-immersion diatribes. A group of grade six immersion students in St. John's spoke of a variety of career options that they would have beyond the government, including airline pilots, customer service representatives, businesspeople, and teachers.[55] Rosemary (Mercer) Vachon, a Newfoundlander married to a French Canadian serviceman, suggested that star Newfoundland MP John Crosbie's leadership ambitions in the Progressive Conservative Party had been thwarted by his unilingualism. Her letter highlighted a theme that divided pro- and anti-bilingualism camps in Newfoundland. Those favouring French immersion often raised the promise of job opportunities outside the province. As Vachon noted, "perhaps many of our offspring will stay in Newfoundland but as our population census shows, many will leave and there is now and will only be an increase in the number of employment opportunities where bilingualism is a necessity all through this country." If French immersion were wiped out, it would be at the cost of their children's future, including the "dream of their son or daughter obtaining the highest post in our Canadian government one day 20 or 30 years hence ... No wonder we are considered goofie Newfies."[56] Even grandparents, such as Philomena

Chafe, thought that the program was necessary because of the opportunities that it might open.[57] Newfoundland's difficult economic times in the 1980s, a major push factor for migration, were an important motivator for promoting opportunities for bilingualism.

These events reflect broader patterns of how issues related to French-language learning had to be addressed in Newfoundland. Jan Finlay joined the local St. John's chapter of CPF when her family moved from Ottawa to Newfoundland in 1982, and she became the provincial branch president in the mid-1980s. Not all of the province's confessional school boards offered immersion, so her daughter attended a Catholic school in order to access EFI. Finlay's organization worked closely with the local francophone population in St. John's on coordinating events and activities. Showing the dynamism of French Canada, including communities outside Quebec, was a key part of how they framed the need for bilingualism and French-language learning, so they brought in francophone entertainers from other provinces, including Janine Tougas of Manitoba. Finlay noted that, in addition to all of the usual pedagogical concerns about immersion, the themes of elitism and diverting school resources away from the English program were constant. Newfoundland's anti-immersion spokespeople tapped into the "come-from-away" discourse: immersion was an import that served non-Newfoundlanders. It was a charge that resonated because of anecdotal evidence. Finlay recalled that about half of her daughter's class came from families who were new to Newfoundland, though this was a less pronounced phenomenon in other communities.[58]

Newfoundland's French immersion programs did not disappear as a result of these debates, but this case demonstrates the importance of sustained engagement at the community level in order to maintain support and mobilize evidence and public opinion in support of French-language education. It also highlights the importance of local circumstances to how French programs were both defended and justified.

Conclusion

Although separated by over 7,000 kilometres, advocates of bilingualism in these Canadian communities experienced similar challenges and employed similar tactics. Direct engagement with parents, media outreach in local papers, and mobilization of pedagogical evidence were key to making the case for improved programs. All of these groups wrestled with variants of issues of elitism and access to the best French program options. But local circumstances and key individuals were also crucial to shaping how these campaigns unfolded. A single trustee's vote could make the difference whether French immersion was offered or not, and local school boards were subject to specific community pressures. Varying provincial policies also affected whether school boards had to offer open access to immersion (as in New Brunswick) or not (as in British Columbia). In some provinces, active francophone community support was key to pressuring school boards for improved programs for English speakers. The national CPF organization and its provincial branches kept in contact with the local chapters in these communities throughout these campaigns.[59] They provided tactical advice, statistics, poll data, and pedagogical material. The stories of local chapters were also related to CPF members in provincial and national newsletters, sharing expertise and learning from their campaigns. Yet each group ultimately had to craft its messages and use tactics that would resonate at the local level, and each group relied on the energies and skills of key volunteers to drive its efforts forward.

8

Shifting Priorities in the Commissioner's Office

D'Iberville Fortier became Canada's third commissioner of official languages in the fall of 1984, fresh from a term as ambassador to Belgium. He was the first francophone and the first Quebecer to occupy the post. His successor, Dr. Victor Goldbloom, a former Quebec MNA and head of the Canadian Council of Christians and Jews, was an anglophone Quebecer and a prominent member of Montreal's Jewish community. As such, he was the first member of one of Canada's official language minority communities to occupy the office.[1] The diplomat and the politician took different approaches to the mandate of their office insofar as their advocacy role was concerned. Overall, both pulled back substantially from the emphasis on individual bilingualism that had been more integral in the terms of Keith Spicer and Maxwell Yalden. Although the individual initiatives of these men are evident in how they managed the affairs of their respective offices and instigated projects related to their conceptions of official languages, one can detect a major shift of emphasis in the direction of duality and language rights during their terms.

The Charter of Rights and Freedoms was a key factor in shaping the new priorities of the commissioner's office. Given the new constitutional rights, the 1980s and 1990s were key decades for official language minority groups fighting for school governance rights and using section 23 of the charter as part of this quest.[2] These were years of intense confrontation in Quebec as its English-speaking population began to redefine itself as a linguistic minority in the province. Anglophone Quebecers challenged the province's language laws in the court system, using both the provincial charter and the federal charter.[3] An increased emphasis on linguistic minority rights was thus not an unexpected new dimension of the commissioners' activism and interventions. The commissioners were sensitive to official language minorities concerned with language rights and possible negative impacts of bilingualism (as a step to linguistic assimilation). They also tread carefully against a constitutional backdrop of the Meech Lake and Charlottetown Accords and the 1995 Quebec Referendum.

Reorienting the Youth Program

This shift in priorities started early in Fortier's mandate and was evident in the Information Branch's Youth Program. Although Fortier inherited a number of initiatives from Yalden's period – Oh! Canada 2, Telephone, and bilingual posters aimed at children, to name but a few – the long-term future of these initiatives was unclear. Christine Sirois, head of the Information Branch, asked Tony Smith, head of Living Dimensions, a consulting firm that worked with the commissioner's office, to pull together a document in 1984–85 about renewal and the future of the branch. Two key factors shaped this renewal. The first factor was that the commissioner wanted to devote new resources to the "second pillar" of official languages policy: a commitment to Canada's linguistic duality beyond the confines of the federal government (the "first pillar"). The second factor was that the Information Branch's budget for production and dissemination of information was the largest discretionary amount in the commissioner's overall budget. The new priority for the branch was to be a "concerted ... effort involving both the public and the private institutions to which the official language minorities relate." This entailed a reallocation of resources toward official language minorities and opinion leaders in the field of language rights and an explicit shift of the content of the Youth Program toward minority communities and official language rights. Smith noted that the Youth Program would need to foster a sense of community pride among young members of official language minority communities, increase awareness among youth of the majority communities of the existence of these minority communities, and "allow the majority to identify with the minority thus creating understanding of minority situations."[4] Accordingly, new projects were identified for each youth demographic to promote awareness of and support for linguistic duality and the rights of linguistic minorities. The promotion of individual bilingualism and second-language learning among majority community members was not identified as part of this new direction.

One of the first Information Branch projects to face discontinuation was Lend an Ear. Intended to be a more extensive audio component to accompany Oh! Canada 2 and Telephone, the kit contained the Telephone record and an audiocassette. The two sides of the cassette were unilingual (one English, one French) and contained recordings of an interview with the "alien" of the Telephone record, a narration of an obstacle course race, and the Telephone song. Conceived to provide age-appropriate audio material to help students with pronunciation, remedying a major perceived weakness of the Oh! Canada 2 kit, the Lend an Ear kit was given a limited production run and tested in the National Capital Region in 1985.[5] The kit was evaluated by Living Dimensions against the new 1985 criteria of the Youth Program "to inform young people about the special official status of the English and French languages in Canada; to increase young people's awareness of where English and French are spoken and by whom; to sensitize young people to linguistic rights seen from a majority and a minority viewpoint."[6] The new policy was to deliver these messages in the first language of the target audience, marking a break from the mixed-language format of the Oh! Canada kits. The kit, however, flopped. The evaluation conducted with teachers found that none of these messages was contained in the kit. This was not surprising given that Lend an Ear was developed prior to adoption of these priorities. More to the point, the teachers thought that the vocabulary was too advanced for their students, so, even as pedagogical second-language teaching material (which the commissioner's office did not intend to produce), the kit was not useful.[7] It was discontinued in 1986 primarily because of its failure to meet these new messaging priorities. Its fate signalled the new direction of the Youth Program. The problematic Oh! Canada 2 kit, with its bilingual comic book, was distributed until its most recent reprint ran out in the late 1980s; it was not reprinted again because "children need to be bilingual to use the material."[8]

The impact of the new policy direction was evident in the first major production developed during Fortier's term. Agenda was designed for grade eleven students. The commissioner's office sought to use this series of school planners to promote positive messages about Canada's official languages and language rights (official language minority rights specifically) across the country. The first version of Agenda, launched for the 1987–88 school year, was distributed through service clubs such as Girl Guides and Boy Scouts.

In subsequent years, the commissioner's office worked directly with school boards, aiming to reach about 50 percent of students in this age cohort. Agenda had a seven-year run until it was discontinued after 1993–94 for budgetary reasons. Its most significant feature was how explicitly its creators and promoters framed its objectives. Ghislaine Frappier, senior officer for the Youth Program, explained that "the objective of Agenda is to inform 15 to 17 year-olds of the fact that English and French are the two official languages of Canada and that, consequently, they have equal status." From this affirmative starting point, she noted that "the objective of Agenda is not to promote bilingualism" and "not to promote second-language learning." Discussing what sorts of material might be included, such as games, telephone lists, and doodle spaces, she noted that Agenda "must not include exercises related to second-language learning."[9] A clearer disavowal of an interest in using this product to promote bilingualism or second-language learning is difficult to envision. Agenda was pitched as an organizational tool that happened to contain messages about duality and language rights. The study guide for teachers developed in 1989 to accompany Agenda maintained this emphasis.[10] A new set of Youth Program priorities was clearly evident.

Making Movies and Choosing Adventures
In line with this new policy directive, the commissioner's office returned to the film studio, working on its first video project since the early 1970s. Targeting five to seven year olds for the first time, the commissioner's office accepted a proposal from Hinton Animation Studios (producer of the popular television series *The Raccoons*) to develop an animated film initially entitled *Curio Birds*, which evolved into *The Magic Mural*. In its final form, it told a fantastical story of two birds, the anglophone Daniel and the francophone Julie, that tumble into a magical mural and begin an adventure involving a snake, a wizard, and a dinosaur. Daniel and Julie work together despite their inability to speak each other's language. The film was meant to convey a pair of key messages aimed at this age demographic: that people can get along even if they do not understand one another's language and that people can do things together even if they do not understand one another's language.[11] These messages were chosen because staff at the commissioner's office believed that concepts of official languages, rights, and even "Canada" were too complicated and sophisticated for young children. The messages centred on tolerance and friendship between people who cannot speak each other's language. The creators were explicitly told that the

movie must "be completely accessible in the *first official language of the reader.* No knowledge of the second official language should be required. *The creation of second language learning exercises must be avoided.*"[12] Preliminary evaluations made it clear that children would not see the video as conveying the message that second-language learning was a good idea, since the birds became friends without being able to understand each other. The consulting team leading the evaluation believed that the film might prime children for this message from their second-language teachers.

Throughout Fortier's and Goldbloom's tenures, the Information Branch struggled with its mandate to produce material that urged acceptance of official languages without explicitly promoting individual bilingualism. As other proposals for videos and information kits were discussed by the advisory committee for the Youth Program, those promoting the message that "bilingual is better" were weeded out as inappropriate.[13] The committee had moved away from a list of eight key messages previously included: "Speaking Canada's two official languages is fun (e.g. travel, new friendships, cultural activities)" and "Speaking Canada's two official languages is useful (e.g. education, careers, business, travel)."[14] As of 1985, all messages that explicitly promoted personal bilingualism had been dropped, and material that required personal bilingualism was to be avoided. However, problems surfaced because the Information Branch contracted out the development of new material, inviting proposals from creative organizations. Many of these proposals still urged bilingualism, even though guidelines for new submissions included clear directives:

> You **must avoid** ... proposals that place emphasis on second language learning. "Learn the other official language" is not the message we wish to transmit; proposals that imply that it is very difficult to be a member of an official language minority and it would be better to be bilingual; and proposals that mix the two languages ... We are looking for material that focuses on the importance of the English and French languages, but that relies on the first official language of the audience to communicate this idea.[15]

In a review of proposals conducted in November 1989, branch officials despaired at the generally low quality of the proposals received and the fact that so many involved translation, vocabulary exercises, or an emphasis on the message "learn the other official language." Most were oriented toward the idea of a travelogue of a trip across Canada and/or the message of triumphing over adversity through both official languages.[16] Many proposals were never developed or were abandoned after development. Despite this official stance against kits that required bilingualism, when considering an activity book pitched by Les Éditions de la Chenelière, advisory committee members observed that "we should avoid using a seal as a character."[17] Not all children, after all, could be assumed to be unilingual!

Eventually, a replacement for Oh! Canada 2 that did not require bilingualism was developed. Adventures in Time was conceived for children ten and eleven years old as an adventure story about two children who travel through time and space learning about Canada and its language groups. Diane and Paul, from a family of both English and French Canadians, travel in a time machine made from a giant clothes dryer, completing their family tree by visiting different times and places in Canadian history and meeting their ancestors. The activity book was modelled on the popular "Choose Your Own Adventure" books, giving readers a variety of "decision points" affecting how the story unfolds.[18] (Unlike the books on which it was based, none of the decision points ends in "certain doom!") The books were developed from 1990 to 1993 and went into distribution in 1994–95.[19] Although successful, Adventures in Time was one of the last kits of its type to be produced and distributed by the branch. By 1992, it was starting to face budgetary constraints that also spelled the end of Agenda.[20]

Myth Busting and Promoting National Unity

In the early 1990s, with constitutional crises constantly in the news, D'Iberville Fortier and Victor Goldbloom redirected many of the informational efforts of the Office of the Commissioner of Official Languages toward adult populations, urging national unity and tolerance in troubled times. Amid a national recession, budgets for the activities that once characterized the Information Branch were unavailable. Nevertheless, the branch made it a priority to counter misinformation about the Official Languages Act (revamped in 1988 thanks in part to urging from Fortier) and federal language policy. The commissioner's office published booklets aimed at adults entitled *Official Languages: Some Basic Facts* and later reworked as *Official Languages: Myths and Realities*. They aimed to dispel myths about Canada's official languages policies. This effort included providing statistics to prove that only a minority of civil service positions (under 30 percent during this period) required bilingualism. Data from public opinion polls were used to show strong Canadian support for the policy and for second-language teaching (discussed in Chapter 9). The booklets clarified, yet again, that the official languages policy was not about "French being shoved down people's throats"[21] but about placing the onus of bilingualism on the government. On the other hand, the booklets noted that becoming bilingual was "an opportunity for personal development" and "a contribution to nation building,"[22] "a welcome opportunity ... for career development" and "a sound investment in our country's future,"[23] and "a personal asset that also represents an asset for the country."[24] The commissioner's office also published a directory of resources aimed at adults who wanted to maintain or improve their skills in French.[25]

Canadian teenagers were also part of this communications objective. The commissioner's office developed another video aimed at older teenagers and the general public, entitled *Two Languages, One Country*. In development in the later years of Fortier's mandate, it was released right at the end of his term and then reworked in the early years of Goldbloom's term. The video was hosted by an animated map of Canada that talked to the audience about Canada's official languages, the Official Languages Act, and language rights in the country.

In between the map's exposition of various myths and facts about languages in Canada, the video featured short clips of teenaged Canadians (and a few adults) speaking about different language issues. They spoke in the official language of their choice, subtitled depending on the version of the video. The main objectives of the video were to have students understand the historical reasons for the special status of English and French in Canada, the language rights that Canadians enjoy under the Constitution and the Official Languages Act, and the role of the commissioner of official languages. A study guide for the kit included a true/false quiz for students to complete before and after watching the video, with statements such as "the fact that Canada has English and French as its official languages means that all Canadians must be bilingual," "in order to work for the federal government you must be bilingual," and "the Office of the COL was formed to promote second-language learning." (For all three, the correct answer was "false.")[26] The map told teenagers watching the video that nowhere in the Official Languages Act does it say anything about Canadians having to be bilingual and that the majority of civil servants did not have to work in both languages. In these respects, *Two Languages, One Country* was typical of the latter phase of information kits produced by the commissioner's office and echoed the messages of the adult-oriented publications.

On the other hand, given the national unity focus of the video and Goldbloom's approach to his office, there was some content on personal bilingualism. The interviews with young Canadians included some who

This animated map of Canada was the host of the video *Two Languages, One Country.* | *Source: Two Languages, One Country,* Office of the Commissioner of Official Languages, 1991.

Among the myths about bilingualism debunked in *Two Languages, One Country* was the claim that Canada's language laws had forced French onto the Corn Flakes box. That decision had been made decades earlier by Kellogg's for marketing reasons. | *Source: Two Languages, One Country,* Office of the Commissioner of Official Languages, 1991.

spoke about what they considered to be the advantages of being bilingual or understanding Canadians from the other language group. A few spoke about the problems of bilingualism or opined that it might be easier if everyone spoke the same language. Although the video's development team were instructed to be careful that nothing in the video was factually incorrect, they were allowed to include clearly demarcated opinion-based material. The study guide for the video included classroom activities such as suggested topics for debate, including "it is important that all Canadians learn to speak both official languages," "bilingualism is not essential to the future of Canada," and "two official languages split a country instead of uniting it."[27] Members of the development team were keenly aware that, in order to be well received by this age group, the video could not sugar-coat the real controversies about official languages and bilingualism. As such, these statements on bilingualism, so assiduously avoided in other Information Branch kits of the period, were included in the form of Canadian public opinion. The commissioner did not take an official stance on these issues in the video, but the debate was nonetheless permitted under the auspices of messages on national unity.

By the mid-point of Goldbloom's term, the Youth Program had largely wrapped up in terms of big, expensive new initiatives. After kits such as Explorations exhausted their print runs, they were not reprinted, and the academic journal *Language and Society*, sponsored by the commissioner's office, ended its run in 1994. The office continued to distribute smaller items, such as posters. Goldbloom chalked up the winding down of the Information Branch's programs to a shift in emphasis of the office's activities and a sense that the time when there was a need for such initiatives had largely passed by the 1990s.[28] Certainly, budgetary constraints were pinching the Information Branch by this point. The full-blown national unity crisis stemming from the constitutional accords and the 1995 Quebec Referendum had also largely superseded an optimistic approach to bilingualism. Moreover, without the second-language learning component, developers had struggled to come up with engaging ideas for the youth kits.

Conclusion

Second-language learning had not lost the personal support of the commissioner of official languages. In 1993, Goldbloom's annual report noted that "we must continue to consider the value of our investments in second-language educational programs and their potential 'revenues' in terms of national harmony, understanding and co-operation. The momentum that has been building over the past quarter-century must not be allowed to abate or we risk sacrificing a national treasure that cannot be replaced."[29] The following year, in a section of his annual report dedicated to individual bilingualism, he commented that

> the motives of Canadians for becoming bilingual may be economic or intel-
> lectual, or both. Is it too naïve to suggest that there is also an act of faith in
> Canada? How many parents simply want to give their children the gift of
> tongues so that they can bridge the linguistic divide and work together to-
> wards common goals? They believe, surely, that knowledge of another lan-
> guage and other cultural values enriches each person, and therefore the
> whole of society.[30]

Goldbloom continued to observe developments in French immersion and second-language learning, and he made supportive speeches. He noted in his 1997 annual report that

> I have been throughout my mandate a strong supporter of second-language
> instruction and have actively cooperated with teachers' associations and
> with parents' organizations such as Canadian Parents for French ... Under
> my aegis our office has continued, in spite of severe budgetary restrictions,
> to fulfil its objectives towards our youth: to promote harmony, understand-
> ing and respect between young English- and French-speaking Canadians.[31]

However, while the Office of the Commissioner of Official Languages had once been a key organizer and initiator of FSL learning campaigns, by the late 1990s it had largely reduced its role to monitoring and supporting the promotional efforts of others.

9

Squaring Off with the Foes of Bilingualism in the Meech Lake Years, 1986–90

As Canadian Parents for French entered its tenth year, its problems largely concerned how to manage and support a successful initiative. The popularity of French immersion was a Canadian phenomenon, with demand outstripping supply. Indeed, school board caps on immersion programs continued to be a huge challenge in the mid-1980s.[1] In Charlottetown in February 1986, 197 parents lined up to register their children for grade one immersion; some waited in line overnight to ensure a spot.[2] The 1987 CPF national conference passed a resolution urging action to combat caps on immersion enrolments, resulting in meetings with provincial education ministers in 1988.[3] In some communities, including Thompson, Manitoba, parents took their school districts to court to fight what they considered a discriminatory transportation policy, a common obstacle to access, and won.[4] The popularity of immersion coexisted with tales of pro-immersion parents who had their driveways littered with nails and received calls threatening their spouses and children if they did not stop fighting for a new French immersion program.[5]

CPF's second decade would prove to be substantially more challenging than its first. In the late 1980s, new constitutional crises and language policies served as flashpoints for anti-bilingualism sentiments. The Alliance for the Preservation of English in Canada (APEC) and other opponents of expanded French-language learning and bilingualism took advantage of political opportunities opened by new language laws such as the Official

Languages Act, 1988, Ontario's French Language Services Act, and Quebec's Bill 178 to mobilize support for their cause. Turmoil over the Meech Lake Accord fuelled anti-Quebec sentiments transferred to a broader discontent over status of the French language. Increasingly, CPF was in direct confrontation with these groups as they turned their ire to French-language educational programs and CPF itself. For most of the latter half of the decade, CPF held its own in the battle for public opinion, but there were clear warning signs that the years ahead would be increasingly rocky.

The Nielsen Task Force
CPF had been feeling fairly secure that, despite a switch from a Liberal to a Conservative government, federal funding for official languages remained a priority. Then came a shock in March 1986. As part of a wide-ranging study of federal expenditures, Deputy Prime Minister Erik Nielsen released the massive report of his task force containing recommendations on options to cut spending, including axing the RCMP's Musical Ride.[6] Although not featured prominently among the recommendations, federal funding for second-language instructional programs was among the potential cuts.

CPF started a Take Your MP to Lunch project to combat this recommendation. Representatives met with their MPs and MLAs to convey the message that "bilingualism in the two official languages is a responsibility of the national government. Excellence in education is an investment in the future and bilingualism is an integral part of a quality education." Members stressed that second-language instruction was helping to turn around public opinion on official-language services for minorities.[7] The provincial directors liaised with the provincial francophone associations to take joint action. The campaign was a success. At its fall meeting with Secretary of State David Crombie, CPF was relieved to learn that the federal government had decided to reject the Nielsen recommendations on second-language instruction.[8] Still, it was a cautionary moment for CPF. Bilingualism was far from being untouchable.

APEC and Ontario's Bill 8
Throughout the 1970s and early 1980s, with the exception of Manitoba, forced into action on the language front because of court decisions, and New Brunswick, implementing its official languages policies, most of the other English-majority provinces had not done much to advance French-language services. Some took a quiet approach to expanding these services but avoided grand gestures that might provoke a backlash. In 1986, Ontario's

Liberal government under David Peterson broke with the incremental approach when it presented Bill 8, the French Language Services Act. The act guaranteed that Ontario's French-speaking citizens had the right to communicate in French with the provincial government and receive government services from the head or central office of any government agency or institution of the legislature as well as from any branch located in certain designated districts. About two dozen districts were covered, including most of the province's major cities and regions with high concentrations of Franco-Ontarians. The act did not automatically apply to institutions funded by the government, such as hospitals or daycare centres, and it was left up to municipalities to determine whether they wanted to be officially bilingual and offer services in both languages.[9]

APEC launched a fight with the Ontario government over Bill 8, claiming that it would lead to anglophones losing jobs to bilingual francophones.[10] It urged its members to attend meetings and hearings in municipalities opting to become bilingual. Bill 8 would be a rallying cry for the alliance over the next few years. APEC also took aim at Canadian Parents for French, dedicating the cover page of a 1986 newsletter to "the unwitting dupes of the Federal government in its insatiable search for ways of strengthening the 'French fact.'" APEC lambasted CPF president Carolyn Hodych, arguing that it was "almost beyond belief" that people like her were demanding "a special education" that was having "extremely detrimental effects on our English-language schools and costing untold millions" while "English-speaking teachers are losing their jobs to French-speaking people from Quebec, France, and other French-speaking countries." APEC claimed that students were being forced to attend schools out of their areas to get English-language education. It strongly endorsed Simon Fraser University linguistics professor Hector Hammerly's contention that "French immersion was a waste of time" because of built-in mistakes in speaking French "which would never be corrected," and it scorned Sharon Lapkin of OISE for defending the program because it was "nice for English-speaking people to be able to communicate with French-speaking people." APEC demanded that the flow of public money to French immersion cease.[11]

Although the CPF board circulated APEC's material to members, it decided not to respond, and to refuse invitations to engage in a direct debate, because "to do so only gave them credibility." The newsletter was added to the CPF crisis kit as an example of hate literature.[12] The national executive met with MPs from eastern Ontario, where APEC was most active, and got the sense that the alliance was not being taken seriously.[13]

Peter Brimelow, *The Patriot Game*

Peter Brimelow was one of the more prominent gurus of APEC and the anti-bilingualism movement of the mid-1980s. A self-described "wandering WASP," born in the United Kingdom in 1947, he lived in Canada in the early to mid-1970s and worked for American senator Orrin Hatch in the late 1970s. Brimelow became an editor for *Forbes* magazine in 1986, later becoming a star of the conservative movement in the 2000s. In 1986, he published *The Patriot Game*, a scathing indictment of the Liberal Party's approach to Canadian identity and politics, particularly the place of Quebec and the French language within Canada.[14] Brimelow saw this approach as a suppression of the natural English majority culture of Canada by the hegemonic ideology propagated by a left-wing, English-speaking minority in conjunction with a united French-speaking majority. The book was a natural successor to the BMG-published books of the late 1970s. Brimelow argued that the natural inclination of Canada's English-speaking majority was toward free-market, liberal policies, with English as the sole language of communication. This inclination had been subverted and cowed into submission by an alliance between "alienated" left-wing anglophone Liberals and their French-speaking allies. Pierre Trudeau's government, Brimelow argued, reshaped the hegemonic narrative of Canada to one in which appeasement of the French Canadian minority was essential to the country's survival. This allowed left-wing English speakers to work together with statist French Canadians to reshape the country.

Brimelow argued that "English Canada's British Heritage has been systematically subverted ... The extraordinary result is that in Canada today, it is the Anglophones and not the Francophones who are the colonized group ... [The Anglophones] have been prevented from following the political patterns of their cultural siblings, America and Britain."[15] This "problem" had subverted the Tory party, which explained how the party of the English majority could elect Brian Mulroney, a Quebecer and an "unknown and quite atypical leader," as its leader over unilingual anglophone John Crosbie, who would have represented the "perfectly natural" desire of anglophones for a "representative leader."[16] However, Brimelow believed that the Liberal hegemony was failing and would give rise to separatism in both Quebec and western Canada.

His starting point was that the Liberal "bedrock" vote was a coalition of minorities alienated from the culture of the majority of English Canada. "Conniving" anglophone minority leaders of this coalition were disaffected from their own community for either family or psychological reasons and led the party of "Western suicide."[17] For Brimelow, a "guilty sensibility of contemporary English Canada" toward the past that had lasted for two generations had led, "by a succession of steps, each apparently as reasonable as the last, English Canadians ... to abandon and forget their original position, which is that Canada was English-speaking with a French community allowed to function internally in French." From his perspective, "there was nothing atrocious about this position. On a world scale of majority attitudes to minorities, it was distinctly amiable." Moreover, Brimelow made the astonishing claim that, "although it is now unpopular to say so in Quebec, the traditional Anglophone position was obviously accepted by French Canadians."[18]

The problem, for Brimelow, was that "it takes nerve to look a minority member in the eye and tell him that at a given point his language and his community must yield to the official language and the national community ... Sometime in this century, English Canada lost its nerve."[19] French immersion was a sign that "the minority has the moral initiative in Canada" because "children of the majority [had] to bear the brunt of acculturation ... when their language is that of the entire continent."[20] Like other critics, Brimelow questioned the efficiency of immersion, claiming that studies in Quebec showed that "significant proportions of the graduates from immersion schools cannot function in French at college level" and that immersion children rarely spoke French at home or in the street. He claimed that the numbers of children in these "heavily subsidized" programs were "derisory" and that "their popularity may well be in part another desperate lunge by middle-class parents trapped by the deteriorating schools common to all North America, and mindful of the element of coercion introduced by the federal government's bilingual hiring preferences."[21] He noted that, for every bilingual anglophone, there were nearly fifteen in Canada who spoke only English, a state of unilingualism that he qualified as "not in any way surprising, perverse or unnatural,"[22] merely part of a normal state of affairs, given that "free people do not generally learn new languages at the request of their governments,"[23] citing the example of Gaelic in Ireland. Brimelow claimed that Canadians were engaged in "a devastating rejection of the bilingualism experiment," evident from "the obstinate non-materialization of significant numbers of bilingual Canadians."[24] He thought that the days of these policies were not likely to endure given what he called English Canada's "resentment of official bilingualism [that,] although amorphous, is profound."[25]

Brimelow's work was particularly popular with APEC because of how it fed into the discourse of victimization. Brimelow claimed, and APEC regularly repeated, that "Ottawa has already shown that it will not scruple to interpret bilingualism as a mandate for an ethnic quota."[26] The bilingual air traffic control crisis of 1976 was special, making headlines because bilingualism was "forced" on controllers, and "the victims of bilingualism are usually too scattered and unorganized to gain the attention of the Anglophone majority, on whom the policy impinges only indirectly."[27] He also quoted from Richard Gwyn's *The Northern Magus* to describe language classes for anglophone civil servants in which they were "sometimes ... reduced to tears by petites *Québécoises* who were either separatists or feminists or both, and who delighted in their revenge."[28] Pity the victims of bilingualism and language learning, and fight the loss of anglophone moral authority at the heart of Canadian bilingualism and official languages policies: these were the rallying cries of *The Patriot Game*.

APEC, NAER, and French Immersion in Brockville
One such "victim" drawn to APEC's message was Faye Garner, a clerk-typist who worked in Brockville's probation office. Garner lost a competition to a francophone for a permanent position in 1985 and apparently was told that this was because she did not speak French. Garner claimed that the woman who got the job was hired by another francophone, despite poorer results on other tests, because of her French-language skills. Garner took her case to the Ontario Human Rights Commission but was turned down because language was not considered a form of discrimination. She then pursued her case through the grievance process of the Ontario Public Service. Her MPP, Progressive Conservative Bob Runciman, an opponent of Bill 8, called her case a clear example of the Liberal government's commitment to covertly make Ontario officially bilingual.[29] In 1986, Garner became the founding president of the Brockville chapter of the Alliance for the Preservation of English in Canada.[30] Her case is an interesting tale of how a personal grievance – whether real or perceived – can lead an individual to crusade against bilingualism and French immersion.

Over the fall and winter of 1986–87, Garner delivered speeches, wrote letters to the editor, and published APEC ads, taking aim at proposals to create a French immersion program in the Leeds and Grenville County Board of Education. Garner claimed that Ottawa was creating an artificial need for the French language, and she took OISE research findings wildly out of context to cast doubt on the program.[31] She claimed that French immersion created so much work that children could not keep up. She also alleged that the Canadian government would pass over English speakers with French-language skills in favour of mother tongue francophones.[32] Brockville APEC ads claimed that francophones were being disproportionately appointed to government positions, that David Peterson planned to make Ontario officially bilingual, that $1.3 million per day was "squandered" to promote French in English Canada, that the dropout rate from French immersion was 40–50 percent, and that the past president of CPF, Carolyn Hodych, had called French immersion "a façade." APEC called for a complete end to government-funded French immersion.[33]

Against this backdrop, the school board voted down a proposal in the fall of 1986 to create a middle French immersion program. Local CPF members did not think that this decision was directly connected to APEC's activities, for this had been the long-standing board position, but they did monitor APEC. The husband of Marilyn Caners, a Brockville CPF member, even attended an APEC meeting. He noted that it attracted fifty people, only three of whom were young men, the rest being conservative senior citizens. His impression was that APEC was gaining some traction largely because Brockville was becoming a retirement community and a haven for anglophone ex-Montrealers who had fled Quebec, bringing their grievances with them.[34] Despite APEC's activities in the region, the school board voted in February 1987 to review the feasibility of starting a middle French immersion program for the fall of 1988.[35]

The local chapter of CPF nevertheless kept close tabs on the activities of Garner and APEC. Gail Vavro, the local chapter president, worried that APEC was having an impact on local trustees. Garner repeated her anti-immersion stump speech – largely based on an anti-immersion piece by Katherine Govier in *Toronto Life* in 1986 – on numerous occasions, including before the school board on March 8, 1987. Garner attacked the program for projected job losses for English staff, for how it would lead to busing of students out of the district, and for the lack of need for such a program in a region with a small French workforce. She deliberately misrepresented OISE researchers, claiming that the initial lag in developing English-language skills was permanent.[36] Her supporters followed this up with a series of letters to the editor, often with the theme of the "unwarranted influence" of French speakers in Ontario.[37] These letters cited approvingly *The Patriot Game* and called for English Canada to wake up and assert its English North American identity. Members of CPF responded calmly and refuted the claims of APEC, citing bilingual job prospects and the optional nature of the program. CPF called on parents to take positive steps to open doors for their children rather than live in "the dream world of English supremacy."[38]

Most trustees seem to have been less concerned with APEC's spectre of domination by Quebec and imposed bilingualism and more inclined to debate the necessity of immersion, with some trustees questioning costs of the program. In October 1987, the school board voted to conduct a survey of parents' interest for a fifty-fifty middle French immersion program in the fall of 1988.[39] A pilot program to start with one grade five class was officially approved by a 7:4 vote of the board in March 1988. Admission would be decided by lottery.[40] This capped a five-year campaign by Brockville CPF. A second class was then added in Kemptville. The vote succeeded despite the argument of Faye Garner and the National Association for English Rights (NAER), her newest affiliation, that 70 percent of parents did not want the program. Trustees who voted no, including Don Davis, claimed that immersion would not make the students bilingual and that the federal government would find reasons other than language to deny anglophones jobs.

The early years of immersion in Leeds-Grenville's school board were tenuous, with a series of votes on maintaining the grade five class and whether to add a follow-up grade six class. The program was under regular threat of cancellation, pitting immersion supporters largely concentrated in Brockville and Kemptville against opponents in Gananoque and more rural areas.[41] Brockville also made national headlines when a group of anti–Bill 8 protesters stomped on the Quebec flag and then tried to light it on fire during a visit by Premier Peterson and his caucus in September 1989.[42] In 1991, seeking some guarantee of program continuity, pro-immersion trustees voted 10:5 to have a board policy that would offer French immersion annually in grade five (and continued in grade six) when numbers and finances permitted. Proponents of the program noted that substantial proportions of the region's graduates ended up seeking employment in the National Capital Region, where bilingualism was key to finding jobs.[43] After six years, despite vocal opposition from APEC, the issue finally seemed to be settled.

The Meech Lake Accord

The ultimately unsuccessful process of ratifying the Meech Lake Accord from 1987 to 1990 created a difficult climate for bilingualism in Canada.[44] A large number of social movement organizations opposed the accord. Some convinced their governments to hold public hearings on it and either temporarily or permanently rescind their support. A number of these groups, encouraged by past prime minister Pierre Trudeau's attack on the deal,[45] were concerned about its implications for linguistic minorities and the role of the federal government in shared-cost programs.

CPF's first round of engagement with the Meech Lake Accord came in late May 1987. The major groups representing minority language communities – Alliance Quebec and the Fédération des francophones hors-Québec – had expressed concern that the new accord did not adequately safeguard linguistic minorities. CPF's analysis echoed this perspective.[46] The crucial issue was the language to be added to the Constitution to recognize Quebec as a "distinct society" and deal with questions of duality. The accord contained wording on "French-speaking Canadians" "centered in Quebec but also present elsewhere in Canada," and "English-speaking Canadians" "concentrated outside Quebec but also present in Quebec," and the roles of governments in dealing with this duality. The Quebec government had a responsibility to "preserve and promote" the distinct identity of Quebec, whereas the other provincial governments and the federal government were to "preserve" the duality as described above.[47] Canadian Parents for French and francophone minority organizations were concerned that there was no visible evidence in the accord of an ongoing commitment by either level of government to recognition, and especially promotion, of official languages.

In response, CPF provincial branch presidents wrote to their respective premiers, asking each provincial government to make a commitment to support and promote the two official languages.[48] National president Susan Purdy wrote to the three federal party leaders expressing her organization's grave reservations about what the accord might mean for the bilingual future of Canada, given the uneven provincial record of commitment to official languages. She called for all of the premiers and the prime minister to make firm commitments to "promote" the two official languages.[49] In a national news release entitled "Accord May Cause Crisis, Group Warns," Purdy stated that "we believe it is the right of all Canadians to become bilingual. If we do not ensure that this is so, we reduce many of our people to the status of second class citizens. We believe all Canadians have the right to feel at home across this land, in either French or English."[50] Purdy feared that the accord might lead to the unravelling of programs such as the Official Languages in Education Program (OLEP), which provinces might opt out of (under Meech Lake's provisions for opting out of shared-cost programs) or the federal government might feel less obligated to fund.

The initial response to these telegrams from federal leaders was not particularly encouraging. None of the three leaders replied directly to CPF's concerns over the future of official languages programs under the accord. Brian Mulroney and John Turner sent generic letters outlining their parties' official stances on the accord.[51] Turner did indicate, though, his desire for "better protection of minority language rights both inside and outside Quebec."[52]

Parliamentary hearings provided an opportunity for CPF to voice its concerns. In August 1987, Susan Purdy, New Brunswick director Berkeley Fleming, and Alberta director Fiona Cleary spoke to the special joint committee of the Senate and House of Commons on the 1987 constitutional accord. Purdy observed that, when it came to language issues, maintaining the status quo was not enough and that the accord should be amended to speak about not just the protection but also the promotion of French outside Quebec. She raised the spectre of a "linguistic curtain" being drawn around Quebec as the only province with a responsibility for promoting French, noting that it would lead to a decrease in the number of envoys for greater openness. She also raised concerns about how amendments to shared-cost programs might affect the OLEP. Citing research and poll data, she argued that federal funding of second-language education was leading to greater openness and a turn-around in public opinion on minority language rights. To address these shortcomings, she wanted wording on "promotion" of language added with reference to the other governments and a mechanism put in place to ensure that provinces that opted out of shared-cost programs still met national objectives. Purdy also called for more courage on the second-language front, arguing that public attitudes toward bilingualism had changed significantly in the past few years. Canada's political reality, she claimed, was lagging behind public opinion, so governments should seize the opportunity to enhance Canadian unity through greater commitment to bilingualism.[53]

Although members of the committee expressed general support for CPF's work, they did not appear to share its concern. Most seemed to think that including the word *preserve* was a major concession from the provinces, a position held by Senator Brenda Robertson of New Brunswick.[54] NDP MP Pauline Jewett seemed to think that the obligation to preserve, in most provincial contexts, would de facto imply the need to promote language rights and programs.[55] On the other hand, CPF's argument resonated in certain academic circles. John Whyte, dean of law at Queen's University, echoed the argument that the Meech Lake Accord might create "unilingual linguistic enclaves" and that its language might indeed be read as opposing the growth of bilingualism. Whyte suggested that halting the spread of bilingualism and following an enclave-based policy could give even more power to the few bilingual citizens able to communicate across those barriers and to the entire nation.[56]

Members of the CPF Alberta chapter made their own presentation to the Senate committee of the whole on the accord, raising specific issues relevant to their province. They feared that Alberta's endorsement of the accord was really not about appreciation of Quebec's demands but about a desire for more control in Alberta over policies, including those on language. They feared detrimental impacts on the francophone minority, where section 23 rights had yet to be fully implemented, and on the promotion of bilingualism to the non-francophone population. Alberta, after all, was where MLA Léo Piquette was forced to apologize for using French in the legislature and where the minister for advanced education mused that money used to teach French would be better spent on Japanese. For CPF Alberta, the opting-out provisions of the Meech Lake Accord held potentially devastating prospects for bilingualism.[57]

These concerns were not addressed via an amended accord. It was not the rights of francophone minorities or bilingual education that fed the massive public backlash against the accord. Instead, it was the rights of anglophones in Quebec, as will be discussed shortly, that fed the anger in many English Canadian communities. However, CPF's response to the Meech Lake Accord demonstrated its worry that the ongoing commitment of the federal government to promoting bilingualism everywhere in the country might be slackening. It also pointed to ongoing concern that many provinces had not fully embraced the idea that they had their own obligations and responsibilities on the language front.

The Official Languages Act, 1988

At the time of the Meech Lake Accord process, the federal government of Brian Mulroney was revisiting the Official Languages Act. Bill C-72 was first announced in 1987 and officially adopted in 1988 as the Official Languages Act, 1988. Among the new provisions were several components of Part V of the act that strengthened the right of civil servants to work in the official language of their choice. The new Part VII, "Advancement of English and French," gave statutory authority to the various activities that the Department of the Secretary of State had been carrying on since the 1970s in promoting the rights of official language minority communities and promoting the two official languages and the learning thereof. Section 43, 1 (b), for instance, gave the secretary of state the authority to take measures to "encourage and support the learning of English and French in Canada," and subsection (e) gave it the power to "encourage and assist provincial governments to provide opportunities for everyone in Canada to learn both English and French."[58]

Canadian Parents for French was very supportive of the revised act. President Susan Purdy expressed her hope that there would also be a renewed commitment to the OLEP rather than the cutbacks in base funding recently suggested. She supported her francophone allies in expressing hope that the government would take a generous approach to an active offer of French government services. Purdy particularly hoped that the new bill would give recognition to the new generation of bilingual Canadians capable in both official languages and appreciative of a heritage that allowed them to speak, read, and write both French and English.[59] CPF drew connections between French immersion and a more tolerant generation of Canadians unafraid of the second language and not prejudiced against it. It urged the federal government to continue supporting both second-language and minority-language education, for they produced the practical advantages of a thoughtful and progressive language policy that increased the number of bilingual Canadians entering the workforce. This enabled governments and the private sector to offer a greater variety of bilingual services to Canadians everywhere.[60] The stronger legislation passed with all-party support, but it was clear that CPF thought it necessary to ensure that the nice words and laws were accompanied by solid moral and financial commitments.

APEC, Jock Andrew, and the Late-1980s Backlash

Although the Official Languages Act, 1988, passed easily, it opened a window of opportunity for anti-bilingualism groups to rally supporters. The Alliance for the Preservation of English in Canada came out swinging against Bill C-72. Although claiming that it was not opposed to either bilingualism or the teaching of French in schools – both doubtful claims given the activities of its members – it was opposed to official bilingualism, which it called "divisive, destructive and discriminatory," and a policy in which Canadians "have had no say." APEC claimed that, if it were allowed to continue, "Canada as a nation will be destroyed" and that it was "humanly impossible to implement a policy and give equality of status and use to both languages." APEC argued that it was not until passage of the OLA in 1968–69 that "problems concerning language began to erupt in this country" and that from that point forward there had been "discrimination against

English speaking people in this country."[61] APEC also rejected the new official languages provisions of the 1982 Constitution.

The alliance vociferously opposed Bill C-72's new provisions on language of work in the civil service as being unworkable and discriminatory.[62] The secretary of state's additional powers to promote the official languages and enhance official language minority groups attracted particular ire. APEC was hostile to these provisions because, it claimed, for every dollar given to French-language groups, only about ten cents went to English-language groups. It further claimed that the government had no interest in fostering the English language in French Canada, but its "attempt to foster the use of the French language in English Canada has been so blatant that the words 'shoving French down our throats' ha[ve] become a common expression in English Canada."[63]

Considering section 133 of the BNA Act as a limiting clause on French, APEC went so far as to claim that "the powers given to the Secretary of State in the proposed Official Languages Act go far beyond the requirements of the Constitution and are an infringement of the right, not only of provinces, of municipalities, of business, labour and volunteer organizations, but are an infringement on the rights of every individual in this country." APEC did not accept the basic premise that the act was about equality, claiming that it was about promoting francophones: "The implementation of the act has been discriminatory right from the very beginning. Even in the hiring of bilingual personnel it has not been enough to be bilingual – one had to be a Francophone."[64] This claim called the validity of bilingual education programs into question.

APEC's Bill C-72 brief was reprinted in Jock Andrew's new book, published in June 1988, entitled *Enough! (Enough French, Enough Quebec)* Andrew alleged that the new Official Languages Act, coupled with provincial French Language Services Acts, comprised the "final moves" of French Canada to make Canada an "entirely French nation," which he claimed had been admitted by former secretary of state Serge Joyal. These acts, Andrew claimed, were designed to bring about "1) The Frenchification of every provincial, regional, city and town government, and their services to the public, across the whole of Canada. 2) The Frenchification of all business, industry, unions, the courts and every enterprise, private or otherwise serving the Canadian public. 3) The Frenchification of all schools and every workplace across Canada."[65] It is difficult to give credence to his conspiracy theory. However, he was invited to speak at APEC gatherings, and his theories were repeated by opponents of bilingualism. Andrew claimed that the revised Official Languages Act would give complete power to the secretary of state, cabinet, and commissioner of official languages to bring about complete Frenchification of the Canadian government public service, Armed Forces, all government agencies and commissions, courts, crown corporations, and all businesses doing business with these corporations. The Meech Lake Accord, he claimed, ratified the "outlawing" of the English language brought about by Bill 101. He asserted that "French Canada has been brought up from birth to hate the 'English' in Canada."[66] He also claimed that the language policy was part of a philosophy of revenge initiated by Pierre Trudeau. The conspiracy theory got thicker; Andrew contended that French Canadian RCMP were planted in every city to spot and report on English speakers who did not agree with Frenchification and that a French CBC crew who filmed three hours of an APEC meeting had passed along their tapes to a Trudeau-created secret police.[67]

Ontario's Bill 8 fuelled his rage. Andrew considered it to be "the instrument by which the English language is to be eliminated from the Province of Ontario."[68] Ontario's French Language Services Act, he wrote, made the main goal of the provincial government the Frenchification of all government services as well as agencies and businesses wanting to receive any provincial money or contract. He claimed that hundreds of thousands of francophones from Quebec and outside Canada were being brought in to fill those French jobs.[69] Bill 8, Andrew believed, gave groups such as the Association canadienne-française de l'Ontario (ACFO) the power to demand French service from a French Canadian whenever they contacted any government institution, and ultimately they wanted that service from every "girl guide cookie salesgirl, lottery ticket salesperson, shopping mall Santa Claus or security guard."[70] In his version of David Peterson's Ontario, nobody was safe from the ravaging hordes of ACFO and its Quebec henchmen.

Andrew believed that it was only a matter of time before speaking English would no longer be permitted by law, so he encouraged all English-speaking Canadians to join and work for APEC, "the finest and most courageous Canadians I have ever met."[71] He urged

> those of you who have been sending your hard-earned savings to the Jim and Tammys, and Jimmy Swaggarts, and Gerry Falwells, in the hope of a better after-life, I suggest your money can be much better spent on APEC in the hope of achieving a better life here and now for you and your children and your grandchildren in the Canada of today and tomorrow.[72]

Andrew made no bones about his hostility toward Quebec, stating that "Quebec and French Canada contributed not one iota to the development and integrity of this country, and very little to its defence in its two world wars."[73] He saw absolutely no need for the French language, noting that, "if we feel compelled to learn a second or third or fourth language, let those languages be ones that do us and Canada some good, such as Russian or Japanese, or Chinese, or Spanish, or Portuguese."[74] Andrew called for steps "to invite ... and if necessary enforce the departure of the state of Quebec from the new Canada."[75]

He also demanded the elimination of French immersion, which he saw as being focused entirely on the French language and the hiring of French Canadian teachers. Although immersion was "not yet compulsory," he believed that every form of propaganda and enticement was being used to lure parents into these programs. He claimed that in some communities parents had no choice but to have their children schooled in French.[76] By the spring of 1989, following passage of the new Official Languages Act by the Progressive Conservative government of Brian "mentally 100% French Canadian" Mulroney,[77] Andrew claimed that, across Canada, French immersion schooling was now no longer the exception but the norm (in a period when less than 10 percent of English Canadians attended these schools). Going further, he believed that immersion schooling "is not intended to teach English-Canadian school children to speak French, but instead to brainwash them into believing that Canada is now a French-speaking country."[78]

Andrew was greatly disheartened that, at the twenty speaking engagements that he had attended since *Enough!* was first published, the leaders of English-speaking communities did not "have the courage to as much as show their noses, let alone the courage to stand up and be counted." He claimed that Bernard Grandmaître, the Ontario minister responsible for French-language services, had wanted his "French-Canadian legions" to break up a gathering of 1,200 who had come to hear Andrew in Sudbury but that "they didn't dare open their mouths." Andrew noted well-attended meetings in Sudbury, Moncton, and Saint John, "where the people have good reason to see what is being done," but he was disappointed that barely forty people turned up to a meeting in Barrie, Ontario, which "has already been designated for Frenchification." From this poor turnout, Andrew opined, English Canadian community leaders were "leaving it to retired school teachers and aging veterans of the Second World War to try to fight this war," and he feared that these people alone were not enough and did not have the necessary political clout.[79]

Andrew drew hope from a new political party willing to stand for one official language of English. He drew readers' attention to Elmer Knutson of Edmonton and the Confederation of Regions (COR) Party, founded to bring about better representation for western Canada in Ottawa via an elected Senate. It also opposed official bilingualism and had run candidates in New Brunswick, Ontario, and western Canada in the 1988 federal election. Andrew believed that the reasonably strong showing of COR in a number of New Brunswick ridings might mean that the party could become the political champion of an anti-bilingualism movement.[80] COR's brief moment in the spotlight came in 1991 when it vaulted into the official opposition in New Brunswick, though it was wiped out in the next election.[81]

Andrew's assessment of the state of anti-bilingualism activism is telling. Although Andrew believed that there was rampant voter anger just waiting to be unleashed, the rallies that he spoke at were not particularly well attended, even by his standards. The most vocal opponents of bilingualism were from an older generation, which set up the conflict as an intergenerational one over visions of Canada and the place of English and French within the country. Although Andrew was disappointed that the anti-bilingualism revolution had not started, his actions and those of APEC were increasingly troublesome to pro-bilingualism organizations.

Bill 178

A Supreme Court ruling on Quebec's language laws added to the linguistic turmoil of the late 1980s. In the *Ford* decision, released on December 15, 1988, the Supreme Court struck down several sections of Quebec's Charter of the French Language that restricted the posting of commercial signs in English.[82] The government of Robert Bourassa announced on December 19 that a new bill would reintroduce the sign laws, invoking the notwithstanding (or override) clause of the Charter of Rights and Freedoms. Bill 178 added the modification that, though outdoor signs had to be in French, indoor signs out of sight from the street could be multilingual, as long as French was predominant. When invoking the notwithstanding clause, Bourassa mused that, had the Meech Lake Accord been in force, the law might have withstood a charter challenge.[83] Critics of the accord saw this as evidence that it would undermine the language rights of Anglo-Quebecers. This became a prominent theme in the publications and rhetoric of APEC and other groups, who saw this as even further evidence that Quebec was anti-English, and therefore English Canada needed to push back against any French-language rights or promotion of bilingualism.

CPF Responds to Anti-Bilingualism Activism

Bill 8 made Ontario a hotbed for APEC activism. The Ontario branch of Canadian Parents for French thus bore the brunt of combatting misinformation. CPF Ontario undertook an information campaign in collaboration with the Ontario government's Office of Francophone Affairs about what Bill 8 actually meant to deal with misinformation on both this bill and the revised OLA. Diane Carlucci, president of CPF Ontario, presented a kit on how it "set the record straight" to the CPF national conference in Banff in 1989. Its campaign against the coalition of opponents of bilingualism – including APEC, the National Association for English Rights (NAER), Alliance Ontario, the Confederation of Regions Party, and the Reform Party – was oriented toward the statement of principle that "bilingualism will unite Canada, and that only if there is harmony between the two languages and cultures will there be continuing opportunities for their children to study French as a second language."[84] CPF tried to advance the message that second-language learning was key to combatting anti-French and anti-bilingualism attitudes.

The challenge was substantial. In the wake of the passage of Bill 8, APEC and Alliance Ontario had launched campaigns to have municipalities declare themselves to be unilingual English. The rhetoric attacking French was wide ranging – and sometimes farcical, with one pamphlet calling French language "demeaning to the female gender, depicting everything feminine that is passive, frivolous or useless."[85] Alliance Ontario, whose most visible spokeswoman was senior citizen Vona Mallory of Barrie, was particularly active, producing a document called "Get the Truth to the People" and calling for information kits to be delivered to offices, schools, mailboxes, car windshields, parks, fairs, and festivals. The alliance held house gatherings to "discuss" French immersion and hand out information to young parents.

The links between Bill 8 and French immersion were tight in the minds of these groups. Alliance Ontario circulated a pamphlet entitled "Questions for French Immersion Parents of Canada," which included a series of statements and questions:

> Do you want your children to be limited in vocabulary? (French language less than a third of the English language)

Have you considered that French is forced on Canadian Society? (No French, no jobs) (legislated bills – C-72, 8 and Meech Lake)

Would you prefer a Communist rule to a Democratic rule? Have you considered Quebec's denial of English rights within our Canadian society? (Bill 178, Quebec).[86]

Other Alliance Ontario material claimed that the government was censoring the latest research on French immersion, that "early age immersion in the French language distorts good English grammar!," and that "French immersion could contribute to French take over of Canada!"[87] CPF was targeted because it received funding from the federal government.

CPF adopted a multi-pronged strategy to combat this campaign. Committees produced documents to counter anti-bilingualism materials. Information on Bill 8 was circulated via CPF Ontario's newsletter. CPF submitted briefs to the 834 Ontario municipalities, gave presentations against the APEC position, and engaged in an active media campaign. As a result, only twenty-three Ontario municipalities held referendums on issues related to bilingualism, and many communities reversed their anti-bilingualism policies. Although this was a difficult period, the adversity brought about closer ties with Franco-Ontarian groups and led to a higher media profile for CPF.

Major newspapers piped up in their condemnation of APEC's activities. *Globe and Mail* columnist Orland French referred to APEC as "an organization about which one writes with fear and trepidation lest someone else think it is a good thing," and that it "fomented anguish and distress among many municipal councils that ought to have known better." He condemned the group whose "paranoia is too thick to be cut with reason."[88] In the fall, as the anti-bilingualism referendum campaigns heated up, the *Globe and Mail* published an editorial about APEC in which it asked "is ignorance catching?" It referred to the group as "an unpleasant organization whose adherents believe the use of the French language should be contained like a contagious illness within the boundaries of the province of Quebec" and who held "the ludicrous notion that English speakers risk becoming an endangered species in Canada." As the editorial observed, "such a notion would be merely laughable but, like other big lies, it conceals a myriad of grimmer deceits and bigotries." It saw this attack on municipal language services as a tactical manoeuvre to scare Ontario and the federal government on the official languages front with a resounding referendum result.[89]

Accordingly, the *Globe* editorialist gave credit to Ontario for resisting this manoeuvre but also criticized the provincial government for not promoting its policies as strongly as it might have.

The anti-bilingualism wave was not limited to Ontario. The BC branch of Canadian Parents for French reported that in 1989 APEC could count about 3,000–4,000 members and four chapters in the province (out of twenty across the country). The group's activities were particularly noticeable in Kelowna, on the Sunshine Coast, and in Nanaimo. CPF BC's assessment of APEC was that it was exclusively white and composed of older members who had no children in the school system.

Yet APEC certainly raised a lot of noise. For example, Nanaimo had a particularly active APEC chapter trying to eliminate French immersion. The district had a fairly well-established early immersion program, plus late immersion and a secondary continuation program, plus an active local Franco-Columbian group.[90] In 1989–90, APEC launched an escalating campaign, including letters to the editor, calls to radio talk shows, pickets at school board meetings, and even anonymous threats to members of CPF. As one CPF member wrote, "this is one discouraged, scared chapter."[91] The provincial branch sent it the crisis kit and offered help in any way possible.

APEC ran ads during the school board election season that used provocative rhetoric:

DO YOU BELIEVE ... That with our national debt approaching $400 billion, we could cut our yearly addition of $30 billion by at least $4 billion if we cut bilingualism and immersion programs. What are we really GIVING OUR CHILDREN – LANGUAGES OR BANKRUPTCY?

DO YOU BELIEVE ... If people in a country like using a language, would they need language police to enforce it?

DO YOU THINK ... In a time like this, our school board can justify spending money on elite separate schools for Immersion Programs, when the dollars should be carefully and fairly used for all children. Be THOUGHTFUL WHEN YOU GO TO THE POLLS.[92]

The Nanaimo CPF chapter reported high levels of stress and exhaustion but ultimately was able to hold on to their programs, with two-thirds of the school board supportive of its efforts.[93]

192 Squaring Off with the Foes of Bilingualism

The 1989 CPF Poll

Amid this turmoil, CPF commissioned a second national poll. Conducted by Environics Research Group as part of its October 1989 Focus Canada National Omnibus survey, the poll contained two components. The first was a survey of 2,079 adult Canadians.[94] The second was a survey of 857 CPF members to elicit a fuller profile of the organization's membership and attitudes.

The most significant finding was that 74 percent of Canadians thought that children in their particular province should learn the other official language in order to become bilingual, with 90 percent of francophones and 69 percent of anglophones giving this response. This support for second-language learning was consistent nation wide, with the highest levels of support among university-educated respondents (81 percent) and in eastern Canada.[95] A majority of respondents in each region was favourable to second-language learning.

Thirty percent of respondents indicated that they had grown more supportive of second-language learning over the past year, versus 15 percent who had become less supportive. Young anglophones aged eighteen to twenty-nine were among those most likely to indicate that they had become more supportive (39 percent). Only in British Columbia could more people be found whose opinions had worsened (25 percent) versus improved (19 percent) on this subject. Asked about the main advantage of learning French, respondents overwhelmingly tilted toward job opportunities, with almost half (49 percent) giving this response, far ahead of personal or intellectual growth (21 percent), or travel (8 percent), with national unity at the bottom with only 3 percent. English-speaking Canadians seemed to be increasingly satisfied with the quality of French education offered to their children.[96]

A majority of English-speaking Canadians also indicated that core French was their preference as a type of French education, with 53 percent picking this option over 17 percent who said French immersion and 19 percent who supported both options. Nationally, 36 percent of English-speaking respondents said that they would enrol their children in French immersion if it were an option, and an additional 10 percent said that they might do so. Support rose starkly with education level.[97] The highest support by region was in Prince Edward Island (62 percent) followed by Toronto (44 percent), whereas the lowest levels of support were in the prairie region at between 26 and 29 percent.

CPF executive members across the country made use of this polling material. They found it useful to have up-to-date statistics to back up their policies and responses to questions from the media, parents, and other interlocutors. It was seen as particularly useful in countering the charges of anti-bilingualism groups to prove that they too had a sense of what the "silent majority" wanted and in discussions with those who did not see the need for French in schools. The material was widely used in submissions to school boards and communications with the media and potential new members.[98]

The poll of CPF members provides a snapshot of members of the organization and how their attitudes and priorities differed from those of the general population. CPF members ranked cultural and intellectual broadening first among the possible advantages of having children learn French, with 30 percent of respondents, and bilingualism itself was named by 29 percent. Better employment opportunities were named by 23 percent (compared with 49 percent of the national sample). Travel and social uses were named by 8 percent, and contributions to national unity barely registered, at only 2 percent. CPF parents were also keen on immersion, with 28 percent wanting it to be the type of French instruction available in schools and another 56 percent wanting both immersion and core French. Only 4 percent gave core French alone as a response.[99] Of the 857 CPF members polled, 818 had children under the age of eighteen. The vast majority were in public schools (89 percent) or separate schools (10 percent), with only 4 percent in a private or independent school. Of the parents with children in schools, the vast majority had their children in some form of immersion.[100] Only 23 percent had children in some form of core French program.[101] This compared with only half of those in the national sample who reported having school-aged children currently taking French.

CPF members were asked questions to gauge their perceptions of public attitudes toward French-language learning. Most members thought that attitudes toward FSL programs in the schools of their particular province had stayed about the same since the past year (42 percent), whereas somewhat more thought that the programs were viewed by the public more positively (25 percent) than negatively (19 percent).[102] Forty-three percent thought that Bill 178 and the new regulations on English on signage in Quebec had a major impact on attitudes toward French, and 47 percent thought that it had at least a minor impact. Most thought that it would have a negative impact on general attitudes toward French, with somewhat fewer parents thinking that it would have an impact on parents' attitudes to FSL programs.[103]

The negativity regarding the Meech Lake Accord was also perceived, by the fall of 1989, to have an impact on the attitudes of Canadians, though somewhat less so than Bill 178. The responses regarding perceived impact on attitudes toward FSL in general and toward FSL for children were about the same as those for Bill 178. Thirty-five percent of CPF members thought that Meech Lake had a major impact on attitudes toward French in general, and another 47 percent thought that it had a minor impact; 92 percent indicated that the impact was negative.

CPF members were less concerned by the impacts of anti-bilingualism groups such as the Alliance for the Preservation of English in Canada and the Confederation of Regions Party. Only 8 percent feared a major impact on attitudes toward French, and another 40 percent thought that there might be a minor impact, with 84 percent thinking that it would be a negative impact.[104] Interestingly, fully a third of those who thought that these organizations were having an impact thought that it might lead to more positive attitudes toward FSL programs. Although there was an undercurrent of worry about the impact of anti-bilingualism groups, it was not a major preoccupation the way that national issues around the Constitution and Quebec's language policies were.

The poll revealed a lot about CPF members. There was some truth to the oft-repeated attack from anti-bilingualism groups that CPF itself represented an elite group, even if that was not necessarily the case for families with children in French immersion. Thirty-three percent of the CPF members who responded to the survey had completed graduate school or other professional education, and another 27 percent had completed university degrees. Only 10 percent had a high school education or less. Fifty-two percent of members worked full time, with another 26 percent in part-time work, and 18 percent were at home full time. Fifty-eight percent described their current (or most recently-held) occupation as professional, with another 12 percent administrators or owners of business, and 15 percent were office workers. Only 4 percent were skilled or semi-skilled tradespeople, and 1 percent each were unskilled workers or farmers/fishers. Ninety-three percent were married or living as couples. Members' spouses tended to fit the same profile, being highly educated, with 84 percent having at least some form of postsecondary education. Ninety-six percent reported English as the language most often spoken at home. The poll did not include a gender breakdown of respondents, though this is not surprising since whole families were treated as members.

The Environics poll gives an interesting snapshot of CPF and its activism. The most active members of the group were those with children aged seven to nine. Overall, members were more than twice as likely as respondents in the general population to be working in a professional occupation or married to someone who was (58 percent versus 23 percent) and almost six times as likely to be university graduates. Active members were also more likely to be at home full time, which speaks to the availability of both their time and their energy for activism. Overall, Environics considered CPF members to fit the profile of "opinion leaders."[105]

CPF's release of the poll information was coordinated by Cynthia Steers. Timing of the release was moved up to mid-February 1990 in an effort to combat much of the negativity surrounding Meech Lake, Bill 178, and APEC. The messages used in press releases, draft letters to the editor, and position statements incorporated key phrases highlighting CPF's non-partisan nature: "The bottom line is we are parents with a concern for our children. We have no political axes to grind." They also stressed the grassroots and populist nature of support for second-language instruction: "Its message is clear: right across this vast land the majority of Canadians want and appreciate our bilingual heritage and want it for their children."[106]

The press releases stressed that the strongest support for second-language learning came from the youngest cohort surveyed. CPF's national press conference made a point of including a secondary school student to speak about the advantages of bilingualism; this strategy was also recommended to local chapters. CPF emphasized the pan-Canadian nature of support, reaffirming that a majority of Canadians in all regions supported the teaching of French in schools. CPF vice-president Pat Brehaut, from Alberta, was actively included in the publicity to emphasize western voices. The strategy appeared to work, with analysis a year later indicating that there had been widespread, positive media coverage and that it had "position[ed] CPF as a voice of reason and optimism for the future."[107]

CPF Outreach and Partnerships

Canadian Parents for French continued to be committed to partnering with francophone minority communities. An opportunity to do so arose in 1988 thanks to funding from the CRB Foundation – a charitable foundation funded by Montreal businessman Charles Bronfman. CPF was given a grant to organize a series of weekends for a project called Rendezvous Canada, bringing together francophone minority children and FSL learners for a weekend spent in French. The first weekends were held in New Brunswick, Prince Edward Island, and Newfoundland.[108] Evaluations showed that immersion students found this approach useful in improving their language understanding and attitudes toward native speakers of

French, while francophones were pleased to discover that immersion students could actually speak French well. However, one challenge was that francophone communities had reservations about the project and trying to grow the francophone community in this manner. The two were different cultural groups, and the merits of tapping into the immersion cohort and francophiles to bolster francophone communities were often resisted or viewed with suspicion.[109] However, additional funding was secured to run Rendez-vous Canada for two more years, covering the remaining provinces. Without the CRB funding (which amounted to another $140,000 over the following two years), programs of this nature were not sustainable from CPF's other revenue streams, becoming increasingly stretched.[110]

The limited number of charitable foundations interested in supporting CPF was an ongoing challenge. CPF proposed a special Canada 125 event in 1992 of a "student travelling road show" of winners of the Festival national d'art oratoire to share what being bilingual meant to them to encourage young people to help create the kind of Canada that they wanted and to promote learning of the second official language as a tool of communication.[111] However, this project had to be scrapped when efforts to secure funding from the Walter and Duncan Gordon Charitable Foundation were not fruitful.[112]

Perhaps as a consequence of professionalization, but typical for a social movement organization well into its second decade, by the late 1980s declining or stagnating membership became a regular theme at CPF meetings. Overall numbers remained relatively stable, but the number of membership renewals was starting to slip significantly.[113] To a certain extent, this is understandable. Involvement in CPF chapters tended to peak when there was an immediate objective, and by the late 1980s many jurisdictions had well-established French immersion programs or improved core French. The generation of parents who became involved in the 1970s and early 1980s was seeing their children graduate and likely felt little direct impetus to remain involved.

For CPF, maintaining solid paid membership numbers was key to efforts to attract corporate sponsorship, maintain federal funding, and combat claims of anti-bilingualism groups such as APEC, whose volunteer numbers were climbing. CPF's membership committee tried a number of initiatives to bolster renewals and sign up new members.[114] By mid-1990, CPF could count 17,005 paid individual/family members (the annual fee was raised to fifteen dollars per year in 1988 and then to twenty-five dollars in 1991). But it was concerned about its long-term viability and its ability to continue to

Learning French Matters transit ad. This advertisement, and others like it, was used by Canadian Parents for French to reach out to Canadians about the value of two official languages in the late 1980s and throughout the 1990s. | *Source:* Mount Allison University Archives, Canadian Parents for French fonds, 2000.23, file 3/10/13: Thirteenth National Conference, Banff – 1989. © Canadian Parents for French.

present itself as a mass movement. Five years later a study of membership to find out why members joined discovered that most did so as a symbolic show of support for bilingualism, French immersion, and FSL. Most did not want to become active volunteers.[115] Given CPF's struggles to secure non-governmental funding, a decline in even the small proportion of revenues from membership was important. (See Appendix 5 for revenue figures.) Finding ways to sign up new members proved to be an ongoing challenge.

One way to promote CPF membership and the organization's overall goals was through national information campaigns. Following on the success of the 1986 Making Choices national campaign, CPF's 1989 campaign, Learning French Matters, featured informational pamphlets and transit advertising with quotations from famous Canadians.[116]

The ad series Leading Canadians Agree: Learning French Matters! took a soft-sell approach to the issue of language, stressing opportunities, learning, and experiences of Canada, though not explicitly mentioning jobs. For instance, astronaut Marc Garneau said that "knowing both languages has opened many doors for me; doors of opportunity and doors of the mind. There's an interesting and exciting world out there, waiting for those who are ready to reach." Nine-year-old Emma Houlston, described as a "transcontinental pilot," said that "French is important to me because I like to travel. It's fun to learn and it helps me make new friends."[117] With other

quotations from NHL star and lawyer Ken Dryden, journalist Mary Lou
Finlay, and heart surgeon Dr. Wilbert Keon, the campaign featured a balance of genders, Canadians of different ages, and an array of occupations.[118]
In all, CPF estimated that the 1989 campaign reached between 3 and 4 million people.[119]

Three years later CPF launched its Learning French Makes a World of
Difference campaign. The campaign was broadened to include a variety of
other initiatives to reach communities that did not have mass transit.[120] Over
the course of the campaign, ads ran in venues including *Canadian Living*
and Air Canada's *En Route* magazine. The youth-oriented cable channel
YTV ran a public service announcement for CPF. Board members were
generally pleased that these campaigns positioned CPF well as a leader on
FSL education issues, though the limited extent to which they reached
beyond major metropolitan centres remained a concern.[121] The same campaign ran again in January 1994 thanks to financial aid from the Department of Canadian Heritage.[122]

Canadian Parents for English/Core French

Maintaining a positive media presence for CPF was important because
opposition to French-language learning efforts, especially immersion, was
increasingly prominent. Over the course of 1989 and 1990, Lori Nash, a
freelance journalist and parent from Orleans, Ontario, disenchanted with
French immersion, from which she had withdrawn her son after kindergarten, started a campaign against these popular programs in the Ottawa-
Carleton region. Within a year, she took her campaign to the national
level, using the name Canadian Parents for English/Core French. It was a
deliberate attack on Canadian Parents for French and would be a thorn in
its side, particularly in eastern Ontario, for several years. There were ties
between this group and APEC (Nash would speak at APEC meetings over
the years), but this group explicitly challenged the French immersion lobby
while claiming to support a good core French system. As will become clear,
however, it often acted as a front for anti-bilingualism and anti-French
activities.

Early documents pertaining to Nash's initiative refer to it simply as
Parents for English. In her speeches, Nash claimed to have been spurred to
action by an information night for parents with kindergarten-aged children
interested in French immersion, when no such night was held for parents
interested in the regular program. The Carleton Board of Education disseminated materials prepared by Canadian Parents for French and allowed

the group to speak at meetings. Nash argued that these materials made parents feel guilty for not choosing French immersion and did not inform them of alternatives. She claimed that the quality of immersion teaching was poor, that teachers' only qualification was the ability to speak French, and that "they certainly can't speak English."[123] She believed that Canada already had problems with English illiteracy and that immersion was now opening the door to illiteracy in two languages. Nash claimed that there were high dropout rates from immersion and that only 23 percent actually obtained a bilingual graduation certificate at the end of high school. She alleged that 16 percent of immersion dropouts landed in special education, implying that immersion was the cause. She questioned CPF's claim to be a volunteer organization, pointing to its support by the Department of the Secretary of State and its paid staff. Nash attacked Marc Garneau and Wilbert Keon for providing quotations for the Learning French Matters campaign because (she claimed) the language of medicine and science was English. Her early speeches were rife with conspiratorial allusions to psychological and educational facts being covered up and an educational establishment in the pocket of Canadian Parents for French. Moreover, she saw French immersion as part of a francophone takeover of English school boards, for there were parents in her son's French immersion class who were French speaking.[124]

Learning disabilities appear to have been the cause of Nash's anti–French immersion crusade. Nash often cited Dr. Ronald Trites on his studies of students with learning difficulties at the Royal Ottawa Hospital.[125] Her arguments also echoed the somewhat conspiratorial tone of a feature article penned by Katherine Govier in *Toronto Life* in 1986 filled with allusions to "little birds" claiming that French immersion researchers were hiding negative dimensions of the program and that parents sending their children to such programs did so to bolster their own social status rather than their children's education.[126] Govier had raised the spectre that English-stream parents thought that French immersion got special treatment with funding, free busing, and additional teachers.[127]

At the time that her article was published, Pat Webster wrote to *Toronto Life* stating that Govier's piece set "a new standard for biased journalism" and that, "after careful and repeated use of innuendo, your writer finally tells the reader that immersion consists of greedy Yuppies foisting another fad on their overburdened and unhappy offspring." Webster noted that "children of farmers in Wellington county, teachers in Sault Ste Marie, steelworkers in Hamilton, salesmen in Goderich ... will be surprised to learn that their parents are Yuppies who take holidays in French-speaking areas, and the parents will be surprised to learn that one of them speaks French and that they have only one child and live-in help." The argument about illiteracy in both languages was a clear echo of Simon Fraser University's Hector Hammerly's ongoing assault on French immersion, which Hammerly had claimed was creating "little butchers of the French language."[128]

By February 1990, Nash's organization had begun to incorporate core French into its branding and was officially going by the name Canadian Parents for English/Core French (CPE/CF). Among its objectives, it listed the promotion of a national syllabus for core French. The rest of the objectives were explicitly hostile to French immersion, including "to actively research and respond to issues that impact negatively on the delivery of English language programming; to provide support for children and their parents in the transition from French immersion to English/Core French; [and] to provide a forum for parents and children to express their concerns and provide information to those encountering difficulties in the French immersion program." The group noted that "more and more parents are questioning the wisdom of educating young children in an unfamiliar language" and raised the spectres of stress and emotional difficulty of French immersion students, the pushing out of English programs from schools, and the busing of English children out of their home communities. Overall, CPE/CF claimed that, "as a result of inequitable resource allocations and inadequate promotion, a misconception has surfaced in the minds of many parents, that English/Core French is a second rate program and a poor educational choice."[129]

The group sought "to encourage quality in English language programming in order that students will achieve the highest personal level attainable in ENGLISH LITERACY." It did not believe at all in French immersion's benefits: "We believe that children in the English/Core French program enjoy a richer, more positive early educational experience than the Early French Immersion Students." They claimed that the English classroom allowed children to communicate effectively with teachers and classmates, promoted easy and free expression of ideas, and provided a learning environment in which self-esteem and confidence could flourish during a critical stage in a child's development. To improve core French, the group promised to lobby for first choice of French teachers, and quality resources and learning environments, and to promote enriched extracurricular activities.[130] It was a forceful, direct attack on the merits of French immersion and took aim at the program in the region where it had been most popular and successful.

Canadian Parents for French countered the CPE/CF documents with information on CPF's active support for core French and how many members had children in this program. It noted that CPF was not a group initiated by the Department of the Secretary of State but resulted from the 1977 conferences funded by the Office of the Commissioner of Official Languages and that it received federal grants only for specific program applications and had to report on how these grants were used. CPF threatened legal action against CPE/CF if misstatements were not removed from its literature.[131]

Jakob Knaus, APEC, and CPE/CF in British Columbia

Canadian Parents for English/Core French also made an impact in the coastal regions of British Columbia, where its rhetoric was coupled with that of the Alliance for the Preservation of English in Canada. As often seemed to be the case, much of this furore centred on a single individual, once again from an older generation. On the Sunshine Coast, this person was Jakob Knaus. An immigrant from Switzerland in his sixties living in Sechelt, he was instrumental in forming a local chapter of APEC and publicizing its activities. Although he claimed that the group had nothing against learning a second language, and that he supported core French, there was a particularly virulent anti-French tone to his interventions. Knaus penned letters hostile to the revised Official Languages Act published by the *Coast News* despite an editorial team that appeared to find his fears of Frenchification farcical (one thought them Monty Pythonesque in their absurdity).[132] Knaus claimed that the new regulations would lead to government offices being completely staffed by francophones: "We had vivid examples of what happens when one minority group usurps the administration and imposes its own rules on the majority. Goebbels and the Nazi's did it in the Third Reich; The Communists did it in the Balkan States. Is this going to repeat itself in Canada?"[133] He referred to an experiment on CBC Newsworld of airing the news in French with English subtitles as "sheer provocation of English speaking Canadians in British Columbia," and he declared that British Columbia had been "contaminated with this French provocation."[134]

After printing letters to the editor in response to the "contamination" letter and a counterpoint editorial from editor John Burnside, the *Coast News* ceased printing APEC's missives. But Knaus was only warming up. He and his sympathizers (he claimed 125 member families in the district) were taking aim at the Sunshine Coast early French immersion program, hoping to eliminate it or at least push it back to no earlier than grade six. They were supported by the other newspaper in Sechelt, published by Richard Proctor, who penned anti-immersion editorials.[135] APEC chapter president John Cook, a retiree living in Gibson, worked with Knaus and APEC supporters to lobby the school board throughout 1989 and into early 1990 to eliminate the program.[136]

After a February 1990 meeting, the school board announced its decision to phase out EFI over the next three years and replace it with a middle immersion program with a grade four entry. The board claimed that this change would strengthen the program, based on research showing that grade four was a better entry point because students in middle immersion tended to be motivated (despite the opposition of the local CPF chapter, representing the parents of 160 students in the early grades of the program). The board cast it as a decision about balancing the needs of "all our students in both English and French programs for a quality education."[137] Carol Adams, chair of the board, took pains to state that the decision was the result of a year-long review, "for the betterment of the school district," and that "APEC was not involved ... I don't like what they do ... We are committed to both languages here and are still open to discussion."[138]

Despite the Sunshine Coast board's distancing itself from APEC, the group claimed victory, believing that its goals were gaining ground rapidly in British Columbia, and it would soon take aim against other French immersion programs.[139] Provincial Liberal leader Gordon Wilson found it hard to believe the school board's claim that APEC had no influence, and he called on the Social Credit government to denounce APEC's bigotry.[140] Local French immersion advocates were disheartened by the decision, arguing that it would make it harder to attract good teachers to the district and claiming that some parents might even move out of the region.

CPE/CF found other adherents in British Columbia, including Mrs. D. Davies of Kelowna, who wrote to the local school boards in an attack on CPF and French immersion, citing in particular the Trites study on children with learning difficulties. She congratulated Quebec's minister of education, Claude Ryan, for protecting children during their formative years by eliminating the teaching of other languages before grade four and the province for becoming "unilingual" French, recognizing the impossibility of bilingualism with only 12 percent of the population belonging to the English-speaking minority. Davies drew the conclusion that British Columbia, with a francophone population of 1 percent, and Canada, with a francophone population of 24 percent, could not be bilingual either. She lambasted CPF for providing information to its members on what she called "how to manipulate school boards, media and the public," and she deemed it "repulsive" that tax dollars supported this campaign.[141]

Knaus and his supporters in APEC also appear to have gravitated to the CPE/CF message. He began circulating a document entitled "French Immersion Often an Unfortunate Choice."[142] It called for the elimination of French immersion and its replacement with core French (which the BC government wanted in place with a grade four start in all school boards by 1992).[143] In addition to CPE/CF's standard arguments, Knaus circulated old canards about the difficulty of following an immersion curriculum, which "can only be reached by the brightest students, because of the difficulty of absorbing the required knowledge in a foreign language." He reiterated claims that these programs were primarily for status-seeking parents and that "parental expectations are placing emotional stress on students which can cause them to fail." He made the economic argument that a program aimed at only 5 percent of the population should, and could, be cut in British Columbia. He raised the spectre of widespread social chaos, claiming that, if learning problems were not detected early, students with university potential would drop out of school, fomenting disruption in the family and causing a great loss to society.[144]

Knaus's document, circulated widely in British Columbia, concluded by urging parents to get a copy of "What You Were Not Told about French Immersion" by Lori Nash.[145] In a number of school districts, teachers or principals tipped Canadian Parents for French off to the existence of the document so that it could respond if the document made it onto the agendas of school districts.[146] In Bulkley Valley, local ministry officials responsible for French-language programs urged that the document be left on the agenda so that CPF could counter it directly, and CPF circulated materials that responded to CPE/CF's claims.[147] It does not appear that the CPE/CF documents reversed school board policies in most districts, but this was a challenge for local CPF chapters, and the links between CPE/CF and APEC were clear. All local branches were asked to report to British Columbia Parents for French on any APEC or anti-French activity in their districts.

APEC and the Mainstream Press

By early 1990, with the national drama on the Meech Lake Accord, APEC's national profile was at its peak. President Ronald Leitch appeared on CTV News in February 1990 to take aim at French immersion. APEC issued press releases claiming a 50 percent dropout rate after three years, alleging, on the

basis of Hector Hammerly's research, that French immersion was producing students not functionally literate in either language. Overall, Leitch
stated, "French immersion is disruptive, inefficient, and costly." He took aim
at CPF, calling it a lobby group funded by federal and Ontario government
contributions, contrasting it with APEC's own volunteer base of 36,000
members.[148]

APEC did not get an easy ride from the mainstream press. In March
1990, Toronto's alternative weekly *NOW* did an exposé on the group, re-
visited the following week in the *Toronto Star*. The articles detailed APEC's
ties with extreme right-wing groups, including the Canadian League of
Rights (CLR), a leading anti-Semitic organization, and other right-wing
groups, including the National Citizens' Coalition. Ron Gostick of the CLR
distributed his Holocaust denial literature after his talks at APEC meetings.
The *NOW* article, by Howard Goldenthal and Wayne Roberts, also made a
great deal of Leitch's ties to Peter Brimelow, who saw bilingualism as just
one part of "Canada's repellent package of leftist social and human rights
policies," and the Northern Foundation, a right-wing group created in opposition to Brian Mulroney's alleged "capitulation to the left and Quebec."
The thesis advanced by Goldenthal and Roberts, endorsed by former NDP
national secretary Gerald Caplan in the *Toronto Star*, was that APEC was
a "stalking horse" for American right-wing extremism, using the language
issue to advance "beyond the lunatic fringe" and gain greater credibility in
Canada.[149]

Hubert Bauch's profile of Ronald Leitch in the Montreal *Gazette* noted
that, compared with some of his followers, he "sounds like a voice of sweet
moderation," but "all sorts of slimy things come crawling out" when one
turned over the "rock of Ron Leitch's rectitude." These "slimy things" included Burlington APEC's vice-president, Ed Hudson, kicked out of the
organization over racist jokes about the United States getting blacks instead
of French Canadians because it had first choice, and Jock Andrew's comments likening French Canada to the AIDS virus. Although Leitch claimed
that there were no official APEC links to Andrew, he began the Ontario
chapter of APEC by mailing Andrew's book to friends in 1977. Bauch referred to *Bilingual Today, French Tomorrow* as "remain[ing] the APEC holy
writ ... replete with distortions, outright untruths and blatant racism."[150]
The problem, from his perspective, was that APEC had suddenly become a
significant player in the constitutional crisis.

CPF Crisis Kits

To help chapters at the community level fight back against the rapid rise of anti-bilingualism groups, the national office of CPF put together information sheets to refute frequently used claims about bilingualism and French-language learning. The first set was distributed in January 1990 by CPF president Kathryn Manzer. She noted that local chapters were likely to run into these new groups first through community newspapers or locally distributed pamphlets. Written propaganda would usually start with some variant of "we are not anti-French, we are only against federal government–enforced bilingualism," before launching into arguments that were anti-French and anti-French-language education. Oral presentations, Manzer noted, tended to be more stridently anti-French, arose from feelings of being threatened, and deliberately aimed at creating an emotionally charged environment. She wanted to provide factual information to help groups resist being pulled into heated, emotional debates. Local members were urged to contact the provincial president or chapter director before engaging in any debates in order to get close-to-home information and advice. All chapters were urged to send in newspaper clippings, pamphlets, and other personal accounts of anti-bilingualism activities in their areas.[151]

The 1990 kit contained responses to seven major claims circulating at the time.[152] In response to the first claim – "Education in French means that our children and our country will become 'frenchified'" – CPF noted that a person does not lose his or her culture or identity simply by speaking, reading, and writing more than one language, though studies did show that immersion students had more positive attitudes toward native speakers of French. To refute the second claim – "Federal Policy on official language bilingualism, and in particular the new *Official Languages Act*, is designed to bring about the frenchification of all schools across Canada" – CPF pointed out that provinces had sole jurisdiction over education and that Ottawa merely provided funding that the provinces could access for minority- and official-languages education.

The next several anti-bilingualism claims were common ones regarding financial costs and pedagogical outcomes of immersion:

Claim 3: French immersion demands so much in terms of money, resources, administration and teachers that it destroys the regular English program.

Claim 4: Only core French should be offered in schools. Half the kids that start in immersion drop out anyway and all students could learn French just as well and at a lower cost in a core program.

Claim 5: French immersion program is for an academic elite. Kids who are enrolled in the regular program are made to feel dumb or are assumed to have learning problems.

Claim 6: French immersion students are not competent in either language. In fact, by enrolling them in French you limit their vocabulary.

For each claim, CPF pointed to the relevant funding statistics and pedagogical research showing that, once started, the programs did not cost substantially more and indicated the learning outcomes of each type of FSL. To the final claim of this kit, the seventh claim, "Parents are being seduced into thinking French immersion is the be-all and end-all and their children can be someone great," which echoed Katherine Govier's *Toronto Life* article, CPF responded by arguing that it was extremely naive to suggest that parents do not consider all options when thinking about their children's education. It further noted that research showed that even children who need remedial education can still thrive in French immersion when supports are provided. These information sheets were useful quick-reference tools for chapters across the country when dealing with opponents of bilingualism and FSL.

Conclusion
By the middle of 1990, the anti-bilingualism movement was gaining steam. APEC claimed that it had more members than CPF, struggling to maintain its paid membership (but succeeding so far). Although the CPF poll conducted in 1989 showed that levels of support for French-language learning were still strong, portents were ominous. There was still an appetite among parents for French immersion and FSL programs for their children, but efforts to expand these programs at the local level encountered more vitriolic opposition. Anti-bilingualism organizations, which used to be active mainly at the national level, became increasingly prominent at both provincial and local levels and more directly adversarial to French-language education. The situation was becoming increasingly volatile and seemed to be unlikely to improve in the near future.

The relationship between CPF and the federal government was likewise becoming increasingly complex. Over the period from 1984–85 to 1989–90, the federal government's contributions to the national CPF budget increased from $243,144 to $515,182 (out of total revenues that rose from $331,168 to $765,914; see Appendix 5).[153] This provided substantial new financial resources that CPF could use in support of initiatives such as the 1989 Gallup poll and the Making Choices and Learning French Matters publicity campaigns. CPF could still count on substantial volunteer energies, and the moral support of between 17,000 and 18,000 paid members. Yet, despite a strong and stable paid membership, the extent of federal backing opened CPF up to widespread criticism from APEC and CPE/CF, which repeatedly took aim at CPF for being a front for, or puppet of, the federal government. The reality of this relationship, as demonstrated in this chapter, was substantially more complex. Although CPF did maintain good relationships with officials in the Department of the Secretary of State (and the Office of the Commissioner of Official Languages), its leaders did not hesitate to act and speak out when the federal government's commitment to national bilingualism seemed to waver, whether in the Nielsen Report or in the Meech Lake Accord. It was a delicate balancing act for this federally funded social movement organization and was about to become substantially more difficult in the austere financial climate and fraught constitutional atmosphere of the early to mid-1990s.

10
Constitutional Crises and Economic Challenges in the Early 1990s

Canada's economy suffered a major recession in the early 1990s, coupled with the rise of neo-liberal policies and political parties. This led to major cutbacks to funding for programs across the board, with significant ramifications in the language sector. Although support for bilingualism in English-speaking Canada did not exactly retreat, it did appear to plateau and stagnate for a variety of reasons. It was as if, having reached a crucial point at which the gains of the 1970s and 1980s could have been solidified, the rug was instead pulled out from underneath. These were difficult years for Canadian Parents for French, which saw its membership, staff, and budget shrink. Yet, despite this difficult political and economic climate, CPF and supporters of bilingualism held on to established programs and defended them from attacks. Although public enthusiasm for the French language itself was waning, Canadians had become aware of the material and intellectual benefits of personal bilingualism in general.

From Meech Lake to Charlottetown

With the failure of the Meech Lake Accord in June 1990, another period of constitutional turmoil erupted. Quebec passed a law mandating a referendum on the future of the province to be held in 1992. The federal government responded by trying to cobble together a new constitutional package to address the failures of Meech Lake. There were two forums for public input into this process, and both were used by pro- and anti-bilingualism groups.

The first forum for public feedback featured an old friend of Canadian Parents for French: Keith Spicer. Tapped to head the Citizens' Forum on Canada's Future, he travelled coast to coast meeting with groups of Canadians. Local CPF chapters emphasized the importance of second-language programs in their submissions. The other forum was a task force of parliamentarians (initially the Castonguay-Dobbie, then the Beaudoin-Dobbie, Committee) that held hearings on the 1991 package of constitutional proposals called Shaping Canada's Future Together. As with the Meech Lake Accord, CPF expressed its concern that there was not really much on official languages in the proposals. In its national brief, CPF stressed the need for language on the value of the English and French languages to Canadians and how they aided both in developing tolerance and understanding and in fostering world competitiveness and trade. CPF urged official support for French and English linguistic minorities and the federal government to retain its power to spend money on French and English as second and minority languages in education in the provinces.[1] The silence on linguistic duality and bilingualism as a pan-Canadian value was of greatest concern to Canadian Parents for French, so it attempted to keep these issues active during this period of constitutional crisis.

A diametrically opposed position emerged from the Alliance for the Preservation of English in Canada, which claimed 42,000 paid members by 1991. APEC had been extremely hostile to the Meech Lake Accord because of the special status that it included for Quebec. APEC referred to the process that led to the 1992 Charlottetown Accord as Meech II. In its booklet *Constitutions Are for People, Not Politicians* and ten pamphlets in its Constitutional Countdown series, the group spelled out an agenda for constitutional reform that aimed to turn back the clock to the pre-1982 constitutional era. APEC also proposed populist reforms that bore close resemblance to the positions of the Reform Party of Canada. Their position papers on both Meech Lake and Charlottetown were nearly identical in content, couched in the discourse of populism and direct democracy, but the reforms were designed to eliminate Canada's official languages policies and special status for Quebec or French Canada.

APEC's core position on both accords was that Canada's official languages policies should be eliminated because "the government should speak to all Canadian people in one language and that language should be the language spoken by the majority of Canadians, namely English."[2] Although conceding that French-language services would need to be provided in Quebec "out of necessity," APEC held that the language rights of section 133 of the British North America Act were intended to be both "permissive" and limiting and were never intended to be extended to the civil service.[3] Only by communicating officially in English exclusively would Canadian unity be achieved. Two official languages created division, not unity, and thus APEC wanted the Official Languages Act and the Charter of Rights and Freedoms – especially its sections on language rights – to be repealed.[4]

APEC believed that there was no historical basis for any special status for the French language in Canada, and it selectively quoted from historian Donald Creighton and Senator Eugene Forsey to make its case that, with the Official Languages Act, the Trudeau government was "bent on a social engineering project without any historical, constitutional, or legal authority."[5] From APEC's perspective, the fact that there had been no explicit mention of the French language in past constitutional documents meant that there should be no such recognition granted in the present. Moreover, since Quebec had been actively pursuing a unilingual provincial policy since the 1970s, APEC concurred with Creighton, who wrote in 1977 that "English Canada's whole bilingual program, which never had any constitutional or cultural justification, has ceased to have any political purpose ... The provinces – and particularly Ontario – that have been promoting French in the schools for purely political purposes should realize that these purposes are now politically meaningless."[6]

Central to APEC's critique of the official languages policy was the contention that it was a smokescreen for discriminatory hiring policies that favoured ethnic francophones. APEC believed that the federal government ultimately did not consider bilingual anglophones to be acceptable. The group claimed that "from the very beginning the government was intent on creating a bilingual elite which would be at the very core of the civil service of this country" and that this process started when the overwhelming majority of bilingual Canadians were ethnically French. APEC alleged that departmental hiring policies set quotas for francophones – as opposed to bilingual employees – and claimed that C-level competency meant hiring only those of francophone descent.[7] It asserted that there were huge dropout rates from the French immersion programs promoted by CPF (a 50 percent rate within the first three years) and that "few if any of the people who continue beyond grade 7 become fluent in the French language." From its perspective, there was no hope for a non-francophone, even one who studied in French immersion, to land a bilingual job. Such jobs, it believed, were being "artificially created."[8]

Ronald Leitch, APEC's national president since 1986, couched his concerns in the guise of a lost British-centric history and tradition. He wrote that "politicians have led the parade of those who would deny Canada's roots" and that, "as an example of the foregoing, British history cannot be taught in Ontario without the permission of the Minister of Education."[9] Changes to Canada's Constitution and language policies since the 1960s, he argued, were threatening the foundations of Canada, rooted in parliamentary democracy and a jury system – both British in origin. In the preface to *Constitutions Are for People, Not Politicians*, Kenneth McDonald of the BMG Publishing group claimed that Trudeau's 1982 Constitution and Charter of Rights and Freedoms were rooted in his distaste for the English tradition of parliamentary supremacy. McDonald argued that Canada's political trajectory had been distorted by a Quebec voting bloc in Parliament, returning to arguments that he had made in the 1970s and echoed in Peter Brimelow's *The Patriot Game*.

According to Leitch and McDonald, the charter had replaced the fundamental principle of the equality of status and rights of individuals with special status for certain groups. Moreover, they argued, "the Official Languages Act, rather than unifying the country, has unleashed bitterness, racial animosity and has contributed to the fracturing of a nation."[10] APEC opposed the proposed Canada clause of the Charlottetown Accord that would spell out certain features of Canada, including duality. All provinces, APEC argued, should be treated symmetrically, and English should be the language used from coast to coast. It claimed historical justification for this approach:

> From a historical point of view we have endeavoured to establish two points: i) where in any geographic area the effective control of that area changes, the language of the person in control becomes the language of the government and the people of that geographic area. (ii) No historical or constitutional documents with respect to what is now Canada provided for any official status for French from 1759 on to Confederation, save and except for section 133 of the BNA Act, 1867.[11]

All of this was linked to a set of proposals for more direct democracy, including recall, referendums, voter initiative, and a new amending formula, that would allow for complete dominance by Canada's English-speaking majority and likely prevent the reinstitution of policies to promote French –

or any other minority rights.[12] The rhetoric supporting these policies was couched in the language of the will of the people, bottom-up democracy, and retaking power from bureaucracies and politicians. It was hardly co-incidental that these policies would also make it possible for a determined English-speaking Canadian majority to strip away any official status for the French language and wipe out any special status that had been acquired by the Quebec government in recent decades.

Don Getty vs. the Elite Consensus on Bilingualism

At the height of the rounds of constitutional reform in the 1990s, Alberta premier Don Getty created a national firestorm when he delivered a speech on January 9, 1992, in which he called official bilingualism an "irritant" that should be "removed from the force of law." He believed that more Canadians could embrace bilingualism if it were voluntary.[13] Politicians of all stripes at both federal and provincial levels marched out to oppose his position, including federal Liberal leader Jean Chrétien, BC and Ontario NDP premiers Mike Harcourt and Bob Rae, and federal Conservative constitutional affairs minister (and fellow Albertan) Joe Clark. They called Getty's statements an attack on bilingualism and an effort to score "cheap political points." Newfoundland Liberal premier Clyde Wells questioned Getty's basic premise of "forced" bilingualism, noting that he was not being forced to use French, nor was the government of Newfoundland forced to operate in French.[14] Even members of Getty's own party broke ranks, including rising cabinet star Nancy Betkowski and former premier Peter Lougheed, who noted that bilingualism "goes to the core, to the very essence of our country ... Bilingualism may not be particularly popular in the province, but it is accepted in terms of priorities."[15] An Angus Reid poll taken the week after the speech showed that only 14 percent of Albertans agreed with his statements and that 26 percent were less likely to support Getty in a provincial election. Fifty-seven percent said that his statements made no difference.[16]

Commissioner of Official Languages Victor Goldbloom intervened in this debate in a speech to Edmonton's Rotary Club. He calmly reiterated that it had never been the purpose of the Official Languages Act to make Canada "uniformly, homogenously bilingual from sea to see," nor was it "about shoving French down the throats of English-speaking Canadians." Rather, it was about "service to the public, about fairness to Canadian citizens." He pointed out that the teaching of French was not compulsory in Alberta schools; rather, it was the decision of each school board. Moreover, only 3 percent of federal public service jobs in Alberta, and only 10 percent at the management level (a grand total of 400), were designated bilingual. Of these positions, over 60 percent were occupied by anglophones, as were eight of the nine bilingual management posts. As Goldbloom noted, though, he did not wish to fight about numbers; instead, he considered this as an issue about "Canadians living together and relating to one another. I want to prevail upon Canadians to feel positively about our country; I seek to motivate English-speaking and French-speaking Canadians to want to keep Canada together." It was a measured intervention stressing that some jobs need to be bilingual for a fair and effective federal public service and in the broader interests of the unity of Canada.[17]

Albertans might not have rallied to Getty's call, but that did not mean that they, or Canadians more generally, thought that Ottawa's official languages policies were a huge success. A Gallup poll of 1,037 Canadians taken in mid-February 1992 showed that 64 percent thought that official bilingualism was a failure, whereas only 26 percent thought that it was a success. Notably, the poll did not ask whether official bilingualism should be abolished, but it gave a reading on whether Canadians thought that it was working as it should be.[18] The poll bore out observations made by *Toronto Star* columnist Geoffrey Stevens, who claimed that Canadians had never fully embraced or believed in bilingualism but were willing to accept it as necessary. He cited a recent Environics poll showing that only a slim national plurality (47 versus 44 percent) thought that Canada should be a country in which both languages are spoken coast to coast versus those who thought that French should be spoken in Quebec and English everywhere else. Support for bilingualism was lower in much of English-speaking Canada. Stevens pointed to University of Toronto historian Michael Bliss's interpretation that there was a consensus in Canada, supported by its political elites, to tolerate the official languages policies as the price of English being respected in Quebec and French in the rest of the country, a consensus being undermined by Quebec's Bill 178 and Getty's attack on official bilingualism.[19]

CPF's national president, Albertan Pat Brehaut, waded into the fray with an op-ed piece in the *Toronto Star*.[20] She observed that much of what existed in Canada was not compulsory bilingualism forced on Canadians by federal legislation but voluntary bilingualism adopted by individual Canadians coast to coast. She pointed to how the new international reality meant that bilingualism would be an economic advantage – one reflected in the education systems of Japan and Europe, Canada's economic competitors – as well as a learning experience that opened one's mind to tolerance of differences in people. Brehaut noted that understanding both official languages helped children to understand better the history, development, and politics of their nation. This built bridges to help Canadians better understand each other. It was with such considerations in mind that 70 percent of English-speaking Canadians had told Environics, in the poll released in 1990, that children should learn French in school to become bilingual.

The 1992 Bad News Poll

Yet public support was starting to flag by 1992, even on the language learning question. Environics conducted another poll in May and June 1992 for Canadian Parents for French on Canadian attitudes toward language learning and bilingualism. The poll was extremely discouraging.[21] This poll, the first taken for CPF since the collapse of the Meech Lake Accord and the founding of the Bloc Québécois, showed a significant decline in support for bilingualism and French-language learning. As a result, when the CPF board met in the fall, President Brehaut urged board members not to release the poll and to use the remaining budget for poll dissemination to engage in other bilingualism promotion activities.[22]

Brehaut qualified the results of the poll as not encouraging but also not devastating. There was definite slippage in support for language learning. In the poll of 2,005 Canadians,[23] 64 percent believed that children should learn French in school to become bilingual. Although this was still a position held by 58 percent of anglophones, it was down 10 percent from the results of 1989. Every province reported lower support, with western Canadian provinces dropping into overall negative territory.[24]

Some of the poll's findings are particularly interesting. There were significantly higher levels of support from non-British European immigrants (67 percent) and immigrants from other parts of the world (72 percent) for children to learn French in schools to become bilingual. And, though a plurality of those polled in each western province opposed the teaching of French in schools, with the strongest opposition in Alberta (61 percent), there was still strong support in eastern Canada, especially in the Atlantic provinces, where at least 66 percent were favourable. Perhaps most interesting was how these attitudes aligned with partisan orientation. Liberal voters remained strongly in favour (70 percent) of learning French in school. Supporters of the other two long-established federal parties also expressed favourable opinions, with a slightly higher margin among Progressive Conservatives (63 percent/33 percent) than among New Democrats (59 percent/ 37 percent). The new Reform Party, emerging out of western Canada's socially conservative base, had supporters who were more likely to oppose learning French than support it, by a margin of 55 percent to 41 percent. It was a clear sign that this new party was providing a voice for anti-bilingualism elements of the Canadian population.[25]

CPF had to address the overall negative trend in responding to its funders and in managing any potential for negative coverage. CPF reported to the Department of the Secretary of State that a majority of Canadians still thought that children should learn French (or English) as a second language in school to become bilingual, and most respondents had not changed their opinions in that regard. However, CPF's national executive committee "did not feel that these findings merited a publicity event such as the news conference which was given to release the 1989 findings. It should be borne in mind that the survey was carried out during the pre-referendum months."[26] Instead, this budget was used to print and disseminate 100,000 more bookmarks from the Learning French Makes a World of Difference campaign to reach uncommitted parents across the country.

CPF's national board developed a strategy to minimize the bad news. Members of CPF were to be told that the poll itself had been delayed and that it took place "during a highly volatile period of constitutional debate when, for many Canadians, political and language issues were especially difficult to separate." As a result, CPF was to inform members that "the political climate has changed considerably since then, leaving us with dated information."[27] Members were to be reassured by estimated enrolments for immersion for 1992–93 showing growth in all regions and figures showing that more students than ever were taking core French (see Appendix 1 for overall immersion enrolments). There is little in CPF's files or published materials to indicate any negative fallout from this poll, or any additional queries from the federal government, suggesting that this somewhat discouraging news was swept under the carpet. CPF knew, though, that it had to increase its efforts to cope with the negative fallout from the constitutional and political crises of the early 1990s.

Ultimately, the referendum on the Charlottetown Accord was defeated both nationally and in most provinces. There was certainly the perception that many voted against the referendum to reject special status for Quebec or entrenched duality. In the weeks and months that followed the referendum, Canadian Parents for French pointed to ongoing high levels of immersion enrolments and core French attendance to refute arguments that the referendum was also a rejection of bilingualism and/or FSL instruction.[28]

Vona Mallory and Alliance Ontario

Turning now from the national level to the local level, in the first few years of the 1990s CPF faced a determined national letter-writing campaign aimed both at French immersion and at FSL instruction – and at CPF itself. The letters appeared in community newspapers across the country, but almost all of them seem to have originated with one woman, Vona Ruth Mallory, of Barrie, Ontario. Born in 1924, Mallory signed her letters with various configurations of her name and affiliations, including Alliance Ontario. The content and tone were always the same. Her widely aimed attack required responses from bilingualism advocates across the country. The most vitriolic letters accused Canadian Parents for French and French immersion advocates of being child abusers. Mallory cited the few researchers hostile to French immersion, using Hector Hammerly to cast doubt on the quality of the French being learned, calling it "Frenglish ... a jargon that is uncorrectable when learned very young,"[29] and Dr. Ronald Trites to claim that early French immersion students developed psychiatric problems.[30] She also twisted research by other scholars, alleging that a Carleton Board of Education study on students who had transferred out of French immersion and were in remedial courses was evidence that French immersion students "required psychiatric treatment." Immersion, Mallory claimed, was "destroying the future potential of your children because of the coercing of a dying language by a tribal segment of our society on them."[31] She alleged that "government-sponsored Francophone organizations ... [were] continually promoting their own language and culture so strongly that young parents do not seem to be able to evaluate the importance of their own Canadian language and culture."[32] Mallory also wildly misrepresented the research of Nancy Halsall, claiming that 77 percent of EFI students dropped out of high school. The study actually said that they did not follow the immersion program through to the point of gaining an immersion certificate at graduation.[33]

Some of Mallory's claims were particularly bizarre, such as her claim that French had one-fifth to one-third of the vocabulary of English, a "multiculturally based ... language that will allow greater future possibilities in the world in every field of work."[34] Mallory demanded that government funding of Canadian Parents for French be stopped "to save our children from child abuse."[35] By 1992, she had taken to writing open letters to CPF president Pat Brehaut under the moniker Mallory, Wood, Campbell, and Associates. They particularly targeted Alberta newspapers, "request[ing] that you and your group start revealing to young parents the possible and probable casualties of early French immersion programs." They claimed that the "rights of English speaking children must be protected instead of nourishing the false pride of parents who are not told the whole truth about the disadvantages of French immersion." The truth, as they saw it, was that dropouts and psychological/behavioural problems stemmed from immersion.[36] Running through all of these letters was the claim that parents were enrolling their children in immersion for their own personal glory, a trope that Mallory picked up from (and referenced) Katherine Govier's 1986 *Toronto Life* article.

Although Mallory's letters were inflammatory, they paled in comparison with her speeches. Her Ottawa speech in November 1991 – "Early French Immersion: Child Abuse? Linguistic Retardation?" – was filled with inflamed rhetoric. Mallory started from the thesis that her "crusade is to expose the casualties of Early French Immersion" and to deal with the "problems with French promotion and domination in Canada" like she would deal with the problems of a spoiled child. Her listeners were treated to a discourse on the fragile state of democracy in Canada: "WE HAVE A SOCIALIST GOVERNMENT IN POWER, and I believe we are headed for a COMMUNIST REGIME if we ... the people ever cease what we are doing to correct the situation." She went on to say that "we have a serious fight on our hands ... 1) to keep our identity as an English-speaking country; 2) to keep from being over-run by French culture and domination on upper and lower levels of our society." To accomplish this, she continued, "our weapons in this battle are truth, and dedication to sharing it and spreading it the width and breadth of our country. A lot of help from prayer is needed."[37]

In her wide-ranging speech, a host of issues unrelated to French immersion cropped up, ranging from her hostility to the metric system – "it originated in FRANCE did you know" – to anti-immigration sentiments. Mallory saw all of this as part of a giant plot of Quebec nationalists to seize control of the government and "Frenchize" Canada with the support of the "mother country" of France. It was these people, she argued, who promoted their language and culture through government-sponsored programs such as EFI. As she phrased it, "young parents may **think** they are doing the right thing by immersing their little children in a *foreign language* all day," but "in ancient China young parents used to bind the feet of their little girls with little or no empathy because they thought it was the right thing to do. Think about it." These parents, she accused, "are guilty of **CHILD ABUSE**. Not only are they guilty of child abuse, but guilty of **CONTRIBUTING TO ILLITERACY**." Mallory demanded a return to an emphasis on "GOOD ENGLISH" as a force for national unity and for building "Citizens of Tomorrow."[38]

Her accusations were published in newspapers across the country, and Mallory gave speeches and appeared on call-in radio shows.[39] Her allegations of child abuse were defamatory and prompted CPF members to respond to them. Their lawyer wrote to the editors and publishers of newspapers that had run her letters, which led to some papers publishing apologies or corrections. The central office also produced a document detailing her claims and refuting them with suitable evidence, often from the authors themselves of the miscited reports (such as Nancy Halsall and Merrill Swain). Pat Brehaut's letter to her community paper, Sherwood Park's *This Week*, noted that Mallory's writings "basically [let] us know that this small group from Barrie, Ontario is opposed to having us learn French."[40] Other writers drew on personal experiences to refute her claims. Harry Schacter, a *Kingston Whig-Standard* journalist and parent of a child in French immersion, penned an op-ed entitled "A Hitler-Like Child Abuser Speaks Out," pointing out that his own son in immersion was reading, writing, and spelling in English better than his brothers, who were educated in English, and that his French was far superior to what he learned in the core FSL program.[41]

Scarborough CPF chapter president Monica Gaudet's response demonstrated how French immersion's demographics were evolving. Gaudet observed that in her school board there were no special qualifications needed to get into the early French immersion program, though the late French immersion program needed an entrance exam. She pointed out that, for most students in Scarborough, French was their third language and that, "increasingly, new immigrants coming to Canada with little knowledge of Canada's history of English-French tensions are embracing this program as an opportunity to give their children a competitive edge." Gaudet had been to an immersion graduation ceremony at which the valedictorian was a male student of Chinese origin. Gaudet, a first-generation Canadian herself of mixed Estonian, Russian, German, and Swiss descent, observed that there were numerous reasons why parents chose immersion for their children, ranging from believing in Canada's dual-language heritage, to realizing that learning languages developed intellectual capacities and helped to overcome prejudices, and to believing that the future belonged to people who could communicate and be open minded. She pointed out the demand for multilingual and bilingual employees in professions linked to marketing products and creating jobs, an observation that pulled immersion away from being linked solely to government jobs.[42]

Although Vona Mallory was effectively an anti-bilingualism army of one, she nevertheless caused trouble for advocates of French-language learning. She was also closely tied to other anti-bilingualism groups and referred her readers and listeners to the work of APEC and Canadian Parents for English/ Core French. It was hyperbolic rhetoric, but it played to the fears and concerns of parents, and it tied in to fears about the decline of English-speaking Canada's control over the country's national identity.

More CPF Crisis Kits
Local chapters that needed to respond to Mallory's letter-writing blitz could draw on CPF's follow-up to its 1990 crisis kits. In August 1991, CPF president Pat Brehaut circulated a second set of responses to claims about French and bilingualism.[43] This series of claims dealt with critics who argued that learning French was pointless, that the time of bilingualism was passing, and that issues of language should be devolved completely to the provinces, allowing Quebec to go its own way with French and letting English predominate elsewhere. The priority was to refute that enrolments in EFI were dropping because there was something wrong with the program. This claim had recently been touted by Link Byfield in the *Western Report*.[44] The response sheet noted that the 1990–91 overall increase in enrolments was only 8 percent, the lowest one-year increase in recent years, but that it was tied partly to overall population decline in the school-aged cohort, and enrolment figures varied substantially from province to province.

Another common claim was that Canadians should not learn French since Quebec might separate, Canada was becoming more multicultural, and other languages were becoming more important. CPF replied that it made sense to learn a language that is part of the country's heritage and because Canada had internationally acknowledged expertise in teaching the two official languages and a bank of resource materials. Bilingual Canadians, CPF noted, were especially well equipped to act as Canada's bridge builders and peacemakers by maintaining a dialogue with Quebecers in French as well as with millions of other French speakers around the world. Heritage languages were an important complement of, not a replacement for, official languages. CPF also cited that 2 million Canadians were learning French as a second language and that Environics polls showed that 74 percent of Canadians wanted a second language to be taught in schools. Finally, in response to the claim that Canada's problems could be solved by giving control over languages to the provinces, with French in Quebec and English elsewhere, CPF showed its allegiance to minority-language communities, noting that they would be left out of such a policy. It further observed that a Canadian Facts survey had recently shown that 57 percent of English-speaking Canadians supported having services made available in minority languages in all provinces. These response sheets were maintained and updated over the years as part of CPF's research and fact-based strategy for responding to the emotional rhetoric of anti-bilingualism organizations.

Secondary Immersion and Attrition

While CPF's major concern in the 1970s and much of the 1980s was creating new programs and expanding French-language learning opportunities, by the early 1990s attrition of students, particularly at the secondary level, had become a pressing concern. This issue manifested itself in different ways. The most vehement critics of French immersion threw around figures claiming that anywhere between 20 and 80 percent of immersion students dropped out of the program. Vona Mallory claimed that at least one out of every five children dropped out of EFI and that this rate increased with every year. She claimed that her figures were based on a study in the Ottawa-Carleton school board and that these dropouts caused serious adjustment problems and sometimes required psychiatric treatment.[45]

Nancy Halsall, the consultant with the Carleton school board who had conducted the study of attrition, said that Mallory's statistic was a misrepresentation of the data. Halsall noted that students left the program for a number of reasons, including moving to other school districts, taking courses offered only in English, or attaining the level of bilingualism that they wished to attain. On the basis of data from one school year in Carleton, Halsall said that it was possible to determine that 3 percent of students in the program from kindergarten to grade eight left immersion specifically to join the regular program, a much lower "dropout" rate than that being claimed.[46] Moreover, though 16 percent of students in special education programs at the elementary level were former French immersion students, immersion was not the causal factor. Halsall was concerned, however, that these students were being transferred out rather than given the supports they needed to stay in immersion.[47]

There was a lack of good scientific data on the extent to which students did leave the immersion stream, the reasons why they did so, and what might address or reduce the degree to which this occurred. Canadian Parents for French commissioned Halsall to work on a study of issues related to immersion retention. A questionnaire was sent in the spring of 1991 to 353 school boards across Canada, focusing on secondary school attrition but also asking about elementary schools.

Halsall's final report was distributed in 1992.[48] It found that at the elementary school level boys were more likely to transfer out of immersion than girls but that socio-economic factors did not play a role. Many students who transferred out of the immersion stream did so for reasons that would not be accepted in the regular stream, such as discontent with the teacher.[49] Only about one-quarter of school boards thought that there might be an issue with attrition at the elementary level, and some had plans to study it.[50] Secondary-level studies pointed to the difficulty of getting hard data, since the school boards did not track students who left immersion. It was hard to define what qualified as "leaving" immersion, since many schools did not have a set stream, merely a number of courses offered in French. The only metric for determining how many students "completed" immersion was whether they had enough credits to qualify for the high school's immersion certificate, if there was one.[51] Three-quarters of school boards thought that there was some loss of secondary students, and half of them thought that it was a problem.

Respondents noted that immersion often ruled out other program choices, including gifted and technical programs, and a number of electives. This was partly because immersion programs were often scattered across multiple dual-track schools rather than being housed in a single immersion centre. However, they also noted that the latter option might be unpopular with students who wanted to attend a local school with their non-immersion friends. Respondents noted the perception that it was easier to get high marks, required for postsecondary admission, in the English stream, though there were no studies on whether this was in fact the case. Teacher quality and parental advice also influenced students' decisions. Halsall pointed to a number of ways in which to address these factors, including expanding French-language course offerings and improving teacher training and recruitment, but she noted that perhaps many students had simply reached their desired levels of bilingualism.[52] She also observed that work needed to be done with teachers, administrators, and guidance counsellors on the circumstances in which they would or would not recommend transferring between the programs.

In response to the Halsall study, CPF launched the initiative Meeting the Challenge of Secondary School Programs in the fall of 1992, capped off with the national CPF conference in Vancouver in the fall of 1993. The campaign involved action on a number of Halsall's key recommendations,[53] including working with school boards on improving teacher training for secondary French immersion, addressing teacher recruitment, developing better special education programs within the immersion stream, and working with guidance and counselling programs. CPF attempted to increase the involvement of parents in lobbying for a broader array of courses in the secondary school immersion programs. It also worked on how to describe the language capacities of immersion graduates for employers and university entrance and how to quantify the value of bilingual graduation certificates. Members discussed research on the issue of grades/marks in the immersion programs and what impact it had on applications for university.[54] It was clear that transfers out of the immersion stream were sometimes caused by perceptions that had to be corrected, but other cases were rooted in real problems that needed to be addressed. Resourcing was a major problem. Without a critical mass of students, it was not possible for schools to offer as extensive an array of courses for students in the immersion stream as for students in the English stream. On the other hand, creating immersion centres fed into the debate over neighbourhood schools and NIMBYism. Regardless, secondary school programs were more central to CPF's activities by the mid-1990s.

A Recessionary Context
The challenge of promoting bilingualism against the backdrop of constitutional issues in the late 1980s and early 1990s was exacerbated by the overall economic context as Canada slipped into a serious recession. Although CPF received some revenue from membership fees, the Department of the Secretary of State was the major funder of its projects and operations. Recession-era budget cuts had significant impacts on its ability to carry out its mission. Early warning signs came in the spring of 1991 when voluntary summer staff reductions, board meeting cancellations, and scaling back of publications were announced.[55] By the end of 1991, CPF, which always ran with slight surpluses, was operating with a budgetary shortfall. In early 1993, it became aware of plans to cut all federal programs by 10 percent, and it began to consider ways to reduce expenses, including cancellation of the high-profile but expensive Festival d'art oratoire.[56] A further 5 percent cut was announced for 1994–95.[57] (See Appendix 5 for federal contributions to CPF's budget.) CPF trimmed programs, reduced board meeting frequency, scaled back major initiatives such as the newsletter, and increased national conference fees.

Funding to the educational programs themselves was also threatened. The Official Languages in Education Program (OLEP) was up for its five-year renewal in 1993. CPF undertook a direct and personalized letter-writing campaign to key figures at both levels of government. It urged members to stress the federal government's competitiveness/globalization/ free-trade agenda and how bilingualism gave Canada an advantage in this global market.[58] Although the OLEP was renewed, it was with reduced funding, with $1.1 billion earmarked for five years, a reduction of $125 million. The new Liberal government of Jean Chrétien, elected in the fall of 1993, did not restore the funds cut by the Conservative administration.[59] This had implications for CPF's ability to convince provinces and school boards to create better FSL and French immersion programs. The budget to expand programs beyond their current levels would not be available from Ottawa, and provinces generally had not stepped up with their own commitments. It is thus not surprising that figures for immersion enrolments in Canada plateaued in the mid-1990s. (See Appendix 1 for figures.) Financial constraints, coupled with a hostile political-constitutional climate, made it much more difficult for advocates of better French programs (themselves operating with reduced funding) to continue to expand and improve these programs. The budget cuts could not have come at a worse time politically.

Lean-Year Partnerships and Campaigns

Despite these cutbacks, Canadian Parents for French continued to maintain some long-running initiatives and even undertook some new ventures. In 1990, CPF published a revised edition of *So You Want Your Child to Learn French!* that was co-edited by Berkeley Fleming and Margaret Whitla. However, no similar publications were undertaken in the financial climate of the 1990s. New projects tended to be done in partnership with other groups or governments, such as *Meeting the Challenge of Secondary School French Programs* in 1992–93 with funding from Canadian Heritage.[60]

One promising new initiative was a partnership with the Society for Educational Visits and Exchanges in Canada (SEVEC) to run a video exchange program launched in early 1992. The project sought ways for anglophone and francophone students to interact, hopefully without the significant costs associated with in-person travel exchanges. Classrooms in English- and French-speaking Canada of FSL students and native francophones would exchange videocassettes with recorded messages and communicate with each other in this way.[61] The program was initially slow to get moving, largely because of a lack of interest in Quebec. By November, sixty classes in

A good sense of humour was always an asset when promoting bilingualism to Canadians. | *Source:* Berkeley Fleming and Margaret Whitla, eds., *So You Want Your Child to Learn French! Second Revised Edition* (Ottawa: Canadian Parents for French, 1990), 128. Illustration by Ted Boothroyd. © Canadian Parents for French.

English-speaking provinces had agreed to participate, but only four classes in Quebec had applied to participate as the "twin" classes, so CPF and SEVEC approached francophone minority classes in the Maritime provinces.[62] By early in 1993, twenty-six classes were involved in active exchanges, with ten pairs of ESL and FSL classes and three pairs of immersion classes trading videos. However, the francophone side of the program continued to be a problem since a number of francophone minority communities expressed concern that the program might contribute to their problems with assimilation.[63] The program did continue to expand for a number of years.[64]

Canadian Parents for French also promoted and co-sponsored a writing contest for young Canadians. Launched in 1993, Write It Up! was a joint venture with Canadian Heritage, the Canadian Association of Second-Language Teachers (CASLT), and the Canadian Association of Immersion Teachers (CAIT). Children aged ten to thirteen were asked to submit essays on what Canada's official languages meant to them. Three thousand children participated in 1993, and the four winning entries were published in CPF's national newsletter.[65] Write It Up! became an annual event, running until 2001, and over time it brought on additional partners. All 4,200 participants in the 1995 competition received a letter from Prime Minister Jean Chrétien.[66]

In 1994, CPF recycled its Learning French Makes a World of Difference publicity campaign materials and once again ran a radio and television campaign to promote learning two official languages. An estimated 2 million Canadians saw or heard the publicity spots aired on sixty-nine radio stations and fourteen television stations across the country, somewhat down in number. Funding was much tighter by the time of this campaign, only possible thanks to a special project grant from Canadian Heritage.[67]

Mid-1990s Restructuring
In the aftermath of the constitutional crises of the early 1990s, and heading into the period around Quebec's second referendum, identifiably Canadian dimensions of bilingualism were less foregrounded in CPF's promotional efforts. For instance, in the winter of 1994, General John de Chastelain, the chief of Canada's defence staff, wrote an article for CPF's newsletter on the importance of languages in an international context, how language skills related to foreign policy and trade, and the connection between Canada's success as an exporting nation and the language dexterity of its citizens. The same issue featured interviews with two former immersion high school students, now an international journalist and a computer programmer making use of their French skills.[68] Newsletters later in the year featured other immersion graduates from Prince Edward Island, Andrew Kinnear and Megan Thomson, who wrote about how having French as a second language helped them in picking up their third languages of Spanish and Indonesian.[69]

CPF had not decided to divorce itself from the national context of bilingualism, but there was clearly a move to incorporate broadly relevant advantages of bilingualism. As CPF president Jan Finlay put it,

knowing both Canadian languages promotes greater tolerance and understanding among Canadians; French is the natural second language for English-speaking Canadians everywhere to learn; reading and understanding

French opens the door to one of the world's great cultures; learning and using a second language stretches the mind and creates mental muscles; knowing a second language makes it easier to learn a third – or a fourth – or even a fifth language. For a nation as committed to international trading and cooperation as Canada, knowing more than one language is invaluable.[70]

French made sense as the logical first language for English-speaking Canadians to learn, but it was also a gateway to multilingualism and other benefits.

The mid-1990s were a period of major transition for CPF. There was a major shake-up at the national office with the resignation of Executive Director Jos Scott in 1994 after fifteen years of service. Budget cuts would soon mean that CPF could no longer afford the services of its communications consultant, Cynthia Steers, who stopped being actively involved with the organization by 1996. Festival Director Alan Roberts and Treasurer Margaret Terry also stepped down in this period. Coupled with the serious budget situation, which saw further cuts of $50,000 in 1995–96, there was a need for restructuring. The new executive director, Elmer Hynes of Prince Edward Island, who had worked for the Department of the Secretary of State for seventeen years, and most recently for the Tax Court of Canada, was seconded to work for CPF for a two-year term, with his salary initially covered by Canadian Heritage.[71] Hynes ultimately served four years with CPF.

His term was largely geared toward financial streamlining, reworked governance, and an end to many high-profile but expensive activities. A review of the Festival national d'art oratoire in early 1994 found that most participants saw it as having ongoing relevance but that it was costly and needed more support from politicians and the media. The report recommended retaining it for the time being.[72] A poll of CPF members found that 50 percent thought it worth maintaining regardless of cost, but perhaps some other direct youth involvement program could be considered.[73] The festival was held again in 1995 but then cancelled. Instead, a new venture with the Canadian Council on Unity and the Terry Fox Centre, called Encounters with Canada, was launched in which FSL students from CPF families spent a week in Ottawa at the Terry Fox Centre.[74] CPF's annual national conference had long served as both an opportunity to disseminate research findings on French second-language learning and a tool for networking and volunteer development. But it was extremely expensive to hold, particularly since CPF usually sponsored the participation of many delegates from each region. A decision was made not to hold the conference in 1996.[75]

Hynes streamlined operations at CPF's national office, and its annual reports and newsletters took on a much more bureaucratic tone. The national office moved to a space-sharing arrangement with CASLT and CAIT in 1996. Canadian Heritage had suggested that the three organizations merge, and though this was resisted there was more resource and space sharing going forward.[76] CPF's national board structure changed from one representative from each provincial branch, plus a national president and vice-president, to a seven-member elected board in 1997–98.[77] As a result of these changes, CPF ran a slight budget surplus by 1997–98. A leaner organization with a more "modern" governance structure was firmly in place by the time Hynes announced his departure.

The Quebec Sovereignty Movement
The spring of 1995 was hardly a sunny time for language issues. The 1993 federal election brought the Bloc Québécois to official opposition status, with the anti-bilingualism Reform Party two seats behind. The fall 1994 election installed a Parti Québécois government in Quebec. Polling showed that Quebec sovereignists could potentially win a referendum.[78]

This new political landscape was troubling. The two main opposition parties in Parliament were no longer committed to the official languages policy. CPF was at a loss about what to do vis-à-vis Quebec. Although there was acute concern about the impacts of Quebec separation on FSL elsewhere in Canada, CPF opted against a media campaign in the province. Quebec's media had shown little interest in either CPF or FSL education, and past outreach initiatives in the province had not been successful. CPF's overall strategy was to position the decision to learn French "as a decision for personal and career growth and not simply a 'political' statement in support of Quebec."[79]

Instead, CPF worked on another type of public initiative to promote FSL that downplayed the Quebec question. CPF planned another information campaign called Learning English and French Opens Doors to Tomorrow, which would celebrate the achievements of students.[80] The campaign aimed to show Canadian support for language learning to help parents make informed decisions when faced with options for the education of their children. CPF hoped to include updated information showing Canadian support for French-language learning. CPF did not have funds for a detailed poll but inserted two questions into the omnibus national telephone survey conducted by COMPAS research from May 4 to 11, 1995, and 703 English-speaking Canadians were part of this poll.[81] The key question, however, did not specifically ask about French second-language instruction, which had been the phrasing of the 1984, 1989, and 1992 polls. Instead, respondents were asked "Do you think that learning a second language, *any* language, is an important part of a good education for Canadian students? [INTERVIEWER NOTE: THE FOCUS IS ON ALL LANGUAGES BESIDES ENGLISH.]" Respondents were then asked to indicate why they did or did not think that it was important. The second question asked "As you may know, many English-speaking children are enrolled in French immersion programs in schools across Canada. Children in French immersion take most of their instruction in French. Overall, would you describe your feelings about French immersion as [very positive/somewhat positive/neither positive nor negative/somewhat negative/very negative]?"[82]

The recast questions had the potential to reduce the political associations attached to learning French, particularly with the question on French immersion coming second. The result was a much more positive poll. Three-quarters of respondents thought that learning a second language was an important part of a good education for Canadian students, and 52 percent thought that it was very important. Supporters gave a variety of reasons, which showed that some, but not all, were thinking in terms of English-French bilingualism. Twenty-two percent noted that it made students more employable, 19 percent noted that Canada is a bilingual country, 15 percent said that it provided a range of personal benefits, and 11 percent said that it was part of a good education. There was a multicultural thrust to some responses, with 12 percent saying that it helps people to understand other cultures and 8 percent saying that Canada is a multicultural country. The small minority (8 percent) who said that learning a second language is not important were overwhelmingly clustered around those who saw no value in or advantage to it (38 percent) and those who thought that other subjects were more important (23 percent). A few argued that Canada is English speaking (12 percent) and that English is an international language (6 percent). A small minority saw language learning as too expensive (9 percent) or not necessary (5 percent).[83]

On the issue of French immersion specifically, only one in five held negative attitudes, with 8 percent declaring very negative attitudes. They were outnumbered 3:1 by those holding positive attitudes. Although these poll results were not directly comparable with the earlier poll results, they were enough to warrant a "good news" press release. National CPF president Jan Finlay observed that "Canadian students need to learn a second language in school today because it will make them more employable – and because

Canada is a bilingual country and French is part of our heritage." Finlay tied the poll to CPF's information campaign, noting that CPF was trying to combat misinformation about FSL and trying to help people make good decisions about language programs. As she noted, "we did the poll because education, in most areas of the country, is in tumult with all programs undergoing some pretty fundamental re-examination ... We are delighted that people are recognizing the need for languages, and the wide availability of French as the obvious choice of a first second-language for our Canadian students." The poll showed ongoing strong support for the general principle of second-language learning. CPF hoped to leverage this into support for French.[84] In subsequent responses to press coverage questioning the cost of French immersion and the cost of bilingualism,[85] Finlay pointed to the strong support for language learning expressed in the poll and the logic that French was the ideal language to learn since it was so widely taught, even before the Official Languages Act.[86]

Beyond the poll, the Learning English and French Opens Doors to Tomorrow campaign launched a new logo for Canadian Parents for French and a new slogan: "Proud of Two Languages." This was part of the Write It Up! challenge for 1995, which asked schoolchildren to write to the prime minister about the importance of French and English in Canada and why they were proud to know both official languages.[87] The campaign stressed the messages that languages are important, that French is the logical second language for Canadian students to learn, and that immersion works.[88] Key figures were asked to provide articles discussing the importance of bilingualism and multilingualism. They included Jocelyne Côté-O'Hara, president of Stentor Telecom Policy, Commissioner of Official Languages Victor Goldbloom, and Tim Reid, president of the Canadian Chamber of Commerce. Reid argued that children needed every advantage that they could be given so that they could go out and create their own opportunities for success, but he also stressed that, when it came to language, Canadians needed to be able to cross borders within their own country before they could think of crossing others.[89] CPF also launched a new video, *Proud of Two Languages*, which featured seven young graduates from French immersion programs who spoke about their experiences learning FSL and the personal and professional benefits that bilingualism provided to them.[90]

CPF stayed out of the 1995 Quebec Referendum campaign despite internal pressures to take a firm stand in support of national unity.[91] In the aftermath of the referendum, CPF's board adopted the following policy statement on national unity: "Congruent with the mission and goals of CPF, we support a united Canada which continues to recognize the value of our two official languages and to provide opportunities for all young Canadians to learn and use English and French."[92] It was a token gesture to board members who had wanted to become more involved, but it kept the issue of language learning front and centre.

Local Engagements with Anti-Bilingualism Activism

Kelowna

The fiscal and political climate of the mid-1990s made work to promote bilingualism at the local level more difficult, but it was not overwhelming. Kelowna, British Columbia, in the heart of the conservative Okanagan Valley, might seem like an odd place to find a success story in fending off the Alliance for the Preservation of English in Canada, but this was the case. Kelowna Parents for French was an active chapter with engaged parents who undertook fundraising activities to enrich the program. Thanks to fundraisers – including sales of T-shirts featuring the legendary Ogopogo – they were able to bring in entertainers such as Matt Maxwell and Charlotte Diamond and host a winter Carnaval.[93] As in other communities across Canada, members successfully mobilized academic studies such as the Gillin Report and the national core French work by H.H. Stern to expand core FSL offerings in the district and to enhance the immersion program.[94] Provincial studies undertaken by the BC Ministry of Education and CPF's polls on demand for quality FSL, coupled with detailed information on federal grants, helped to create and support programs in the district. By 1990, Kelowna Parents for French had enough money in the bank that the interest alone paid for most activities, such as scholarships and attendance at the national Festival d'art oratoire. It claimed between 125 and 150 members, and the district had core FSL for grades six to twelve and immersion for grades kindergarten to twelve, with reduced options at the senior secondary level.[95]

Over the late 1980s and early 1990s, Kelowna Parents for French had successfully fended off periodic challenges from APEC, using CPF crisis kit materials. These challenges included an APEC campaign to reverse Kelowna's 1990 declaration as a bilingual community.[96] The Kelowna chapter also defeated a challenge to immersion in the 1990 school district elections. It worked closely with the local French cultural centre, creating an information packet sent to all election candidates and the media with short, direct refutations of APEC's claims.[97] All of the elected candidates were supportive of immersion, and the one incumbent who hated the program lost in a squeaker by two votes. Other challenges in the early 1990s were also confronted and defused.

In 1995, there was another APEC volley against Kelowna's immersion programs. National office director Pauline Leitch submitted a letter to the *Kelowna News* criticizing French immersion and asking "why should the general public have to pay extra so that some students can take French immersion?" Leitch claimed that bilingual English speakers would not have access to jobs because "it seems bilingual English-speaking people don't have the right accent. Let's not get into a discussion of the English accent of our Prime Minister and most of the French-speaking politicians." She then engaged in some race-baiting, calling on English-speaking Canadians to wake up, claiming that the top five political jobs in the country were occupied by francophones from Quebec and listing a series of francophone political appointees, including the governor general.[98]

The most recent issue involved expanding French immersion to a second school, Westbank Elementary School. Anti-immersion trustee Nicki Hokazono, backed by APEC in the past, had returned to the board after her 1990 defeat, and she solicited input from parents on the question of French immersion in the *Kelowna Daily Courier* in March 1995. Hokazono raised the issue of overcrowding in schools chosen as immersion centres and claimed that the money spent on immersion would be better spent on other programs.[99] Her call prompted letters with headlines such as "Yuppies Should Pay the Tab for French Immersion" from Judith Harris of Peachland. Harris expressed the opinion that there was no point in funding French immersion given Quebec's impending departure from Canada. "I think it unwise and foolhardy to go on spending our tax dollars on a select few people – who are probably well off enough to pay for their own children's French lessons should they so desire them."[100] Ninety-three of 100 callers to AM radio station CKIQ opposed the expansion of French immersion in their district (not an entirely surprising outcome, given the demographics of talk radio listeners).[101] Eugene Boiselle and APEC members handed out anti-immersion leaflets at Kelowna malls claiming that the expansion would lead to overcrowding and division along linguistic lines in the schools.[102] Once more, the rhetoric of French immersion as a program for the elite at the expense of programs for the majority was promoted.

APEC's overall goal of eliminating publicly funded immersion in Kelowna was countered thanks to efficient information mobilization. Proponents of immersion were able to point out that it would be foolish for Kelowna to forgo federal grants.[103] If Hokazono had an issue with OLEP funding, Vivian

Turgeon observed, it made more sense to bring it up with Ottawa rather than deprive residents of Kelowna. Turgeon and other CPF members noted that many other special programs got funding, including special education, First Nations and ESL, and many other courses, including instrumental music, that not all students took.[104] They called on Hokazono to be upfront about the fact that her issue was with the "French" part of French immersion rather than hide behind rhetoric about overcrowding or saving tax dollars. As Turgeon noted, the program was no more elitist in its admission process than any other optional program or sport offered in the schools, and all the children played together in the schoolyard. In his speech to the District 23 school board, Joe Gordon observed that APEC had a history of claiming to speak for a vast constituency, but the 1990 Environics poll for CPF showed that 55 percent of British Columbians supported having children learn French in schools, and a sizable proportion wanted immersion as an option. He cited statistics from the Okanagan French immersion program that showed minimal loss of students from year to year and overall program growth. Gordon was tired of APEC's sniping at an effective education program, and he called on school board members, most of whom had endorsed French immersion at the November 1993 candidates' forum, to continue to do so.[105]

Existing programs continued, but the school board did vote against expansion of the program to Westbank in 1995.[106] In many respects, Kelowna was a good example of what was happening with immersion by the mid-1990s. Although there was virulent anti-immersion rhetoric from a small cohort of the population, for the most part authorities were publicly supportive of the program and its objectives and were unwilling to scale the program back. However, in tight financial times, and lacking additional federal funds, expansion often was not approved. Although surveys showed that parents would enrol their children if a local school offered the program, the distance of the commute was a disincentive. This might help to explain the plateauing numbers in French immersion in other jurisdictions in the mid-1990s.

Ottawa-Carleton

In 1994–95, another wave of anti-immersion sentiment swept through Ottawa-Carleton. It was connected to Lori Nash's Canadian Parents for English (renamed as Ottawa-Carleton Parents for Excellence in Education and claiming fifty member families[107]) and Hector Hammerly, but it included some new players and an increased media profile.

This wave was primed by a feature-length article by Carol Milstone in *Saturday Night* in September 1994 that was largely a litany of anti-French immersion critics. She centred her critiques on Orleans, Ontario, where Nash resided, and the Carleton Board of Education. The article claimed that research by critics of immersion – Hector Hammerly and Ronald Trites especially – was ignored or suppressed by supporters of immersion. Millstone went so far as to claim that the "powerful national lobby group" called Canadian Parents for French had assumed a gatekeeper position in vetting and blocking research in the interest of protecting the "sacred cow" of immersion. She outlined the limitations of immersion claimed by its critics – on grammar and proficiency in particular – and devoted a lot of space to Hammerly and his theories of how "superior levels of French proficiency" could be attained. Ignoring the Halsall study, Millstone claimed that CPF hid or ignored the issue of attrition. She also quoted local psychologists on the struggles of children with learning difficulties in immersion and parents on the stigma of either not enrolling or removing children from immersion. Millstone did not quote a single expert who favoured immersion to refute the claims of the critics, picking only people who could support her article's claim that "when it comes to French immersion parental faith has been shaped by false hopes, false promises, and false illusions – all fuelled by the government of Canada's bilingual dream machine."[108]

Millstone's feature was a nice bit of advance publicity for Hammerly's newest venture. In December 1994, Hammerly appeared on CBC Radio, wrote op-eds in the *Ottawa Citizen* and *Vancouver Sun,* and placed ads in the *Globe and Mail,*[109] pitching his new "diagnostic test" for children in French immersion to determine if there were flaws in their French. The ad interpellated "French immersion parents: Research studies show that the French of most immersion students is poor. How good is your child's French? Find out with the specialist-designed bilingual French Immersion Test (FIT)."[110] Hammerly's letters to the editor denouncing immersion appeared in community newspapers across the country.[111] The op-eds repeated his usual line about "Frenglish" being spoken by immersion students and claimed that second-language instruction should be started at a much later age, using a structured, drill-based manner to produce proper grammar. In April 1995, he sent a letter to school principals across the country promoting the school version of his FIT.[112]

Anti-immersion rhetoric tended to get greater media exposure when it came from an academic with a university position, so Hammerly could not be easily ignored. CPF members and immersion students wrote letters that outnumbered those favourable to his op-eds.[113] Long-time immersion researcher Merrill Swain penned a counter piece, dismissing his cover-up theory as a farce, noting that research on immersion's flaws had been published as early as 1975 and that since then there had been advances in teaching methodology. Over twenty years of research had come from OISE, McGill, Ottawa, and Simon Fraser attesting to immersion's strengths, she noted, and "their work, unlike Hammerly's, is based on results from many thousands of students, and has been published in peer-reviewed journals."[114] Indeed, Simon Fraser University distanced itself from Hammerly and told him to quit using the university's name in connection with his project, which had not been passed by the university's ethics review committee.[115] André Obadia, a French professor at Simon Fraser University, wrote a scholarly response to Hammerly. Obadia obtained a copy of the Hammerly test and had it evaluated by colleagues who were experts in second-language pedagogy. They were "revolted" by the test, observing that it showed that Hammerly, a linguist, knew nothing about how students in immersion learned French. What he proposed for language learning was straight-up behaviourism, demanding perfect speech utterances from day one – a model that could only work in a controlled laboratory setting. The test was described by one of Obadia's colleagues as perhaps suitable for third-year translation students in university.[116]

While Hammerly continued to be hailed as an expert by organizations critical of immersion and bilingualism more broadly, and was the "go-to" person for anti-immersion news articles,[117] his work was a nuisance more than a genuine threat to the pedagogy. Nevertheless, it provided fodder for critics and kept whisper campaigns and rumour mills on FSL and French immersion effectiveness alive. Hammerly was a visible presence who had to be dealt with on a regular basis, using the most current pedagogical research.[118]

The final major figure to introduce in this Ottawa-Carleton story is Don Bell, a professional engineer and management consultant in Kanata and an ex-CPF member. Bell now thought that immersion was a legal form of segregation that pulled good students into it and streamed immigrant, visible minority, and low-income children, along with those with learning disabilities and behavioural problems, into the English-only stream. Bell now believed that the bilingual capabilities of immersion graduates were not worth the cost of what he thought was a two-tiered system. He wanted to see a move toward an enhanced core FSL program for all students.[119] This was not a new argument in the nation's capital, where the popularity of immersion and the large number of students in the program led to some stark contrasts between the two streams. Some critics called it "scholastic apartheid" and "a quasi-private school system going on in the public school system."[120] Bell had some clout as a former CPF parent who now thought that the solution was to end immersion altogether rather than improve supports for other students to enhance inclusiveness.

In March 1995, Don Bell, Carol Millstone, and Lori Nash organized a public forum on the "pros and cons" of French immersion in Ottawa, and it attracted a crowd of 350 people.[121] A pre-forum article in the *Ottawa Citizen* told the tale of Bell's son Andrew, claiming that French immersion classes were smaller and had better-motivated students.[122] The article built the case that a two-tiered system was being created in Carleton and observed that a new group called Ottawa-Carleton Parents for Excellence in Education was organizing a forum to examine the issue of immersion. The article provided some balance by citing CPF leaders, Ottawa and Carleton trustees, and curriculum experts who countered the allegations of elitism while acknowledging that more needed to be done to provide supports for children with special education needs and to attract children of immigrants.

Although CPF president Jan Finlay was invited to the forum, the room was stacked with anti-immersion representatives, including Hector Hammerly and Geoffrey Wastenays, a well-known APEC spokesman who claimed that French immersion had "literally destroyed" the life of his son.[123] It was an emotional forum, to the extent that a radio announcer commented on air about the impoliteness of some of the participants, noting that Hammerly interrupted Finlay's presentation. Montreal *Gazette* columnist William Johnson noted that "some of [French immersion's] current critics have undermined what could be legitimate criticisms by grossly overstating their case, by attacking the person and motivation of professionals who have researched FI, rather than being intelligent participants in an open debate."[124] It did not help that Nash maintained that many parents in her neighbourhood sent their children to immersion because "they did not want colored people in their class and that was why they were going into immersion."[125] While raising emotions, the forum did not curtail immersion in the National Capital Region.

Nash's anti-immersion activism would continue on and off for the next five years, including appearances at APEC meetings, articles published in APEC's newsletter, and op-eds and letters published in Ottawa-area newspapers, including the *Ottawa Citizen*. Her later writings took on a more strident anti–French Canadian tone, arguing that CPF's advocacy was "an example of the 'Stockholm syndrome' where the captive comes to admire the captor."[126] Nash decried the expansion of francophone rights and French services in Ottawa, arguing that it created more and more jobs requiring French-language proficiency, leading to a flood of francophone commuters from Quebec into Ontario, jobs that could be filled by anglophone Ottawans. She claimed that all of these bilingual positions were filled by francophones because "anglophones have no opportunity to become well spoken beyond a functional level in French. Bilinguals with fluent French are francophones."[127] In other writings, Nash continued to claim that immersion was elitist and did not work. She wanted the Ottawa school boards to move to a system in which all students could take extended French (a standard forty-minute-per-day core French lesson, plus one other subject in French), claiming that this approach would solve various problems – including uneven teacher workloads, classroom organization, and busing out of neighbourhood schools – and trumpeting "equality of opportunity" for all students.[128] CPF and its supporters continued to counter her allegations and claims, noting in 1998, for example, that core French now used the communicative methodology pioneered in immersion.[129]

Conclusion

By the end of 1995, Canada and Canadian Parents for French had weathered a tumultuous decade on the constitutional front and much more virulent anti-bilingualism campaigns than in the past. The public mood on language and accommodation was less generous than in the past, and with hard economic times the financial resources to support expanded programs to support bilingualism were drying up. The expansionary era had ground to a halt, and most French immersion and core French initiatives were treading water at best, maintaining the status quo, and doing their best to resist cutbacks. Bilingualism's supporters were feeling a bit battered but hoped that, with CPF's organizational restructuring and improvement in the economy, it might be possible to regroup and revitalize their efforts.

11

A Millennial Reprieve

The late 1990s provided a reprieve for Canadian Parents for French as Canada moved away from the harsh economic times and constitutional conflicts of the late 1980s to mid-1990s. Good news arrived in 1998 with the announcement of a four-year period of guaranteed minimum funding for CPF from Canadian Heritage, plus project funding for the next two years to improve communication and increase membership.[1] The organization also got a welcome boost from a Canadian Chamber of Commerce statement endorsing FSL programs in Canadian schools. Chairman Gerald Pond and President Timothy Reid noted that "communication between the two principal language groups is essential to the fostering of an efficient economic climate ... [and] to developing further language abilities to support our communication efforts in rapidly developing international markets." They went on to argue that "an increasingly prosperous Canada will have a far greater probability with a competently English and French bilingual generation and the strong support of our business community."[2] In November 1998, CPF partially revived its national conference, holding a joint event with the Canadian Association of Second Language Teachers (CASLT) and the Canadian Association of Immersion Teachers (CAIT).

All was not completely rosy yet. As the Official Languages in Education Program (OLEP) agreement lapsed in 1998, the program was initially subject to an 11.6 percent cut above the 30 percent reduction of the prior five years. CPF urged members to redouble their efforts to push the Canadian

238

government to increase funding for second-language programs.[3] By the time the new five-year protocol was signed in 1999, thanks partly to the efforts of CPF, funding for the OLEP was increased.[4]

New CPF executive director Robin Wilson, entering the position in March 1999, embodied the links between CPF and the Ottawa policy community. His background included working for five years with the Office of the Commissioner of Official Languages and for three years with the Treasury Board Secretariat's Official Languages Branch.[5] With increased Canadian Heritage funding for the national office and provincial branches, it was possible for CPF to revive activities that had been placed on hold and launch new initiatives. A research officer was added to the national office in 1999. In 2000, CPF was once again able to host its own national conference, and it would continue to do so on a biennial basis.

By 1998, CPF membership had plummeted to below 10,000 members in fewer than 130 chapters (down more than 7,000 members since the outset of the decade). An aggressive membership campaign, coupled with a shift in the funding model to direct more membership revenues to individual chapters, contributed to a period of sustained growth.[6] With greater activity, and the capacity for greater outreach to recruit members, President Joan Netten was able to report that membership figures were up by 22.5 percent in three years. Canadian Heritage funding made it possible to launch a membership campaign in 2001–2 called I'm Learning French Because ... , which communicated the value of teaching FSL and being a CPF member.[7] The grassroots strength of the movement rebounded, and CPF was back to 17,000 members and 170 active chapters by the fall of 2002, and it continued to increase in subsequent years, crossing the 20,000 threshold.[8] By 2003, in partnership with Glendon College at York University, CPF revived the Concours national d'art oratoire, with competition categories for core French, core special, extended French, immersion, and francophone students.[9] After a year at Faculté St-Jean at the University of Alberta, CPF entered into a long-term partnership to hold the event annually at the University of Ottawa, which offered scholarships to winners.

Francophone Partnerships

Partnerships continued to be key to CPF's approach through the late 1990s. Beyond office- and conference-sharing arrangements with CASLT and CAIT, both second-language organizations, there was increased partnership with francophone organizations, supporting work being done by Canadian Heritage and the Office of the Commissioner of Official Languages to increase the profile and appreciation of the value of two official languages. This fit nicely with the new organizational slogan: "Proud of Two Languages/Nos deux langues, notre fierté." This became the theme of the annual writing competition – started as Write It Up! in 1993, aimed at ten to thirteen year olds – rebranded as Proud of Two Languages in 1997, with high school students as the target group.

In 1998, CPF was invited to send a delegation to the Jeux de la francophonie canadienne. It did so for the Memramcook Games held in conjunction with the 1999 Sommet de la francophonie in Moncton, New Brunswick.[10] Another delegation of francophile students participated in the jeux of 2002 in Quebec City. This was part of a new partnership with the Fédération de la jeunesse canadienne-française and a broader engagement with the Canadian and international francophonie.[11] CPF enhanced its commitment to duality, in addition to bilingualism, with its revised vision statement of "a Canada where French and English live in mutual respect with understanding and appreciation of each other's language and culture and where linguistic duality forms an integral part of society."[12] CPF's stature as a francophile organization led to increased involvement in francophone gatherings, including the Nineteenth Biennale of the French Language held in Ottawa-Hull in 2001. Having struggled to make connections with francophone minority communities throughout the 1980s and early 1990s, by the turn of the millennium CPF was a partner in the Dialogue project run by the Fédération des communautés francophones et acadiennes du Canada.[13]

The State of French-Second-Language Education in Canada 2000
As part of its growing capacity for activity, CPF undertook a major new project to produce an annual report on FSL issues across Canada. With a foreword by John Ralston Saul, co-patron of CPF (along with his wife, Governor General Adrienne Clarkson), *The State of French-Second-Language Education in Canada 2000* was featured in a full-page article in *Maclean's* and then launched in events in major cities across the county in late August 2000, coupled with interviews on CBC and other TV, radio, and print media outlets. The report outlined areas of existing strength and plans for action in each province. By this point, nearly 2.5 million children in Canada were enrolled in core French classes and over 317,000 in immersion.

It is striking how the priorities for action at the turn of the millennium were all too familiar. These priorities included acute French teacher shortages, the need to provide remedial help for students in French immersion, the need for a transparent process of allocating FSL funds, the need to evaluate current FSL teaching methods and adopt new ones informed by research, and the need to eliminate barriers to entry to FSL programs.[14] It was a case of *plus ça change, plus c'est la même chose*. Despite over two decades of work, the challenges facing second-language instruction remained constant. With a hint of fatigue, CPF's 1998–99 annual report noted "that parents and teachers, children and decision-makers, move through their respective roles over the years and new ones coming on to the scene have to be told all over again."[15]

The 2000 COMPAS Poll

In April 2000, CPF commissioned a COMPAS opinion poll to gauge the strength of support for language learning, and 1,428 English-speaking Canadian residents were surveyed. In the top-level results of the poll released in its newsletter, CPF reported that 87 percent of Canadians believed that "the ability to speak more than one language is very important in this period of growing international trade" and that 78 percent believed that learning a second language was important for students, the same level reported in 1995.[16]

It is somewhat telling that the other major question found that "nearly half" of respondents continued to think it important for English-language children to learn French specifically as part of their education. This was well down from the 74 percent of the 1989 poll and a significant drop from the 64 percent of the unreleased 1992 poll. Although slightly less than half of anglophones – 48 percent – thought it important for children to learn French in school, 31 percent thought it very important. Canadian Parents for French prepared a Q&A sheet for media inquiries. It included the fact that support for French-language learning was significantly lower in western Canada. CPF observed that,

> since the Anglophone majority is, in many areas, higher in the western area of the country, it can sometimes be difficult for people to recognize the potential of bilingualism. It is not necessary to live in an area where French is spoken on a regular basis, since FSL programs have a variety of benefits for any student. People in all parts of Canada can benefit from second language education.[17]

The full poll, available on CPF's website (launched in 1997), gave additional details on how attitudes to language and language learning were evolving. It appears that attitudes toward FSL learning were not becoming more negative per se but drifting toward apathy. People had firmer impressions of the outcome of French immersion as it became more established. Although generic support for language learning and FSL was expressed, there was less support for measures that might lead to increased FSL teaching in the regular classroom. This bridge between abstract principles and realities of in-classroom changes directly affecting children continued to be where slippage occurred. Finally, there continued to be significant demographic divides along gender, region, age, and education lines when it came to questions of language.

On the key question of whether learning French in school was important, overall support had slipped from 52 percent in 1995 to 48 percent in 2000. But opposition had also declined from 27 percent to 25 percent. The greatest growth, up to 26 percent, was respondents who had no strong opinion. The demographic divide was stark, with far more women (54 percent) than men (43 percent) considering French-language learning important and significantly higher levels of support among those with university education (54 percent) than those with a public (41 percent) or high school (44 percent) education. The regional divide pitted 80 percent of Atlantic Canadians and 51 percent of Ontarians against much lower levels in British Columbia (33 percent), Alberta (42 percent), and Manitoba and Saskatchewan (35 percent). These represented 20–30 percent drops in support in some categories since 1989.[18]

Those who had indicated support for French-language learning were now most likely to cite reasons related to Canada as a bilingual country with a bilingual and bicultural heritage (36 percent). Job opportunities, while still a popular answer, had dropped significantly over the decade, given by about one in four respondents (23 percent). A variety of personal growth and educational benefits rounded out the field.[19] Of those who said that learning French was not important, 30 percent thought that other languages were more important, and this reason had doubled in significance over the past five years. Another 27 percent said that they saw no value or advantage in learning French, and a smattering of reasons related to Quebec accounted for another 15 percent of respondents.[20]

Attitudes toward French immersion programs remained constant over the five-year period, with those with positive opinions outnumbering those with negative opinions three to one (57 percent to 18 percent).[21] Perceptions of regular second-language programs (core French) were slightly more positive (64 percent versus 17 percent). The poll probed perceptions of core FSL and French immersion programs' strengths and weaknesses. Perhaps the most significant finding was that respondents split evenly about whether French immersion students spoke French fluently upon completion of the program, with 35 percent saying that they did and 34 percent saying that they did not. Significant minorities thought that French immersion meant that "problem" students were left in the regular programs (20 percent) and that immersion programs were attracting the "best" students (26 percent), both of which were long-standing critiques related to elitism and streaming.[22]

On "core" French, over two-thirds (68 percent) thought that one period of French per day was not enough for students to become bilingual, whereas almost 22 percent thought that it would suffice. Sixty-four percent thought that core French should be part of the basic curriculum of English schools (versus 29 percent who did not), and 59 percent thought that one period of French per day was an asset (versus 29 percent who did not). However, for the proposal that there should be more than one period in French per day in the basic school system, only 45 percent agreed, versus 43 percent opposed. Canadians appeared to recognize the limitations of core FSL as a means of language learning but did not appear to feel strongly overall that this was a problem that deserved additional classroom time.[23]

Overall, women, respondents aged eighteen to twenty-nine, Atlantic Canadians, and those with more education were more likely to voice supportive attitudes toward French-language learning broadly and French immersion specifically. Those with university educations were less likely to believe that immersion graduates did not speak French well upon graduation or that they performed poorly in other subjects. Western Canadians were more likely to voice negative opinions on French immersion and related issues, though BC residents were on par with Ontarians in believing that learning any second language was part of a good education, and residents in the prairie provinces were as likely as Ontarians to believe that French immersion helped people to get jobs. Overall, western Canadians were about as likely as Ontarians to think that the ability to speak more than one language was an asset in this period of growing international trade (this was the formulation of the statement on language learning that got the most support, at 87 percent of Canadians). Residents of communities with populations of less than 100,000 expressed the most negative attitudes toward French-language issues.[24]

Parents' status was a crucial variable. Respondents with younger children were more likely than those with older children to have positive views of

French-language issues. Respondents with children were more likely than those without children to think that multilingualism was an asset in a period of international trade. They were also, notably, less likely to believe that French immersion programs had the best students in them or that students in immersion programs performed less well in other subjects, such as math or science. Direct exposure to French-language programs seemed to diminish negative attitudes toward them.

In light of the poll's findings, CPF continued to try to distance FSL learning from Canadian politics. It touted how the benefits of fluency in more than one language extended far beyond the political realm. These included economic and cultural benefits that stemmed from a quality education and social benefits that flowed from gathering confidence and esteem by communicating in a second language. CPF highlighted other pedagogical benefits, including that language development enhanced learning in other subjects. To combat those who claimed that the priority needed to be "core topics" such as math and science, CPF argued that increased literacy in two languages often made it easier for students to deal with abstract concepts. On the long-running question about why students should learn French, and not another global language such as Japanese, Mandarin, or Spanish, CPF used the gateway argument:

> These other languages are important, especially within specific industries, and once a second language is learned, it is that much easier to learn a third or fourth language. We can look to Europe as an example, where the education system provides children with the opportunity to learn three to five languages ... Many careers here [in Canada], especially those within the federal public service, tourism, and export industries, require employees to be familiar, if not fluent, with both English and French.[25]

By 2000, CPF's overall message foregrounded the educational and career benefits of French-language learning and placed the national dimensions in the background. CPF noted that Canadians had identified employment opportunities, personal growth, and quality education as reasons why FSL programs were important. It added that

> learning and using a second language stretches the mind and creates mental flexibility. Learning a second language makes learning a third or fourth language easier. Learning French allows you to truly experience another of the world's cultures. Knowing a second language is a competitive edge in

the world of business and trade. Fluency in both of Canada's official languages promotes tolerance and understanding among Canadians.[26]

It stressed that it was easiest to start with widely taught French and then progress to other third and fourth languages.

Given concerns about attrition rates in FSL learning and softening public support for learning French, CPF began running a series of conferences called French for the Future. The brainchild of CPF co-patron John Ralston Saul, these conferences aimed to give high school students insights into the opportunities that their bilingual capacities would bring them as they entered postsecondary education and the workforce. These conferences featured presentations by representatives from business, government, and education in an effort to promote the wide array of options – including those outside the government sphere – that English-French bilingualism could provide in terms of job and career opportunities.[27]

Doubling the Numbers

At the turn of the century, rumours swirled that enrolment in French immersion was on the decline. It was an allegation that members of CPF feared could lead to a bandwagon effect and fuel the criticisms of opponents of the method. However, President Joan Netten pointed out that overall in Canada participation in French immersion was stable. For the past five years, participation in French immersion accounted for 6.5 percent of Canada's total school population – representing about 10 percent of students in FSL classes. Although some provinces saw dipping numbers, they were up in other locations. Netten noted that school-age populations in Canada were declining but that French immersion's share of that population was constant. Moreover, the perpetual problems affecting French immersion enrolment remained, including demand exceeding supply in terms of classroom space, caps on enrolment, transportation issues, and other structural factors.[28]

The Official Languages in Education Program was renewed once again in 2003. By this point, the federal government had balanced its budget, and it appeared that Jean Chrétien's administration was interested in legacy projects. When announcing the new OLEP protocol, Minister of Intergovernmental Affairs Stéphane Dion and Minister of Heritage Sheila Copps connected this funding to a new action plan for official languages. *The Next Act: New Momentum for Canada's Linguistic Duality* set an objective of doubling the number of fifteen to nineteen year olds who had a working knowledge of their second official language to 50 percent by 2013.[29] Funding for the OLEP protocol was boosted by $751 million, an increase of 90 percent compared with the previous agreement. There was a separate injection of $137 million for second-language learning alongside the regular funds for minority-language education, which had been the federal government's priority for the past two decades.[30] This doubled the amount that the federal government had spent on this sector over the past five-year agreement.

Dion singled out the goal of responding more effectively to the desires of parents and students for access to high-quality immersion programs. As he observed, anglophone Canadians were less bilingual than the British – the least bilingual of Europeans – and this put Canadian competitiveness at stake. He stated that "many Canadians appreciate that linguistic duality does not just reflect our past. It is part of the future of a prosperous Canada in a world of growing trade where, increasingly, the ability to communicate in many languages is valued more and more." Once again, the issue of global competitiveness provided the crux of the argument for improved bilingualism and second-language learning in Canada. Although Dion also nodded to how this provided "access to a broader cultural heritage and contrib[utions] to their personal enrichment," these cultural/personal dimensions were clearly secondary justifications for immersion and increased bilingualism.[31]

Anti-Bilingualism Activism
In the aftermath of the 1995 Quebec Referendum, the Alliance for the Preservation of English in Canada continued to publish its newsletter, but it faded on the national stage. Its rhetoric became more virulently anti-Quebec, and President Ronald Leitch adopted the catchphrase "no more prime ministers from Quebec" in his writings and in the group's activities during the run-up to the 1997 federal election. Although not explicitly endorsing the Reform Party, APEC was certainly repeating many of its positions. Leitch became fixated on the declining role of the monarchy and the British connection. Several articles in APEC's newsletter called for a return to English Canada's "heritage" and referred readers to a book written by John Farthing entitled *Freedom Wears a Crown*, which praised the role of the monarchy in Canada and denounced English Canadians who sacrificed their heritage to ally with French Canadians for power.[32] Much of APEC's newsletter was filled with stories from members who had written to

complain about things such as French predominance on packaging or signage, and it reprinted apologies received from companies. APEC appeared
to be convinced that the Canadian government was levying pressure on US
companies to "give preference to the French language" on product labelling
destined for the Canadian market, though the group was unable to find
evidence to prove this.[33] It also routinely published statistics on how many
francophones worked in each federal department, in an effort to prove
anti-English discrimination.

APEC clearly continued to think that promoting English-French bilingualism through the school system was a waste. One article noted that,

> had we directed the billions wasted on French to training in the important
> languages, we would be better placed to exchange with, trade with and
> teach many of the other peoples of the world. While English is the main
> language, others are regionally significant and growing in importance:
> Spanish, German, Japanese, Mandarin, Chinese and Russian. Each is of
> greater significance than French, which has noticeably declined from the
> important place it had in the mid nineteenth century.[34]

Other articles called on members to sign petitions against French immersion, cheered declining enrolment in immersion in the occasional jurisdiction, such as Thunder Bay,[35] and claimed that the commissioner of official
languages himself would not hire French immersion graduates to work in
his office (where 73.4 percent of employees were francophones).[36]

APEC also published another book from Kenneth McDonald. *The Monstrous Trick*, published in 1998, aimed to show "how radicals from the
French Canadian minority that is anchored in Quebec first invaded, then
dominated, the Federal Government in Canada." The "trick" in question was
"the way Canada's centuries-old tradition of inherent freedom and responsibility under the common law and sovereign parliaments was changed to
the Quebec civil code model of legislated rights and entitlements under a
central authority."[37] Between 1967 and 1997, McDonald claimed, French
Canadians "overthrew Canada's system of government" through stealth and
political acumen. The book was largely a litany of the complaints that APEC
and the BMG group had raised for years, including the charter, which they
saw as limiting freedom, and the decline of parliamentary supremacy and
the monarchy, which McDonald argued "ensured minorities were treated
justly; the majority does not oppress them."[38] Official bilingualism was cast

as a means of gaining power for French Canadians as well as "their anglophone counterparts from Montreal ... who learned the other language in childhood," and this "began to appeal to elites in English Canada as well. The effect was to create a 'New Class' of politicians, bureaucrats, academics and journalists who bought into bilingualism as the means to personal advancement."[39] As far as McDonald was concerned, Jock Andrew's 1977 predictions had come true, and the Quebec-based prime ministers had facilitated an overthrow of Canada at the expense of English Canadian heritage. Although the book would have appealed to die-hard APEC supporters, it did not attract mainstream media attention. McDonald probably would have chalked that up to the media conspiracy against his views.

By the late 1990s, APEC was fading in influence and did not seem to be a major irritant for groups such as Canadian Parents for French. In February 2000, Leitch changed the name of the group to Canadians Against Bilingualism Injustice (CABI), which placed ads during the 2000 federal election. The board then changed the name again in 2001 to Canadian Network for Language Awareness (CNLA). This was a response to attrition and an effort to attract new members, but ultimately it failed. The CNLA survived less than two more years. In September 2002, it wrapped up its operations, citing a lack of financial means to continue its work and the increasing difficulty of educating Canadians about "language concerns." President John deRinzy suggested that members direct their support to one of a number of Ottawa-based groups working against bilingualism, including the Human Rights Institute of Canada, English-Language Advocates, and Canadians for Language Fairness.[40] Of these groups, the last one became the most active anti-bilingualism group, though it largely focused on issues pertaining to the national capital.

The passage of time greatly weakened the leadership of anti-bilingualism forces, not routinely regenerated as CPF's leadership had been. Ronald Leitch passed away in 2006 at age eighty-six. The saga of CPF and Hector Hammerly ended on a rather odd note when he was forced to take early retirement from Simon Fraser University in 1997 over a scandal involving threats against his departmental colleagues and members of the university administration.[41] He passed away in 2006. Vona Mallory did not significantly revive her efforts on the anti-French front, and she died in 2011 at age eighty-six. Lori Nash, of Canadian Parents for English/Core French, largely faded from the media on the French issue after 2000, concentrating her efforts instead on library advocacy and literacy programs until she passed away in 2012.[42] Jock Andrew retreated from public engagement on the language issue, believing that the battle had been lost. With no prominent new torch bearers emerging on the anti-bilingualism front, and even the national Conservative Party shying away from criticisms of official languages policies after the re-merger of the Reform/Canadian Alliance Party with the Progressive Conservative Party, the main challenge to French immersion and FSL in Canada shifted away from organized social movements and toward the occasional media critic or locally based resistance.

Conclusion

We Learned French!
Well, Many Canadians Did

Numbers, Trends, and Considerations

If I had written this book at the turn of the millennium, my concluding assessment of the efforts to promote bilingualism in English-speaking Canada likely would have been more positive but still mixed. Over the past decade, Statistics Canada has reported slippage in the overall percentage of Canadians, particularly English-speaking Canadians, who report that they can communicate in both official languages, after four decades of steady, if not wildly impressive, growth. The decade from 2001 to 2011 was the first since 1961 in which Canada's total population growth rate outstripped its bilingual population growth rate. Of greatest concern for future trends, there has been a significant drop in the percentage of anglophones aged fifteen to nineteen who report being able to conduct a conversation in both official languages; the figure stood at 11 percent in 2011, down from 15 percent in 1996. The percentage of students at primary and secondary school levels taking core French as a second language has been falling since 1991, down from 53 percent of that age cohort to 42 percent by 2011.[1] Although it is possible to explain away, or at least mitigate, some of these trends, they are nevertheless troubling for proponents of English-French bilingualism in English-speaking Canada.

On the other hand, for the period covered in this book, the story is a significantly more positive one of modest but noteworthy gains in English-French bilingualism and bilingual education opportunities. The most impressive figure was the total number of bilingual Canadians. Even when Quebec is removed from the equation (bilingualism rates are at their highest in that province, particularly among anglophones), the number of bilingual Canadians living outside Quebec rose from 892,000 in 1961 to 2,323,900 in 2001 and then to 2,466,800 in 2011. As a percentage of the population, this was a rise from 6.9 percent in 1961 to 10.3 percent in 2001 and then a slight dip to 9.7 percent in 2011. A number of provinces posted significant gains in their bilingualism rates over this fifty-year period, including British Columbia (up from 3.5 percent to 6.8 percent), Prince Edward Island (7.6 percent to 12.3 percent), Alberta (4.3 percent to 6.5 percent), New Brunswick (19 percent to 33.2 percent), and Ontario (7.9 percent to 11 percent). No province showed either an absolute or a percentage decline below the 1961 starting point.

Canada's bilingual population continues to be concentrated in the "bilingual belt" from Ontario to New Brunswick, but there has been significant growth in both total numbers and percentages outside this region. The concentration of bilingual speakers in the region has not increased (87 percent in 1961, 86 percent in 2011), despite major growth in bilingualism among anglophone Quebecers and in the National Capital Region of Ottawa-Gatineau. Until the decade from 2001 to 2011, growth in the bilingualism rate outstripped growth in the population rate, though the gap between these two figures did narrow after being twice the total population growth rate (outside Quebec) from 1961 to 1981. Although enrolment in core FSL declined significantly, French immersion numbers, after stalling in the 1990s, have continued to rise. From 23,000 students when Canadian Parents for French was launched in 1977, enrolment rose to 267,000 by 1992 and stood at 341,000 in 2011.[2] This figure masks the fact that demand for French immersion continues to exceed space for students in many districts. Clearly, the pro-bilingualism advocacy of actors such as Canadian Parents for French and the Office of the Commissioner of Official Languages reached many Canadians.

Statisticians posit a partial mitigating factor for the declining rate of bilingualism outside Quebec from 2001 to 2011. They observe that this was a period of particularly high immigration, and the rate of bilingualism among immigrants whose mother tongue is not English is substantially lower than among the Canadian born. Outside Quebec, 11 percent of Canadian-born residents report being bilingual, versus only 6 percent of immigrants. Interestingly, the highest rates of English-French bilingualism are reported among Canadian-born residents whose mother tongue is other than English, followed by Canadian-born residents whose mother tongue is English, followed by English mother tongue residents, followed by immigrants with other mother tongues.[3] Another curious but unrelated dimension of bilingualism among anglophones outside Quebec is that the rates of bilingualism are 4–5 percentage points higher among girls than boys aged ten to nineteen, indicating a gender dynamic at play in addition to an ethnic component.

Educational Factors

Progress, or lack thereof, in promoting bilingualism among English-speaking Canadians was intimately tied up with broader issues related to education policy. It was not possible simply to "teach more French," part of a much broader matrix involving the delivery of education and philosophies on how the public education system should function. Some of the crucial issues might never be completely resolved one way or the other. There is a seemingly intractable debate over whether public education systems should be differentiated and provide options, specialized programs, and separate classrooms for different types of learners or whether there should be a standardized classroom for all types of learners to provide equal education and social integration. There is also the question of how to cope with a chronically underfunded public education system with the concomitant growth of class sizes and a shrinking resource pool for "extras." This fuels ongoing quarrels over any new program that might be perceived to give "special treatment" to *any* group within the public education system. There was potency in the rhetoric of anti-elitism and anti-streaming used by opponents of French immersion programs in particular. This was a powerful tool in the hands of those who saw no value in French, and it could convince self-described progressives who felt uncomfortable with their children getting special treatment or contributing to class or racial segregation in the public school system.[4]

As an educational innovation, French immersion was subject to debates that went beyond the overarching goal of bilingualism. Some of these debates were based on the pedagogy of language learning and raised questions about the French proficiency of graduates and the methodology used to teach French. Others related to how certain groups, including those with special learning needs, were marginalized from the program. These debates often were not constructive. Opponents of French immersion did not always critique the programs in good faith by proposing ways to improve them to address perceived weaknesses, such as incorporating more formal grammar training or fighting for special needs teachers in the immersion stream. Rather, they argued that the program should be scrapped altogether as a failure. This fuelled the tendency of some defenders of the program to retrench their positions and become wary of raising any critiques of the ongoing programs. Many feared that even constructive critiques would be used as excuses to cancel the program or not launch new pilots. It was not the most constructive and productive way to launch an educational innovation, nor was it the healthiest environment for improving the program. Yet there was evolution in pedagogy and methodology over these decades.

The Value of Bilingualism

Trends in FSL learning were also shaped by broader considerations of the value of bilingualism and the French language. Some of these trends remained constant over time, whereas others shifted. Anglocentrism was on the more intractable side. Many English-speaking Canadians continued to perceive little or no value in learning *any* second language, believing that English was growing in international importance in all fields, in addition to its dominance in North America. They felt perfectly comfortable in their monolingualism. Others, confronted with the issue of French-language learning, deflected it with the argument that it made more sense, on a global scale, for Canadians to learn a language such as Mandarin or Spanish. Many people who made this argument had no intention of actually adhering to it.

Over the latter half of the twentieth century, it did become harder to argue that French was an ascendant international language. Although it was true, and promoted by the commissioner of official languages and Canadian Parents for French, that French was spoken on every continent and was an official language in dozens of countries, many of these countries were not major international powers or major trade partners with Canada. French continued to be an international language for diplomacy and had official status in bodies such as the United Nations, the European Union, and the Olympics. However, news stories pointed to the rising stars of Asia as economic powers and trade partners, and thus the benefits of Mandarin- or Japanese-language skills, or to Canada's increasing trade integration with Latin America, for which Spanish or even Portuguese might be more useful.

The progressive disengagement of Quebec's provincial elites and elected representatives in Ottawa from broader national debates in the 1990s and early 2000s might also have led many Canadians to see less merit, from the standpoint of national unity, in learning French. Quebec's perceived disengagement from English-speaking Canada might have fostered negative views of French. This view certainly resonated in the most prominent anti-French activist literature, which often played on the line "why learn French when Quebec doesn't care about what the rest of Canada does?"

On the other hand, many English-speaking Canadians, and particularly English-language media, business, and political elites, have embraced the value of French-language skills in a national context. It has become increasingly rare to see federal leadership candidates who lack at least basic competency in the other official language. In the private sector, business leaders have made many positive statements about the merits of bilingualism. Polls of Canadian attitudes, combined with the evidence of how Canadians educated their children in this period, showed that individual bilingualism gained strength as an English Canadian value, even if primarily an aspirational one for many. Far from the majority of English Canadians could actually speak both official languages, but the idea that they *should* be able to became, for many, part of how they conceptualized Canadian identity.

There has also been a growing consensus that second-language learning has many other positive benefits beyond its economic dimensions. Psychologists have been producing increasing numbers of research studies on the overall cognitive benefits of second-language learning in terms of brain development and maintaining cognitive function.[5] The side benefits of language learning in terms of how individuals develop other skills are more widely recognized. Learning French as a second language is not only viewed as part of being a good Canadian or helping one to secure a government job but also seen as part of an enriched and enhanced education that spurs one's intellectual and psychological development, with a wide array of secondary benefits. Over the past fifty years, the values attached to personal bilingualism have developed and branched out in new directions.

Social Movement Mobilization
The overall levels of bilingualism in English-speaking Canada and the trends of second-language learning participation seem to indicate that neither pro- nor anti-bilingualism social movements emerged as clear victors. Certain factors seem to have worked in each side's favour.

Any failure to advance the cause of bilingualism among English-speaking Canadians tended to be celebrated as a victory by anti-bilingualism groups. A number of factors, particularly those linked to path dependency, tended to work in their favour. Whenever there was an effort to increase the amount of time dedicated to FSL or to create French immersion, it meant a shift from the status quo operations of a school or school board. Inertia was on the opponents' side. Creating new programs often entailed potential disruptions that could be cast in a negative light. Some of these were the practical implications of path dependency. Once hired, teachers were normally assumed to be employed until retirement. The prospect of replacing English-speaking teachers with French immersion teachers was viewed in a negative light. Anti-bilingualism activists could often win their case simply by pointing out the disruptions that might be caused by a new innovation. Path dependency was also key to the overarching argument of why change should not occur. It was more difficult for bilingualism's advocates to mobilize an argument around "levelling the playing field" or "reaching out to francophones/minorities" than it was for opponents to insist that past practices – having francophones learn English and assume the burden of bilingualism – had always worked and would continue to work. Path dependency was thus a passive aspect of the political opportunity structure that worked in the favour of opponents of new programs to enhance bilingualism.

There were also a number of resources that opponents of bilingualism mobilized. Their chief weapon was fear.[6] The materials and speeches produced by groups such as APEC and Canadian Parents for English/Core French and individuals such as Vona Mallory and Jock Andrew played heavily on emotional triggers rooted in fear. The fears were diverse but often included the loss of power, status, privilege, and control by English Canadians faced with the rising influence of "the French." It is not surprising that these fears were often articulated by, and appealed to, individuals from an older generation, largely of English speakers whose identities were anchored in a British Canadian model. These were the individuals most likely to fear that "their" Canada was at risk of being lost.

Economic fears, such as loss of English speakers' jobs to bilingual individuals, were powerful motivators. The ability to mobilize financial concerns was also key. Education has never been cheap, and in times of economic recession it was relatively simple to raise concerns over the added costs of new French programs (and to inflate those costs!) and tie them to the nation-wide cost of bilingualism (though these figures were often highly contestable[7]). Given how Canada's public education systems were funded, it was often possible to use the cost of French programs as a wedge issue, steering the debate into one over the best allocation of scarce resources rather than the best type of education possible.

Anti-bilingualism organizations also positioned themselves as outsiders or underdogs in their rhetoric. Paradoxically, given that their members came from the English Canadian majority, with the entrenched power attached to that status, they were able to cast themselves, at least to their supporters, as underdogs, as anti-government protectors of the "little guy" who would get run over by French Canadians (and their quisling anglophone allies) in the rush to make Canada more French. By positioning themselves as the antithesis of the government-supported Canadian Parents for French, they could mobilize tens of thousands of Canadians to make individual donations to their cause. Indeed, having mobilized so many supporters was considered a form of success by the anti-bilingualism movement's leaders. This worked well in conjunction with the anti-elitism rhetoric targeted at French immersion programs. Groups opposed to bilingual programs often used class-based language to vilify the upper-middle-class parents who were the most visible faces of the French immersion movement. Although some might have believed their own rhetoric, few of them actually seemed to be concerned with crafting French programs that would be accessible to all socio-economic classes, learning capacities, races, and genders.

Pro-bilingualism social movements and their allies mobilized a substantially different set of resources and took advantage of different dimensions of the political opportunity structures in order to make gains in French program offerings, the number of English-speaking Canadians who took advantage of those opportunities, and the thousands of Canadians whom they mobilized to become involved in the movements. Their message was framed in a much more positive discourse on opportunity, excellence, growth, personal development, and openness to and tolerance of others. Because so much of this debate centred on education, proponents of bilingualism could cast themselves, at least partly, as altruists seeking the best opportunities for children (sometimes but not always their own) and building a "better" Canada for tomorrow. That being said, many parents who supported French immersion programs were also motivated by the prospects of advantages for their children – smaller class sizes, better students in the classrooms, more motivated teachers – even if these benefits dissipated over the years as programs became more established and administrators tried to keep the costs and class sizes comparable to those of the regular program. The material and personal benefits of bilingualism, on the other hand, were potent tools to motivate supporters. Leaders of CPF and its predecessors were also careful to combat any impressions of elitism. They knew that French programs could be torpedoed if they appeared to be for a select elite, so they worked to expand these programs as far as possible to provide opportunities for all who wanted to take advantage of them.

The pro-bilingualism groups were also able to mobilize a host of tangible resources. In the early decades covered by this study, they were able to use the unpaid volunteer labour of young mothers who did almost all of the logistical and practical work of convincing school boards to adopt new programs. Indeed, throughout the decades, gender has been a crucial aspect of the pro-bilingualism movement. Women by far comprised the majority of the leadership and volunteer base of Canadian Parents for French. Although men have played larger roles in recent years, the movement is still heavily reliant on the volunteer efforts of Canadian mothers, and women have been most of the organization's executives and paid staff.

The pro-bilingualism movement also benefited from ongoing research in university contexts that supported its arguments and from researchers willing to speak publicly on its behalf. Media allies in major newspapers and on radio and television programs diffused its message in supportive ways. Within the school boards and education ministries, key individuals provided encouragement and direct support to the parents. The Office of the Commissioner of Official Languages supplied initial financial support to bring together groups interested in these issues and then provided ongoing moral and informational supports. Indeed, there was a strong element of path dependency in how this office operated. Keith Spicer's initial decision to engage in advocacy for personal bilingualism and establish a commitment to the youth option paved a path followed to varying degrees by his successors. The financial supports provided by the Department of the Secretary of State and Canadian Heritage to official languages programs in education and Canadian Parents for French itself were crucial in making these programs less financially onerous and allowing CPF to ease some of the burden on its volunteers by hiring some paid staff. Although this federal funding opened CPF up to the criticism that it was a paid pro-government agitator, as discussed in Chapter 9, the movement had a stable membership base even without this funding, which demonstrated the commitment of members to its objectives. Overall, federal funding was beneficial to the organization in terms of the initiatives that it could pursue, despite the headaches that it created in responding to critics.

In many respects, despite the inertia-related path dependency discussed above, the political opportunity structure was favourable to pro-bilingualism groups, at least for the first two decades of this period. For Canada, Quebec's

Quiet Revolution of the early 1960s kicked off that decade's "cycle of contention" (to employ Tarrow's term). Responding to the new wave of Quebec
nationalism, the federally sponsored B&B Commission launched a new era
of serious attention to and interest in bilingualism. Diefenbaker's 1960 Bill
of Rights contributed to an increased discussion of human rights and
"rights talk," which coupled with broader North American and Western
European social movement trends. By the end of the decade, Canada had
seen major developments in the second-wave women's movement, peace
and anti-nuclear activism, Aboriginal activism, the student movement, and
the launch of the gay and lesbian rights movement, among others.[8] In the
early 1970s, the federal government became intimately engaged with this
"social movement society" and began directly funding many of the organizations associated with these social movements.[9] Even the sense of crisis regarding Quebec separatism in the late 1960s and 1970s could be considered
a positive feature of the political opportunity structure, for it created an opening to consider new approaches to the language issue. Many well-meaning
Canadians thought that their actions in this respect could have positive re-
percussions for national unity.

By the late 1960s, all three major political parties at the national level
were in support of the official languages policies. That consensus would not
break down until the late 1980s, with the rise of the Reform Party, and then
creation of the Bloc Québécois in the 1990s. Media elites, including major
columnists with the *Globe and Mail, Toronto Star,* and Montreal *Gazette,*
were keen supporters of bilingualism, and their positions were echoed in
newspapers across the country, including many small community papers.

The model of the political opportunity structure also helps to explain the
problems that the pro-bilingualism social movement ran into over time. A
succession of recessions in the 1970s, 1980s, and 1990s led to reductions in
federal funding for second-language education programs and ultimately for
CPF. In turn, the drying up of federal dollars made provinces less willing to
expand their French immersion programs, and this had marked consequences in the 1990s, when enrolment plateaued. Demographic trends, particularly the declining birth rate and shrinking school-aged population in the
1970s, which never recovered to baby boom levels, limited the opportunities for program innovation because of structural inflexibility in the education system (e.g., an unwillingness to fire surplus teachers). The constitutional
fatigue, mixed with some antipathy toward Quebec, that set in after the late-
1980s and early-1990s efforts to amend the Constitution meant that the res-
ervoir of goodwill for official languages was notably shallower. Although

Raymond Mougeon posits that the late-1990s end to immersion growth was the result of English Canadians losing faith in the program and the job opportunities that it might create,[10] I think that he neglects the importance of the structural factors that impeded the growth of French-language programs. These factors made it substantially more difficult, at least in the short term, for advocates to push for these programs.

Bilingualism among English-Speaking Canadians

Beyond social movement activity, concrete structural factors and conspicuous absences help to explain why the increase in personal bilingualism among English-speaking Canadians has been modest. A couple of hurdles pose ongoing and real structural challenges. Human resources are central in this regard. Although laying off English-speaking teachers to make way for French immersion programs was perceived as a threat, the flip side was the challenge of finding enough francophone teachers to staff these positions. Most provinces did and continue to experience serious teacher shortages for their French programs, whether francophone minority schools, French immersion, or core FSL. There simply are not enough native francophone teachers living in or willing to move to many provinces, and the ideal for immersion programs in particular is to have a native speaker as the model for students. Many provinces did create French immersion teacher training programs at their universities (e.g., Simon Fraser and Regina), but the demand still outstripped what these programs could supply. Beyond the teachers, the literature on second-language learning indicated that having opportunities to interact with native speakers of the target language, preferably in a natural setting, was highly beneficial to perfecting colloquial speech and syntax. Canada's very geography, both physical and human, works against such opportunities. Far too many French-language learners live thousands of kilometres away from major francophone centres. Although exchange programs have helped, distance is still a major barrier for many Canadians.

One can also consider the absence of leadership on some dimensions of the bilingualism issue. Although the federal government funded language education programs and pro-official languages groups, its actions were somewhat contradictory in terms of its faith in the "youth option." Despite calls dating back to the late 1970s from the commissioner of official languages to do away with the civil service "bilingual bonus" and to phase out on-the-job second-language training, the federal government has never done so. I would argue that this plays subtly into the public impression that bilingualism is not a core job requirement for federal civil servants (like math skills are for engineers) but a "bonus," "add-on," or "frill" – a burden for which the federal government feels the need to apologize and assumes the financial and moral obligation to compensate. In more recent years, waffling over whether positions with bilingualism explicitly stated as a job require-ment – such as when the auditor general was replaced in 2011 – would be filled by bilingual individuals has reinforced the impression that even the federal government might not be fully committed to requiring bilingualism for key positions.

Most provincial governments and local school boards have shown only tepid commitment to better second-language programs. Their support has almost always been conditional on dollars flowing from Ottawa, and rarely have provinces committed substantial additional funds of their own for this purpose. There have been exceptions, though, such as when Ontario re-structured its funding formulas in response to the Gillin Report in the 1970s, or Manitoba's Bureau d'éducation française, which put a premium on ex-panding French immersion programs. But these examples are the excep-tion.[11] An example of this lack of leadership or engagement occurred in New Brunswick in the 2000s when its early French immersion programs came under attack for siphoning off the best students and leaving most of the spe-cial needs students in the regular English programs. Rather than proposing a reworking of immersion to provide funding for special needs supports to keep those students in the immersion stream, the Willms Report called for an end to immersion in early grades to prevent streaming. This provided the basis for the policy direction taken in New Brunswick for several years.[12] The provinces have not fully integrated French immersion as a "normal" part of their educational offerings. Even after four decades it is treated as an add-on, subject to cuts in hard economic times and caps on enrolment.

For its part, the private sector in Canada has been passive about bi-lingualism. Although some corporate leaders were willing to make public statements or pen short op-eds for CPF's public awareness campaigns about the need for bilingualism and second-language skills in the private sector, that was about the limit of their involvement. CPF struggled for years to get corporate funding for its core activities and campaigns, with only lim-ited success, such as in-kind funding from Air Canada for air travel and a few sponsors for its public-speaking festivals. The initiative of Stewart Goodings to have a private sector–run campaign to promote language learning – the BilinguAction proposal – fell flat in the mid-1980s when none of the corporate leaders was willing to take the lead. Leadership on bilingualism, it seemed, was a government responsibility in the minds of corporate Canada's leaders.

Epilogue: Moving Forward

As a historian, perhaps I am not the best person to predict what will happen in the future. But since I am routinely asked how past experience might inform what we, as a society, will do in the future, I will offer the following thoughts and suggestions on what those committed to enhancing bilingualism among English-speaking Canadians might do in the future. Historians are often the Cassandras of the policy-making world, but it's worth making the attempt!

At the fundamental level, money is needed to make progress in second-language learning and the education system more broadly. When there have been financial incentives and supports, the programs have grown. When they are cut back, progress stalls. However, there has been far too much expectation that the federal government alone would provide leadership and funding for these programs. Provincial governments and local school boards, half a century after bilingualism became a real part of Canada's identity policies, should be shouldering more of this responsibility themselves, on top of what Ottawa provides.

On the leadership question, there is a need to stop apologizing and being defensive about bilingualism. English-French bilingualism, as long as it is conceptualized as "the price to pay" for national harmony or functional government, will have negative connotations. It will continue to be considered the medicine that must be coaxed down the resistant throats of Canadians. Groups such as Canadian Parents for French have already taken steps to put a more positive spin on bilingualism by emphasizing the cognitive, intellectual, and personal benefits that flow from it. More needs to be done to convert bilingualism from a bitter tonic into a delicious cocktail to be quaffed and savoured as part of the enjoyments, benefits, and privileges of being Canadian.

Outreach to groups that have been less included in past initiatives is also needed. Recent research shows that newer immigrants to Canada are less likely to learn French. Although CPF has undertaken a campaign to appeal to parents from new immigrant communities, more needs to be done to convince recent immigrants that learning both English and French will be an asset for them and their children. Given the gender divide in bilingualism among young anglophone Canadians, more also needs to be done to reach boys, more likely to drop the study of languages.

There is also an elephant in the room regarding language learning. Although there is merit to the "youth option" of teaching languages when Canadians are already in the school system, the corollary has been the seeming abandonment of any broad initiative to support language learning by adults who are not civil servants. There were initial proposals on tax credits or family-oriented language exchanges in the early days of CPF, but they quickly ran into roadblocks at the government or corporate level, and the BilinguAction campaign fizzled. Canada's approach seems to have been that, if you missed your opportunity to become bilingual in school, you are on your own as an adult to find and pay for a privately run program. If subsidized language-learning opportunities for adults do exist, they are not well publicized or promoted. Creating and promoting these opportunities would also help to reduce the perception that language-learning opportunities exist only for a select segment of Canada's population and are possible only during a limited window of one's life. This approach would also diminish the justification for full-time, fully funded, second-language training programs for civil servants. Indeed, I would argue, Ottawa needs to end the bilingual bonus and announce a date after which it will cease paying for full-time French training for its employees (or grandfather in existing civil servants but make no more provisions for those hired after a certain date). This is necessary to establish that the government considers language skills to be core skills comparable to any other skills expected of employees hired for certain jobs.

Within education communities, including ministers of education, bureaucrats, researchers, school board officials, trustees, and teachers, it would be nice to see a renewed commitment to making second-language programs the best that they can be. Broad informational campaigns on what reasonably can be expected from the French-language instructional programs of English Canadian schools would also be helpful. Despite decades of research and analysis, public perception and anticipation – and this even applies to university French professors – are that French immersion should be turning out graduates with near-perfect grammar and syntax and with communication skills close to those of native francophones. Canada's English-language schools do not produce perfect written or oral communication skills in English, yet our French immersion programs are routinely called failures for being unable to reach these thresholds, which they have not been intended to meet for decades. Greater public awareness of what these programs can produce in terms of bilingualism would help to reduce criticisms and "whisperings" about alleged failures. However, this should not be taken as an excuse to retrench into a defence of the status quo. Core French programs can continue to be improved, particularly in terms of oral communication, and immersion requires more work on grammar and syntax, among other things. Moreover, after more than three decades of research and criticism, resources need to be invested to allow special needs students to stay in French immersion when their learning disabilities or behavioural issues are not explicitly linked to the second language. An emphasis on improving our French programs, rather than calling for the "experiment" to be scrapped, would certainly improve the discourse on them.

English-speaking Canadians might be faced with motivational challenges related to learning French, but the opportunities to enrich a French-language learning program outside the classroom are now far superior to those that existed in the 1960s and early 1970s. Over the decades covered in this book, French-language radio and television were dramatically expanded across the country via the Radio-Canada network. The present era of digital radio and digital cable (along with Netflix and other on-demand entertainment programming) has opened up a universe of pleasant options for reinforcing one's French-language learning in a more leisurely setting. Although it seems clichéd to say it, the era of the Internet and rapid expansion of digital telecommunications have meant that in-person communication, whether written or face to face, across the globe is now possible in ways that could only be dreamed about in science fiction when Canada launched its bilingual adventure. Although an in-person immersive experience of weeks or months in a predominantly francophone environment is still the best way to perfect one's French-language skills, it is now possible to gain access to an array of native French accents and colloquial expressions beyond what a single classroom teacher could provide a few decades ago.

Canada is well positioned to achieve excellence with its second-language programs and has built a strong teaching and research infrastructure to support further growth. Canada could also provide, if we want to engage in a bit of nationalistic chest-thumping, global leadership in how a majority community can engage in widespread learning of the minority community's language rather than force all the effort onto the minority. What remains to be seen is whether the determination and financial will to continue and enhance this process with confidence still exist in twenty-first-century Canada. Canadians, and their country, will benefit greatly if this proves to be the case.

Appendices

APPENDIX 1

French immersion enrolments, by province, 1976–77 to 1997–98

	National	NL	PEI	NS	NB	QC	ON	MB	SK	AB	BC	YT	NT
1976–77	17,763*	56	304	46	2,504	n/a	12,363	1,290	338	n/a	862	n/a	n/a
1977–78	37,881	95	541	127	3,179	17,800	12,764	1,667	407	n/a	1,301	n/a	n/a
1978–79	26,004*	193	820	363	3,763	n/a	15,042	2,521	1,208	n/a	2,094	n/a	n/a
1979–80	47,667	279	1,023	491	4,501	17,500	16,333	3,113	1,286	n/a	3,141	n/a	n/a
1980–81	53,170	392	1,280	590	5,532	18,000	17,119	4,286	1,603	n/a	4,368	n/a	n/a
1981–82	60,727	551	1,465	865	7,390	18,500	18,352	5,770	2,175	n/a	5,659	n/a	n/a
1982–83	106,713	742	1,644	869	9,162	17,500	57,971	7,580	3,061	n/a	8,184	n/a	n/a
1983–84	135,809	970	1,833	894	11,009	17,833	65,310	9,090	4,018	14,523	11,500	171	151
1984–85	158,289	1,437	2,181	1,099	12,820	18,178	76,527	11,043	5,011	16,983	12,632	186	192
1985–86	180,345	2,015	2,492	1,859	14,530	18,006	87,819	12,581	5,965	19,017	15,590	247	250
1986–87	202,736	2,621	2,514	2,421	15,368	18,391	98,809	14,619	7,503	21,194	18,744	291	261
1987–88	221,314	2,979	3,033	3,490	15,458	18,750	108,000	16,395	8,398	22,779	21,404	318	310
1988–89	240,541	3,641	3,165	4,410	16,452	19,000	116,697	17,779	9,476	24,921	24,292	342	366
1989–90	265,579	3,980	3,271	4,900	16,425	28,717	125,000	19,024	10,440	26,182	26,900	360	380
1990–91	284,503	4,715	3,371	5,343	17,100	30,800	135,900	19,604	10,713	28,200	27,984	369	404
1991–92	285,277	5,165	3,511	5,500	14,987	32,000	137,000	19,669	10,851	28,000	27,780	391	423
1992–93	297,788	4,938	3,539	7,433	14,749	32,442	149,195	19,518	10,799	26,659	27,681	399	436
1993–94	301,201	4,515	3,312	8,006	16,004	33,327	147,125	19,724	11,003	28,196	28,974	423	444
1994–95	308,521	5,054	3,462	9,965	16,597	33,333	151,583	19,292	10,796	28,043	28,995	693	438
1995–96	307,034	5,074	3,385	10,916	15,880	35,551	150,005	18,999	10,404	26,676	29,184	452	508
1996–97	312,553	4,615	3,431	11,599	18,363	32,968	154,787	18,674	10,325	27,147	29,729	429	486
1997–98	315,683	4,531	3,228	12,213	20,968	37,429	153,298	18,133	9,444	26,766	28,765	425	483

Notes: [*] Excludes Quebec; [n/a] Data not available.
Source: Annual reports of the Office of the Commissioner of Official Languages, 1977–98.

APPENDIX 2

Total FSL (core and immersion) enrolment, by province, and as a percentage of total student enrolment

		1970–71	1977–78	1982–83	1987–88	1992–93	1997–98
Newfoundland	Total school enrolment	160,830	156,168	141,652	136,228	122,024	101,608
	Total FSL enrolment	59,730	67,791	72,717	77,145	71,802	57,723
	FSL as percentage	37	43	51	57	59	57
PEI	Total school enrolment	31,826	27,628	23,559	24,747	24,383	24,213
	Total FSL enrolment	14,355	16,495	15,578	16,110	15,410	14,202
	FSL as percentage	45	60	66	65	63	59
Nova Scotia	Total school enrolment	207,509	198,097	173,636	169,478	166,092	160,909
	Total FSL enrolment	72,597	88,991	96,048	101,229	95,427	88,909
	FSL as percentage	35	45	55	60	57	55
New Brunswick	Total school enrolment	115,233	101,550	95,522	138,531	93,200	89,441
	Total FSL enrolment	80,013	70,629	71,069	72,500	74,829	71,320
	FSL as percentage	69	70	74	52	80	80
Ontario	Total school enrolment	1,906,532	1,950,308	1,642,698	1,823,800	1,987,927	2,093,881
	Total FSL enrolment	783,252	883,269	896,225	1,044,300	1,102,294	1,172,993
	FSL as percentage	41	45	55	57	55	56
Manitoba	Total school enrolment	206,542	221,408	186,707	199,389	196,619	192,212
	Total FSL enrolment	95,379	85,619	88,334	106,525	106,112	93,479
	FSL as percentage	46	39	43	53	54	49

		C1	C2	C3	C4	C5	C6
Saskatchewan	Total school enrolment	246,567	216,248	197,038	203,499	196,235	192,413
	Total FSL enrolment	84,878	53,804	49,554	92,877	120,622	98,381
	FSL as percentage	34	25	51	46	61	51
Alberta	Total school enrolment	425,987	439,804	433,858	452,605	509,197	530,570
	Total FSL enrolment	138,842	111,338	106,184	162,678	189,184	161,838
	FSL as percentage	33	25	24	36	37	31
British Columbia	Total school enrolment	526,991	527,769	491,109	491,309	572,439	615,522
	Total FSL enrolment	145,851	161,110	167,345	209,856	254,761	279,953
	FSL as percentage	28	31	34	43	45	45
Yukon	Total school enrolment		5,394		4,896	5,774	6,370
	Total FSL enrolment		2,285		2,695	3,832	4,021
	FSL as percentage		42		55	66	63
NWT	Total school enrolment		12,717		13,386	16,121	17,534
	Total FSL enrolment		3,200		4,046	4,669	3,332
	FSL as percentage		25		30	29	19
Canada	Total school enrolment	5,195,849	5,178,753	4,311,732	4,694,048	4,981,293	5,087,106
	Total FSL enrolment	2,330,227	2,240,949	2,177,955	2,485,011	2,673,855	2,665,959
	FSL as percentage	45	43	51	53	54	52

Source: Annual reports of the Office of the Commissioner of Official Languages, 1977–98.

APPENDIX 3

Elementary core french enrolments, by province, and as percentage of elementary school–aged children

		1970–71	1977–78	1982–83	1987–88	1992–93	1997–98
Newfoundland	English elementary population	101,977	93,440	82,407	68,101	58,875	47,594
	Elementary FSL enrolment	21,835	33,585	37,518	36,802	33,786	27,204
	Elementary FSL percentage	21.4	35.9	45.5	54	57.4	57.2
PEI	English elementary population	18,818	13,284	11,128	10,302	10,287	9,996
	Elementary FSL enrolment	3,561	7,351	6,598	6,059	5,772	5,144
	Elementary FSL percentage	18.9	55.3	59.3	58.8	56.1	51.5
Nova Scotia	English elementary population	121,894	100,529	91,476	83,723	81,078	78,616
	Elementary FSL enrolment	12,642	30,025	44,588	46,049	40,778	36,572
	Elementary FSL percentage	10.4	29.9	48.7	55	50.3	46.7
New Brunswick	English elementary population	61,923	49,019	48,242	36,619	40,406	36,531
	Elementary FSL enrolment	37,305	29,563	31,328	31,989	33,800	30,530
	Elementary FSL percentage	60.2	60.3	64.9	87.4	83.6	83.6
Ontario	English elementary population	1,356,705	1,221,579	1,076,654	1,025,700	1,077,128	958,087
	Elementary FSL enrolment	514,173	650,136	660,873	690,000	754,429	594,317
	Elementary FSL percentage	37.9	53.2	61.7	67.3	70	62
Manitoba	English elementary population	104,466	110,831	98,291	90,035	88,290	86,187
	Elementary FSL enrolment	39,739	42,576	46,174	48,640	49,318	46,622
	Elementary FSL percentage	38.0	38.4	47	54	55.9	54.1

Saskatchewan						
English elementary population	133,514	110,382	107,226	106,539	100,381	95,251
Elementary FSL enrolment	6,950	4,928	8,269	40,776	61,264	51,824
Elementary FSL percentage	5.2	4.5	7.7	38.3	61	54.4
Alberta						
English elementary population	230,433	216,656	229,053	234,000	251,353	258,257
Elementary FSL enrolment	58,235	52,435	50,756	65,524	79,932	75,870
Elementary FSL percentage	25.3	24.2	22.2	28	31.8	29.4
BC						
English elementary population	333,340	305,574	293,029	278,999	308,427	292,849
Elementary FSL enrolment	18,558	75,740	83,747	91,223	127,477	106,830
Elementary FSL percentage	5.6	24.8	28.6	32.7	41.3	36.5
Yukon						
English elementary population		3,545		2,836	3,307	3,058
Elementary FSL enrolment		1,346		1,430	2,570	2,313
Elementary FSL percentage		38		50.4	77.7	75.6
NWT						
English elementary population		8,801		9,103	9,729	10,039
Elementary FSL enrolment		2,100		2,244	2,732	1,803
Elementary FSL percentage		23.9		24.7	28.1	18
Canada						
English elementary population	3,314,995	2,813,991	2,587,284	2,548,637	2,617,838	2,414,409
Elementary FSL enrolment	1,052,482	1,144,515	1,198,601	1,312,736	1,436,433	1,205,600
Elementary FSL percentage	31.7	40.7	46.3	51.5	54.9	49.9

Source: Annual reports of the Office of the Commissioner of Official Languages, 1977–98.

APPENDIX 4

Secondary core french enrolments, by province, and as percentage of secondary school-aged children

		1970–71	1977–78	1982–83	1987–88	1992–93	1997–98
Newfoundland	English secondary population	58,853	62,453	59,245	64,962	57,953	49,216
	Secondary FSL enrolment	37,895	34,111	34,457	37,364	33,078	25,988
	Secondary FSL percentage	64.4	54.6	58.2	57.5	57.1	52.8
PEI	English secondary population	13,008	13,171	12,431	10,908	9,972	10,365
	Secondary FSL enrolment	10,794	8,603	7,336	7,018	6,099	5,830
	Secondary FSL percentage	83	65.3	59	64.3	61.2	56.2
Nova Scotia	English secondary population	85,615	91,545	82,160	78,463	74,200	65,985
	Secondary FSL enrolment	59,955	58,839	50,591	51,690	47,216	39,944
	Secondary FSL percentage	70	64.3	61.6	65.9	63.6	60.5
New Brunswick	English secondary population	53,310	58,930	47,280	40,505	38,366	31,942
	Secondary FSL enrolment	42,708	37,887	30,579	25,052	26,830	19,822
	Secondary FSL percentage	80.1	64.3	64.7	61.9	69.9	62.1
Ontario	English secondary population	549,827	612,574	566,044	597,600	665,639	887,470
	Secondary FSL enrolment	269,079	220,369	177,381	246,300	198,670	425,378
	Secondary FSL percentage	48.9	36	31.3	41.2	29.8	47.9
Manitoba	English secondary population	102,076	100,707	88,416	87,734	83,488	82,651
	Secondary FSL enrolment	55,640	41,376	34,580	41,490	37,276	28,724
	Secondary FSL percentage	54.5	41.1	39.1	47.3	44.6	34.8

Saskatchewan						
English secondary population	113,053	104,075	89,812	87,194	83,865	86,302
Secondary FSL enrolment	77,928	48,469	38,224	43,703	48,559	37,113
Secondary FSL percentage	68.9	46.6	42.6	50.1	57.9	43
Alberta						
English secondary population	195,554	215,899	204,805	193,937	228,702	242,514
Secondary FSL enrolment	80,607	58,903	55,428	74,375	82,593	59,202
Secondary FSL percentage	41.2	27.3	27.1	38.4	36.1	24.4
BC						
English secondary population	193,651	220,894	198,080	188,985	234,311	291,048
Secondary FSL enrolment	127,293	84,069	75,414	97,229	99,603	144,358
Secondary FSL percentage	65.7	38.1	38.1	51.4	42.5	49.6
Yukon						
English secondary population		1,849		1,696	1,990	2,779
Secondary FSL enrolment		939		947	863	1,283
Secondary FSL percentage		50.8		55.8	43.4	46.2
NWT						
English secondary population		3,916		3,973	5,908	6,838
Secondary FSL enrolment		1,100		1,492	1,501	1,046
Secondary FSL percentage		28.1		37.6	25.4	15.3
Canada						
English secondary population	1,880,854	1,957,415	1,724,448	1,682,457	1,842,285	2,113,098
Secondary FSL enrolment	1,277,745	1,058,599	872,641	946,661	939,634	1,144,676
Secondary FSL percentage	67.9	54.1	50.1	56.3	51	54.2

Source: Annual reports of the Office of the Commissioner of Official Languages, 1977–98.

APPENDIX 5

Canadian Parents for French budget: Revenues and expenditures, 1982–2001

Year	CPF national revenues from memberships	CPF national revenues from federal government sources	Total CPF national revenues	Total CPF national expenditures
1982–83	13,254[a]	145,508	187,516	214,585
1983–84	25,842[b]	190,000	252,254	235,904
1984–85	37,558	243,144	331,168	313,537
1985–86	44,683[c]	354,333	480,739	480,226
1986–87	55,595	271,105	438,957	426,756
1987–88	57,140[d]	321,344	502,363	540,101
1988–89	61,175	392,146	572,508	575,063
1989–90	49,546[e]	515,182	765,914	764,598
1990–91	n/a[f]	n/a	n/a	n/a
1991–92	n/a	n/a	533,102	519,004
1992–93	77,385	452,372	650,678	646,129
1993–94	79,680	444,115	682,021	648,133
1994–95	70,520	395,021	598,000	614,934
1995–96	65,015	461,232	679,487	685,238
1996–97	58,423	325,058	459,650	490,948
1997–98	58,090	296,144	415,204	411,177
1998–99	56,197	512,493	666,962	680,629
1999–2000	57,408	735,595	900,153	898,034
2000–01	27,830[g]	1,038,309	1,234,950	1,229,811

n/a   Figures not available.

a   Family membership was initially set at five dollars per family in 1979.

b   Family membership was raised to ten dollars per family in 1983.

c   A three-year family membership category was created in 1986, at twenty-five dollars.

d   Membership fees were raised to fifteen dollars per family or forty dollars for three years.

e   The way in which membership revenues were calculated was changed in 1989–90 to spread the three-year memberships across the years to which they were applied.

f   Membership fees were raised to twenty-five dollars per family or sixty dollars for three years.

g   The allocation of membership fees was altered so that 65 percent went to local chapters, 25 percent to provincial branches, and 10 percent to the national office.

Source: Annual reports and newsletters of Canadian Parents for French.

Notes

Introduction: Canada's Bilingualism Conundrum

1 Graham Fraser, *Sorry, I Don't Speak French: Confronting the Canadian Crisis that Won't Go Away* (Toronto: McClelland & Stewart, 2006).

2 Pierre Elliott Trudeau, "Why Are They Forcing French down Our Throats?" (Ottawa: Department of the Secretary of State, 1969).

3 Throughout this book, unless otherwise noted, "bilingualism" will refer to English-French bilingualism. Many Canadians, of course, spoke more than one language but not both official languages.

4 Jock Andrew, letter to the author, July 14, 2010.

5 I have already explored the issue of federal initiatives and funding for the language education sector in *Bilingual Today, United Tomorrow: Official Languages in Education and Canadian Federalism* (Montreal: McGill-Queen's University Press, 2005). On the official language minority groups program, see Leslie A. Pal, *Interests of State: The Politics of Language, Multiculturalism, and Feminism in Canada* (Montreal: McGill-Queen's University Press, 1993). On the ill-fated bilingual districts program, see Daniel Bourgeois, *Canadian Bilingual Districts: From Cornerstone to Tombstone* (Montreal: McGill-Queen's University Press, 2006). On minority-language education governance under the Charter of Rights and Freedoms, see Michael Behiels, *Canada's Francophone Minority Communities: Constitutional Renewal and the Winning of School Governance* (Montreal: McGill-Queen's University Press, 2004). Other scholars have considered institutional bilingualism outside governments, including David Cameron and Richard Simeon, eds., *Language Matters: How Canadian Voluntary Associations Manage French and English* (Vancouver: UBC Press, 2009).

6 José E. Igartua, *The Other Quiet Revolution: National Identities in English Canada, 1945-71* (Vancouver: UBC Press, 2006).

7 Bryan Palmer, *Canada's 1960s: The Ironies of Identity in a Rebellious Era* (Toronto: University of Toronto Press, 2009).
8 C.P. Champion, *The Strange Demise of British Canada: The Liberals and Canadian Nationalism, 1964–1968* (Montreal: McGill-Queen's University Press, 2010).
9 Matthew Hayday, "Fireworks, Folk-Dancing, and Fostering a National Identity: The Politics of Canada Day," *Canadian Historical Review* 91, 2 (2010): 287–314.
10 Kenneth McRoberts, *Misconceiving Canada: The Struggle for National Unity* (Toronto: Oxford University Press, 1997), xii.
11 Eva Mackey, *The House of Difference: Cultural Politics and National Identity in Canada* (Toronto: University of Toronto Press, 2002), 19–22.
12 Marcel Martel et Martin Pâquet, *Langue et politique au Canada et au Québec: Une synthèse historique* (Montréal: Éditions Boréal, 2010); Marcel Martel and Martin Pâquet, *Speaking Up: A History of Language and Politics in Canada and Quebec* (Toronto: Between the Lines, 2012).
13 On this question in particular, scholars usually consider the impacts of "subtractive bilingualism," in which the acquisition of a second language is linked to concerns about assimilation and loss of cultural identity. See, for instance, Rodrigue Landry et Réal Allard, "Choix de la langue d'enseignement: Une analyse chez des parents francophones en milieu bilingue soustractif," *La revue canadienne des langues vivantes* 44 (1985): 480–500; Rodrigue Landry et Réal Allard, "Contact des langues et développement bilingue: Un modèle macroscopique," *La revue canadienne des langues vivantes* 46 (1990): 527–53. There is limited research on the politics of "additive bilingualism" among dominant or majority populations around the world; such bilingualism is the acquisition of a second language that does not threaten the cultural identity of an individual or his or her skills in a mother tongue.
14 These questions tend to animate and inform most scholarship presented, for instance, at the biennial conferences of the International Academy of Linguistic Law. See http://www.iall-aidl.org/. There is extensive Canadian scholarship on this topic, particularly in the French language. See, for instance, Linda Cardinal, dir., *Le fédéralisme asymétrique et les minorities linguistiques et nationales* (Ottawa: Éditions Prise de parole, 2008); Jean-Pierre Wallot, dir., *La gouvernance linguistique: Le Canada en perspective* (Ottawa: Presses de l'Université d'Ottawa, 2005); Joseph-Yvon Thériault, Anne Gilbert, et Linda Cardinal, dirs., *L'espace francophone en milieu minoritaire au Canada* (Montréal: Éditions Fides, 2008); Marcel Martel et Martin Pâquet, dir., *Légiférer en matière linguistique* (Québec: Presses de l'Université Laval, 2008).
15 Raymond Tatalovich, *Nativism Reborn? The Official English Language Movement and the American States* (Lexington: University Press of Kentucky, 1995).
16 James Crawford, *At War with Diversity: US Language Policy in an Age of Anxiety* (Clevedon: Multilingual Matters, 2000); Carol L. Schmid, *The Politics of Language: Conflict, Identity, and Cultural Pluralism in Comparative Perspective* (Oxford: Oxford University Press, 2001).
17 Philippe Van Parijs, *Linguistic Justice for Europe and for the World* (Oxford: Oxford University Press, 2011).
18 Tarah Brookfield, *Cold War Comforts: Canadian Women, Child Safety, and Global Insecurity* (Waterloo: Wilfrid Laurier University Press, 2012), 86–87. Other scholars,

including Frances Early and Marie Hammond-Callaghan, also raise the issue of respectability in their work on Voice of Women.

19 David S. Meyer and Sidney R. Tarrow, "A Movement Society: Contentious Politics for a New Century," in *The Social Movement Society: Contentious Politics for a New Century,* ed. David S. Meyer and Sidney R. Tarrow (Lanham: Rowman and Littlefield, 1998), 1–28.

20 Excellent articles on this subject appear in Howard Ramos and Kathleen Rodgers, eds., *Protest and Politics: The Promise of Social Movement Societies* (Vancouver: UBC Press, 2015). See, in particular, Judy Taylor, "No to Protests, Yes to Festivals: How the Creative Class Organizes in the Social Movement Society"; Dominique Clément, "The Social Movement Society and the Human Rights State"; Dominique Masson, "Institutionalization, State Funding, and Advocacy in the Quebec Women's Movement."

21 Leslie A. Pal, *Interests of State: The Politics of Language, Multiculturalism, and Feminism in Canada* (Montreal: McGill-Queen's University Press, 1993).

22 Clément, "The Social Movement Society"; Kevin Brushett, "Guerrilla Bureaucrats: New Social Movements and the New Ottawa Men 1960–1980," paper presented at the Canadian Historical Association Annual Meeting, May 2014; Andrew Nurse, "Pyrrhic Victory: Opposition to Freeway Development and the Crisis of Civic Activism, Halifax 1971–73," paper presented at the Canadian Historical Association Annual Meeting, June 2013.

23 See, for instance, Theda Skocpol, "Bringing the State Back In: Strategies of Analysis in Current Research," in *Bringing the State Back In,* ed. Peter B. Evans, Dietrich Rueschemeyer, and Theda Skocpol (Cambridge, UK: Cambridge University Press, 1985), 3–37.

24 Paul Pierson, *Politics in Time: History, Institutions, and Social Analysis* (Princeton: Princeton University Press, 2004).

25 Both neo-pluralist and historical institutionalist approaches to public policy and social movement activism contrast sharply with older pluralist models of governance that see the state as a relatively neutral arbiter among individuals who organize into groups to make demands on the state or Marxist models that see the state as an agent of the capital class in a struggle among individuals subdivided into social classes. I am indebted to Miriam Smith for her concise and readable synthesis of the major approaches to social movements. See Miriam Smith, *A Civil Society: Collective Actors in Canadian Political Life* (Toronto: Broadview, 2005), 19–45.

26 See, for example, Sidney Tarrow, *Power in Movement: Social Movements and Contentious Politics,* 2nd ed. (Cambridge, UK: Cambridge University Press, 1998); Doug McAdam, John D. McCarthy, and Mayer N. Zald, eds., *Comparative Perspectives on Social Movements: Political Opportunities, Mobilizing Structures, and Cultural Framings* (Cambridge, UK: Cambridge University Press, 1996); Suzanne Staggenborg, *Social Movements,* 2nd ed. (Toronto: Oxford University Press, 2012), 13–28.

27 Smith, *A Civil Society,* 38–39.

28 Tarrow, *Power in Movement,* 141–60.

29 Among the authors who have considered the evolution of collective behaviour theory and its relationship to the political process and resource mobilization model,

see Maurice Pinard, *Motivational Dimensions in Social Movements and Contentious Collective Action* (Montreal: McGill-Queen's University Press, 2011), 3–35.

30 See, for example, Alberto Melucci, "Getting Involved: Identity and Mobilization in Social Movements," *International Social Movement Research* 1 (1988): 329–48; Donnatella Della Porta and Mario Diani, *Social Movements: An Introduction,* 2nd ed. (Malden: Blackwell, 2006), 64–134.

31 Smith, *A Civil Society,* 33–36. See also Miriam Smith, ed., *Group Politics and Social Movements in Canada,* 2nd ed. (Toronto: University of Toronto Press, 2014).

32 Pierre Vallières, *White Niggers of America,* trans. Joan Pinkham (Toronto: McClelland and Stewart, 1971).

Chapter 1: Bilingualism and Official Languages in Canada

1 Marcel Martel et Martin Pâquet, *Langue et politique au Canada et au Québec: Une synthèse historique* (Montréal: Éditions Boréal, 2010); Marcel Martel and Martin Pâquet, *Speaking Up: A History of Language and Politics in Canada and Quebec* (Toronto: Between the Lines, 2012).

2 Matthew Hayday, *Bilingual Today, United Tomorrow: Official Languages in Education and Canadian Federalism* (Montreal: McGill-Queen's University Press, 2005).

3 British North America Act, 1867, 30-31 Vict., c. 3 (United Kingdom).

4 An Act to amend and continue the Act 32-33 Victoria, chapter 3; and to establish and provide for the Government of the Province of Manitoba, 1870, 33 Vict., c. 3.

5 Martel et Pâquet, *Langue et politique,* 109.

6 Jean Delisle, "Fifty Years of Parliamentary Interpretation," *Canadian Parliamentary Review* 32, 2 (2009): 27–32.

7 Martel et Pâquet, *Langue et politique,* 110.

8 See Kenneth McRoberts, *Quebec: Social Change and Political Crisis, 3rd Edition with a Postscript* (Toronto: McClelland and Stewart, 1993), for an excellent overview of these transformations.

9 "Montreal Mayor Opposes Name of New Hotel," *Globe and Mail,* April 1, 1955; Robert Duffy, "MPP's Act: Controversy Keeps Pace with Hotel," *Globe and Mail,* November 24, 1955; Marc V. Levine, *The Reconquest of Montreal: Language Policy and Social Change in a Bilingual City* (Philadelphia: Temple University Press, 1990), 37, 209–10.

10 "Gordon Remark about French Brings Protests," *Globe and Mail,* November 26, 1962; Thomas Sloan, "Quebec Students Burn CNR Head in Effigy: Four Persons Injured," *Globe and Mail,* November 29, 1962.

11 Martel et Pâquet, *Langue et politique,* 142.

12 Royal Commission on Bilingualism and Biculturalism (RCBB), *Report of the Royal Commission on Bilingualism and Biculturalism. General Introduction and Book 1: The Official Languages* (Ottawa: Queen's Printer, 1967), xxi.

13 André Laurendeau and Patricia Smart, eds., *The Diary of André Laurendeau, Written during the Royal Commission on Bilingualism and Biculturalism, 1964–1967,* trans. Patricia Smart and Dorothy Howard (Toronto: James Lorimer, 1991), 90–91.

14 Ibid., 85.

15 Quoted in ibid., 107–8.

16 Ibid., 59.

17 RCBB, *A Preliminary Report of the Royal Commission on Bilingualism and Bicultur-alism* (Ottawa: Queen's Printer, 1965), 13.

18 Canada, *House of Commons Debates,* April 6, 1966, 3915 (Pearson, PM).

19 Ibid., 3917–23 (Diefenbaker, MP; Lewis, MP; Caouette, MP; Thompson, MP).

20 Daniel Bourgeois, *Canadian Bilingual Districts: From Cornerstone to Tombstone* (Montreal: McGill-Queen's University Press, 2006), 73.

21 Hayday, *Bilingual Today,* 57–59.

22 Martel et Pâquet, *Langue et politique,* 159–60; Hayday, *Bilingual Today,* 46, 89–90.

23 Matthew Hayday, "Reconciling the Two Solitudes? Language Rights and the Con-stitutional Question from the Quiet Revolution to the Victoria Charter," in *Debating Dissent: Canada and the Sixties,* ed. Lara Campbell, Dominique Clément, and Gregory Kealey (Toronto: University of Toronto Press, 2012), 244.

24 A variation on this perspective was raised by Commissioner Jaroslav Rudnyckyj, who included a separate statement in the B&B report on the need to recognize regional languages of First Nations and immigrant communities. RCBB, *Report of the Royal Commission ... Book 1,* 155–69. See also Aya Fujiwara, *Ethnic Elites and Canadian Identity: Japanese, Ukrainians, and Scots, 1919–1971* (Winnipeg: University of Manitoba Press, 2012); Kenneth McRoberts, *Misconceiving Canada: The Struggle for National Unity* (Toronto: Oxford University Press, 1997), 117–36.

25 Treasury Board of Canada, "Official Languages in the Public Service of Canada," 1973 (pamphlet containing the June 1973 text of the resolution adopted by Parliament and Treasury Board Circular 1973–88 dealing with the identification of language requirements and policies on staffing of bilingual positions).

26 Bourgeois, *Canadian Bilingual Districts,* 196–97.

27 Canadian Heritage, *Official Languages: Myths and Realities* (Ottawa: Minister of Supply and Services Canada, 1994), 23; Keith Spicer, *Life Sentences: Memoirs of an Incorrigible Canadian* (Toronto: McClelland and Stewart, 2004), 97–98.

28 Hayday, *Bilingual Today,* 90; Quebec, Commission of Inquiry on the Position of the French Language and on Language Rights for Quebec, *Report of the Commission of Inquiry on the Position of the French Language and on Language Rights for Quebec* (Quebec: Government of Quebec, 1972).

29 Sanford Borins, *The Language of the Skies: The Bilingual Air Traffic Control Conflict in Canada* (Montreal: McGill-Queen's University Press, 1983).

30 Hayday, *Bilingual Today,* 161.

31 Statistics Canada, "Births – 2008" (Ottawa: Industry Canada, 2011), 12, http://www.statcan.gc.ca/pub/84f0210x/84f0210x2008000-eng.pdf.

32 Hayday, *Bilingual Today,* 171.

33 Peter Russell, *Constitutional Odyssey: Can Canadians Become a Sovereign People?,* 3rd ed. (Toronto: University of Toronto Press, 2004), 145–46.

34 Hayday, *Bilingual Today,* 172; Canadian Parents for French, "Focus on French Second Language Education: A Canadian Parents for French Position Paper on the Renewal of the Official Languages in Education Program and a New Protocol for Agreements" (Ottawa: CPF, 1997), i.

35 Russell, *Constitutional Odyssey,* 229–35.

36 Hayday, *Bilingual Today,* 172.

Chapter 2: From *Chez Hélène* to the First French Immersion Experiments

1 Louise was played by Madeleine Kronby, who would later advise the commissioner of official languages on the Oh! Canada kit for children.

2 "The Tan Gau Demonstration," in *Seminar Report – "Teaching Modern Languages," Chateau Laurier, Ottawa, 21–23 November 1963,* ed. Gerald Nason, 123–25.

3 From what I have been able to determine from available sources, this was not Wallace Lambert of McGill University, who appears later in this chapter.

4 John Fitzgerald, "From Singer to Judge: Helene Finds New Beginnings Invigorating," Montreal *Gazette,* June 12, 1978.

5 "Emphasis on Spoken French," Montreal *Gazette,* September 29, 1961.

6 "Chez Helene Marks Its 500th Telecast Today," Montreal *Gazette,* June 15, 1962.

7 Baillargeon did get a nice exit package. She was named to the Order of Canada in 1974 and then appointed to the Canadian Citizenship Court.

8 L. Ian Macdonald, "'I Will Be Lonesome for the Love of the Children,'" Montreal *Gazette,* May 4, 1973.

9 Richard F. Lewis, "CBC Sesame Street: A Description and Discussion of Issues," *Canadian Journal of Communication* 17, 3 (1992), http://www.cjc-online.ca/index.php/journal/article/view/683/589.

10 "Enrichment – French outside the Classroom," *Canadian Parents for French Newsletter,* December 8, 1979, 6.

11 "Bonjour Sesame (Canada)," *MuppetWiki,* http://muppet.wikia.com/wiki/Bonjour_Sesame_%28Canada%29. The expanded Canadian edition featuring the Canadian Muppet characters Basil the polar bear, Louis the otter and Dodi the mail carrier debuted in 1987. http://muppet.wikia.com/wiki/Sesame_Park.

12 Edith Mitchell, Information Services, CBC, to Mrs. Fritz Spiess, July 15, 1960, Personal Files of Gunild Spiess (hereafter PFGS); Robert Gauthier, Director of French Instruction, Ontario Department of Education, to Mrs. Fritz Spiess, June 21, 1961, PFGS.

13 McKee Avenue French committee, report to McKee Avenue Home and School Executive, n.d., PFGS; interview with Gunild Spiess, June 16, 2009.

14 Interview with Gunild Spiess, June 16, 2009; French committee report, December 8, 1969, PFGS; French program committee report, January 19, 1970, PFGS; oral French committee report, March 12, 1971, PFGS; oral French instruction notice, PFGS.

15 The North York Board of Education extended compulsory French down to grade six in the late 1960s; report of the French committee, (1974?), PFGS.

16 Canadian Parents for French found evidence of an immersion-style experimental class at Cedar Park School in the West Island School Commission in Quebec in 1958. "Who Had the First Immersion Public School?," *Canadian Parents for French National News* 29 (1985): 5.

17 "Two Language School Planned for Toronto," *Globe and Mail,* August 25, 1962; Penny Longley, "Children Learn French in City's Newest School," 1962, http://50.tfs.ca/our-history/.

18 This included the Bassetts, the Batas, and the Eatons, with later classes including children from the Mirvish and Sifton families, among many others.

19 "One Man Campaigns for Bilingualism, Sets Up French Sschools in Metro," *Globe and Mail,* July 15, 1965.

20 Toronto French School, "Our History – TFS," 2014, http://50.tfs.ca/our-history/.
21 "School Asks for Federal Aid at B-B Hearing," *Globe and Mail*, December 2, 1965.
22 Kitchener-Waterloo Bilingual School, "The Kitchener-Waterloo Bilingual School – Our History," 2014, http://www.kwbilingualschool.com/school-17-history.html.
23 Interview with Carmeta Abbott, March 6, 2014.
24 Zena Cherry, "After a Fashion: French Week Aims to Help French School," *Globe and Mail*, May 27, 1966.
25 Wendy Dey, "New School for French Students," *Toronto Daily Star*, January 15, 1971; Nora McCabe, "Davis Opens New $780,000 French School," 1971, http://50.tfs.ca/our-history/.
26 "Private Schools Eligible for Bilingualism Subsidy," *Globe and Mail*, August 17, 1977.
27 Judy Steed, "Immersed in a Dream," *Globe and Mail*, December 10, 1988.
28 W. Harry Giles, "On parle français ici, but Not Very Well," *Globe and Mail*, June 20, 1991; André Picard, "French Future Doesn't Depend on a Parisian Accent," *Globe and Mail*, June 25, 1991.
29 Marlene Habib, "First Person – Harry Giles, Founder of the Giles School," *Globe and Mail*, September 22, 2008.
30 Wallace E. Lambert and G. Richard Tucker, *Bilingual Education of Children: The St. Lambert Experiment* (Rowley, MA: Newbury House, 1972), 3–4.
31 Olga Melikoff, "Parents as Change Agents in Education: The St. Lambert Experiment," in ibid., 220–22.
32 "French Immersion Changed Canada," Montreal *Gazette*, March 20, 2006; Ingrid Peritz, "'Language Bath' Parents Earn a Merci Beaucoup," *Globe and Mail*, March 22, 2006; "40th Anniversary of First French Immersion Model in Canada Celebrated," *CPF National News* 101 (2006): 1–2.
33 Melikoff, "Parents as Change Agents," 222–23.
34 Ibid., 224–26.
35 Ibid., 227–30.
36 Ibid., 230–31.
37 Lambert and Tucker, *Bilingual Education of Children*, 8–34.
38 Melikoff, "Parents as Change Agents," 232–34.
39 Brief of the Association of (English-Speaking) Catholic Principals of Montreal to the Commission of Inquiry on the Position of the French Language Rights in Quebec, cited in Lambert and Tucker, *Bilingual Education of Children*, 4–5.
40 Lambert and Tucker, *Bilingual Education of Children*, 200–7.
41 Margaret Caughey, "What's What about the CCC," in *What's What for Children Learning French, Second Edition*, ed. Elaine Isabelle (Ottawa: Mutual Press, 1976), 89.
42 Glenna Reid, "Introduction," in *What's What for Children Learning French*, ed. Glenna Reid (Ottawa: Mutual Press, 1972), 1–2.
43 C.A. Brigden, "French for Children," in *What's What for Children*, ed. Eve Kassirer (Ottawa: Beauregard Press, 1967), 50.
44 Ibid., 51.
45 Interview with Louise Moore, June 23, 2009; interview with Mary Stapleton, June 23, 2009.
46 Interview with Mary Stapleton, June 23, 2009.

47 Calgary French and International School, "Our History – Calgary French and International School," 2014, http://www.cfis.com/main/our-school/history.

48 Most of the material in this section comes from interviews with Mary Stapleton and Louise Moore, with some additional technical material from the Calgary French and International School website, http://www.cfis.com.

Chapter 3: Playing Games with the Language Czar

1 Donald Savoie, *Power: Where Is It?* (Montreal: McGill-Queen's University Press, 2010).

2 Paul Pierson, *Politics in Time: History, Institutions, and Social Analysis* (Princeton: Princeton University Press, 2004); Miriam Smith, *A Civil Society? Collective Actors in Canadian Political Life* (Peterborough: Broadview Press, 2005), 31.

3 Smith, *A Civil Society?*

4 Leslie A. Pal, *Interests of State: The Politics of Language, Multiculturalism, and Feminism in Canada* (Montreal: McGill-Queen's University Press, 1993).

5 Matthew Hayday, *Bilingual Today, United Tomorrow: Official Languages in Education and Canadian Federalism* (Montreal: McGill-Queen's University Press, 2005).

6 C. Michael MacMillan, "Active Conscience or Administrative Vanguard? The Commissioner of Official Languages as an Agent of Change," *Canadian Public Administration* 49, 2 (2006): 161–79; Carl Hugh Cosman, "The Commissioner of Official Languages: Language Ombudsman, Watchdog, and Advocate" (MA thesis, University of Guelph, 1990).

7 Paul G. Thomas, "The Past, Present, and Future of Officers of Parliament," *Canadian Public Administration* 46, 3 (2003): 287–314; Sandra Dumoulin, "Le commissariat aux langues officielles: Un acteur institutionnel au coeur de l'administration publique fédérale (1969–2006)," in *Légiferer en matière linguistique*, dir. Marcel Martel et Martin Pâquet (Québec: Les Presses de l'Université Laval, 2008), 107–28; Maria L. Kurylo, "Canada's Commissioner of Official Languages: The Unexplored Concept of the Officer of Parliament" (MA thesis, University of Saskatchewan, 2000).

8 Cosman, "Commissioner of Official Languages," 34.

9 Kathryn Blaze Carlson, "Oh, the Humanities! Language Czars Losing Their Voice," *National Post,* May 30, 2012.

10 Royal Commission on Bilingualism and Biculturalism (RCBB), *Report of the Royal Commission on Bilingualism and Biculturalism. General Introduction and Book 1: The Official Languages* (Ottawa: Queen's Printer, 1967), 138–41.

11 Ibid.

12 Canada, *House of Commons Debates,* May 16, 1969, 8811 (McIntosh, MP).

13 Canada, *House of Commons Debates,* May 20, 1969, 8835 (McIntosh, MP).

14 Canada, *House of Commons Debates,* May 16, 1969, 8790 (Stanfield, MP); Canada, *House of Commons Debates,* May 20, 1969, 8871 (Dinsdale, MP); Canada, *House of Commons Debates,* May 23, 1969, 9015 (Horner, MP).

15 Canada, *House of Commons Debates,* May 26, 1969, 9060 (Diefenbaker, MP).

16 Canada, *House of Commons Debates,* May 26, 1969, 9066 (Diefenbaker, MP).

17 The seventeen MPs were Bert Cadieu (C-SK), Robert Coates (C-NS), John Diefenbaker (C-SK), Walter Dinsdale (C-MB), Cliff Downey (C-AB), Deane Gundlock (C-AB), Jack Horner (C-AB), Stanley Korchinski (C-SK), John McIntosh

(C-SK), Harry Moore (C-SK), George Muir (C-MB), William Ritchie (C-MB), Stan Schumacher (C-AB), Robert Simpson (C-MB), William Skoreyko (C-AB), Richard Southam (C-SK), and Donald Stewart (C-MB).

18 Canada, *House of Commons Debates,* June 18, 1969, 10346–47 (McQuaid, MP).
19 Canada, *House of Commons Debates,* June 18, 1969, 10352 (Woolliams, MP).
20 Canada, *House of Commons Debates,* June 18, 1969, 10368 (Turner, MP).
21 Canada, *House of Commons Debates,* July 7, 1969, 10925.
22 Keith Spicer, *Life Sentences: Memoirs of an Incorrigible Canadian* (Toronto: McClelland and Stewart, 2004), 91.
23 Official Languages Act, 1969, R.S.C. 1970, c. O-2.
24 Commissioner of Official Languages (COL), *First Annual Report, 1970–1971* (Ottawa: Information Canada, 1971), 2–3.
25 Ibid., 3–6.
26 Ibid., 9.
27 Ibid., 94.
28 Ibid., 95.
29 Pierre Elliott Trudeau, "Why Are They Forcing French down Our Throats?" (Ottawa: Queen's Printer, 1969).
30 COL, *Second Annual Report, 1971–1972* (Ottawa: Information Canada, 1973), 47.
31 One of the earliest major studies in this regard was Gilles Bibeau, dir., *Rapport de l'Étude indépendante sur les programmes de formation linguistique de la Fonction publique du Canada,* 1975.
32 COL, *Second Annual Report,* 2.
33 Ibid., 12.
34 COL, *Fourth Annual Report, 1973–1974* (Ottawa: Information Canada, 1975), 12.
35 COL, *Third Annual Report, 1972–1973* (Ottawa: Information Canada, 1974), 26, 31.
36 COL, *Fifth Annual Report, 1975* (Ottawa: Information Canada, 1976), 54, 84.
37 COL, *Sixth Annual Report, 1976* (Ottawa: Information Canada, 1977), 39.
38 COL, *Second Annual Report,* 48.
39 National Film Board (NFB) of Canada and COL, *Bons Amis,* NFB, 1974.
40 COL, *Fifth Annual Report, 1975* (Ottawa: Information Canada, 1976), 26.
41 Ibid., 30–32.
42 *The "Oh! Canada" Kit: An Evaluation Report, August 1978,* Library of the Office of the Commissioner of Official Languages.
43 Benedict Anderson, *Imagined Communities: Reflections on the Origins and Spread of Nationalism, Revised Edition* (London: Verso, 2006), 170–78.
44 James A. Leith, "Pedagogy through Games: The *Jeu de l'oie* during the French Revolution and Empire," *Proceedings – Consortium on Revolutionary Europe: 1750–1850* 22 (1993): 166–91.
45 I am not entirely sure how my parents got their hands on the kit, since I was born in 1977, just as the distribution was winding up, yet I can recall playing the record on my Fisher Price record player in the early 1980s. Tracking down copies of the kit over three decades after the print run ended proved to be easy. Mention of the kit to friends and colleagues born in the late 1960s and 1970s quickly yielded fond recollections of playing the game, and some still knew the words to "Bonjour, My Friend."

46 Robert Gillin, Ontario Ministry of Education, to Keith Spicer, June 17, 1975, Library and Archives Canada (LAC), RG 122, accession 1992–93/041, box 11, file 0590-5-3-1, vol. 1.

47 André Obadia, Carleton Board of Education, memo to V.A. Caron, Superintendent of Curriculum Services, re: Oh! Canada survey, November 24, 1975, LAC, RG 122, accession 1992–93/041, box 11, file 0590-5-3-1, vol. 1. My translations are "very good for the advancement of bilingualism and for attitudes"; "it proves to students that the study of a second language can be pleasant and easy. Once we have achieved this objective, I think we have won the battle."

48 Marie-Christine Demessine and René Enguehard (Newfoundland), report on Oh! Canada, November 17, 1975, LAC, RG 122, accession 1992–93/041, box 11, file 0590-5-3-1, vol. 1.

49 P.J.H. Malmberg, Deputy Minister of Education, New Brunswick, to Keith Spicer, November 9, 1976; Julian Koziak, Minister of Education, Alberta, to Keith Spicer, November 24, 1976; G.H. Waldrum, Deputy Minister of Education, Ontario, to Keith Spicer, November 17, 1976, all in LAC, RG 122, accession 1992–93/041, box 11, file 0590-5-3-1, vol. 1.

50 John Fraser to Keith Spicer, January 1976, LAC, RG 122, accession 1992–93/041, box 11, file 0590-5-3-1, vol. 2.

51 Robert Stanbury to Keith Spicer, December 29, 1975, LAC, RG 122, accession 1992–93/041, box 11, file 0590-5-3-1, vol. 2.

52 Pierre Blanchard, Principal, École secondaire Gamelin, Hull, to Maxwell Yalden, November 17, 1977, LAC, RG 122, accession 1992–93/041, box 11, file 0590-5-3-1, vol. 2. My translation is "a gem for our English teachers."

53 L.M. Ready, Associate Deputy Minister of Education, Saskatchewan, memo to M. Richer, Secretary General of Council of Ministers of Education, Canada, July 8, 1975, LAC, RG 122, accession 1992–93/041, box 11, file 0590-5-3-1, vol. 1.

54 Demessine and Enguehard, report on Oh! Canada.

55 Raymond Hébert, Sous-ministre adjoint, Department of Education, Manitoba, to Keith Spicer, December 13, 1976, LAC, RG 122, accession 1992–93/041, box 11, file 0590-5-3-1, vol. 1.

56 Henri Tanguay, Commission Scolaire, Outaouais-Hull, to Keith Spicer, June 10, 1977; Jean-Pierre Prud'homme, evaluation report, June 9, 1977, both in LAC, RG 122, accession 1992–93/041, box 11, file 0590-5-3-1, vol. 2.

57 My translation is "the methodology and the approach ... could have disastrous impacts on the language of our children."

58 Jacques-Yvan Morin, memo to Quebec school boards, August 12, 1977, LAC, RG 122, accession 1992–93/041, box 11, file 0590-5-3-1, vol. 2. My translations are "learning of Frenglish," "weak, if not trivial," and "fight with great difficulty for the survival and recognition of their language."

59 COL, "The 'Oh! Canada' Kit: An Evaluation Report," August 1978, LAC, RG 122, accession 1992–93/041, box 11, file 0590-5-3-1, vol. 5; COL, "Survey Finds the 'Oh! Canada' Kit a Success," news release, August 3, 1978, LAC, RG 122, accession 1992–93/041, box 11, file 0590-5-3-1, vol. 5.

60 Stephen Acker, Executive Assistant to COL, to Paula Wegrich, January 17, 1978, LAC, RG 122, accession 1992–93/041, box 11, file 0590-5-3-1, vol. 3.

61 Gabrielle Kirschbaum, briefing document for Maxwell Yalden, November 30, 1977, LAC, RG 122, accession 1992–93/041, box 11, file 0590–5-3–1, vol. 2.

62 Keith Spicer to D.S. Macdonald, Minister of Finance, copied to Monique Bégin, Minister of Revenue, November 8, 1976, LAC, RG 122, series A-1, accession 1997–98/632, box 22, file 1140–7, vol. 1. Handwritten note from R.R. indicates that this was discussed verbally with Macdonald, who replied favourably.

63 Monique Bégin to Keith Spicer, December 21, 1976, LAC, RG 122, series A-1, accession 1997–98/632, box 22, file 1140–7, vol. 1.

64 Keith Spicer to D.S. Macdonald, Minister of Finance, November 8, 1976, LAC, RG 122, series A-1, accession 1997–98/632, box 22, file 1140–7, vol. 1.

65 Otto Lang to Keith Spicer, February 1977, LAC, RG 122, series A-1, accession 1997–98/632, box 22, file 1140–7, vol. 1.

66 Keith Spicer to Claude Taylor, President and CEO, Air Canada, and Robert Bandeen, President and CEO, CN Rail, January 24, 1977, LAC, RG 122, series A-1, accession 1997–98/632, box 22, file 1140–7, vol. 1.

67 Robert Bandeen, President and CEO, CN Rail, to Keith Spicer, February 16, 1977; Claude Taylor, President and CEO, Air Canada, to Keith Spicer, March 2, 1977; G.C. Campbell, VIA Rail, to Keith Spicer, April 15, 1977, all in LAC, RG 122, series A-1, accession 1997–98/632, box 22, file 1140–7, vol. 1.

68 "Travel Canada" Task Force, briefing notes, June 21, 1977, LAC, RG 122, series A-1, accession 1997–98/632, box 22, file 1140–7, vol. 2.

69 Pierre Trudeau to Maxwell Yalden, September 26, 1977, LAC, RG 122, series A-1, accession 1997–98/632, box 22, file 1140–7, vol. 2. My translation is "it must be recognized that a project such as this depends, above all, on the Canadian population."

70 Interview with Keith Spicer, October 7, 2011.

71 COL, *Annual Report 1977* (Ottawa: Information Canada, 1978), 30.

72 Interview with Keith Spicer, October 7, 2011.

Chapter 4: Social Movement Activism, 1969–76

1 "Written Opposition to Bill Light, Mostly from Edmonton: Trudeau," *Globe and Mail*, October 30, 1969.

2 Val Ross, "Thorson's Last Stand," *This Weekend* (*Globe and Mail*), October 9, 1976; "Canada Not Bilingual, People Brainwashed, Women's Group Hears," *Globe and Mail*, January 25, 1968.

3 Letter to the editor, *Globe and Mail*, June 7, 1974 (the letter was not printed), LAC, MG31 E38 (R5018–10-X-E), file 10, vol. 18.

4 Reverend Hugh MacPhail to Joseph T. Thorson, August 12, 1972, and reply of Thorson to MacPhail, October 11, 1972, LAC, MG31 E38 (R5018–10-X-E), file 12, vol. 18.

5 "Canada Not Bilingual, People Brainwashed, Women's Group Hears," *Globe and Mail*, January 25, 1968.

6 "Opponent Vows to Challenge Language Bill," *Globe and Mail*, June 3, 1969.

7 Ibid.; "Thorson Leads League Fighting Special Status," *Globe and Mail*, June 4, 1969.

8 "Dual Nationalist Nonsense for Canada, Thorson Says," *Globe and Mail*, April 30, 1971.

9 Agnes Enns to J.T. Thorson, April 25, 1971, LAC, MG31 E38 (R5018–10-X-E), file 13, vol. 18.

10 Single Canada League membership form, LAC, MG31 E38 (R5018–10-X-E), file 11, vol. 18.
11 Henry Luck to J.T. Thorson, (April 1971?), and reply from Thorson to Luck, June 11, 1971, LAC, MG31 E38 (R5018–10-X-E), file 13, vol. 18.
12 R.W.F. James to J.T. Thorson, n.d., and reply from Thorson to James, December 22, 1971, LAC, MG31 E38 (R5018–10-X-E), file 11, vol. 18.
13 J.T. Thorson, *Wanted! A Single Canada* (Toronto: McClelland and Stewart, 1973), 8–9.
14 Ibid., 9–10.
15 Ibid., 47, 52–53.
16 Ibid., 49.
17 Ibid., 83, 67.
18 Ibid., 57.
19 Ibid., 60.
20 Ibid., 111–12.
21 See ibid., 113, 115, 117–18.
22 Ibid., 138.
23 Ibid., 132.
24 Ibid., 154.
25 Ibid., 141.
26 Ibid., 154.
27 Ross, "Thorson's Last Stand."
28 Royce Firth, "Dead Horses and Unrelenting Bias in a Singular Monotone," *Globe and Mail*, April 21, 1973.
29 Ross, "Thorson's Last Stand."
30 Thorson, *Wanted*, 153.
31 *Thorson v. Attorney General of Canada*, [1975] 1 S.C.R. 138.
32 *Jones v. A.G. of New Brunswick*, [1975] 2 S.C.R. 182.
33 "Join the Single Canada League – Advertisement," *Globe and Mail*, June 8, 1974.
34 Ross, "Thorson's Last Stand."
35 "Joseph T. Thorson: Ex-Minister Fought Languages Act," *Globe and Mail*, July 6, 1978.
36 William Busby to J.T. Thorson, February 6, 1968, and Canadian National Association flyer, LAC, MG31 E38 (R5018–10-X-E), file 14, vol. 11.
37 Ibid.
38 J.T. Thorson to William Busby, February 6, 1968, LAC, MG31 E38 (R5018–10-X-E), file 14, vol. 11.
39 "The British North America Act – Section 133 – Advertisement," *Globe and Mail*, January 24, 1970.
40 "Consultants Study Aspects of Independent West Canada," *Globe and Mail*, February 18, 1970.
41 "New Party Stirs Political Dust," *Globe and Mail*, January 9, 1971.
42 "One-Language Party Will Contest Seats," *Globe and Mail*, April 1, 1977.
43 "'Decent' People's Political Party," *Globe and Mail*, July 13, 1970.
44 "Anti-Quebec Turnout Not True Picture: MP," *Globe and Mail*, January 16, 1971.
45 "Dominion of Canada Party – 'Nous ne sommes pas des bigots,'" *Évangeline*, septembre 10, 1973.

46 Ibid.
47 Flo E. Frawley, letter to the editor, *Globe and Mail,* July 20, 1978.
48 Flo E. Frawley, letter to the editor, *Globe and Mail,* June 30, 1984.
49 Flo E. Frawley, letter to the editor, *Globe and Mail,* August 19, 1972.
50 Frawley passed away in Calgary in 1997 at age eighty-three.
51 Voice of Canada League to supporters, n.d., LAC, MG31 E38 (R5018–10-X-E), file 14, vol. 11.
52 The quotations above are from LAC, MG32 B35 (R3611–0-0-E), file S.O.S. Bilingualism Notes, vol. 133.
53 "Advertisement – Our Government: Racist and Arrogant," *Globe and Mail,* June 25, 1976.
54 Geoffrey Stevens, "Words, Words, Words," *Globe and Mail,* June 26, 1976.
55 Winnett Boyd with Kenneth McDonald, *The National Dilemma and the Way Out* (Richmond Hill, ON: BMG Publishing, 1975), 83–93.
56 Kenneth McDonald, *The Monstrous Trick* (Toronto: APEC Publishing, 1998), 24–25.
57 Kenneth McDonald, *Red Maple: How Canada Became the People's Republic of Canada in 1981* (Richmond Hill, ON: BMG Publishing, 1975), 8.
58 Ibid., 72.
59 Ibid., 73–74.
60 Ibid., 74.
61 Glenna Reid, "Introduction," in *What's What for Children Learning French,* ed. Glenna Reid (Ottawa: Mutual Press, 1972), 2.
62 Diana M. Trent, "Why Bilingualism? An Anglophone Point of View," in *What's What for Children Learning French,* ed. Glenna Reid (Ottawa: Mutual Press, 1972), 3–4.
63 Ibid., 4–5.
64 Rockcliffe's school board was amalgamated with the Ottawa Board of Education in 1970.
65 Jean Daniel, "Ottawa Public Schools"; Barbara Green and Dorothy Pratt, "Ottawa Separate Schools"; Joan Pond, "Carleton Core Programs"; Betty Stewart, "Carleton Immersion," in *What's What for Children Learning French,* ed. Glenna Reid (Ottawa: Mutual Press, 1972), 26–45.
66 Donalda Hilton, "Television and Radio," in *What's What for Children Learning French,* ed. Glenna Reid (Ottawa: Mutual Press, 1972), 76–77.
67 Interview with Jan Finlay, September 16, 2013.
68 Thomas Wells, Minister of Education, to Gérard Pelletier, September 28, 1972, Archives of Ontario (hereafter AO), RG 2–200, accession 17121, box 2, file Fed/Prov – Projets de rattrapage 1972.
69 Beth and John Mlacak to W.R. McGillivray, April 9, 1973, Personal Files of Beth Mlacak (hereafter PFBM).
70 W.R. McGillivray to Mr. and Mrs. J.S. Mlacak, May 14, 1973, PFBM.
71 Beth Mlacak to Sidney Handleman, May 1, 1973; Sidney Handleman to Thomas Wells, May 10, 1973, both in PFBM.
72 G.A. Fossey, Principal, W. Erskine Johnston Public School, to John and Beth Mlacak, June 1973, PFBM; interview with Beth Mlacak, June 18, 2011.
73 G.A. Fossey to John Mlacak, October 24, 1973, PFBM.

74 Interview with Beth Mlacak, June 18, 2011.

75 Ibid.; John Mlacak, Carleton Board of Education, submission re: immersion, 1973; John and Beth Mlacak to J. Sevigny, Chairman, Carleton Board of Education, February 14, 1974, both in PFBM.

76 Beth Mlacak to W.R. Dakin, Chair, Carleton Board of Education, March 30, 1976, PFBM; Beth Mlacak, "Immersion – There May No Longer Be a Choice," *Kanata Standard*, April 2, 1976.

77 Keith Spicer, "Foreword," in *What's What for Children Learning French (Second Edition)*, ed. Elaine Isabelle (Ottawa: Mutual Press, 1976), ii.

78 H.P. Edwards, "Bilingual Education Programs: Attitudes and Expectancies," in *What's What for Children Learning French (Second Edition)*, ed. Elaine Isabelle (Ottawa: Mutual Press, 1976), 3.

79 Peggy Wightman, "French Immersion: A Canadian Experiment," in *What's What for Children Learning French (Second Edition)*, ed. Elaine Isabelle (Ottawa: Mutual Press, 1976), 24.

80 R.L. Trites, "Children Who Have Difficulty in Early French Immersion," in *What's What for Children Learning French (Second Edition)*, ed. Elaine Isabelle (Ottawa: Mutual Press, 1976), 29–31.

81 Valerie Kennett, "Programs in Ottawa-Carleton Schools," in *What's What for Children Learning French (Second Edition)*, ed. Elaine Isabelle (Ottawa: Mutual Press, 1976), 42–54.

82 Florence Fraser, "Teacher Education in Ontario," in *What's What for Children Learning French (Second Edition)*, ed. Elaine Isabelle (Ottawa: Mutual Press, 1976), 64.

83 Elaine Isabelle, "Postscript," in *What's What for Children Learning French (Second Edition)*, ed. Elaine Isabelle (Ottawa: Mutual Press, 1976), 88.

84 Interview with Beth Mlacak, June 18, 2011.

85 Ontario Ministry of Education, *Report of the Ministerial Committee on the Teaching of French* (1974), 1. This document is commonly referred to as the Gillin Report.

86 Ibid., 26.

87 Ibid., 15–18.

88 Ibid., 26–28. This could be done through variable combinations of time per day in French lessons at the various grade levels (whether reached through twenty minutes per day for grades one to three, forty minutes per day for grades four to six, or thirty minutes per day for grades one to six, or some other combination).

89 Ibid., 22–23. The basic level, which could be accomplished through the regular "core" program, meant a vocabulary of between 3,000 and 3,500 words and a fundamental knowledge of the language's grammar, pronunciation, and idiom. This level would allow a person to be understood in basic conversation, read standard texts with the aid of a dictionary, have some knowledge of French-speaking communities, and be able to recommence study of French at a higher level later in life. Middle-level students, through extended French (at least one other subject taught in French), could read books and newspapers with occasional help from a dictionary, understand television news and programs, and participate adequately in conversations. They would have absorbed knowledge of the culture, society, economy, customs, government, and institutions of a French-speaking community and could function well in

that community after a few months of residence. At the top level, attainable through French immersion, graduates could take higher education in a bilingual educational institution, accept training or employment in the other language, and live in a French-speaking community after a short period of training and participate easily in conversations. They could understand and share the emotional attitudes and values held by members of the community since they would possess a core of ideas, knowledge, and concepts available to the native speaker.

90 Ontario Ministry of Education, *Teaching and Learning French as a Second Language: A New Program for Ontario Students* (1977), 8–9.

91 Loren Lind, "Brown School Parents Win: Total Immersion in French for Two Kindergartens," *Globe and Mail*, May 30, 1972.

92 Loren Lind, "Provincial Spending Ceiling Stymies French Classes in Metro Schools," *Globe and Mail*, October 18, 1971.

93 McKee Home and School, brief to the North York Education and Community Council on teaching French in the North York Public School System, October 15, 1973, PFGS.

94 *Brian Public School Newsletter*, June 17, 1975, PFGS.

95 Minutes of Educom Educational Research Liaison Committee meeting, October 9, 1974, PFGS.

96 Dave Toole, "Metro Hampering French Instruction" *North York Mirror*, December 4, 1974; minutes of Educom Educational Research Liaison Committee meeting, January 15, 1975, PFGS; Educom Educational Research Liaison Committee, memo to Chairman and Board, North York Board of Education, April 9, 1975, PFGS.

97 Kathryn Manzer, Parent Group for Extended French, to Thomas Wells, Minister of Education, March 3, 1975, PFGS; Thomas Wells to Kathryn Manzer, April 7, 1975, PFGS.

98 Interview with Marion Langford, June 16, 2009.

99 "French Class Demand 'Very High' in Toronto," *Globe and Mail*, April 25, 1973.

100 Norman Webster, "French Language Education: For Anglophone Bigots, the Going Is Tough," *Globe and Mail*, December 1, 1973; Norman Webster, "Bilingualism: Patriotic Duty Ignored," *Globe and Mail*, October 28, 1974; Norman Webster, "Immersion in French for Ontario," *Globe and Mail*, October 29, 1974; Norman Webster, "A Way to Master French," *Globe and Mail*, January 23, 1975.

101 Gunild Spiess, "How a Group of Like-Minded Women Brought about Change in Attitudes toward French Language Instruction in Our Schools," 2009, PFGS.

102 Interview with Gunild Spiess, June 16, 2009.

103 Correspondence between Gunild Spiess and Marion Langford, June 15, 1975, PFGS; minutes of the Work Group on French Program meeting, July 7, 1975, PFGS.

104 Marion Langford to Judy Jordan, July 23, 1975, Personal Files of Marion Langford (hereafter PFML).

105 Interview with Marion Langford, June 16, 2009; interview with Gunild Spiess, June 16, 2009.

106 Material from the Management and Academic Program Committee of the North York Board of Education, September 29, 1975, PFGS.

107 Thomas Wells to Jean MacLeod, President, University Women's Club of North York, Canadian Federation of University Women, December 29, 1975, PFGS.

108 North York Board of Education, report on feasibility study of further expansion of FSL programs, November 2, 1977; agenda of the Educational Program Committee meeting, November 16, 1977, PFGS.

109 Ontario Parents for French, brief to Thomas Wells, and cover letter from Pat Webster, June 14, 1977, PFGS; Pat Webster to Ontario Parents for French members, July 14, 1977, PFGS.

Chapter 5: Canadian Parents for French and Its Adversaries, 1977–86

1 Keith Spicer, "Words of Welcome," Parents' Conference on French Language and Exchange Opportunities Program, March 1977, 1, PFBM.

2 Ibid., 2; interview with Keith Spicer, October 7, 2011.

3 Spicer, "Words of Welcome," 3–4.

4 "Agenda," Parents' Conference on French Language and Exchange Opportunities Program, March 1977, PFBM.

5 Ibid.

6 "Appendix 1 – Revised Recommendations of the Parents' Conference on French Language and Exchange Opportunities," Parents' Conference on French Language and Exchange Opportunities Program, March 1977, PFBM; "Introduction," *Canadian Parents for French Newsletter* 1 (1977): 1.

7 Keith Spicer, "Strasbourg Goose Syndrome," *Canadian Parents for French Newsletter* 1 (1977): 1.

8 "Appendix 1 – Revised Recommendations," 1–5.

9 Jean-Luc Pépin, "French Second Language Programs and National Unity," *Canadian Parents for French Newsletter* 2 (1978): 2.

10 Canadian Parents for French – New Brunswick Branch, brief to the Task Force on Canadian Unity, 1978, Mount Allison University Archives (hereafter MAUA), Canadian Parents for French fonds (hereafter CPF fonds), 2000.23/2/1; Canadian Parents for French – Manitoba Branch, brief to the Task Force on Canadian Unity, 1978, MAUA, CPF fonds, 2000.23/3/1/1.

11 Mary Lou Morrison, brief to the Task Force on Canadian Unity, October 6, 1977, MAUA, CPF fonds, 2000.23/3/10/1.

12 Canadian Parents for French, minutes of the first Annual General Meeting, October 15, 1977, MAUA, CPF fonds, 2000.23/3/10/1.

13 Canadian Parents for French, minutes of the first meeting of the Board of Directors, October 16, 1977, MAUA, CPF fonds, 2000.23/3/10/1.

14 Executive Secretary, CPF, report to the Board of Directors and alternates, December 1, 1977, MAUA, CPF fonds, 2000.23/2/1.

15 Canadian Parents for French, *So You Want Your Child to Learn French! A Handbook for Parents* (Ottawa: Mutual Press, 1979), 3.

16 Canadian Parents for French, minutes of the meeting of the Board of Directors, February 11–12, 1978, MAUA, CPF fonds, 2000.23/3/1/1.

17 Interview with Janet Poyen, September 2012.

18 Ibid.

19 Poyen and Gibson had worked together extensively in BC Parents for French. Judy Gibson, email to the author, June 29, 2015.

20 "A look at the future," *Canadian Parents for French Newsletter* 7 (1979): 1.

21 Canadian Parents for French, National Office Budget, 1978, MAUA, CPF fonds, 2000.23/3/1/2.
22 Canadian Parents for French, minutes of the meeting of the Board of Directors, June 3–4, 1978, MAUA, CPF fonds, 2000.23/3/1/2.
23 Canadian Parents for French, minutes of the meeting of the Board of Directors, October 12, 1978, MAUA, CPF fonds, 2000.23/3/1/3; Canadian Parents for French, minutes of the meeting of the Board of Directors, January 19–21, 1979, MAUA, CPF fonds, 2000.23/3/1/4.
24 *Canadian Parents for French Newsletter* 3 (1978); *Canadian Parents for French Newsletter* 6 (1979).
25 Canadian Parents for French, minutes of the meeting of the Board of Directors, January 25–27, 1980, MAUA, CPF fonds, 2000.23/3/1/5.
26 Canadian Parents for French, minutes of the meeting of the Board of Directors, June 3–4, 1978, MAUA, CPF fonds, 2000.23/3/1/2.
27 Canadian Parents for French, minutes of the meeting of the Board of Directors, January 25–27, 1980, MAUA, CPF fonds, 2000.23/3/1/5.
28 David Macdonald, Secretary of State, to Janet Poyen, October 10, 1979, Personal Files of Janet Poyen (hereafter PFJP).
29 Janet Poyen, "Report on a Pilot Study to Assess Information Gathered on Parents' Reactions to French Second Language Learning," 1980, MAUA, CPF fonds, 2000.23/2/13/1.
30 "A National Study on French Language Learning in Canada (Phase 1)," project proposal, May 14, 1980, MAUA, CPF fonds, 2000.23/2/13/1.
31 Robert C. Williston, report on findings of 1979–80 survey on parents' reaction to French second-language learning, MAUA, CPF fonds, 2000.23/2/13/1.
32 Canadian Parents for French questionnaire, PEI raw data, 1980, MAUA, CPF fonds, 2000.23/2/13/2.
33 Canadian Parents for French – British Columbia Chapter, profile, November 1, 1980, MAUA, CPF fonds, 2000.23/2/13/4.
34 Evaluation of Canadian Parents for French pilot study on parents' reactions to French second-language learning, 1979–80, May 9, 1980, MAUA, CPF fonds, 2000.23/2/13/4.
35 Canadian Parents for French, minutes of the fourth Annual General Meeting, November 8, 1980, MAUA, CPF fonds, 2000.23/3/1/5.
36 "National Project Shows Strong Parent Interest in French Language," *Canadian Parents for French Newsletter* 10 (1980): 3.
37 Evaluation of the CPF national study, phase 2, 1981–82, MAUA, CPF fonds, 2000.23/3/1/5.
38 "Membership Fees to Be Collected," *Canadian Parents for French Newsletter* 6 (1979): 5.
39 Canadian Parents for French, minutes of the fourth Annual General Meeting, November 8, 1980, MAUA, CPF fonds, 2000.23/3/1/5.
40 Canadian Parents for French, minutes of the meeting of the Board of Directors, January 19–21, 1979, MAUA, CPF fonds, 2000.23/3/1/4.
41 Canadian Parents for French, minutes of the meeting of the Board of Directors, January 25–27, 1980, MAUA, CPF fonds, 2000.23/3/1/5.

42 Canadian Parents for French, minutes of the meeting of the Board of Directors, January 22–24, 1980, MAUA, CPF fonds, 2000.23/3/1/5.

43 J.V. Andrew, *Bilingual Today, French Tomorrow: Trudeau's Master Plan and How It Can Be Stopped* (Richmond Hill, ON: BMG Publishing, 1977), 107.

44 Ibid., 111.

45 Ibid., 59.

46 Ibid., 88.

47 Ibid., 122.

48 Winnet Boyd, "Preface," in ibid.

49 APEC does not appear to have maintained any formal archive of these newsletters, and my efforts to locate them have yielded only sporadic issues.

50 "Anti-Bilingualism Leader Says She's No Bigot," Montreal *Gazette*, March 17, 1979.

51 Hubert Bauch, "He Likes Being Called Bigot," Montreal *Gazette*, April 15, 1990.

52 David Somerville, *Trudeau Revealed by His Words and Actions* (Richmond Hill, ON: BMG Publishing, 1978).

53 Sam Allison, *French Power: The Francization of Canada* (Richmond Hill, ON: BMG Publishing, 1978).

54 Ibid., 58–63.

55 Ibid., 86–92.

56 William Johnson, "View from Quebec: French-Bashing New Literary Genre," *Globe and Mail*, October 2, 1978.

57 J.V. Andrew, *Backdoor Bilingualism: Davis's Sell-Out of Ontario and Its National Consequences* (Richmond Hill, ON: BMG Publishing, 1979), 32–33.

58 Ibid., 51–60.

59 Ibid., 62–97. The reference to Pelletier as Goebbels is on page 80, and the Hitler references are on pages 81 and 92.

60 Ibid., 37.

61 Ibid., 99.

62 Ibid., 158–59.

63 "Learning Difficulties," *Canadian Parents for French Newsletter* 8 (1979): 4.

64 Fred Genesee, "The Suitability of French Immersion for Students Who Are at-Risk: A Review of Research Evidence," 18–20, http://www.psych.mcgill.ca/perpg/fac/genesee/Suitability%20of%20Immersion%20for%20At-Risk%20Students.pdf.

65 G. Paul Olson and George Burns, "Immersed for Change: Politics and Planning in French Immersion," 1982, MAUA, CPF fonds, 2000.23/2/31/2. This paper drew on findings from their longer study *Immersion and Politics in French Immersion: Analysis, Discussion, and Recommendations on the Social Effects of Implementation in Northeastern Ontario Communities* (Toronto: Ontario Institute of Studies in Education, 1982).

66 "French Immersion Creating Bilingual 'Elite,' Professor Says," Montreal *Gazette*, June 4, 1984; Linda Diebel, "The Rise of a Bilingual Canadian Elite," *Maclean's*, July 4, 1983, 22–24; Paul McGrath, "An Immersion Inundation," *Maclean's*, October 1, 1984, 73–74.

67 Olson and Burns, "Immersed for Change."

68 "Teapot Tempest: Immersion Schools and the Burns-Olson Report," *CPF National Newsletter* 17 (1982): 6.

69 "Burns Responds to 'Elitism' Issue," *CPF National Newsletter* 20 (1982): 1.

70 George E. Burns, "Charges of Elitism in Immersion Education: The Case for Improving Program Implementation," *Contact* 2, 2 (1983): 2–8.

71 Canadian Parents for French, minutes of the meeting of the Board of Directors, January 22–24, 1982, MAUA, CPF fonds, 2000.23/3/1/5.

72 Canadian Parents for French – Saskatchewan, "Remedial and Enrichment Instruction in French Immersion Programs – A Survey," 1985, MAUA, CPF fonds, 2000.23/3/5/2. Statistics in the following two paragraphs are from this source.

73 Canadian Parents for French, minutes of the meeting of the Board of Directors, January 18–19, 1986, MAUA, CPF fonds, 2000.23/3/1/6.

74 "Special Needs: A Consultant's View," *CPF National Newsletter* 24 (1983): 10.

75 Mary Jane Cioni, "So, Johnny's Report Wasn't Wonderful: Helping Your Child Cope with Problems in School," *CPF National Newsletter* 30 (1985): 4.

76 "Must Make Special Learning Needs Normal – Fortier," *CPF National Newsletter* 32 (1985): 3.

77 Margaret Bruck, "Attitude Provides the Key to Greater Immersion Success," *CPF National Newsletter* 32 (1985): 9.

78 Fred Genesee, "Immersion for All? Research Probes Suitability for below Average Students," *CPF National Newsletter* 34 (1986): 1.

79 Matthew Hayday, *Bilingual Today, United Tomorrow: Official Languages in Education and Canadian Federalism* (Montreal: McGill-Queen's University Press, 2005).

80 Francis Fox to Janet Poyen, May 12, 1980, PFJP.

81 Janet Poyen to Ronald Duhamel, December 17, 1980, PFJP; Canadian Parents for French, brief to the Council of Ministers of Education, Canada, 1981, PFJP; notes on a meeting between the Committee for Non-Governmental Organizations of the Council of Ministers of Education, Canada, and representatives of Canadian Parents for French, June 15, 1981, PFJP.

82 Notes on a meeting between Huguette Labelle and Canadian Parents for French representatives, February 9, 1981, PFJP.

83 Janet Poyen to Huguette Labelle, March 9, 1981, PFJP; Canadian Parents for French, "Federal-Provincial Agreement on Bilingualism in Education Funding," position paper, and summary sheet, 1981, PFJP.

84 Janet Poyen to Jean Chrétien, September 30, 1981, PFJP.

85 Camille Laurin to Janet Poyen, May 11, 1981, PFJP.

86 Canadian Parents for French, minutes of the fourth Annual General Meeting, November 8, 1980, MAUA, CPF fonds, 2000.23/3/1/5.

87 Hayday, *Bilingual Today*, 140–41.

88 Canadian Parents for French, minutes of the meeting of the Board of Directors, October 26–27 and 30, 1983, MAUA, CPF fonds, 2000.23/3/1/5; Canadian Parents for French, minutes of the meeting of the Board of Directors, October 2 and 6, 1985, MAUA, CPF fonds, 2000.23/3/1/6.

89 *Société des Acadiens du Nouveau-Brunswick Inc. v. Minority Language School Board No. 50* (1983), 48 N.B.R. (2d) 361.

90 "CPF Endorses Core and Improved P.R.: Opposes New Brunswick Restrictions," *CPF National Newsletter* 24 (1983): 3.

91 Stuart Beaty, memo to D'Iberville Fortier, December 18, 1986, LAC, RG 122, series A-1, accession 1997–98/632, box 19, file 1140-2-2, vol. 7; André Creusot, reflections

on the Tenth Congress of CPF, 1986, LAC, RG 122, series A-1, accession 1997–98/632, box 19, file 1140–2-2, vol. 7.

92 Stuart Beaty, memo to Maxwell Yalden, May 31, 1984, LAC, RG 122, series A-1, accession 1997–98/632, box 19, file 1140–2-2, vol. 4.

93 Canadian Parents for French, minutes of the meeting of the Board of Directors, June 1–3, 1984, MAUA, CPF fonds, 2000.23/3/1/5.

94 Special item of business, Board of Directors meeting with Secretary of State representatives re: funding, February 1984, MAUA, CPF fonds, 2000.23/3/1/5.

95 Canadian Parents for French, minutes of the meeting of the Board of Directors, October 26–27 and 30, 1983, MAUA, CPF fonds, 2000.23/3/1/5.

96 Interview with Stewart Goodings, July 8, 2009.

97 Canadian Parents for French, minutes of the meeting of the Board of Directors, October 22–24, 1982, MAUA, CPF fonds, 2000.23/3/1/5.

98 Ibid.

99 Sharon Lapkin, Merrill Swain, and Valerie Argue, *French Immersion: The Trial Balloon that Flew* (Toronto: OISE Press, 1983).

100 Canadian Parents for French, minutes of the meeting of the Board of Directors, October 26–27 and 30, 1983, MAUA, CPF fonds, 2000.23/3/1/5.

101 Canadian Parents for French, minutes of the meeting of the Board of Directors, February 3–5, 1984, MAUA, CPF fonds, 2000.23/3/1/5.

102 Canadian Parents for French, minutes of the meeting of the Board of Directors, June 1–3, 1984, MAUA, CPF fonds, 2000.23/3/1/5.

103 Canadian Parents for French, minutes of the meeting of the Board of Directors, January 25–27, 1985, MAUA, CPF fonds, 2000.23/3/1/6.

104 Canadian Parents for French, minutes of the meeting of the Board of Directors, June 7–9, 1985, MAUA, CPF fonds, 2000.23/3/1/6.

105 For more on the history of ParticipACTION, see work by Victoria Lamb Drover, including "ParticipACTION, Healthism and the Crafting of a Social Memory (1971-1999)," *Journal of the Canadian Historical Association* 25, 1 (2014): 277–306.

106 Pamela Wiggins, memo to Christine Sirois, July 28, 1983, LAC, RG 122, series A-1, accession 1997–98/632, box 19, file 1140–2-2, vol. 4.

107 Perhaps thinking along the same lines, board game manufacturer Canvesco of Winnipeg started selling a game called Biwords in 1983, in which teams earned points by correctly translating words from English into French or vice versa, with the choice of word determined by the roll of a die.

108 Stewart Goodings to Maxwell Yalden, November 14, 1983, LAC, RG 122, series A-1, accession 1997–98/632, box 19, file 1140–2-2, vol. 4.

109 Christine Sirois, memo to Commissioner, January 31, 1984, LAC, RG 122, series A-1, accession 1997–98/632, box 19, file 1140–2-2, vol. 4.

110 Maxwell Yalden, handwritten note to Stuart Beaty, February 2, 1984, LAC, RG 122, series A-1, accession 1997–98/632, box 19, file 1140–2-2, vol. 4.

111 Stuart Beaty, memo to M. Yalden, February 2, 1984, LAC, RG 122, series A-1, accession 1997–98/632, box 19, file 1140–2-2, vol. 4.

112 Stewart Goodings, memo to Maxwell Yalden, February 28, 1984, LAC, RG 122, series A-1, accession 1997–98/632, box 19, file 1140–2-2, vol. 4.

113 "'Linguistic Participaction': A Report on a Feasibility Study Conducted by Canadian Parents for French under Contract to the Office of the Commissioner of Official Languages," 1985, LAC, RG 122, series A-1, accession 1997–98/632, box 18, file 1140–2, vol. 5.
114 Keith Spicer, "'A Linguistic Participaction?' An Informal Preliminary Survey for Canadian Parents for French," October 19, 1984, LAC, RG 122, series A-1, accession 1997–98/632, box 18, file 1140–2, vol. 5.
115 "'Linguistic Participaction.'"
116 "Language Vital, Says Exporter," *CPF National Newsletter* 30 (1985): 3.
117 "Major Magazine Reports – CPF and Immersion: The Achievements and the Future," *CPF National Newsletter* 30 (1985): 6.
118 Canadian Parents for French, minutes of the meeting of the Board of Directors, May 13–14, 1983, MAUA, CPF fonds, 2000.23/3/1/5.
119 Helen Wilkes, "How Immersion Has Changed Core," *CPF National Newsletter* 26 (1984): 1.
120 Canadian Parents for French, minutes of the meeting of the Board of Directors, June 7–9, 1985, MAUA, CPF fonds, 2000.23/3/1/6.
121 Canadian Parents for French, minutes of the meeting of the Board of Directors, November 30–December 1, 1985, MAUA, CPF fonds, 2000.23/3/1/6.
122 Canadian Parents for French, *Bilingual University Education for Anglo-Ontarians*, conference program, September 30–October 1, 1983; "Are Universities Ready for Your Child?" and "Universities: What Changes Are Needed," *CPF National Newsletter* 20 (1982): 7–10.
123 Marjorie Loughrey, "French for the Post-Secondary French-Speaking Student," *CPF National Newsletter* 29 (1985): 5.
124 Canadian Parents for French, minutes of the meeting of the Board of Directors, October 2 and 6, 1985, MAUA, CPF fonds, 2000.23/3/1/6.
125 Canadian Parents for French, minutes of the meeting of the Board of Directors, June 6–8, 1986, MAUA, CPF fonds, 2000.23/3/1/6.
126 Canadian Parents for French, minutes of the meeting of the Board of Directors, June 1–3, 1984, MAUA, CPF fonds, 2000.23/3/1/5.
127 "Quebecers Show Most Interest in Bilingual Classes," press release on the Gallup report, September 1983, Canadian Parents for French National Office Files (hereafter CPFN), file Surveys/Opinion Polls. Surveyed were 1,070 Canadians (both English and French speaking), and the poll was considered accurate within a 4 percent margin, nineteen times out of twenty. The poll provided a rough measure of English-speaking Canadian opinion, since provinces other than Quebec would include some members of francophone communities and exclude the Montreal anglophone population.
128 Canadian Parents for French, minutes of the meeting of the Board of Directors, June 1–3, 1984, MAUA, CPF fonds, 2000.23/3/1/5.
129 Synopsis of the results of a Gallup survey conducted in the summer of 1984 for Canadian Parents for French, CPFN, file Surveys/Opinion Polls. Respondents were asked whether they thought that children living in their province should learn French at school so that they could become bilingual. If they said no, they were asked why they objected to French-language education. If they said yes, they were asked what

they thought the main advantage would be for children who learned French and became bilingual. Respondents were asked what type of French instruction they thought was preferable – French as a subject, early French immersion, late French immersion, or bilingual instruction. Gallup asked respondents whether they were satisfied with the French instruction that they had received and for the reasons for any dissatisfaction. They were also asked whether they thought that French should be a compulsory subject at the elementary and secondary school levels and whether it should be a compulsory entrance or graduation requirement for universities. Finally, they were asked if they could recall the name of specific Canadian organizations that promoted French as part of the school curriculum.

130 The regions were British Columbia, the prairie region, Ontario, Quebec, and Atlantic Canada, and special subcategories for New Brunswick and Manitoba, in the midst of language-related political crises.

131 Gallup National Omnibus, conducted for Canadian Parents for French, June–July 1984, CPFN, file Surveys/Opinion Polls.

132 Even in the older age categories, support was consistently over 60 percent. Ibid., 13–16.

133 This opinion was expressed most strongly by labourers (22.4 percent) and in Ontario (18.8 percent).

134 This issue of other languages being more frequently spoken than French was most significant in the prairie region (16.3 percent), among those with a public school education (16.9 percent), and among those earning under $10,000 per year. Overall, another 4 percent did not think that French should be taught in schools because English was not spoken or taught in Quebec, and about 3 percent cited the costs of French-language programs.

135 Ibid., 17–20.

136 New Brunswickers (82.4 percent) and Atlantic Canadians overall (66 percent) gave this response most frequently, compared with 44.8 percent in Ontario, 38.7 percent in the prairie region, and 28.4 percent in British Columbia.

137 Most regions were close to this figure, though there was a significant dip in Atlantic Canada (5.3 percent); the highest level of support for this answer was in British Columbia (18.6 percent).

138 This response was somewhat more popular in British Columbia and Ontario.

139 Ibid., 21–24.

140 Ibid., 25–28.

141 The highest support for this option was in New Brunswick (81.7 percent) and Atlantic Canada (70.8 percent), with numbers dropping below 60 percent in all regions west of Quebec, bottoming out at 51.9 percent in British Columbia.

142 Ibid., 29–32.

143 Ibid., 33–36. Drawing comparisons in terms of levels of satisfaction is somewhat difficult given how prevalent the absence of French education was in certain categories: 63.1 percent of those who had only an elementary school education had never taken French, and almost half (45.3 percent) of those over the age of fifty fell into this category. The highest levels of dissatisfaction with the quality of their French education were in Atlantic Canada, where 25 percent of respondents, and 30 percent of New Brunswickers, said that they were not at all satisfied.

144 Other frequently given responses included that there was not enough oral or conversational French taught and that there was an overemphasis on formal French and grammar.
145 Ibid., 37–40.
146 It was also a question with a clear gender divide, with men opposing it by 51.3 percent to 44.7 percent, with women more clearly in support of it (55.2 percent to 41 percent).
147 There was also a clear correlation with experience, since 63.1 percent of those satisfied with their French instruction supported mandatory elementary courses, versus only 36.1 percent of respondents who had not taken French.
148 The opposition was evident in all age categories and most occupations, though a slight majority of professionals and executives would support it. University-educated respondents gave plurality support to this option, though only barely (49.3 percent to 47.5 percent). Upper-middle-income earners ($20,000 to $30,000) were slightly supportive, whereas all other income classes were not. The clearest lines of alignment here are with levels of satisfaction, since those who were very satisfied with their instruction would have supported it by a clear majority (57.8 percent to 37.2 percent), whereas those who had never taken French were the most opposed (37.7 percent versus 56.4 percent).
149 Ibid., 41–56.
150 Gallup poll release, 1984, CPFN, file Surveys/Opinion Polls.
151 Cynthia Steers, memo to CPF chapter contact persons, September 14, 1984, CPFN, file Surveys/Opinion Polls.
152 CPF news release, September 27, 1984, CPFN, file Surveys/Opinion Polls.
153 Ibid.
154 Canadian Parents for French, minutes of the meeting of the Board of Directors, June 7–9, 1985, MAUA, CPF fonds, 2000.23/3/1/6.
155 Unprompted, 87.5 percent of Canadians could not identify the name of any organization that promoted French as part of the regular school curriculum. Gallup National Omnibus, conducted for Canadian Parents for French, June–July 1984, CPFN, file Surveys/Opinion Polls, 57–64.
156 "Reception Launches New Book, CPF Information Campaign," *CPF National Newsletter* 33 (1986): 1.
157 Canadian Parents for French, minutes of the meeting of the Board of Directors, June 6–8, 1986, MAUA, CPF fonds, 2000.23/3/1/6.
158 Cynthia Steers, "Issues Management and Canadian Parents for French," May 6, 1986, MAUA, CPF fonds, 2000.23/3/1/6.

Chapter 6: Internationalization and Higher Education

1 Keith Spicer, *Life Sentences: Memoirs of an Incorrigible Canadian* (Toronto: McClelland and Stewart, 2004), 87.
2 Maxwell Yalden, *Transforming Rights: Reflections from the Front Lines* (Toronto: University of Toronto Press, 2009), 21.
3 Interview with Maxwell Yalden, October 28, 2011.
4 "Preliminary Report to the Commissioner of Official Languages – Elementary Project," 1978, LAC, RG 122, accession 1995–96/063, box 5, file 0590–6, vol. 1; Oh!

Canada 1979, note by Madeleine Kronby, November 17, 1978, LAC, RG 122, accession 1995–96/063, box 5, file 0590–6, vol. 1.

5 Diana Trafford, memo to Christine Sirois, October 22, 1979, LAC, RG 122, accession 1995–96/063, box 5, file 0590–6, vol. 1.

6 Information Branch, Office of the Commissioner of Official Languages, "'Trousse citoyen du monde – Citizen of the World' Kit Being Prepared by the Office of the Commissioner of Official Languages. Progress Report and Proposal Regarding Co-Operation with the Council of Ministers of Education Canada," September 11, 1979, LAC, RG 122, accession 1992–93/041, box 7, file 0590–4-1, vol. 2.

7 Christine Sirois to Boyd Pelley, September 11, 1979, LAC, RG 122, accession 1992–93/041, box 7, file 0590–4-1, vol. 2.

8 Advisory Committee of the CMEC, meeting re Explorations kit agenda, May 13, 1980, LAC, RG 122, accession 1992–93/041, box 7, file 0590–4-1, vol. 8.

9 Don Blenkarn to Maxwell Yalden, November 20, 1980, LAC, RG 122, accession 1995–96/063, box 5, file 0590–6, vol. 1.

10 Responses to world languages map generally and to Oh! Canada 2 and Explorations, May 13, 1982, LAC, RG 122, accession 1995–96/063, box 5, file 0590–6, vol. 4.

11 Ronald Clark, "O Canada 2: An Evaluation Survey of Kit Users," November 1981; "The Oh! Canada 2 Kit: Summary Results of Independent Evaluation Studies," November 18, 1981; Anthony H. Smith, Gila Hanna, and Sharon Lapkin, "The Explorations Kit: Summary Results of an Independent Evaluation Study," October 1981, all in LAC, RG 122, accession 1995–96/063, box 5, file 0590–6, vol. 4.

12 Christine Sirois, memo to Commissioner Yalden, October 29, 1981, LAC, RG 122, accession 1995–96/063, box 6, file 0590–6-4, vol. 2.

13 Patrick Gaudreau, memo to Deputy Commissioner, LAC, RG 122, accession 1995–96/063, box 5, file 0590–4-1, vol. 12. By 1986, 500,000 kits had been distributed, and smaller print runs of tens of thousands of copies were periodically authorized in the late 1980s.

14 Minutes of the meeting of June 2–3, 1986, LAC, RG 122, accession 1995–96/063, box 5, file 0590–4-1, vol. 12.

15 Tony Smith, Living Dimensions, memo to Tina van Dusen re Final Report on Explorations, May 7, 1986, LAC, RG 122, accession 1995–96/063, box 5, file 0590–4-1, vol. 12.

16 Anthony Smith, Gila Hanna, and Sharon Lapkin, "Oh! Canada 2: An Evaluation – A Survey of Ten Curriculum Experts," October 1981, 7, LAC, RG 122, accession 1995–96/063, box 5, file 0590–6, vol. 4.

17 Ibid., 20.

18 Information Branch, Office of the Commissioner of Official Languages, "The Oh! Canada 2 Kit: Summary Results of Two Independent Evaluation Studies," September 22, 1982, LAC, RG 122, accession 1995–96/063, box 6, file 0590–6-4, vol. 2.

19 Clark, "O Canada 2."

20 Christine Sirois, memo to Commissioner Yalden, January 19, 1984, LAC, RG 122, accession 1995–96/063, box 6, file 0590–6-5.

21 Maxwell Yalden to Bette Stephenson, Minister of Education and of Colleges and Universities, Ontario, and to David Macdonald, February 5, 1980, LAC, RG 122, series A-1, accession 1997–98/632, box 20, file 1140–3, vol. 1.

22 Annual report of Bilingual Exchange Canada, 1980, LAC, RG 122, series A-1, accession 1997–98/632, box 20, file 1140–3, vol. 2.

23 Notes for opening remarks by Maxwell Yalden to the annual conference of the Bilingual Exchange Secretariat, November 18, 1981, LAC, RG 122, series A-1, accession 1997–98/632, box 20, file 1140–3, vol. 3.

24 H.K. Fisher, Deputy Minister of Education, Ontario, to Jane Dobell, Bilingual Exchange Secretariat, December 9, 1982, LAC, RG 122, series A-1, accession 1997–98/632, box 20, file 1140–3, vol. 5.

25 COL, *Annual Report 1977* (Ottawa: Information Canada, 1978), 16.

26 Ibid., 33.

27 Ibid., 17.

28 Jeanne, memo to M. Morin, April 11, 1978, in response to the question in the Ontario legislature from Sean Conway to Bill Davis, LAC, RG 122, series A-1, accession 1997–98/632, box 20, file 1140–4, vol. 1.

29 Jeanne, memo to Maxwell Yalden, May 16, 1978, LAC, RG 122, series A-1, accession 1997–98/632, box 20, file 1140–4, vol. 1.

30 Lorne Laforge, "Report on the Study of the Requirements of Canadian Colleges and Universities Concerning Knowledge of the Second Official Language," October 1979, LAC, RG 122, series A-1, accession 1997–98/632, box 20, file 1140–4, vol. 3.

31 G. Grant Clarke, Deputy Executive Director, Council of Ontario Universities (COU), memo to members of COU, December 19, 1979, LAC, RG 122, series A-1, accession 1997–98/632, box 20, file 1140–4, vol. 4.

32 Eileen Sarkar, memo to Maxwell Yalden, April 9, 1981, LAC, RG 122, series A-1, accession 1997–98/632, box 20, file 1140–4, vol. 4.

33 Compte rendu de la réunion de l'association des directeurs des départements d'études françaises des universités de l'Ontario, avril 3, 1981, LAC, RG 122, series A-1, accession 1997–98/632, box 20, file 1140–4, vol. 5.

34 "Commissioner to Address French Language Policy at UNB," press release, November 17, 1981, LAC, RG 122, series A-1, accession 1997–98/632, box 20, file 1140–4, vol. 6.

35 Donald Savage to Maxwell Yalden, March 25, 1982, LAC, RG 122, series A-1, accession 1997–98/632, box 20, file 1140–4, vol. 6.

36 Research and Analysis Division, Association of Universities and Colleges of Canada, memo to A.K. Gillmore, September 7, 1982, LAC, RG 122, series A-1, accession 1997–98/632, box 20, file 1140–4, vol. 8.

37 G.R. Branton, University of Victoria, to Maxwell Yalden, July 16, 1982; Gilles Lalande, Deputy Commissioner, to G.R. Branton, August 20, 1982, both in LAC, RG 122, series A-1, accession 1997–98/632, box 18, file 1140–1, vol. 3.

38 Sally Andrews, memo to Maxwell Yalden, December 6, 1983, LAC, RG 122, series A-1, accession 1997–98/632, box 21, file 1140–4, vol. 11.

39 Elaine Limbrick, Acting Dean of Humanities, to Maxwell Yalden, March 8, 1984, LAC, RG 122, series A-1, accession 1997–98/632, box 21, file 1140–4, vol. 12.

40 G.R. Branton, Chair, University of Victoria Senate Committee on Academic Standards, to Sally Andrews, February 3, 1983, LAC, RG 122, series A-1, accession 1997–98/632, box 21, file 1140–4, vol. 9.

Chapter 7: Canadian Parents for French and Local Activism, 1977–87

1 For fuller details on the Sackville case, see Matthew Hayday, "Mad at Hatfield's Tea Party: Federalism and the Fight for French Immersion in Sackville, New Brunswick, 1973–1982," in *Mobilizations, Protests, and Engagements: Canadian Perspectives on Social Movements,* ed. Marie Hammond-Callaghan and Matthew Hayday (Halifax: Fernwood Publishing, 2008), 145–63.

2 Interview with Vanessa Bass, March 21, 2007; *Canadian Parents for French New Brunswick Newsletter* 5 (1981).

3 "Board Considers French Immersion," *Communiqué* Spring/Summer (1982): 4; Canadian Parents for French British Columbia files (hereafter CPFBC), file Prince Rupert; Pete Lester, memo, March 20, 1981, CPFBC, file Prince Rupert.

4 Gail Holmgren to Dorthy Graham and Trustees of School District 52, September 22, 1981, CPFBC, file Prince Rupert.

5 Press clippings of French immersion advertisements, CPFBC, file Prince Rupert.

6 "Parents to Petition School Board for a French Immersion Class," January 1982, CPFBC, file Prince Rupert.

7 Gail Holmgren to District Rep, August 7, 1983, CPFBC, file Prince Rupert; "Board Considers French Immersion," *Communiqué* Spring/Summer (1982), 4, CPFBC, file Prince Rupert.

8 Mayor P.J. Lester to Gail Holmgren, January 21, 1982, CPFBC, file Prince Rupert; Graham Lea, MLA for Prince Rupert, to Susan Tickson, January 25, 1982, CPFBC, file Prince Rupert; Jim Fulton, MP for Skeena, to Susan Tickson, February 8, 1982, CPFBC, file Prince Rupert.

9 Guidelines for program management, CPFBC, file Prince Rupert.

10 Gail Holmgren and Elaine Jaltema, "French Immersion Education Option," CPFBC, file Prince Rupert.

11 Gail Holmgren to District Rep, August 7, 1983, CPFBC, file Prince Rupert.

12 J.M. Lowe, Superintendent of Schools, to Gail Holmgren, June 22, 1983, CPFBC, file Prince Rupert.

13 Gail Holmgren to School Board Trustees, June 26, 1983, CPFBC, file Prince Rupert.

14 Jim Carr, President, Prince Rupert District Teachers' Association, to Dal McCrindle, Chairman, Board of School Trustees, District 52, October 21, 1983, CPFBC, file Prince Rupert.

15 School District 52 (Prince Rupert), Parent Survey – French Immersion Programs, January 18, 1984, CPFBC, file Prince Rupert.

16 Prince Rupert Parents for French, "Rationale for Multiple Lead French Immersion Classes," presented to Board of School Trustees, February 1984, CPFBC, file Prince Rupert.

17 School District 52 (Prince Rupert), report on the meeting of the education committee, March 8, 1984, CPFBC, file Prince Rupert.

18 "Board Refuses Immersion Plan," *Prince Rupert Daily News,* March 14, 1984.

19 "Editorial: Parents Shouldn't Give up Cause," *Prince Rupert Daily News,* March 16, 1984.

20 Gail Holmgren to Service Clubs, Political Parties, City Council, MLA, MP, March 17, 1984, CPFBC, file Prince Rupert.

21 Elaine Jaltema to Board of School Trustees, March 21, 1984, CPFBC, file Prince Rupert.
22 Helen Stamnes to Gail Holmgren, April 12, 1984, CPFBC, file Prince Rupert.
23 Interview with Elaine Jaltema, October 16, 2013.
24 Interview with Yvonne Rolston, November 4, 2013; Anne Hohmann, "Early French Immersion Education in Saanich School District," May 1986, CPFBC, file Saanich.
25 Yvonne Rolston, email to the author, November 4, 2013.
26 Interview with Yvonne Rolston, November 4, 2013.
27 Hohmann, "Early French Immersion Education."
28 Elizabeth Martman to Rubymay Parrott, Chairperson, and Trustees, Saanich School District 63, February 25, 1985, CPFBC, file Saanich.
29 Yvonne Rolston to Rubymay Parrott, March 6, 1985, CPFBC, file Saanich.
30 Joe Lott, transcript of CBC interview with Gail Hulnick on the early French immersion program in School District 63 (Saanich), April 16, 1986, CPFBC, file Saanich.
31 Petition of physicians caring for children on the Saanich Peninsula, 1986, CPFBC, file Saanich.
32 Saanich Parents for French, information sheet, April 16, 1986, CPFBC, file Saanich.
33 Malcolm Macaulay to Yvonne Rolston, April 23, 1986, CPFBC, file Saanich.
34 Saanich Parents for French, committee on early French immersion and preschool-age children, "What about Me? A Brief in Support of Having the Choice of Immersion for Our Pre-School Age Children When They Begin Kindergarten Fall of 1987 and beyond in School District No. 63 (Saanich)," April 28, 1986, CPFBC, file Saanich.
35 Saanich Parents for French, "News release," April 28, 1986, CPFBC, file Saanich.
36 Presentation to school board meeting, May 12, 1986; petition presented May 26, 1986, CPFBC, file Saanich.
37 Bonnie Heyldig to Chairman of the Board and Trustees, April 27, 1986, CPFBC, file Saanich.
38 Janet and Chris Wakefield to Chairman of the Board and Trustees, April 25, 1986, CPFBC, file Saanich.
39 "Attention South Zone Parents," June 5, 1986, CPFBC, file Saanich.
40 July Mas and Maryonne Henry to Chairman and Trustees, School District 63 (Saanich), May 13, 1986, CPFBC, file Saanich.
41 Summary of Saanich presentation to National Canadian Parents for French, June 5, 1986, CPFBC, file Saanich.
42 Catou Lévesque, President, Société Historique Franco-Colombienne, to Board of School Trustees, June 9, 1986; Michel Babin, President, l'Association des franco-phones de Nanaimo, to Board of School Trustees, June 16, 1986; Mark Rose, MLA for Coquitlam-Moody, to Pierre Lapointe, President, Fédération Franco-Colombienne, June 26, 1986; Pierrette Woods, Directrice, l'Associations des parents du programme cadre de français, to Board of School Trustees, June 26, 1986, all in CPFBC, file Saanich.
43 Saanich Parents for French, newsletter, January 1987; R.W. Gowin, retired Co-ordinator of French Programs for School District 63, open letter to the press, February 16, 1987, CPFBC, file Saanich.
44 Reasons for Judgment of the Honourable Madam Justice Proudfoot between Barbara Whittington, Bruce Whittington, Jo-Anne Schenck, Andrew Scheck [sic], Lise

Webb, Maureen Woodward, Michael Woodward, Diane Jereb, and Marjon Jereb (Plaintiff) and the Board of School Trustees of School District No. 63 (Saanich), September 2, 1987, CPFBC, file Saanich.

45 Yvonne Rolston to Pierre Gaudet, Department of the Secretary of State, September 7, 1987, CPFBC, file Saanich.

46 Yvonne Rolston and Jan Garnett, email to the author, November 4, 2013.

47 CPF Annual Report, 1986–87, CPFN.

48 Frank Galgay, "French Immersion: A Luxury We Can't Afford," *St. John's Telegram,* November 22, 1986.

49 Susan Knight and Nina Beresford, "Quality French for All: A Canadian Birthright," *St. John's Telegram,* November 29, 1986.

50 Letter to the editor, *St. John's Telegram,* November 29, 1986.

51 E.R. Patrick, letter to the editor, *St. John's Telegram,* December 3, 1986.

52 Letter of February 5, 1987, quoted in Rosemary (Mercer) Vachon, letter to the editor, *St. John's Telegram,* March 4, 1987.

53 Fed Up (pseudonym), letter to the editor, *St. John's Telegram,* n.d., MAUA, CPF fonds, 2000.23/4/5.

54 Frustrated Proud Taxpayer (pseudonym), letter to the editor, *St. John's Telegram,* April 27, 1987.

55 Letter to the editor, *St. John's Telegram,* (March 1987?), MAUA, CPF fonds, 2000. 23/4/5.

56 Rosemary (Mercer) Vachon, letter to the editor, *St. John's Telegram,* March 4, 1987.

57 Philomena Chafe, letter to the editor, *St. John's Telegram,* (November/December 1986?), MAUA, CPF fonds, 2000.23/4/5.

58 Interview with Jan Finlay, September 16, 2013.

59 Indeed, most of the case studies in this chapter have been reconstructed largely on the basis of provincial and national files of correspondence with local branch presidents.

Chapter 8: Shifting Priorities in the Commissioner's Office

1 Dyane Adam, a Franco-Ontarian, was the fifth commissioner and the first woman to hold the post, though her term falls outside the scope of this book.

2 Michael Behiels, *Canada's Francophone Minority Communities: Constitutional Renewal and the Winning of School Governance* (Montreal: McGill-Queen's University Press, 2004).

3 Garth Stevenson, *Community Besieged: The Anglophone Minority and the Politics of Quebec* (Montreal: McGill-Queen's University Press, 1999).

4 Living Dimensions, "Information Branch Strategy and Renewal – Draft," May 21, 1985, LAC, RG 122, accession 1995–96/063, box 6, file 0590–6-5.

5 Living Dimensions, "Lend an Ear Questionnaire," May 22, 1985, LAC, RG 122, accession 1995–96/063, box 6, file 0590–6-5.

6 Living Dimensions, "Lend an Ear: Summary of Available Evaluative Material and Recommendations," March 1986, LAC, RG 122, accession 1995–96/063, box 6, file 0590–6-5.

7 Tina van Dusen, memo to Patrick Gaudreau, March 11, 1986, LAC, RG 122, accession 1995–96/063, box 6, file 0590–6-5.

8   Package of proposals for information kits from June 29, 1990, LAC, RG 122, file 0590–15, vol. 135.

9   Ghislaine Frappier, Senior Officer, Youth Program, to Achim Krull, October 31, 1989, LAC, RG 122, accession 1995–96/063, box 6, file 0590–13, vol. 3.

10 Marilyn Amendola via Peter Rainboth, memo to D'Iberville Fortier, and evaluation notes on Agenda, November 14, 1989, LAC, RG 122, accession 1995–96/063, box 6, file 0590–13, vol. 3.

11 Project schedule for and description of the Magic Mural, November 18, 1988, LAC, RG 122, accession 1995–96/063, box 6, file 0590–16, vol. 1.

12 Letter of understanding between Jean Larose, Senior Program Officer (Youth), and Carl McMullin, Hinton Animation Studios, May 27, 1988, LAC, RG 122, file 0590–15, vol. 135.

13 Advisory Committee – Youth Program, minutes of the meeting of January 21–22, 1988, LAC, RG 122, accession 1995–96/063, box 6, file 0590–16, vol. 1.

14 Guidelines for idea development and material on the Youth Program, 1984, LAC, RG 122, file 0590-3-DOC, vol. 133.

15 Patricia Morisette, cover letter to vendors invited to submit proposals for information kits, June 29, 1990, LAC, RG 122, file 0590–15, vol. 135.

16 Anthony Smith, "Review Paper – Request for Proposals," November 20, 1989, LAC, RG 122, file 0590-2-DOC, vol. 133.

17 Advisory Committee – Youth Program, minutes of the meeting of January 21–22, 1988, LAC, RG 122, accession 1995–96/063, box 6, file 0590–16, vol. 1.

18 Overview of booklet for ten to eleven year olds, February 10, 1993, LAC, RG 122, file 0590–15, vol. 135.

19 Anthony H. Smith, "Evaluation of Adventures in Time," February 12, 1995, LAC, RG 122, file 0590–20, vol. 135, vol. 1.

20 Ghislaine Frappier, memo to Marc Demers, February 24, 1992, LAC, RG 122, file 0590-1-1989, vol. 42.

21 Office of the Commissioner of Official Languages (hereafter OCOL), *Official Languages: Some Basic Facts* (Ottawa: Minister of Supply and Services Canada, 1991), 15.

22 Ibid.

23 OCOL, *Official Languages: Basic Facts* (Ottawa: Minister of Supply and Services Canada, 1993), 17, 25.

24 Canadian Heritage, *Official Languages: Myths and Realities* (Ottawa: Minister of Supply and Services Canada, 1994), 10.

25 OCOL, *Keeping Up Your Skills – and More – in French* (Ottawa: Minister of Supply and Services Canada, 1993).

26 *Two Languages, One Country* draft study guide, November 16, 1989, LAC, RG 122, file 0590-2-DOC, vol. 133.

27 Ibid.

28 Interview with Victor Goldbloom, May 11, 2012.

29 COL, *Annual Report 1993* (Ottawa: Minister of Supply and Services Canada, 1994), 144.

30 COL, *Annual Report 1994* (Ottawa: Minister of Supply and Services Canada, 1995), 11.

31 COL, *Annual Report 1997* (Ottawa: Minister of Public Works and Government Services Canada, 1998), 9.

Chapter 9: Squaring Off with the Foes of Bilingualism in the Meech Lake Years, 1986–90

1 Carolyn Hodych, "Alarm Clocks Shouldn't Determine Immersion Entry," *CPF National Newsletter* 33 (1986): 1–2.

2 Lisa Ferguson, "Long Wait to Register," *Charlottetown Guardian*, February 1986, reproduced in *CPF National Newsletter* 33 (1986): 3.

3 Canadian Parents for French, minutes of the meeting of the Board of Directors, October 20–21 and 25, 1987, MAUA, CPF fonds, 2000.23/3/1/7; Canadian Parents for French, minutes of the meeting of the Board of Directors, January 22–24, 1988, MAUA, CPF fonds, 2000.23/3/1/7.

4 "Around the Provinces – Manitoba," *CPF National Newsletter* 34 (1986): 5.

5 Deborah Whale, "A Thousand Horror Stories: The Fight for Survival," *CPF National Newsletter* 33 (1986): 3.

6 Joel Ruimy, "Nielsen Report Lists Options to Control Ottawa Spending: Cut Tax Breaks, Job Training to Save Billions, PM Urged," *Toronto Star*, March 11, 1986.

7 Canadian Parents for French, minutes of the meeting of the Board of Directors, June 6–8, 1986, MAUA, CPF fonds, 2000.23/3/1/6.

8 Canadian Parents for French, minutes of the meeting of the Board of Directors, November 5–9, 1986, MAUA, CPF fonds, 2000.23/3/1/6.

9 French Languages Services Act, R.S.O. 1990, c. F.32.

10 "Best of Luck, Faye Garner," *APEC Newsletter* 9, 6 (1986): 4.

11 "Canadian Parents for French," *APEC Newsletter* 9, 6 (1986): 1–2.

12 Canadian Parents for French, minutes of the meeting of the Board of Directors, November 5–9, 1986, MAUA, CPF fonds, 2000.23/3/1/6.

13 CPF Annual Report, 1986–87, CPFN.

14 Peter Brimelow, *The Patriot Game* (Toronto: Key Porter, 1986).

15 Ibid., 16–17.

16 Ibid., 19–21.

17 Ibid., 58, 50–51.

18 Ibid., 55.

19 Ibid., 56.

20 Ibid., 82.

21 Ibid., 81.

22 Ibid., 80.

23 Ibid., 96.

24 Ibid., 80.

25 Ibid., 94.

26 Ibid., 96.

27 Ibid., 94.

28 Ibid., 86.

29 "Rights Commission Won't Pursue Issue," *Brockville Recorder and Times,* September 24, 1986, MAUA, CPF fonds, 2000.23/3/5/1.

30 Marilyn Caners to Susan Purdy, February 12, 1987, MAUA, CPF fonds, 2000.23/3/5/1.
31 Faye Garner, letter to the editor, November 27, 1986, MAUA, CPF fonds, 2000. 23/3/5/1.
32 "Not Everyone Favors French Immersion," *Brockville Recorder and Times*, November 15, 1986, MAUA, CPF fonds, 2000.23/3/5/1.
33 APEC ads in *Brockville Recorder and Times*, December 3, 1986, and January 14, 1987, MAUA, CPF fonds, 2000.23/3/5/1.
34 Marilyn Caners to Susan Purdy, February 12, 1987, MAUA, CPF fonds, 2000. 23/3/5/1.
35 Gary Lupton, "Leeds and Grenville Board Re-Thinks French Program," *Kingston Whig-Standard*, February 13, 1987.
36 Faye Garner, "Oral Presentation to Trustees and Board Committees Opposing French Immersion," March 9, 1987, MAUA, CPF fonds, 2000.23/3/5/1.
37 Thomas A. Sagar, letter to the editor, *Brockville Recorder and Times*, March 9, 1987, MAUA, CPF fonds, 2000.23/3/5/1.
38 Mrs. L. Ellinor, letter to the editor, *Brockville Recorder and Times*, March 18, 1987, MAUA, CPF fonds, 2000.23/3/5/1.
39 Murray Hogben, "French-Immersion Pilot Pleases Parents' Group," *Kingston Whig-Standard*, October 21, 1987.
40 Jack Walker, "Leeds, Grenville Board Approves French Immersion," *Ottawa Citizen*, March 15, 1988.
41 Shawn Thompson, "Board's Tie Vote Defeats French Immersion Program," *Kingston Whig-Standard*, April 10, 1990; "Leeds-Grenville: Board Won't Add Immersion Classes," *Ottawa Citizen*, May 15, 1990.
42 Jack Walker, "Anti-Bilingual Protesters Greet Peterson, " *Ottawa Citizen*, September 7, 1989.
43 Shawn Thompson, "Immersion Voted in As Automatic Option," *Kingston Whig-Standard*, February 12, 1991.
44 Some of the best accounts of how this process unfolded can be found in Peter Russell, *Constitutional Odyssey: Can Canadians Become a Sovereign People*, 3rd ed. (Toronto: University of Toronto Press, 2004); Alan Cairns, *Charter versus Federalism: The Dilemmas of Constitutional Reform* (Montreal: McGill-Queen's University Press, 1992); Alan Cairns, *Reconfigurations: Canadian Citizenship and Constitutional Change* (Toronto: McClelland and Stewart, 1995); and Michael Behiels, ed., *The Meech Lake Primer: Conflicting Views of the 1987 Constitutional Accord* (Ottawa: University of Ottawa Press, 1989).
45 Pierre Trudeau, "'Say Goodbye to the Dream' of One Canada," *Toronto Star*, May 2 7, 1987.
46 Notes for a presentation from Alliance Quebec to the Commission des institutions, May 20, 1987, MAUA, CPF fonds, 2000.23/2/15; Jos Scott, memo to CPF Directors, May 29, 1987, MAUA, CPF fonds, 2000.23/2/15.
47 1987 Constitutional Accord, s. 1, http://www.pco-bcp.gc.ca/aia/index.asp?lang=eng &page=hist&doc=meech-eng.htm.
48 Berkeley Fleming, telegram to Richard Hatfield, May 31, 1987, MAUA, CPF fonds, 2000.23/2/15.

49 Susan Purdy, telegram to Brian Mulroney, John Turner, Ed Broadbent, and Senators, June 1, 1987, MAUA, CPF fonds, 2000.23/2/15. The same telegram was sent by each provincial CPF director to his or her respective premier.
50 Canadian Parents for French, "Accord May Cause Crisis, Group Warns," news release, June 1, 1987, MAUA, CPF fonds, 2000.23/2/15.
51 Susan Purdy to Ed Broadbent, June 17, 1987, MAUA, CPF fonds, 2000.23/2/15; Susan Purdy to Brian Mulroney, June 19, 1987, MAUA, CPF fonds, 2000.23/2/15; John Turner to Susan Purdy, July 22, 1987, MAUA, CPF fonds, 2000.23/3/5/3.
52 John Turner to Susan Purdy, July 22, 1987, MAUA, CPF fonds, 2000.23/3/5/3.
53 Minutes of proceedings and evidence of the Special Committee of the Senate and the House of Commons on the 1987 Constitutional Accord, August 6, 1987, 41–61, MAUA, CPF fonds, 2000.23/2/15.
54 Ibid., 60.
55 Ibid., 56–57.
56 Marjorie Nichols, "Meech Lake Provision May Stop Bilingualism," *Ottawa Citizen*, August 22, 1987, MAUA, CPF fonds, 2000.23/2/15.
57 Canadian Parents for French Alberta, brief to the Committee of the Whole Senate on the Meech Lake Constitutional Accord, January 1988, MAUA, CPF fonds, 2000.23/3/5/3.
58 Official Languages Act, 1988, R.S.C. 1985, c. 31 (4th supp.).
59 Canadian Parents for French, "Bill C-72: An Act Respecting the Status and the Use of the Official Languages of Canada – A Presentation to the Legislative Committee of the House of Commons of Canada by Dr. Susan Purdy," April 1988, MAUA, CPF fonds, 2000.23/3/5/3.
60 Canadian Parents for French, "CPF President Claims Immersion Is Producing a Tolerant Generation," April 28, 1988, MAUA, CPF fonds, 2000.23/3/5/3.
61 Ron Leitch, President, Alliance for the Preservation of English in Canada, "A Brief Opposing Bill C-72, Proposed Official Languages Act for Canada, Presented April 1988 to the Legislative Committee for Bill C-72," reproduced in J.V Andrew, *Enough! (Enough French, Enough Quebec)* (Kitchener, ON: Andrew Books, 1988), 136.
62 Ibid., 134.
63 Ibid.,136.
64 Ibid., 137–38.
65 Ibid., back cover.
66 Ibid., vi.
67 Ibid., 12.
68 Ibid., 8–9.
69 Ibid., i–iv.
70 Ibid., 25.
71 Ibid., vii.
72 Ibid., 52–53.
73 Ibid., 43.
74 Ibid., 42.
75 Ibid., 45.
76 Ibid., 72–73.
77 Ibid., 44.

78 Ibid., 159.
79 Ibid., 171.
80 Ibid., 172–73.
81 Matthew James J. Baglole, "'Many Closet Supporters Will Come Forward': New Brunswick's Confederation of Regions Party," in *Mobilizations, Protests, and Engagements: Canadian Perspectives on Social Movements*, ed. Marie Hammond-Callaghan and Matthew Hayday (Halifax: Fernwood Publishing, 2008), 164–85; Geoffrey R. Martin, "We've Seen It All Before: The Rise and Fall of the New Brunswick Confederation of Regions Party, 1988–1995," *Journal of Canadian Studies* 3, 1 (1998): 22–38.
82 *Quebec v. Ford et al.*, [1988] 2 S.C.R. 712.
83 Russell, *Constitutional Odyssey*, 145–46.
84 Diane Carlucci, "How CPF Ontario Set the Record Straight," 1989, MAUA, CPF fonds, 2000.23/3/10/14.
85 Diane Carlucci, "How CPF Ontario Set the Record Straight."
86 Ibid.
87 Alliance Ontario, "Early French Immersion Facts" handout. Reproduced in Diane Carlucci, "How CPF Ontario Set the Record Straight."
88 Orland French, "Ranting without Reason," *Globe and Mail*, June 14, 1988.
89 "Editorial: The Fearful Anglophones," *Globe and Mail*, September 19, 1988.
90 Nanaimo Chapter, information sheet, 1983, CPFBC, file Nanaimo.
91 Handwritten note on Nanaimo Chapter information sheet, April 1989, CPFBC, file Nanaimo.
92 Diane Dodd, district rep for Nanaimo Chapter, to Lois Wade, and attached anti-immersion ad from local paper, November 12, 1990, CPFBC, file Nanaimo.
93 Nanaimo Chapter information sheet, 1990, CPFBC, file Nanaimo.
94 The poll had a national margin of error of 2 percent, nineteen times out of twenty.
95 Environics Research Group, "Canadian Attitudes towards French Second Language Education: A National Survey Commissioned by Canadian Parents for French," February 1990, CPFN, file Surveys/Opinion Polls. Support was particularly high in Quebec (91 percent), Toronto (81 percent), and Nova Scotia (81 percent), and it was lower, though still a majority, in western Canada, ranging from a high of 61 percent in Manitoba to 55 percent in British Columbia. Although most endorsed by Liberals (80 percent), support was also high among Progressive Conservatives (75 percent) and New Democrats (73 percent). Women were slightly more favourable to second-language learning than men (77 percent versus 70 percent), and professionals were slightly more favourable than unskilled workers (78 percent versus 71 percent).
96 Seventy-seven percent indicated that they were satisfied, and only 12 percent said that they were either somewhat or thoroughly dissatisfied.
97 The lowest support for this option, at 29 percent, was among those with less than nine years of education, and it rose to 49 percent among university graduates.
98 Agenda item from Canadian Parents for French, meeting of the Board of Directors re Environics poll, June 1990, CPFN, file Surveys/Opinion Polls.
99 Eighty-seven percent said that, if they had children going through the school system, they would enrol them in French immersion if it were an option.

100 Seventy-nine percent had children in early immersion, 3 percent in middle immersion, 5 percent in late immersion, and 15 percent in continuation of immersion at the secondary level.

101 Environics Research Group, "Canadian Attitudes towards French Second Language Education: Tables for Membership Survey," February 1990, CPFN, file Surveys/Opinion Polls.

102 Ibid. About 15 percent did no't know or had no answer.

103 Of those who thought that Bill 178 had an impact, 96 percent thought that it led to more negative attitudes toward French in their province. They believed that it would have somewhat less impact on attitudes to FSL, with 19 percent thinking that it had a major impact and 53 percent a minor impact. Of those who thought that it had an impact, 86 percent thought that it led to more negative attitudes, versus 12 percent who actually thought that it might lead to more positive attitudes. Only 12 percent thought that it would have a major impact on parents' attitudes toward FSL for their own children, and 40 percent thought that it would have a minor impact. Twenty-eight percent of that subgroup thought that it might have a positive impact on that decision, whereas 69 percent thought that it would have a negative impact.

104 Only 5 percent and 37 percent perceived a major or minor impact on attitudes toward FSL instruction, with 79 percent thinking that it would be more negative. The number of parents who thought that anti-bilingual activities would lead to an impact at the level of FSL decisions made by parents was even less (only 6 percent and 30 percent perceiving a major or minor impact), and almost a third (32 percent) thought that the result would be a backlash leading to more positive attitudes.

105 Environics Research Group, "Canadian Attitudes towards French Second Language Education. Final Report. National Omnibus Study and Membership Study," February 1990, CPFN, file Polls.

106 Cynthia Steers, *Media Relations: National Poll Release*, booklet, June 1991, CPFN, file Polls.

107 Ibid.

108 Canadian Parents for French, minutes of the meeting of the Board of Directors, January 22–24, 1988, MAUA, CPF fonds, 2000.23/3/1/7.

109 Canadian Parents for French, minutes of the meeting of the Board of Directors, October 12–13 and 16, 1988, MAUA, CPF fonds, 2000.23/3/1/7.

110 Canadian Parents for French, minutes of the meeting of the Board of Directors, October 25–26 and 29, 1989, MAUA, CPF fonds, 2000.23/3/1/8.

111 Canadian Parents for French, minutes of the meeting of the Board of Directors, January 26–28, 1990, CPFN; Canadian Parents for French, minutes of the meeting of the Board of Directors, June 8–10, 1990, MAUA, CPF fonds, 2000.23/3/1/8.

112 Canadian Parents for French, minutes of the meeting of the Board of Directors, February 1–3, 1991, MAUA, CPF fonds, 2000.23/3/1/8.

113 Canadian Parents for French, minutes of the meeting of the Board of Directors, February 3–5, 1989, MAUA, CPF fonds, 2000.23/3/1/8.

114 Canadian Parents for French, minutes of the meeting of the Board of Directors, June 2–4, 1989, MAUA, CPF fonds, 2000.23/3/1/8.

115 Canadian Parents for French, minutes of the meeting of the Board of Directors, February 17–19, 1995, CPFN.

116 Canadian Parents for French, minutes of the meeting of the Board of Directors, October 12–13 and 16, 1988, MAUA, CPF fonds, 2000.23/3/1/7.
117 "Leading Canadians Agree: Learning French Matters!," bus poster, 1989, MAUA, CPF fonds, 2000.23/3/10/13.
118 All of them, however, were of European descent.
119 Canadian Parents for French, minutes of the meeting of the Board of Directors, June 2–4, 1989, MAUA, CPF fonds, 2000.23/3/1/8.
120 Canadian Parents for French, minutes of the meeting of the Board of Directors, April 3–5, 1992, MAUA, CPF fonds, 2000.23/2/6/2.
121 Canadian Parents for French, minutes of the meeting of the Board of Directors, November 11–15, 1992, CPFN.
122 Canadian Parents for French, minutes of the meeting of the Board of Directors, November 17–21, 1993, CPFN; Canadian Parents for French, minutes of the meeting of the Board of Directors, May 27–29, 1994, CPFN.
123 Lori Nash, Parents for English, CPFN, file Press Clippings.
124 Ibid.
125 Brian Amaron, "French Immersion Produces 'Semi-Linguals,' Speaker Says," *Brockville Recorder and Times,* February 28, 1990, CPFN, file Press Clippings.
126 Katherine Govier, "French Submersion," *Toronto Life,* March 1986, 31-33, 49-56.
127 Kate Merry, fax to Jos Scott, September 10, 1990, CPFN, file Press Clippings.
128 Pat Webster to Marq de Villiers, Editor, *Toronto Life,* April 3, 1986, CPFN, file Press Clippings.
129 Canadian Parents for English/Core French, brochure, February 1990, CPFN, file Press Clippings.
130 Ibid.
131 Isaac Piotrkowski to Canadian Parents for English/Core French, June 20, 1990, CPFN, file Press Clippings.
132 Ellen Fritty, "Comic Overtones in French Debate," *Coast News,* August 14, 1989; John Burnside, "En bas les bigots," *Coast News,* September 4, 1989.
133 Jakob Knaus, "New Bill C-72 Has Disastrous Impact," letter to the editor, *Coast News,* August 21, 1989.
134 Jakob Knaus, "French Newscast Found 'Contaminating,'" letter to the editor, *Coast News,* September 4, 1989.
135 Fabian Dawson, "Hint of Racism Clouds Sunshine Coast: District Polarized over French Immersion," *Vancouver Province,* March 25, 1990.
136 Ann Rees, "Stop French Classes, Schools Urged," *Vancouver Province,* February 13, 1990.
137 Chris Rose, "School Board to Cut Early French Plan," *Vancouver Sun,* February 14, 1990.
138 Dawson, "Hint of Racism."
139 Deborah Wilson, "Anti-French Group Praises Elimination of Early Immersion," *Globe and Mail,* February 15, 1990.
140 Dawson, "Hint of Racism."
141 Kate Merry, fax to Jos Scott, September 10, 1990; Mrs D. Davies to school boards, appended to fax, CPFN, file Press Clippings.

142 Jakob Knaus, "French Immersion Often an Unfortunate Choice," October 1991, CPFBC, file Bulkley Valley.
143 Jos Scott, fax to Kate Merry, December 3, 1991, CPFN, file Press Clippings.
144 Jakob Knaus, "French Immersion Often an Unfortunate Choice."
145 Jakob Knaus to District Parents Advisory Council, November 11, 1991, CPFBC, file Bulkley Valley.
146 Lorraine Cassidy, memo to Karen McKeown, and Karen McKeown, fax to Lorraine Cassidy, December 2, 1991, CPFBC, file Bulkley Valley.
147 Comox/Courtenay Chapter, report, March 1990, CPFBC, file Comox/Courtenay; Comox Valley Chapter, information sheet, March 1992, CPFBC, file Comox/Courtenay.
148 APEC, press release, February 27, 1990, CPFN, file Press Clippings.
149 Gerald Caplan, "A Stalking Horse for the Ultra-Right? Anti-French Alliance Has Kept Ties with Extremist Organizations," *Toronto Star,* March 18, 1990.
150 Hubert Bauch, "He Likes Being Called Bigot," Montreal *Gazette,* April 15, 1990.
151 Kathryn Manzer, memo to Chapter Presidents, Directors, and Provincial Presidents, January 15, 1990, CPFN, file Press Clippings.
152 "CPF Responses to claims against French," January 1990, CPFN, file Press Clippings. Early drafts of the CPF crisis kit were first circulated to board members in 1986. "CPF Crisis Kit," November 1986, MAUA, CPF fonds, 2000.23/2/31/1.
153 Provincial branches received separate funding, in many cases, from regional offices of the Department of the Secretary of State.

Chapter 10: Constitutional Crises and Economic Challenges in the Early 1990s
1 Canadian Parents for French, minutes of the meeting of the Board of Directors, October 18–20, 1991, MAUA, CPF fonds, 2000.23/3/1/8.
2 Alliance for the Preservation of English in Canada (hereafter APEC), "A Presentation to the Standing Joint Committee of the Senate and of the House of Commons on Official Languages," March 28, 1990, 3, Office of the Commissioner of Official Languages Library (hereafter OCOLL), file APEC.
3 Ibid., 6–7.
4 Ibid., 5–6.
5 Ibid., 9.
6 Donald Creighton, "No More Concessions," *Maclean's,* June 27, 1977, 27, quoted in ibid. For further discussion of Creighton's 1977 article and his stance on bilingualism and Quebec, see Chapter 13 of Donald Wright, *Donald Creighton: A Life in History* (Toronto: University of Toronto Press, 2015).
7 APEC, "A Presentation to the Standing Joint Committee," 12–14.
8 Ibid., 19–20.
9 Ronald Leitch, *Constitutions Are for People, Not Politicians* (Thornhill, ON: APEC, 1991), 3.
10 Ibid., 22.
11 Ibid., 15–16.
12 Ibid., 23–28; APEC, "Constitutional Countdown," pamphlets, OCOLL, file APEC.
13 Ian Mulgrew, "Premier Don Getty Wants Official Bilingualism Abolished, Legislated ...," *Toronto Star,* January 10, 1992.

14 Edison Stewart, "Getty Language Stand Stirs Outrage," *Toronto Star,* January 11, 1992.
15 "Editorial: Battling Bilingualism," *Toronto Star,* February 10, 1992.
16 "14% Back Getty on Bilingualism," *Toronto Star,* January 17, 1992.
17 Victor Goldbloom, "Address to the Downtown Edmonton Rotary Club," January 30, 1992, OCOLL.
18 Alan Barnes, "Official Bilingualism a Failure, 64% Tell Poll," *Toronto Star,* March 12, 1992.
19 Geoffrey Stevens, "Canadians Have Never Believed in Bilingualism," *Toronto Star,* January 19, 1992.
20 Pat Brehaut, "Corn Flakes, and Other Myths of Bilingualism," *Toronto Star,* January 27, 1992.
21 Pat Brehaut, memo to National Executive Committee Members, August 25, 1992, and Environics Research Group, "Public Attitudes toward Learning French in School," May 18–June 14, 1992, CPFN, file Surveys/Opinion Polls.
22 Jos Scott, memo to Directors, December 8, 1992, CPFN, file Surveys/Opinion Polls.
23 The poll had a margin of error of 2.2 percent nineteen times out of twenty at the national level.
24 Environics Research Group, "Public Attitudes toward Learning French in School."
25 Ibid.
26 Canadian Parents for French, report to the Department of the Secretary of State on the project to update the survey on Canadians' attitudes toward official language acquisition, 1992, CPFN, file Surveys/Opinion Polls.
27 Jos Scott, memo to Directors, December 8, 1992, CPFN, file Surveys/Opinion Polls.
28 Canadian Parents for French, minutes of the meeting of the Board of Directors, November 11–15, 1992, CPFN.
29 Vona Mallory, "Parents for French Brochures Full of Untruths," letter to the editor, *Alberta Coronation,* April 17, 1990, CPFN, file Press Clippings.
30 Vona Mallory, "Early French Immersion Called Child Abuse," letter to the editor, *Windspeaker,* February 17, 1992, CPFN, file Press Clippings.
31 Mallory, "Parents for French Brochures Full of Untruths."
32 Ruth Mallory and group, letter to the editor, *Metro 1 (Winnipeg),* November 20, 1990, CPFN, file Press Clippings.
33 Mallory, "Early French Immersion."
34 Mallory, Wood, Campbell, and Associates, letter to the editor, *Morinville Gazette,* September 22, 1992; Mallory, "Early French Immersion"; report from the education committee, 1992, CPFN, file Press Clippings.
35 Mallory, "Early French Immersion."
36 Mallory, Wood, Campbell, and Associates, letter to the editor.
37 Vona Mallory, "Early French Immersion – Child Abuse? Linguistic Retardation?," November 28, 1991, CPFN, file Press Clippings.
38 Ibid.
39 Description of Vona Mallory for Canadian Parents for French Board of Directors meeting, November 1992, CPFN, file Press Clippings.
40 Pat Brehaut, letter to the editor, *This Week,* October 17, 1992, CPFN, file Press Clippings.

41 Harry Schacter, "A Hitler-Like Child Abuser Speaks Out," *Kingston Whig-Standard,*
    February 8, 1992, CPFN, file Press Clippings.

42 Monica Gaudet, letter to the editor, *Scarborough News,* July 20, 1992, CPFN, file
    Press Clippings.

43 Pat Brehaut, memo to Chapter Presidents, Directors, and Provincial Presidents,
    August 29, 1991, CPFN, file Press Clippings.

44 Link Byfield, "Bilingualism: Good News in the War on Ignorance" and "A Nasty
    Knock to French Immersion," *Western Report,* September 17, 1990, CPFN, file Press
    Clippings.

45 Variants of this letter and its allegations appeared in papers across the country, in-
    cluding Mallory, "Parents for French Brochures."

46 Pro forma response letter from CPF to letters by Vona Mallory, CPFN, file Press
    Clippings. Information on the dropout rates was obtained via a conversation be-
    tween Executive Director Jos Scott and Dr. Nancy Halsall.

47 Nancy Halsall, *Immersion/Regular Program Study* (Nepean, ON: Carleton Board of
    Education, 1989), cited in Nancy Halsall, *Attrition/Retention of Students in French
    Immersion with Particular Emphasis on Secondary School* (Ottawa: CPF, 1991).

48 Canadian Parents for French, minutes of the meeting of the Board of Directors,
    October 18–20, 1991, MAUA, CPF fonds, 2000.23/3/1/8; Halsall, *Attrition/Retention
    of Students.*

49 Halsall, *Attrition/Retention of Students,* 6.

50 Ibid., 13.

51 Ibid., 7.

52 Nancy Halsall, "Secondary School French Immersion – Much to Celebrate," *CPF
    National Newsletter* 57 (1992): 2.

53 CPF Annual Report, 1993–94, CPFN.

54 Canadian Parents for French, minutes of the meeting of the Board of Directors, April
    3–5, 1992, CPFN.

55 Canadian Parents for French, minutes of the meeting of the Board of Directors, May
    24–26, 1991, MAUA, CPF fonds, 2000.23/3/1/8.

56 Canadian Parents for French, minutes of the meeting of the Board of Directors,
    February 6–7, 1993, CPFN.

57 Canadian Parents for French, minutes of the meeting of the Board of Directors,
    February 25–26, 1994, CPFN.

58 Canadian Parents for French, minutes of the meeting of the Board of Directors,
    February 6–7, 1993, CPFN.

59 Canadian Parents for French, minutes of the meeting of the Board of Directors, June
    11–13, 1993, CPFN.

60 Canadian Parents for French, minutes of the meeting of the Board of Directors,
    February 6–7, 1993, CPFN.

61 Canadian Parents for French, minutes of the meeting of the Board of Directors, April
    3–5, 1992, MAUA, CPF fonds, 2000.23/2/6/2.

62 Canadian Parents for French, minutes of the meeting of the Board of Directors,
    November 11–15, 1992, CPFN.

63 Canadian Parents for French, minutes of the meeting of the Board of Directors,
    February 6–7, 1993, CPFN.

64 CPF Annual Reports, 1994–95 and 1995–96, CPFN.
65 Canadian Parents for French, minutes of the meeting of the Board of Directors, June 11–13, 1993, CPFN.
66 CPF Annual Report, 1995–96, CPFN.
67 Canadian Parents for French, minutes of the meeting of the Board of Directors, November 17–21, 1993, CPFN.
68 General John de Chastelain, "Languages in an International Context," and Anne McIlroy and Bill Mlacak, "Two Canadians with a World View: Immersion Led to Adventures Abroad," *CPF National News* 64 (1994): 3.
69 Andrew Kinnear, "Learning a Third Language Is Surprisingly Easy," and Megan Thompson, "French Immersion Helped Me Learn Indonesian," *CPF National News* 66 (1994): 3.
70 Jan Finlay, "CPF Briefs Languages Committee," *CPF National News* 67 (1995): 1, 4.
71 Canadian Parents for French, minutes of the meeting of the Board of Directors, May 27–29, 1994, CPFN.
72 Canadian Parents for French, minutes of the meeting of the Board of Directors, February 25–26, 1994, CPFN.
73 Canadian Parents for French, minutes of the meeting of the Board of Directors, May 27–29, 1994, CPFN.
74 CPF Annual Report, 1995–96, CPFN.
75 "Annual General Meeting," *CPF National News* 71 (1996): 2.
76 Canadian Parents for French, minutes of the meeting of the Board of Directors, October 5–7, 1996, CPFN.
77 CPF Annual Report, 1997–98, CPFN.
78 Guy Lachapelle, "The 1995 Quebec Referendum: How the Sovereignty Partnership Proposal Turned the Campaign Around," *Quebec Studies* 24 (1997): 180–96.
79 Canadian Parents for French, minutes of the meeting of the Board of Directors, May 27–29, 1994, CPFN.
80 "CPF Launches New Information Campaign," *CPF National News* 68 (1995): 1.
81 The poll was considered to be accurate within 3.8 percentage points nineteen times out of twenty.
82 COMPAS, "Language Instruction and French Immersion in Canadian Schools – Results Summary," May 1995, CPFN, file Surveys/Opinion Polls.
83 Ibid.
84 Canadian Parents for French, "New Poll Reveals Languages Important to Canadians," press release, June 20, 1995, CPFN, file Surveys/Opinion Polls.
85 Ron Eade, "The High Cost of Bilingualism," *Ottawa Citizen,* August 5, 1995.
86 Jan Finlay to Brian Sarjeant, *Ottawa Citizen,* August 10, 1995, in response to a series of articles by Ron Eade, including ibid.
87 "Write It Up! Is Back," *CPF National News* 67 (1995): 1.
88 "Learning English and French Opens Doors to Tomorrow," *CPF National News* 69 (1995): 1.
89 Tim Reid, "Guest Editorial: International Thinking Is a Reality of Our Youth," *CPF National News* 71 (1996): 1.
90 "CPF's New Video – *Proud of Two Languages,*" *CPF National News* 70 (1996): 12.
91 Interview with Jan Finlay, September 16, 2013.

92 CPF Annual Report, 1996–97, and Canadian Parents for French, minutes of the meeting of the Board of Directors, June 14–16, 1996, CPFN.

93 Kelowna CPF, executive meeting, April 29, 1986; Kelowna CPF, information sheet, 1986; Kelowna CPF, information sheet, 1990; Kelowna CPF, information sheet, 1991, all in CPFBC, file Kelowna. Matt Maxwell was a particularly popular entertainer on the core French and French immersion circuit in Canada in the 1980s and 1990s, well known for his song "C'est l'Halloween."

94 Carolyn Jones to M.G. Pendharkar, Superintendent, School District 23, Central Okanagan, January 31, 1986, CPFBC, file Kelowna.

95 Kelowna CPF, information sheet, 1990, CPFBC, file Kelowna.

96 Ibid.

97 *Kelowna Parents for French Newsletter,* October 1990; *Kelowna Parents for French Newsletter,* November 1990; Lynn Gillon to Kate Merry, November 23, 1990, all in CPFBC, file Kelowna.

98 CBC Kelowna, fax containing a letter from Pauline Leitch to the *Kelowna News,* April 4, 1995, CPFBC, file Kelowna.

99 Vivian Turgeon to Nicki Hokazono and Trustees of School District 23, March 9, 1995, CPFBC, file Kelowna.

100 Judith A. Harris, "Yuppies Should Pay the Tab for FI," letter to the editor (unknown newspaper), March 10, 1995, CPFBC, file Kelowna.

101 J.P. Squire, "Critics Rally Against French Immersion," *Kelowna Daily Courier,* March 12, 1995, CPFBC, file Kelowna.

102 "Anti-French Activists Deliver 1000 Leaflets," *Kamloops Daily News,* March 13, 1995, CPFBC, file Kelowna.

103 Vivian Turgeon to Nicki Hokazono and Trustees of School District 23, March 9, 1995, CPFBC, file Kelowna.

104 Kelowna Parents for French to School District 23 Trustees, March 15, 1995, CPFBC, file Kelowna.

105 Joe Gordon, fax to Joanne Teraguchi, speech that he delivered to School District 23 re French immersion, March 15, 1995, CPFBC, file Kelowna.

106 "Non to French Immersion: Kelowna Trustees Reject Administration's Bid to Expand It," *Western Report,* April 24, 1995.

107 Julia Elliott, "French Immersion Not Producing Bilingual Students, Professor Says," *Ottawa Citizen,* March 28, 1995, CPFN, file Press Clippings.

108 Carol Milstone, "False Immersion," *Saturday Night,* September 1994, 12-18.

109 Kate Merry, memo to Jan Finlay, Elmer Hynes, and Cynthia Steers re Hector Hammerly, December 12, 1994; Hector Hammerly, "French Immersion Still Failing," *Ottawa Citizen,* December 15, 1994; Hector Hammerly, "Écoutez!," *Vancouver Sun,* January 3, 1995, all in CPFN, file Press Clippings.

110 Jan Finlay, memo to CPF Directors, December 9, 1994, and attached letter to the editor from Hector Hammerly, "Immersion Pupils Speak Bad French," CPFN, file Press Clippings.

111 Owen Wilkinson, CPF Selkirk, fax to CPF National Office re Hammerly letter to the editor, December 19, 1994, CPFN, file Press Clippings.

112 Hector Hammerly to School Principals, and attached forms, April 12, 1995, CPFN, file Press Clippings.

113 "Helen," note to Jan Finlay, Laura van Loon, Cynthia Steers, and Elmer Hynes, January 9, 1995, CPFN, file Press Clippings.

114 Merrill Swain, "French Immersion Criticism Has Far More Heat than Light," *Ottawa Citizen*, January 10, 1995, CPFN, file Press Clippings.

115 Bruce Clayman to Joanne Teraguchi, May 1, 1995, CPFN, file Press Clippings.

116 André Obadia, "Le test Hammerly," *Inform APPIPC*, avril 1995, CPFN, file Press Clippings.

117 Michael Jenkinson, "Parlez-vous Frenglish?" *Alberta Report*, March 29, 1995, CPFN, file Press Clippings.

118 "Helen," memo to CPF Directors re Hammerly, September 6, 1995; Yvonne Hébert, "Responding to the Critics of Immersion: Hector Hammerly and *Saturday Night*," workshop for CPF Alberta, May 27, 1995, both in CPFN, file Press Clippings.

119 Don Bell, "French Immersion Failing: Ontario Needs One Quality French Program for All Elementary Students," *Ottawa Citizen*, January 12, 1994, CPFN, file Press Clippings.

120 See Ray Ridgway, "French Immersion Leading to Segregation in Schools," *Ottawa Citizen*, May 25, 1993; and Angela Mangiacasale, "Immersion at 25: Many Wonder Whether It's Working and Who Should Pay for It," *Ottawa Citizen*, February 26, 1994, both in CPFN, file Press Clippings.

121 Julia Elliott, "French Immersion Not Producing Bilingual Students, Professor Says," *Ottawa Citizen*, March 28, 1995, CPFN, file Press Clippings.

122 Joanne Laucius, "Education for the Élite," *Ottawa Citizen*, March 15, 1995, CPFN, file Press Clippings.

123 Jan Finlay, "Some Valuable Lessons to Be Learned," *CPF National News* 68 (1995): 4; William Johnson, "Fight Against Immersion Is Being Fought Unfairly," *Montreal Gazette*, March 31, 1995, CPFN, file Press Clippings.

124 Johnson, "Fight Against Immersion."

125 William Johnson, "Under Attack," *Montreal Gazette*, March 29, 1995, CPFN, file Press Clippings.

126 Lori Nash, "Nation's Capital Key to French Immersion in Canada," *APEC Ottawa Newsletter* 11, 2 (1997): 2, CPFN, file Press Clippings.

127 Lori Nash, "Anglophone Job-Seekers Disadvantaged," *Ottawa Citizen*, February 9, 1998.

128 Lori Nash, "The Best Language-Education Compromise," *Ottawa Citizen*, March 26, 1998.

129 Joan Netten, "The Facts about French Immersion," *Ottawa Citizen*, March 27, 1998.

Chapter 11: A Millennial Reprieve

1 "President's Message: New Funding Agreements Help Revitalize CPF," *CPF National News* 76 (1998): 2.

2 "Canadian Chamber of Commerce Endorses French Second Language Programs in Canadian Schools," *CPF National News* 77 (1998): 1–2.

3 Kate Merry, "Federal Government Cuts Funding for French Second Language Funding," *CPF National News* 77 (1998): 1–2.

4 Carole Barton, "President's Report," in CPF Annual Report, 1998–99, CPFN.

5 "New Executive Director Looks for Strong Representation across Canada," *CPF National News* 80 (1999): 3.

6 Robin Wilson, "Looking Back – Looking Ahead," *CPF National News* 90 (2002): 5.

7 Ibid.

8 CPF Annual Report, 2000–1, CPFN; "President's Message: 25th Anniversary Highlights," *CPF National News* 90 (2002): 3.

9 "CPF National Concours d'art oratoire 2003," *CPF National News* 92 (2003): 1; "French Language Public Speaking Competition Is a Huge Success," *CPF National News* 93 (2003): 1–2.

10 CPF Annual Report, 1999–2000, CPFN.

11 CPF Annual Reports, 1997–98 and 1998–99, CPFN.

12 CPF Annual Report, 1997–98, CPFN.

13 CPF Annual Report, 2000–1, CPFN.

14 "CPF Launches *The State of French-Second-Language Education in Canada 2000,*" *CPF National News* 84 (2000): 1.

15 CPF Annual Report 1998–99, CPFN.

16 COMPAS, *Canadian Parents for French Survey of French Second Language Issues,* May 2000, CPFN, file Surveys/Public Opinion Polls.

17 Q&A re 2000 COMPAS poll, April 2000, CPFN, file Surveys/Public Opinion Polls.

18 COMPAS, *Canadian Parents for French Survey,* 2–3.

19 These included personal benefits (9 percent), part of a good education (8 percent), good to know a second language (7 percent), and an understanding of French culture (6 percent).

20 COMPAS, *Canadian Parents for French Survey,* 5–6.

21 Ibid., 7–11. Majority positive opinions existed in all demographic cohorts but were highest among women, Atlantic Canadians, and those with more education.

22 Ibid., 8. About 18 percent continued to believe that immersion students were outperformed in subjects such as math or science.

23 Ibid., 10–11.

24 Ibid., 12–17.

25 Q&A re 2000 COMPAS poll, April 2000, CPFN, file Surveys/Public Opinion Polls.

26 Ibid.

27 CPF Annual Report, 2000–1, CPFN.

28 "French Immersion Remains Stable," *CPF National News* 86 (2001): 7.

29 Sheila Copps, "'GOOD NEWS' Says Minister of Canadian Heritage," *CPF National News* 92 (2003): 2–3.

30 "CPF's Work Pays Off: Funding Increases for FSL Programs Announced," *CPF National News* 92 (2003), 1–2.

31 Stéphane Dion, "Bilingualism Gives Canada a Competitive Edge: Extracts from a Speech at Hugh McRoberts Secondary School, Richmond, BC," *CPF National News* 92 (2003): 4.

32 Ron Leitch, "Freedom Wears a Crown," *APEC Newsletter* 20, 4 (1996): 2; John Farthing, *Freedom Wears a Crown* (Toronto: Kingswood House, 1957).

33 "U.S. Product Labelling," *APEC Newsletter* 19, 5 (1996): 2.

34 Rideau Banks (pseudonym), "Bilingualism Revealed a Bankrupt Tragedy," *APEC Newsletter* 20, 4 (1996): 3.

35 "French Immersion Declining," *APEC Newsletter* 20, 3 (1997): 4.

36 "Commissioner Should Be Fired," *APEC Newsletter* 20, 1 (1997): 4.

37 Kenneth McDonald, *The Monstrous Trick* (Toronto: APEC Books, 1998), back cover.

38 Ibid., 8.

39 Ibid., 5.

40 Margaret Mercer, Executive Director, and John DeRinzy, President, to Canadian Network for Language Awareness Members, September 2002, OCOLL, file Canadians Against Bilingualism Injustice.

41 Gordon Clark, "Prof Gets Buyout," *Vancouver Province*, July 15, 1997; Neal Hall, "Professor Barred from SFU Campus," *Vancouver Sun*, April 19, 1997.

42 Fred Sherwin, "'Queen' of Queenswood Heights Succumbs to Cancer at Age 62," *Orleans Online*, March 1, 2012, http://www.orleansonline.ca/pages/N2012030101.htm.

Conclusion: We Learned French! Well, Many Canadians Did

1 Jean-François Lepage and Jean-Pierre Corbeil, *The Evolution of English-French Bilingualism in Canada from 1961 to 2011* (Ottawa: Statistics Canada, 2013), 1–4. All figures in this chapter are from this document unless otherwise stated.

2 Ibid., 3.

3 Ibid., 5–6.

4 Joshua Ostroff, "Is 'Immersion' the French Word for 'Elitist'?," *Toronto Star*, February 24, 2014.

5 Fred Genesee, "The Bilingual Advantage," *CPF Magazine* 2 (2014): 16–18; Suvarna Alladi et al., "Bilingualism Delays Age at Onset of Dementia, Independent of Education and Immigration Status," *Neurology* 81, 22 (2013): 1938–44. Some of the leading Canadian research has been conducted by Ellen Bialystok. See Ellen Bialystok, *Bilingualism in Development: Language, Literacy, and Cognition* (New York: Cambridge University Press, 2001); F.I. Craik, E. Bialystok, and M. Freedman, "Delaying the Onset of Alzheimer Disease: Bilingualism as a Form of Cognitive Reserve," *Neurology* 75, 19 (2010): 1726–29.

6 Not unlike the members of Monty Python's Spanish Inquisition.

7 Edmund Aunger, "Academic Research vs. Political Propaganda: Lessons from the Fraser Institute's Study of Minority-Language Education," *Academic Matters: The Journal of Higher Education* (2014), http://www.academicmatters.ca/2014/03/academic-research-vs-political-propaganda-lessons-from-the-fraser-institutes-study-of-minority-language-education.

8 See Miriam Smith, *A Civil Society* (Toronto: Broadview, 2005), 69–73; Suzanne Staggenborg, *Social Movements*, 2nd ed. (Toronto: Oxford University Press, 2012), 67–69; Lara Campbell, Dominique Clément, and Gregory S. Kealey, eds., *Debating Dissent: Canada and the Sixties* (Toronto: University of Toronto Press, 2012).

9 See Leslie A. Pal, *Interests of State: The Politics of Language, Multiculturalism, and Feminism in Canada* (Montreal: McGill-Queen's University Press, 1993); Howard Ramos and Kathleen Rodgers, eds., *Protest and Politics: The Promise of Social Movement Societies* (Vancouver: UBC Press, 2015).

10 Raymond Mougeon, "L'immersion française peut-elle rapprocher les deux solitudes?," in *Introduction aux études canadiennes: Histoires, identités, cultures*, dir.

Colin Coates and Geoffrey Ewen (Ottawa: Presses de l'Université d'Ottawa, 2012), 215.

11 See Matthew Hayday, *Bilingual Today, United Tomorrow: Official Languages in Education and Canadian Federalism* (Montreal: McGill-Queen's University Press, 2005), for more on this.

12 J. Douglas Willms, "The Case for Universal French Instruction," *Policy Options* 29 (2008): 91–96. While I was revising this book in the fall of 2014, the recently elected Liberal government in New Brunswick announced plans to reverse this policy and return to a grade one start for early French immersion.

Unpublished Primary Sources

Interviews
Carmeta Abbott, March 6, 2014
Vanessa Bass, March 21, 2007
Jan Finlay, September 16, 2013
Berkeley Fleming, February 6, 2007
Judy Gibson, June 22, 2009
Victor Goldbloom, May 11, 2012
Stewart Goodings, July 8, 2009
Elaine Jaltema, October 16, 2013
Barbara Jardine, March 26, 2007
Marion Langford, June 16, 2009
Beth Mlacak, June 18, 2011
Louise Moore, June 23, 2009
Janet Poyen, June 22, 2009, and September 6, 2012
Yvonne Rolston, November 4, 2013
Keith Spicer, October 7, 2011
Gunild Spiess, June 16, 2009
Mary Stapleton, June 23, 2009
Patterson Webster, June 14, 2011
Maxwell Yalden, October 28, 2011

Archives of Ontario
RG 2–200, Council on French-Language Schools

Canadian Parents for French British Columbia
Miscellaneous files

Canadian Parents for French National Office
Miscellaneous files

Library and Archives Canada
MG31 E38 (R5018–10-X-E), Joseph Thorarinn Thorson fonds
MG32 B35 (R3611–0-0-E), Walter Gilbert Dinsdale fonds
RG 122, Office of the Commissioner of Official Languages

Mount Allison University Archives
2000.23, Canadian Parents for French fonds

Office of the Commissioner of Official Languages
Miscellaneous library files

Personal Files
Carmeta Abbott (consulted but not directly cited)
Berkeley Fleming (consulted but not directly cited)
Judy Gibson (consulted but not directly cited)
Marion Langford
Beth Mlacak
Janet Poyen
Gunild Spiess

Index

Muppets, 278n11. *See also Sesame Street* (TV program)

Nanaimo (BC): APEC activism and CPF, 191; francophone association, 157

Nash, Lori, 198–200, 203, 232–33, 235–36, 247–48

National Association for English Rights (NAER), 178, 180, 189

National Capital Region (NCR). *See* Carleton (ON); Ottawa (ON)

National Citizens' Coalition, 204

National Core French Study, 126, 134, 230

The National Dilemma and the Way Out (McDonald and Boyd), 86–87, 111

National Foundation for Educational Research (NFER), 96

national identity: Canadian, 5, 9–10, 17, 21–22, 36, 40–41, 53, 58, 66–68, 79–83, 86, 88, 110–11, 171, 176, 179, 217, 253. *See also* British Canada; national unity

national unity, 18–19, 36, 38, 55, 72, 78, 81, 88, 96, 102–3, 108, 115, 130, 132, 135, 143, 168–72, 184, 189, 192–93, 210, 219, 229–30, 260

Nazi: references by anti-bilingualism groups, 113, 201, 218, 290n59

Neale, Valerie, 44

Neatby, Jacqueline, 89

neo-pluralism, 13, 275n25

Netten, Joan, 238, 244

New Brunswick: anti-bilingualism activism, 187–88; attitudes to French and bilingualism, 108, 130, 250, 294nn136–38, 294n141, 294n143; collaboration between CPF and francophones, 195, 239; CPF activities, 103, 106, 121, 149–50; French immersion policy, 150, 162, 259, 316n12; minority language education vs immersion, 121; Official Languages Act, 29; university language

requirements, 146; Willms report, 259. *See also* Acadians; Atlantic Canada; Confederation of Regions (COR) Party; Jones, Leonard; Société des Acadiens du Nouveau Brunswick (SANB); *and enrolment statistics in appendices; names of individual communities*

New Democratic Party, 28, 35, 215

new social movements theory, 15

Newfoundland and Labrador: debates on value of bilingualism, 159–61; government position on bilingualism, 212; Rendez-vous Canada weekend, 195. *See also* Atlantic Canada; Ferryland (NF); St. John's (NF); *and enrolment statistics in appendices*

The Next Act: New Momentum for Canada's Linguistic Duality (federal action plan), 244

Nielsen, Erik, 174

Nielsen Task Force, 174

North York (ON): Core French programs, 39–40, 94–98; French immersion pilot, 96

Northern Foundation, 204

The Northern Magus (Gwyn), 178

Northern Telecom, 125

Nova Scotia: APEC membership in, 111–12; attitudes to French, 305n95. *See also* Atlantic Canada; Halifax (NS); *and enrolment statistics in appendices*

Nurse, Andrew, 12

nursery schools, 41, 51, 89

Obadia, André, xii, 69, 91, 100, 123, 234

October Crisis, 29–30, 79. *See also* Front de libération du Québec (FLQ)

Odyssey Program, 33

Office of the Commissioner of Official Languages. *See* Commissioner of Official Languages

officers of Parliament, 8, 55–57, 74–75. *See also* Commissioner of Official Languages

Printed and bound in Canada by Friesens
Set in Segoe and Warnock by Artegraphica Design Co. Ltd.
Copy editor: Dallas Harrison
Proofreader: Sophie Pouyanne